Teaching Sport Concepts and Skills

A Tactical Games Approach

SECOND EDITION

Teaching Sport Concepts and Skills

A Tactical Games Approach

SECOND EDITION

Stephen A. Mitchell

Judith L. Oslin

Linda L. Griffin

HUMAN KINETICS

Library of Congress Cataloging-in-Publication Data

Mitchell, Stephen A., 1959-
    Teaching sport concepts and skills : a tactical games approach /
Stephen A. Mitchell, Judith L. Oslin, Linda L. Griffin.—2nd ed.
        p. cm.
    Griffin's name appears first on earlier edition.
    Includes bibliographical references.
    ISBN 0-7360-5453-7 (soft cover)
    1.   sports—Study and teaching 2.   Coaching (Athletics)   I. Oslin,
Judith L., 1950- II. Griffin, Linda L., 1954- III. Title.
    GV361.M65 2005
    796' .07—dc22

                                                    2005020525

ISBN-10: 0-7360-5453-7
ISBN-13: 978-0-7360-5453-9

The Web addresses cited in this text were current as of September 15, 2005, unless otherwise noted.

Acquisitions Editor: Bonnie Pettifor; **Developmental Editor:** Ragen E. Sanner; **Assistant Editors:** Carmel Sielicki, Mandy Maiden; **Copyeditor:** Jocelyn Engman; **Proofreader:** Ann M. Augspurger; **Permission Manager:** Dalene Reeder; **Graphic Designer:** Bob Reuther; **Graphic Artist:** Kathleen Boudreau-Fuoss, Denise Lowry; **Photo Manager:** Sarah Ritz; **Cover Designer:** Keith Blomberg; **Photographer (cover):** Sarah Ritz; **Photographer (interior):** © Human Kinetics, except where otherwise noted; **Art Manager:** Kelly Hendren; **Illustrator:** Accurate Art, Keri Evans; **Printer:** Versa Press

Printed in the United States of America   10   9   8   7   6   5   4   3   2

Human Kinetics
Web site: www.HumanKinetics.com

United States: Human Kinetics, P.O. Box 5076, Champaign, IL 61825-5076
800-747-4457
e-mail: humank@hkusa.com

Canada: Human Kinetics
475 Devonshire Road Unit 100, Windsor, ON N8Y 2L5
800-465-7301 (in Canada only)
e-mail: orders@hkcanada.com

Europe: Human Kinetics
107 Bradford Road, Stanningley, Leeds LS28 6AT, United Kingdom
+44 (0) 113 255 5665
e-mail: hk@hkeurope.com

Australia: Human Kinetics
57A Price Avenue, Lower Mitcham, South Australia 5062
08 8277 1555
e-mail: liaw@hkaustralia.com

New Zealand: Human Kinetics
Division of Sports Distributors NZ Ltd., P.O. Box 300 226 Albany, North Shore City, Auckland
0064 9 448 1207
e-mail: info@humankinetics.co.nz

For Carolyn.

— Steve

I would like to dedicate this book to my PETE colleagues
at Kent State University: Connie Collier, Mary LaVine,
Steve Mitchell, and Dave Toothaker.
Thank you for your unconditional love and support
and most of all for letting me be me.

— Judy

To my siblings Mark, Charlene, and Christopher
for their support and belief in me.

— Linda

Contents

Preface

We are pleased to write this second edition of *Teaching Sport Concepts and Skills: A Tactical Games Approach*. We received many positive comments on the original book and also many requests for an expanded version. We hope this book satisfies these requests and the growing enthusiasm for tactical games teaching. Some of you already have knowledge and experience of tactical games teaching, perhaps gained from reading and using ideas in the original book, but others may not. Do not be concerned if you fall into the latter category. We begin this book with a thorough review of tactical games teaching and build a sound conceptual understanding before providing sport-specific lesson plans. We have also added a chapter addressing tactical transfer, which is the understanding of how to solve the common problems presented across situations in similar game types. We have argued for tactical transfer for several years, and in this chapter we present both anecdotal and research evidence to support our contention that learning to solve the problems presented by one game can facilitate understanding of how to solve problems in other games. A sound conceptual understanding is important to your ability to implement a tactical games approach, so we hope you will find part I of the book helpful.

In part II we have carefully reviewed the original work, particularly the sport-specific chapters providing lesson plans. In tactical games teaching the quality of teacher questioning is very important and we have gone to some lengths to review and revise the suggested questions to ensure that they are consistent with lesson goals and game conditions and that they are focused to elicit student responses that identify the need for skill practice. Within skill-practice segments we have made stronger efforts to address broader ranges of student ability by providing task extensions where appropriate to increase challenge when the need arises.

We have added chapters on lacrosse, rugby (at the insistence of one of our student teachers), cricket (to add international appeal and to broaden our attention to striking and fielding games), and bowling (to broaden our attention to target games). We hope these chapters will be a useful resource as you plan tactical games lessons. Two of the additional chapters are written by guest authors Kathleen Howarth and Adrian Turner, and we appreciate their expertise and contributions.

We have retained the emphasis on learner assessment that we emphasized in the original version, but we have also expanded the assessment chapter to address psychomotor, cognitive, personal and social, and affective assessments in terms of standards-based curriculum and to provide examples of assessment integrated into lessons. The assessment chapter is a key component of part III of the book. Also in part III we describe how tactical games teaching in middle and high schools fits with the overall K-12 tactical games curriculum and offer suggestions to enable teachers to make a successful start in teaching tactical games. Part III is an expansion of the original work and draws on the experiences of colleagues who have changed the way they teach games.

This edition also includes a professionally produced DVD that shows some of the lessons in action. This tool will be effective not only in showing you how to implement the theory behind the tactical games approach, it will also help you teach others in either a teacher-coach preparation setting or in a youth/school setting. The volleyball segments show complete question and answer sessions, highlighting for you an effective method for making sure students are processing the lesson properly. A simple menu of demonstrated games makes it easy to find what you wish to review for yourself or to show others. Within the text of the lessons, you can watch for the following icon to call attention to a particular lesson or game that has been included on the DVD.

Games teaching and learning is a substantial part of most physical education curricula, and games playing provides an exciting and interactive environment for learning in all domains. We hope that this book will challenge all who read it. For those who have experience with tactical games teaching, we challenge you to take it to other areas of the curriculum, to maximize the potential of tactical transfer through effective curriculum design, and to assess learning outcomes across all domains. For those of you who are new to the idea of tactical games teaching, we challenge you to think deeply, to question your current practice as it relates to games teaching, and to adopt a new, student-centered approach to games teaching and learning.

Acknowledgments

We would like to thank all of the teachers, teacher educators, and students majoring in physical education at Kent State University, who have used many of the lessons in the first edition of this book and provided feedback, numerous ideas, and encouragement for a second edition. We hope this book serves as an example of how we all make each other better and physical education better for children. Likewise, we would like to acknowledge the following people: UMass PETEs, especially Alisa James, Karen Pagnano, Kevin Patton, Mary Henninger, Heidi Bohler, Jen Fisette, and Eric Carpenter; Deb Sheehy for pushing our thinking; Springfield College preservice teachers and Diane Lorenzo; and Joy Butler for her willingness to debate, her spirit of collegiality, and her friendship.

Our thanks to photographer Tom McGrew and especially to the middle school students in the photographs in chapter 7. They are Alex Bower, Tyler Jastromb, Jack Maynard, Caitlin McGrew, Kelsey McGrew, Katie Mitchell, Matthew Mitchell, and Alanah Timbrook.

Tactical Games Teaching

CHAPTER 1

Using This Book

Teaching Sport Concepts and Skills: A Tactical Games Approach, Second Edition, adds to the range of content of our first book. It answers the *why, what,* and *how* of games teaching by providing both a rationale for rethinking games teaching and a greater range of materials that teachers can use in schools. In part I, we challenge you as the teacher to rethink how you select and teach games and address games tactics when planning games units. We present reasons and organizational structures for implementing a tactical games approach and introduce frameworks to break each game into tactical problems, on-the-ball skills, and off-the-ball movements. We describe levels of tactical complexity so you can teach games in a developmentally appropriate manner, and we present a simple format for planning tactical games lessons. In chapter 3 we address the central concept of transfer across games.

In part II, we apply a tactical approach to specific games and sport teaching. We cut across the games classification system and offer tactical applications for invasion games, including soccer, basketball, rugby, and lacrosse; net and wall games, including volleyball, badminton, and tennis; striking and fielding games, including softball and cricket; and target games, including golf and bowling.

Chapters 4 through 14 address the *how to* question by outlining lesson plans to use in secondary settings. We have designed each lesson to challenge students to solve a tactical problem.

Lessons begin with a developmentally appropriate game form that is followed with skill or movement tasks that lead to the reapplication of these skills in another game. In each lesson we provide you with the tactical problem, lesson focus, and lesson objective. We present each lesson in the tactical format that we advocate and we suggest a teaching progression of game, questions, practice, and game. For each game, we provide you with the goal (e.g., attack using the forearm pass) and conditions (e.g., size of playing area and specific rules). After initially playing each game, ask your students the questions we provide that address what to do when playing and how to do it. Use the practice tasks listed after the questions to help your students develop their tactical awareness of movements and skills. We also provide teaching cues to assist your instruction. We suggest you

end with another game to reinforce the objective of the lesson.

These chapters are building blocks for developing your own units. You may choose to review content with your students by practicing previous levels before moving to the next level of tactical complexity. Each chapter provides you with ideas to enhance your units, but we encourage you to be creative. For example, you can include aspects of sport education, such as the roles of coaches, officials, and managers; organize units into sport seasons; or use cooperative learning, such as peer tutoring. We also encourage you to organize tournaments for your units.

An approach that places tactical awareness at the heart of games teaching and learning helps your students develop their problem-solving skills as they choose their physical and cognitive actions in games. As you move through the chapters on specific games and sports, we encourage you to make them your own by adapting them for your students, your school, your facilities, and your equipment.

In part III, we discuss games curriculum, assessment, and implementation. In chapter 15 we describe the evolution of tactical games education from a teaching approach to a curriculum model and address the integration of the tactical games model with other curriculum models. Part III also addresses the authentic assessment of games teaching and learning, a critical issue if our subject is to retain standing within the K-12 school curriculum. In an approach to games teaching that emphasizes improved game performance, we must use more than isolated skill tests to measure student achievement. Chapter 16 presents the Game Performance Assessment Instrument (GPAI) for measuring the components of effective game performance and also provides assessment ideas for the cognitive and affective domains.

Chapter 17 provides suggestions for starting your journey from the traditional methods of games teaching to a tactical approach. We have derived these suggestions from questions posed at our teacher development workshops and from feedback offered by physical educators working with a tactical approach in their schools. These educators have found the approach rewarding for themselves and their students, though their journeys have not been without difficulties. We are extremely grateful for their participation, and their suggestions will help you smooth your implementation of a tactical approach.

The benefits of the book are twofold. First, it benefits you as a teacher by encouraging you to rethink your games teaching. It provides units and lessons for specific games as well as tools for creating your own units and lessons. Second, it benefits the learner by accommodating individual instruction rather than pacing instruction to the entire class (Jones 1982). Though instruction might focus on particular tactical problems and skills associated with a certain level of complexity, you can individualize your instruction by giving advanced performers more complex skills for the specific tactical problem they are addressing.

Our text provides a complete package for teaching games, linking skills with tactics, and identifying common elements of games. The games classification system described in chapters 2 and 3 encourages students to identify similarities among games, thereby assisting them in transferring understanding from one game to another, a concept further addressed in chapter 3. This notion of transfer is also true for teachers in that the games presented in chapters 4 through 14 represent different types of games classified according to the tactics they employ. This makes similarities among games easier to identify. For example, having used the materials in the soccer chapter, teachers can easily apply the soccer lesson plans to a tactically similar game such as floor hockey.

We hope these ideas open your mind about games teaching. As with learning any new method, implementing a tactical approach will challenge you to think differently about games and sport teaching. Believe in your professional ability and challenge yourself to grow.

CHAPTER 2

Tactical Games Explanation and Review

About two-thirds of a typical physical education curriculum involves games teaching and learning. We believe that, given this emphasis, physical educators must try to teach games effectively. Many people, particularly fitness advocates, have viewed sports and games negatively, labeling them as elitist, overly competitive, and not conducive to developing health and fitness. This negativity perhaps stems from an emphasis on large-sided, zero-sum games in which the winners and losers are obvious and active participation is minimal for many students. We believe that sports and games can be fun, educative, and challenging and can enhance health and self-esteem. Although games teaching should remain a valuable part of the physical education curriculum, we concede that the way games have traditionally been taught is problematic. This is the reason we wrote this book.

Many physical educators teach both the skills and tactics of games but have problems linking these components. For example, in units on basketball in which classes spend several days covering passing, dribbling, and shooting, skill development is not apparent during subsequent lessons on game play. Skills have usually been taught in isolation, out of their tactical context. The approach we outline in this book links tactics and skills by emphasizing the appropriate timing of skill practice and application within the tactical context of the game.

Tactical awareness, critical to game performance, is the ability to identify tactical problems that arise during a game and to respond appropriately. Responses might be on-the-ball skills, such as passing and shooting, and off-the-ball movements, such as supporting and covering. For example, a tactical problem in soccer is for the team to maintain possession of the ball. Players maintain possession by selecting and executing passing, ball-control, and support skills. In a tactical approach, students are placed in a game situation that emphasizes maintaining possession *before* they identify and practice solutions such as passing, ball control, and support. Another tactical problem in soccer is defending space. Players defend space by marking opponents, pressuring the player with the ball, covering for teammates, and clearing the ball from danger areas. The link between skills and tactics enables students to learn about a game and improve their performance, especially because game tactics provide the opportunity for applying game-related motor skills.

Rationale for a Tactical Approach

We believe that traditional games teaching in schools has done little to educate students about games playing. The tactical approach we advocate in this book promotes interest in learning games, understanding of game play, and ability to play games.

Interest and Excitement

The traditional approach to games teaching is technical and focuses on teaching skills in answer to the question "How is this skill performed?" For example, instruction in badminton often develops the techniques of service, overhead clear, drop shot, and smash by concentrating on specific critical elements of these skills. Though this format might improve technique, it has been criticized for teaching skills before students can grasp their significance within the game. As a result, students lose the context of the skill and games teaching becomes a series of textbook drills (Pigott 1982).

Drills often lead students to ask, "Why are we doing this?" or "When can we play a game?" For example, you might hear these questions during a volleyball lesson in which students must pass or set the ball against a wall. For many students, particularly those who are less skilled, the game is characterized by aimless participation following a breakdown of techniques for passing and setting. This frustrates both students and teacher. It is possible that the only thing many children learn about games is that they cannot perform the necessary complex skills (Booth 1983). In addition, skilled students often perceive isolated drills as tedious and irrelevant to their performance during game play.

> **Tip Box**
>
> **The tactical approach aims to improve students' game performance by combining tactical awareness and skill execution.**

A tactical approach provides an exciting alternative through which students can learn to play games. Our research and the experience of others indicate that students find a tactical approach motivational and that teachers prefer it (Berkowitz 1996; Burrows 1986; Griffin, Oslin, and Mitchell 1995; Mitchell, Griffin, and Oslin 1994). Another attractive feature of a tactical approach is its sequential nature, which eliminates redundancy in games teaching for you and your students.

Knowledge As Empowerment

Although skill execution is critical to game performance, deciding *what to do* in game situations is just as important. French and Thomas (1987) state that "mistakes commonly observed in young children in various sports may stem from a lack of knowledge about what to do in the context of a given sport situation" (p. 17). Furthermore, Bunker and Thorpe (1986) have proposed that the uniqueness of games lies in the decision-making processes that precede the use of appropriate techniques. Not understanding the game impairs the student's ability to identify the correct technique for a situation. Bunker and Thorpe (1986) have also suggested that an increased understanding of games, achieved through teaching for tactical awareness, empowers children to easily and skillfully solve the problems each game situation poses.

The next time you teach a games lesson, observe the differences between the performances of students with high and low abilities. You will see more proficient skill execution by students with greater ability, but you will also notice better game-related decision making and skill selection in response to specific situations. Enhanced decisions reflect greater knowledge of the game, an observation supported by the research of McPherson (McPherson 1994, 1995).

Transfer of Understanding and Performance

A tactical focus may help your students carry understanding from one game to another. For example, tactical problems in soccer, field hockey, and basketball, all of which are invasion games, are similar. In our experience the best novice soccer players are those with experience of other

invasion games, because they already understand the spatial aspects of soccer. Invasion games are tactically similar even though they require completely different skills. We can make a similar case for net and wall games (e.g., badminton, tennis), striking and fielding games (e.g., softball, cricket), and target games (e.g., golf, bowling) (Werner and Almond 1990). These similarities enable us to group games according to their tactics. We define invasion games as those in which the goal is to invade an opponent's territory. Net and wall games involve propelling an object into space so an opponent is unable to make a return. In fielding and run-scoring games the goal is to strike an object, usually a ball, so that it eludes defenders. In target games the performer propels an object, preferably with great accuracy, toward a target. We elaborate on the importance and implications of tactical transfer in chapter 3.

Physical educators have suggested that a tactical focus in games teaching suits both the elementary and secondary levels (Bunker and Thorpe 1982; Doolittle and Girard 1991; Mitchell, Oslin, and Griffin, 2003). In this book we address how physical educators can use a tactical approach to enhance students' game performance at different developmental stages by identifying, sequencing, and teaching the tactical problems of specific games at successive stages of development. We offer frameworks for games, provide a broader definition of game performance, and identify levels of tactical complexity for each game.

Game Frameworks

An initial concern for those wishing to tactically teach games and sport is developing frameworks for identifying and breaking down relevant tactical problems, a process originated by Spackman (1983). By selecting teaching materials from a framework, you ensure that students become familiar with the game and that any skills you teach relate to the game context. An example of how you can use a framework is in table 2.1. The example uses soccer, which is taught at all developmental levels, and provides a framework that identifies tactical problems and the off-the-ball movements and on-the-ball skills necessary for solving these problems.

Table 2.1 identifies the major tactical problems in scoring, preventing scoring, and restarting play. To score, a team must solve the progressively complex problems of maintaining possession of the ball, attacking the goal, creating space while attacking, and using that space effectively. Each tactical problem includes relevant off-the-ball movements and on-the-ball skills. For example, to maintain possession of the ball, players must support teammates who have the ball and must pass and control the ball over various distances. You can develop similar frameworks for other games by asking yourself two questions:

- What are the problems in scoring, preventing scoring, and restarting play?
- What off-the-ball movements and on-the-ball skills are necessary to solve these problems?

Game Performance

The two questions of the previous section suggest that a tactical approach defines game performance as more than simply executing motor skills. In table 2.2 we recognize that movements made by players who do not have the ball are important and should be considered in games teaching. For example, a player who can pass the ball accurately is of limited value unless she has potential receivers who have moved to support her. Off-the-ball movements are often ignored in favor of on-the-ball skills, but you should teach these movements to maximize students' performance. We believe in this strongly because, in any game, players possess the ball, Frisbee, or puck only briefly during play. Consider 30 minutes of a soccer game played by

Table 2.1 Tactical Problems, Movements, and Skills in Soccer

Tactical problems	Off-the-ball movements	On-the-ball skills
SCORING		
Maintaining possession of the ball	• Dribbling for control • Supporting the ball carrier	• Passing—short and long • Control—feet, thigh, chest
Attacking the goal	• Using a target player	• Shooting, shielding, turning
Creating space in attack	• Crossover play • Overlapping run	• First-time passing—1v2 • Crossover play • Overlapping run
Using space in attack	• Timing runs to goal, shielding	• Width—dribbling, 1v1, crossing, heading • Depth—shielding
PREVENTING SCORING		
Defending space	• Marking, pressuring, preventing the turn, delaying, covering, making recovery runs	• Clearing the ball
Defending the goal	• Goalkeeping—positioning	• Goalkeeping—receiving the ball, shot stopping, distribution
Winning the ball		• Tackling—block, poke, slide
RESTARTING PLAY		
Throw-in—attacking and defending		• Executing a quick throw
Corner kick—attacking and defending		• Short, near- and far-post corners
Free kick—attacking and defending		

teams of 6 players. Dividing 30 minutes by 10 outfield players (each team has a goalkeeper) demonstrates that each outfield player possesses the ball for an average of only 3 minutes! What are the outfield players doing the remainder of the time? They are moving to appropriate positions to attack or defend and deciding how to contribute to the game. Yet in physical education, we rarely teach these aspects of game performance.

Therefore we provide you with a broad definition of game performance. Game play involves not only the execution of motor skills but also components such as

- making decisions,
- supporting teammates who have the ball,
- marking or guarding opponents,
- covering teammates,

- adjusting position as play unfolds, and
- ensuring adequate court or field coverage by means of a base position.

This expanded definition of game performance has implications for your goals, selected content, and chosen assessment procedures. Expanded goals and content appear in each of the sport-specific chapters, and ideas for assessment are presented in chapter 16.

Levels of Tactical Complexity

Having identified important tactical problems and their associated skills for a particular game, you

Tactical problems	LEVELS OF TACTICAL COMPLEXITY				
	I	II	III	IV	V
SCORING					
Maintaining possession of the ball	· Dribbling · Pass and control—feet	· Supporting player who has ball		· Pass—long · Control—thigh, chest	
Attacking the goal	· Shooting	· Shooting · Turning	· Target player		
Creating space in attack			· First-time passing	· Overlap	· Crossover
Using space in attack				· Width—dribbling, crossing, heading	· Depth—timing of runs
PREVENTING SCORING					
Defending space		· Marking, pressuring the ball	· Preventing the turn	· Clearing the ball	· Delaying, covering, recovering
Defending the goal		· Goalkeeper position, receiving, throwing			· Making saves, kicking or punting
Winning the ball			· Tackling—block, poke	· Tackling—slide	
RESTARTING PLAY					
Throw-in	· Throw-in				
Corner kick	· Short kick		· Near post		· Far post
Free kick			· Attacking		· Defending

Table 2.2 Levels of Tactical Complexity for Soccer

must ensure that the tactical complexity of the game matches the students' development. Some tactical problems are too complex for novice players to understand. For example, novice players might understand the need to maintain possession of the ball and to attack the goal because those are the basic requirements for scoring goals. On the other hand, it would be unrealistic to expect these players to understand more advanced concepts, such as using width and depth when attacking, because this understanding comes from experience playing the game (see table 2.2).

You might present the same tactical problem at successive stages of development. Consider the problem of defending space in soccer. We can reasonably expect novice players to appreciate that defense is needed to prevent opponents from scoring. In its simplest form, defense involves marking, or guarding, an opponent in order to deny access to the ball. However, only as their tactical awareness develops do students appreciate the need for players to defend as a team by delaying the opponent's attacks and covering for teammates challenging for the ball. You may add to the complexity of game understanding as tactical awareness develops. That is, as students improve their tactical understanding, games should involve problems of increasing complexity. If you can identify levels of tactical complexity, matching development becomes a process of planning versions of the game for students at varying stages of awareness. The key question you address is "How tactically complex do I want the game to be?" In contrast, the question you address in a technical approach is "What skills should I teach in my unit?" Table 2.2 identifies possible levels of tactical complexity in soccer.

As indicated in table 2.2, you can increase the complexity of each tactical problem as students develop their understanding and skills. To play the game in its simplest form, students need only to understand maintaining possession of the ball, attacking the goal, and restarting play. Therefore, in teaching soccer to novice players (level I), you might first ensure that students appreciate these activities and then provide solutions to these tactical problems. Level I skills include basic short passing, receiving, shooting, throwing the ball in, and using a short corner to restart when appropriate. Teaching longer passing to young students is inappropriate because it is unnecessary in small-sided games and few students possess the necessary strength. Thus you might revisit maintaining possession at a later level (perhaps IV) by addressing long passing when your students can see its value and can perform advanced skills.

Having introduced soccer in its most basic tactical form, at level II you can further develop student understanding and skill. You can show students that by supporting the player with the ball they increase the probability of their team retaining possession. Developing an awareness of the need to defend space and the goal is also appropriate for level II students, because they will have begun considering ways of preventing opponents from scoring. Simple tactical problems at level II include denying space to opponents who are close to the ball or goal and positioning the goalkeeper in order to decrease the size of the goal to the smallest possible target. When students understand the need for these tactics, they can practice relevant movements such as marking (or guarding) and skills such as basic goalkeeping. Finally, revisiting basic starts and restarts allows the game to take a complete but modified form, facilitating development at the next level.

As indicated in table 2.2, you might teach more advanced tactical problems, such as creating and using space in attack, at a later stage. At level III students can progress to creating space as they attack the goal. At this time you might revisit the problem of defending space by introducing the concept of pressuring the player with the ball. You could also introduce the problem of winning the ball and teach simple tackling skills. Confront the problem of winning the ball again at level IV with work on slide tackling. Level IV students might also address more advanced solutions for creating and using space. At level V, students should understand the problems presented by the game and employ more advanced tactics and skills. The exact level at which students should explore a tactical problem and its associated skills depends on task complexity and student understanding and skill. We recommend that when working with novice players, you begin with essential tactical problems related to scoring and preventing scoring. As you address more complex solutions to tactical problems, the game will increasingly resemble its mature form.

Individualizing Instruction

As you know, within any class students vary in their levels of understanding and performance. To individualize instruction, you can present advanced performers with the more complex solutions to a specific tactical problem. For example, when you teach novice soccer players to maintain possession of the ball by accurate short passing and receiving, some students progress faster than others. You may introduce more skillful students to the concept of support or to longer passing techniques in order to continue to challenge them. Similarly, novice softball players learning to defend space by fielding the ball and accurately throwing to first base progress at different rates. You could introduce students with higher abilities to the concept of defending the base or to the footwork involved in covering first base. In other words, you can increase the level of tactical complexity within the specific tactical problem being addressed. Doing so is sound developmental teaching.

Teaching Tactical Awareness and Skill Acquisition

In this section we outline using a tactical approach to teach an individual game lesson. Notice the use of small-sided games to expose students to specific tactical problems and the importance of the teacher's questioning to provoke critical thinking and problem solving.

Tactical Model

A critical question we now address is "How do I teach for tactical awareness within the physical education lesson?" Bunker and Thorpe (1982) suggest a six-stage model for games teaching, Teaching Games for Understanding, which has usefully guided physical educators. To illustrate its approach, we consolidated the model into three stages, which we present in figure 2.1.

The outline in figure 2.1 suggests that teaching for tactical awareness should start with a game, or more precisely, a game modified to represent its advanced form and exaggerated to present students with tactical problems (Thorpe, Bunker, and Almond, 1986). For example, a tactical problem in badminton is to set up the attack by creating space on the opponent's side of the net. You might begin with a half-court singles game because it represents the full-court game but is played on a narrower court. The narrowness exaggerates the need to play shots to the back and front of the court to create space.

Young or novice students will be unable to play the advanced form of most games because of limited tactical understanding and skill. The game form should relate to student development. Consider the dimensions of playing areas, the numbers participating, and the equipment used when choosing a game form. If you establish a developmentally appropriate form, students' play can represent the advanced game. For example, small-sided volleyball games played in smaller areas with lighter balls and lower nets use the same principles, problems, and skills found in the full game.

Critical Conditions and Questions

Students gradually learn the rules of games through the conditions you apply. After the initial game, questions are necessary, and the quality of your questions is the key to fostering students' critical

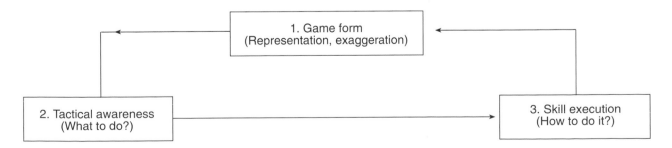

FIGURE 2.1   A tactical approach to games teaching.

thinking and problem solving. First, ask about the goal of the activity, and then ask students what they must do to achieve that goal (i.e., what skills or movements they must use to be successful). Questioning why certain skills or movements are required might also be appropriate. Once students are aware of what they need to do and why, you can ask them how they should perform the necessary skills. These questions help students identify what they ought to practice, thus leading to the practice phase of the lesson. The following example illustrates the process.

Establish an appropriate game form, such as 2 versus 2 (2v2) soccer in a restricted (20 × 20 yard/meter) playing area with an objective of making a specific number of consecutive passes (such as four). This objective forces students to confront what they must do to maintain possession. Appropriate teacher–student questioning might go as follows:

- Teacher: What was the goal of that game?

  Students: For your team to keep the ball for four passes.

- Teacher: What does your team have to do to keep the ball for four consecutive passes?

  Students: Pass the ball.

- Teacher: Yes, and what else?

  Students: You also have to receive passes.

- Teacher: OK. You have to be able to pass and receive the ball. How many teams managed to make four consecutive passes? (It is likely that only a few pairs made this target because passing is difficult in a 2v2 game.)

- Teacher: Well, perhaps some practice with passing and receiving would be good.

The quality of your questions is critical, and these questions should be an integral part of your planning. Literature on tactical games teaching, be

Tip Box

It is essential when modifying or conditioning any game that you encourage students to think tactically. By changing the rules, you exaggerate playing conditions to ensure that players ask, "What must I do to succeed in this situation?"

it the original work of Bunker and Thorpe (1982), the Australian conception of *Game Sense* (Den Duyn, 1997), or our own *Teaching Sport Concepts and Skills and Sport Foundations for Elementary Physical Education* (2003), has consistently emphasized the importance of asking quality questions. Proponents of *Game Sense* provide good general advice on the types of questions you might ask students. These questions fall into three categories:

- Time: "When is the best time to . . . ?"
- Space: "Where is or where can . . . ?"
- Risk: "Which choice is safest and which is most risky?

We encourage you to develop questions that are meaningful to your students. You can never anticipate all the answers you might receive, even when questioning secondary students, so be prepared to probe and perhaps ask a forced-choice question ("Do you think this or that?") to focus response. Questioning is not a teaching skill easily mastered and it does not come naturally to everyone. At first it is acceptable to be plan dependent and to write questions on notecards if necessary. Note cards may seem mechanical but with practice you will develop natural questioning skills for the varied situations of your students and gymnasium.

Continuing the previous example, through a developmentally appropriate game and through skillful questioning students have realized that accurate passing and swift ball control are essential. At this point formal practice of passing and control becomes appropriate. During this practice, you can describe how to perform the necessary skills and movements by using teaching cues related to the critical elements of each technique. Note that although passing and receiving have become the focus of the lesson, you didn't initially inform students of this focus. Rather, you led them to identify the lesson focus through a well-designed modified game and through skillful questioning. Many teachers new to a tactical approach find it difficult to withhold this information at the start of a lesson. Avoid providing too much information early in the lesson because it detracts from the problem-solving process. Conclude a lesson with game play that reinforces the skills practiced. The reproducible planning format at the end of this chapter should help you identify and understand the phases of a lesson.

The students' learning continues lesson by lesson, and you continue to modify the game so students can explore new aspects of tactical awareness. For example, you could introduce a 3v3 game, providing all players with an extra passing option so that they must effectively support the player with the ball. When students understand the need for good support, you can teach off-the-ball supporting movements before returning to the game. Thus you progressively develop game performance. You can extend the problem of maintaining possession by adding either a small goal or a target player at each end of a rectangular playing area. Ask, "How can we get the ball past the defense?" At this point students must think in terms of passing the ball between defenders, or splitting the defense, an essential tactic for penetrating in attack.

Summary

To conclude this chapter, we reemphasize four essential points of a tactical approach to games teaching.

1. **Consider the tactical problems to address during your unit and decide on the complexity of the solutions to these problems.** These decisions depend on the experience and ability of your students. We provide tactical frameworks and levels of tactical complexity throughout this book, and you can easily develop these frameworks and levels for other games within the same category by using our examples.

2. **Within each lesson students practice skills after they have experienced a game form that presents a tactical problem requiring that skill.** In this way they appreciate the need for the skill and broaden their view of skill development to include both off-the-ball movements and on-the-ball skills. The timing of practice is a critical component of a tactical approach. As the teacher, you should modify initial game forms so students can confront tactical problems.

3. **Link the initial modified game and the skill practice through your questions. The quality of these questions is critical.** Questions must first draw students' attention to the tactical problem and then to potential solutions to the problem. You cannot assume that you will always get the answer you are expecting (these are students after all), but experience in this approach will enable you to think on your feet, probe further, and guide students to responses. Don't assume that students are versed in terminology, such as *overhead clear* or *drop shot*. Rather, expect students to talk about *long* and *short* shots, at which point you can introduce correct terminology before skill practice.

4. **Having practiced skills, students have the opportunity to apply their improved skills and tactical understanding in game play.** By providing your students with this opportunity, you increase the probability that they will understand the value of skills in the relevant game context. Chapter 17 provides detailed suggestions on how to implement a tactical approach.

The sport-specific chapters in this book provide suggestions for teaching tactically in a variety of games and sports. The chapters vary in length and the levels of tactical complexity vary from game to game. For example, invasion games tend to be more tactically complex than net and wall games, so we have identified five levels of tactical complexity for soccer but only three for badminton.

Each chapter contains a framework of problems, movements, and skills to assist you in breaking down the game tactically. We also suggest levels of tactical complexity to give you an idea of how to developmentally sequence your teaching. We suggest several lessons for each level, but these are only outlines with little detail on equipment and management procedures. For the sake of space we have restricted each outline to the tactical problem being addressed, the lesson focus, the lesson objective, an initial game form, teacher questions with likely student responses, practice ideas with teaching cues, and a closing game form. This abbreviated format provides a greater breadth of material to get you started.

Finally, we suggest that before focusing on unit content, you take the first one to two lessons in each activity to teach students how to set up and run small-sided games. This will help them understand the playing boundaries and game rules and routines that make the learning environment run smoothly. If you choose to integrate tactical games teaching with Sport Education (more on this in chapter 15), you should organize your environment so that students understand their own roles and the routines for beginning and ending class. Practice student roles as well as class rules and routines during the first one or two lessons.

Planning Format for Tactical Games Lessons

Game _____ Lesson # _____ Grade level _____

Major components of the plan are **bolded**, while points for the teacher to consider are *italicized.*

Tactical problem: What is the tactical problem addressed during the lesson?

Lesson focus: What is the focus in terms of how the tactical problem will be solved?

Objectives: What are the major cognitive and psychomotor learning objectives?

1. **Game:** *What is the modified game being played?*

   Conditions: *What conditions will you put on the game to ensure that students address the tactical problem?*

   Goal: *What performance goal will you give to the students?*

   Questions: *After initial game play, what questions might you ask (and what answers do you anticipate) to help students focus on the tactical problem and its solution?*

2. **Practice task:** *What skill practice will help students solve the tactical problem when they return to game play?*

   Goal: *What performance goal will you give to the students for the skill practice?*

   Cues: *What teaching cues will you use to assist skill acquisition?*

   Extension: *How might you extend the skill practice to make it harder or easier to match content with varying abilities of students?*

3. **Game:** *What modified game may help students apply newly learned skills to solve the tactical problem during play?*

   Conditions: *What conditions will you put on the game to ensure that students use the skills learned to address the tactical problem?*

   Goal: *What performance goal will you give to the students for the game?*

4. **Closure:** *What would be an appropriate closure or ending discussion for the lesson?*

From *Teaching Sport Concepts and Skills: A Tactical Games Approach,* Second Edition, by Stephen A. Mitchell, Judith L. Oslin, and Linda L. Griffin. Champaign, IL: Human Kinetics.

CHAPTER 3

Transfer of Tactical Learning

The principle of transfer in tactical games teaching is sufficiently important to warrant its own discussion. *Transfer of learning,* a commonly applied principle in education, is well documented in the literature on motor learning as the basis for sequencing skills and concepts to be learned (Magill 1993). Transfer may be positive when the learning of one skill or concept aids the learning of another. For example, learning to throw a ball overhand positively affects learning the tennis service because of the biomechanical similarities of these skills. Conversely, transfer might be negative when the learning of one skill or concept interferes with the learning of another, as is the case where a novice performer moves from learning the badminton underhand forehand drive to learning the tennis forehand drive. Racket weight and technical differences (the wrist is used much more in badminton) might cause negative transfer. Transfer might also be zero if learning one skill or concept has no effect on learning another.

There is research literature supporting the principle of transfer in motor skill acquisition (Dan Ota and Vickers 1998; Singer, DeFrancesco, and Randall 1989; Wrisberg and Liu 1991), with most of this literature investigating the relative effects of blocked or variable practice trials on transfer. However, there is a lack of research investigating the transfer of understanding in physical activity, which is surprising considering the abundance of literature confirming transfer of learning in other educational areas. Studies in literacy suggest that children are able to transfer learning strategies across reading tasks and among subjects such as reading, writing, and world geography (Benson 1997; McAloon 1994). Similarly, researchers in linguistics report that learning to read and write in one foreign language can benefit the learning of another (Berman 1994; Tucker 1996). Transfer has also been supported in technology. Beard (1993) has argued for the positive transfer of computer skills to new computer tasks, while Harvey and Anderson (1996) have identified positive transfer across computer languages. Finally, Toh and Woolnough (1994) have determined that the science skills of planning, performing, communicating, and interpreting transfer to other scientific areas of study.

Transfer of Tactical Knowledge in Games

Given the findings just described, it seems reasonable to speculate that understanding transfers positively among tactically similar games. Though historically games have been grouped in different ways for different reasons, we use the classification system suggested by Almond (1986), which is presented in table 3.1. The system divides games into invasion, net and wall, striking and fielding, and target games:

- **Invasion games.** In invasion games teams score by moving a ball (or other projectile) into another team's territory and either shooting into a fixed target (a goal or basket) or moving the projectile across an open-ended target (across a line). To prevent scoring, one team must stop the other from bringing the ball into its territory and attempting to score. Solving these offensive and defensive problems requires similar tactics in various invasion games even though many of the required skills are different. For example, while

Table 3.1 Games Classification

Invasion	Net/Wall	Striking/ Fielding	Target
· Basketball (FT)	· Net	· Baseball	· Golf
· Netball (FT)	· Badminton (I)	· Softball	· Croquet
· Team handball (FT)	· Tennis (I)	· Rounders	· Bowling
· Water polo (FT)	· Table tennis (I)	· Cricket	· Lawn bowling
· Soccer (FT)	· Pickleball (I)	· Kickball	· Pool
· Hockey (FT)	· Volleyball (H)		· Billiards
· Lacrosse (FT)	· Wall		· Snooker
· Speedball (FT/OET)	· Racquetball (I)		
· Rugby (OET)	· Squash (I)		
· Football (OET)	· Handball (H)		
· Ultimate Frisbee (OET)			

FT = focused target; OET = open-ended target; I = implement; H = hand.

Adapted, by permission, from L. Almond, 1986, Reflecting on themes: A games classification. In *Rethinking games teaching,* edited by R. Thorpe, D. Bunker, and L. Almond (Loughborough University), 71-72.

players must understand the need to shoot in order to score in both floor hockey and team handball, the striking and throwing skills used to shoot in these two games are very different. Movement off the ball is common across all invasion games. Offensive players must move without the ball and position themselves so that they can receive passes from teammates and threaten the goal. The defensive components of invasion games are also similar in that players must mark or guard opponents and must pressure the ball carrier before attempting to win the ball. Effective decision making is critical, with players deciding whether to pass, shoot, or move with the ball and deciding when, where, and how to move when they do not individually possess the ball.

• **Net/Wall games.** In net/wall games, teams or individual players score by hitting a ball into a court space with sufficient accuracy and power so that opponents cannot hit it back before it bounces once (as in badminton or volleyball) or twice (as in tennis or racquetball). In all of these games shot placement is at a premium in that players must hit to open spaces in order to win points. Court awareness is important so that a player can move an opponent around the court in order to create the spaces needed to attack. On the other hand, players must also defend spaces, usually on their side of the net, to best position themselves to return the ball. Players need to decide on their own strengths and weaknesses, and on those of opponents, before selecting and executing skills. Decisions by any player must also account for the court positioning of all players involved in a game.

• **Striking/Fielding games.** In striking/fielding games such as softball, baseball, and cricket, players on the batting team must strike a ball with sufficient accuracy and power so that it eludes players on the fielding team and gives the hitter time to run between two destinations (bases or wickets). As in a net/wall game, players attempt to place the ball in gaps between fielders in order to maximize the run scoring of each hit. Decisions regarding where (accuracy) and how (power or placement) to hit a ball are based on the positioning of fielders and on the type of ball or pitch delivered. To prevent scoring, players on the fielding team must position themselves so they can gather and throw a ball to the base or wicket to which the hitter is running

before the hitter reaches it. Fielding decisions, particularly those concerning a fielder's positioning, are based on the relative strengths and weaknesses of the pitcher or bowler and of the batter, and also (perhaps) on the score in the game.

• **Target games.** In target games, players score by throwing or striking a ball to a target. Some target games are unopposed (e.g., golf, tenpin bowling) while others are opposed (e.g., lawn bowling, croquet, shuffleboard) in that one participant is allowed to block or hit the opponent's ball. In opposed target games, players prevent scoring by hitting the opponent's ball to a disadvantageous position relative to the target. Decision making is much more individualized than in other game categories, primarily focused on the player's own personal strengths and weaknesses or perhaps on equipment, such as in selecting a club before a shot in golf.

The classification system presented in table 3.1 was originally developed so that teachers could select from several game types to expose children to a variety of activities (Almond 1986). The weakness of selecting across types is that it is unlikely to lead to deep tactical learning and improved game performance within any category. Lack of depth is an issue because performance enhancement in any game will probably not result from the typical unit of 6 to 8 lessons used when variety of experience is the basis for content selection.

Table 3.1 emphasizes games tactics rather than skills. If your students are well versed in tactics, the carryover of performance from one game to another within a category will be more effective than when skills are emphasized in isolation. To clarify, the skills used in soccer, basketball, and field hockey are different, and if instruction focuses on these skills there will be little carryover from one game to another. However, because the games

> **Tip Box**
>
> **Select from within rather than across game categories. Doing so provides students with a deeper understanding of effective game performance by identifying similarities among games within each category.**

are tactically similar, focusing on tactical problems can lead to positive transfer among games. Several teachers have found this transfer to be the greatest benefit of using a tactical approach to games teaching. For example, a sixth-grade teacher began a series of units on invasion games by focusing eight lessons on the tactical problems of maintaining possession of the ball and attacking the goal in soccer. She then applied the same tactical problems to ultimate Frisbee and floor hockey during consecutive units of similar lengths. Her students were able to transfer understanding of one game to another, particularly how to move when not in possession of the ball, Frisbee, or puck. Other teachers and student teachers have reported similar outcomes.

Considering the conceptual arguments we have just presented, it is perhaps surprising that only a few studies have investigated the extent to which knowledge and tactical understanding transfer from performance of one game to another. One of our studies indicated a positive transfer of performance in high school students moving from badminton to pickleball (Mitchell and Oslin 1999b). Game performance was videotaped for each game, and students answered structured questions regarding the similarities between badminton and pickleball and how learning one might help in performing another. The students demonstrated transfer of both game performance and cognitive knowledge. Martin (2004) conducted a similar study using the invasion games of ultimate Frisbee and team handball, novel activities for the sixth-grade boys involved in the units. This study also noted positive transfer when students moved from ultimate Frisbee to team handball, particularly in passing decisions and offensive support.

Implications for Curriculum Development

The concept of transfer underpins a tactical approach to games teaching. Given its support in the education literature, and more recently in the physical education literature, transfer has some implications for selecting content during curriculum development. Simply, if students transfer cognitive learning such that playing one game helps the learning of another, it might be wise to consecutively teach games with similar tactical goals in order to capitalize on their similarities. In addition to obtaining breadth of experience across two or more different games, students might achieve depth of tactical learning within the same games category. Tables 3.2 and 3.3 demonstrate consecutive units in both invasion games and net games.

Table 3.2 presents sample content selection for eight lessons of soccer followed by eight lessons of field hockey for middle school students. Clearly these students will develop the understanding that soccer and field hockey are essentially the same game played with different implements and that what they learn in solving the problems of one game applies to the other. We have not included a chapter on field hockey in this book, and again we emphasize that transfer is also a feature of tactical games teaching for you as the teacher. Teachers who do not know much about field hockey could apply what they know about soccer (or basketball or ice hockey or team handball) to field hockey. In doing so you will realize that you know more than you think you do about many games.

Table 3.3 presents sample content for badminton and pickleball units. Again, we have not included a pickleball chapter in this book (it is very similar to tennis). As in the example of invasion games, students will soon appreciate the similarities of the two net games. The sequence of lessons in table 3.3 emphasizes three problems and corresponding solutions of net games, which are shown in table 3.4.

Summary

Clearly the concept of transfer is central to teaching and learning games tactics. Though the research literature supporting the transfer of tactical understanding is limited, many of you can recall anecdotal examples of students who have successfully applied knowledge of one game to another. In our experience, players in field hockey easily adapt to the spatial aspects of soccer, despite being soccer novices, because of their good understanding of positions and movements. Likewise we have witnessed a cross-cultural transfer where players with

Table 3.2 Consecutive Units on Invasion Games

Lesson	SOCCER		FIELD HOCKEY	
	Tactical problem	Solution—skill or movement	Tactical problem	Solution—skill or movement
1	Maintaining possession of the ball	Dribbling under control—using multiple surfaces of the foot to change direction	Maintaining possession of the ball	Dribbling under control—using correct side of the stick and stick manipulation
2	Maintaining possession of the ball	Passing and receiving with inside and outside of the foot	Maintaining possession of the ball	Passing and receiving—using push pass and cushioning the ball
3	Maintaining possession of the ball	Supporting teammates who have the ball—moving to open space	Maintaining possession of the ball	Supporting teammates who have the ball—moving to open space
4	Attacking the goal	Shooting a static or moving ball	Attacking the goal	Shooting a static or moving ball
5	Attacking the goal	Dribbling around defenders to shoot (combining lessons 1 and 4)	Attacking the goal	Dribbling around defenders to shoot (combining lessons 1 and 4)
6	Defending space	Marking opponents and pressuring the ball in small-sided game play	Defending space	Marking opponents and pressuring the ball in small-sided game play
7-8	All	6v6 round-robin tournament play	All	6v6 round-robin tournament play

Table 3.3 Consecutive Units on Net Games

Lesson	BADMINTON		PICKLEBALL	
	Tactical problem	Solution—skill or movement	Tactical problem	Solution—skill or movement
1	Setting up to attack	Overhead forehand clear for depth in the opponent's court—creating space in the front court	Setting up to attack	Forehand groundstroke for depth in the opponent's court—creating space in the front court
2	Setting up to attack	Overhead backhand clear for achieving depth in the opponent's court	Setting up to attack	Backhand groundstroke for achieving depth in the opponent's court
3	Setting up to attack	Initiating play with an underhand clear (service) to push the opponent back	Setting up to attack	Initiating play with a flat underhand service to the receiver on the baseline
4	Setting up to attack	Using a drop shot to bring the opponent forward to use the space in the front court	Setting up to attack	Using approach shot to position at the net and threaten the space in the front court

(continued)

Table 3.3 (continued)

| Lesson | BADMINTON | | PICKLEBALL | |
	Tactical problem	Solution—skill or movement	Tactical problem	Solution—skill or movement
5	Winning the point	Using a smash into the front court to exploit a weak clear or poor drop shot	Winning the point	Using a volley from the net to exploit the advantageous position at the net
6	Defending space	Recovering to center court in between skill attempts	Defending space	Recovering to center of the baseline in between skill attempts
7-8	All	Round-robin tournament play—preferably singles	All	Round-robin tournament play—preferably singles

Table 3.4 Scoring Tactics

Problem	Solution
How do I set myself up so I can attack my opponent?	By pushing my opponent to the back of his or her court to open up space in the front.
How do I take advantage of this space to win a point?	By attacking the space I created in the front court with a smash, drop shot, or volley. (Though these shots differ in the techniques used in various net games, the principle of attacking space in the front court is the same.)
How do I prevent my opponent from scoring?	By positioning myself in the best place from which I will be able to return most of my opponent's shots. (Again, the best position varies with different net games. Base position for badminton is the actual center of the court so a player can reach both drop shots and clears. In pickleball, because the ball is allowed to bounce once on the receiver's side, the base position is at the center of the baseline. Nevertheless, the principle of returning to a base position from which space is most easily defended is common to both games.)

cricket experience understand the principles of baseball and softball, including offensive principles such as ball placement and defensive principles such as backing up bases and adjusting fielding position for right- and left-handed hitters.

Several teachers have raised the concern that they are not games experts but instead possess expertise in a specific area such as swimming or gymnastics, and so they lack the confidence to teach games tactically. Learn one game from each category and apply your knowledge to other games within the same category as a way of getting started in tactical games teaching. The chapters in part II cover each game category, including at least two games per category, and have been written to simplify the task of transfer. For example,

much of the chapter on soccer can be applied to teaching offensive and defensive principles in team handball or field hockey, and much of the chapter on tennis can be applied to pickleball. We hope these chapters are useful resources for your games teaching.

Tip Box

The principle of transfer applies to the teacher. Remember that many games are similar and therefore if you know one game from each category, you will know the principles of other games within the same category.

PART II

Lesson Plans for Tactical Games Teaching

CHAPTER 4

Soccer

This chapter illustrates a tactical approach to teaching soccer, an invasion game. Before starting, remember that two critical points form the basis for the lesson format. First, students practice for skill development *after* they have played a game form that presents a tactical problem requiring that skill. As the teacher, you can modify game forms so that students confront various problems. You can also ask questions that encourage students to think of solutions. Second, having practiced a skill, students have the opportunity to apply their improved skill and tactical awareness in a game. By providing this opportunity you increase the probability that students will understand the value of skills in the relevant game context.

In this chapter, we make the following assumptions about facilities, equipment, and students' experience:

1. Soccer is taught outdoors, though you can teach some lessons indoors.

2. There is one soccer ball for every two students. Where you have more than two students for one ball, you can adjust for most activities.

3. Cones are available for marking the suggested playing areas. It would be advantageous to permanently mark a series of 10- by 10-yard/meter grids (10 by 10 yards is ideal, but you could vary the grids according to available space). The 10-yard markings on an American football field can be useful when marking play areas.

4. The size and weight of the soccer balls match students' development (i.e., younger students use smaller and lighter balls). It may also be necessary to use smaller or larger playing areas, depending on student development. Bear in mind that players with lower abilities need more space, not less, because greater space gives them more time to control and use the ball (assuming they stay spread out).

5. Students have some experience playing soccer. We assume this because soccer was probably addressed to some extent at the elementary level, perhaps in combination with other invasion games as we suggest in *Sport Foundations for Elementary Physical Education: A Tactical Games Approach* (2003). Therefore, games start with 1v1 but move quickly to 3v3 and 6v6. We do not overtly address the 11v11 game but accept that at the high school level, both teachers and students will want to spend some time in full-field play (if class size permits). We have limited game development to 6v6 because it requires less extensive positional knowledge on the part of either the teachers or the players. For a better understanding of the positional demands of the full-field game, consult one of the many available texts on soccer coaching.

All the lessons in this chapter begin with a game form. When determining the size of the teams for these game forms, consider the appropriate group size for skill practice. Keep students in their teams during skill practice to facilitate transitions among lesson stages.

It is up to you to ask questions and give answers that will help the students to have the fullest and most useful experience.

For ease of reference, we include the tactical framework and levels of tactical complexity for soccer once more in tables 4.1 and 4.2. We briefly describe activities before beginning the specific lesson at each level.

Table 4.1 Tactical Problems, Movements, and Skills in Soccer

Tactical problems	Off-the-ball movements	On-the-ball skills
SCORING		
Maintaining possession of the ball	• Dribbling for control • Supporting the ball carrier	• Passing—short and long • Control—feet, thigh, chest
Attacking the goal	• Using a target player	• Shooting, shielding, turning
Creating space in attack	• Crossover play • Overlapping run	• First-time passing—1v2 • Crossover play • Overlapping run
Using space in attack	• Timing runs to goal, shielding	• Width—dribbling, 1v1, crossing, heading • Depth—shielding
PREVENTING SCORING		
Defending space	• Marking, pressuring, preventing the turn, delaying, covering, making recovery runs	• Clearing the ball
Defending the goal	• Goalkeeping—positioning	• Goalkeeping—receiving the ball, shot stopping, distribution
Winning the ball		• Tackling—block, poke, slide
RESTARTING PLAY		
Throw-in—attacking and defending		• Executing a quick throw
Corner kick—attacking and defending		• Short, near- and far-post corners
Free kick—attacking and defending		

Table 4.2 Levels of Tactical Complexity for Soccer

Tactical problems	I	II	III	IV	V
SCORING					
Maintaining possession of the ball	• Dribbling • Pass and control—feet	• Supporting		• Pass—long • Control—thigh, chest	
Attacking the goal	• Shooting	• Shooting • Turning	• Target player		
Creating space in attack			• First-time passing	• Overlap	• Crossover
Using space in attack				• Width—dribbling, crossing, heading	• Depth—timing runs

(continued)

Soccer   **29**

Tactical problems	I	II	III	IV	V
PREVENTING SCORING					
Defending space		· Marking, pressuring the ball	· Preventing the turn	· Clearing the ball	· Delaying, covering, recovering
Defending the goal		· Goalkeeper positioning, receiving, throwing			· Making saves, kicking or punting
Winning the ball			· Tackling—block, poke	· Tackling—slide	
RESTARTING PLAY					
Throw-in	· Throw-in				
Corner kick	· Short kick		· Near post		· Far post
Free kick			· Attacking		· Defending

Level I

At level I, we suggest that students focus on maintaining possession of the ball and attacking the goal, because these are the fundamental tactical problems for invasion games. At this level we answer what to do and how to do it by focusing on players' actions when they possess the ball. Dribbling, passing, controlling the ball, and shooting are the primary solutions to maintaining possession and attacking the goal. We suggest beginning with dribbling since it is the natural inclination of the novice soccer player upon receiving the ball and it allows players to move the ball away from opponents who are trying to regain possession. Adding simple restarts when the ball goes out of bounds at the side- or goal line enables a small-sided game to evolve at this level.

We do not recommend that you pay attention to defense at level I, though you could easily do so by using level II lessons. Our rationale for focusing only on the tactical problems of scoring is threefold. First, besides making students aware

When students are first learning soccer, focus on the fundamentals of dribbling.

that each team should try to prevent the other from scoring, spending time on defense is not necessary for a modified game of soccer. Players need only to focus on the essential tactical problems for a game to take place, these being maintaining possession and attacking the goal. Unless teams seek solutions to these problems, a modified game does not represent the mature form. Second, we believe early success motivates students and it would be counterproductive to focus on preventing offensive success at level I. Third, due to time constraints, it is not possible to focus on all aspects of the game during an initial instructional unit.

Lesson 1 ⊙   Level I

Tactical Problem
Maintaining possession of the ball

Lesson Focus
Dribbling to control the ball

Objective
Move the ball into space to avoid opponents and move the ball forward using controlled actions.

GAME 1

Setup
1v1 played in an area 20 by 10 yards/meters marked with cones at each end. The dimensions can vary for this beginning game. It is possible to play without lines—just spread out the cones marking each game to allow for movement between them (from end to end) and don't be too concerned if one game overflows into another (overflow will only be temporary and the players will still be working on their dribbling).

Goal
Stop the ball on the opponent's line (between the cones) to score.

Conditions
- After a goal is scored, the ball is returned to the player who conceded the goal.
- The player who scored must retire to halfway down the playing area.

Questions
Q: What is the goal of this game?
A: Get to the opponent's line and stop the ball.

Q: So how do you get the ball to the line?
A: Dribble.

Q: What problem does the opponent give you?
A: She's in the way. You have to keep the ball away from her while you dribble.

Q: How many parts of the foot can you use as you dribble?
A: Six—the inside, outside, instep (i.e., the laces), sole, heel, and toe. (Teachers often fail to consider all of these surfaces as useful for ball manipulation, instead focusing on the inside of the foot. While the inside of the foot is important, the outside is equally important for dribbling and the other surfaces are crucial for changing direction.)

PRACTICE TASK

Setup

Free dribbling within a specified area (of sufficient size matched to the number of students). Give one ball to each student or have students share a ball if necessary. Call "turn" or "speed up" or "slow down" (or anything else that forces change in direction or speed).

Goals

- Closely control the ball while dribbling.
- Quickly change speed and direction.

Cues

- Keep the ball close.
- Use all parts of both feet.
- Turn and move away at high speed.

Extensions

- Teacher becomes the defender (along with some other students)—beat the defenders.
- 1v1 possession game in 10 by 10 yards/meters. Player 1 tries to keep the ball away from player 2 for 5 seconds.

GAME 2

Repeat game 1.

Lesson 2   Level I

Tactical Problem
Maintaining possession of the ball

Lesson Focus
Passing and receiving balls on the ground with inside of foot

Objectives
- Make accurate and firm short passes.
- Use one touch to control and set up next move.

GAME 1

Setup

3v3 possession game in 30 by 20 yards/meters (see figure 4.1)

Goal

Make five consecutive passes.

Questions

Q: *What must you do in this game?*
A: Keep the ball.

Q: *How can your team keep the ball?*
A: Pass.

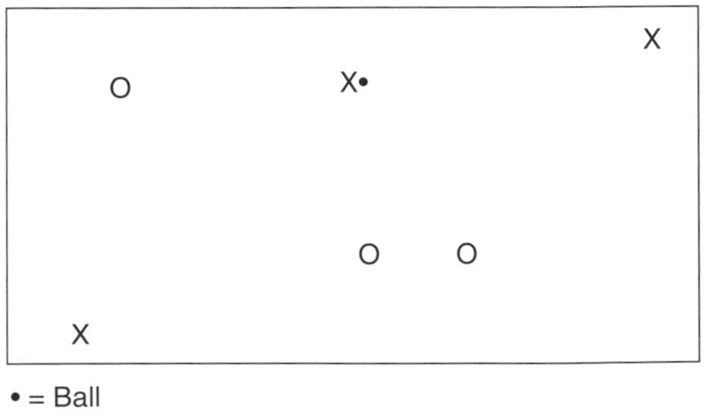

• = Ball

FIGURE 4.1

PRACTICE TASK

Setup
Partner (or triad) practice approximately 10 yards/meters apart; practice pass and control

Goals
- Use one touch to control and set up the next pass.
- Firmly and accurately pass using insides of both feet.

Cues
- Passing
  - Face the direction you are passing.
  - Keep nonkicking foot next to the ball.
  - Use inside of foot and square foot to the ball.
  - Strike the ball through its center.
- Receiving
  - Get in line with the ball as it comes.
  - Use one touch with the inside of your foot to set yourself up for the next pass.

Extension
Pass and move to another space. The receiver has to look up and find the player who moved in order to give the next pass. Encourage the receiver to look twice—once as the ball is on the way and once after he has it under control—before passing.

GAME 2

Setup
3v3 in 30 by 20 yards/meters, narrow goal, no goalkeeper (see figure 4.2)

Goals
- Quick control and setup.
- Firm and accurate passing.
- Heads up for vision.
- Score in the small goal.

Conditions
- Maximum of three touches before passing (depending on abilities of students).
- Ball must stay below head height (the head-height rule).

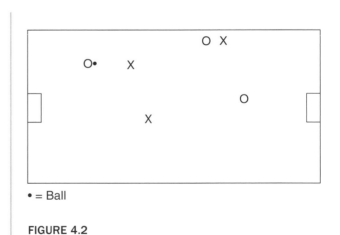

• = Ball

FIGURE 4.2

Lesson 3 Level I

Tactical Problem
Maintaining possession of the ball

Lesson Focus
Passing and receiving balls on the ground with outside of foot

Objectives
- Accurate and firm short passes.
- One touch to control and set up for next move.

GAME 1

Setup
3v3 possession game in 30 by 20 yards/meters (see figure 4.3)

Goal
Make five consecutive passes.

Questions

Q: *What must you do in this game?*
A: Keep the ball.

Q: *How can your team keep the ball?*
A: Pass.

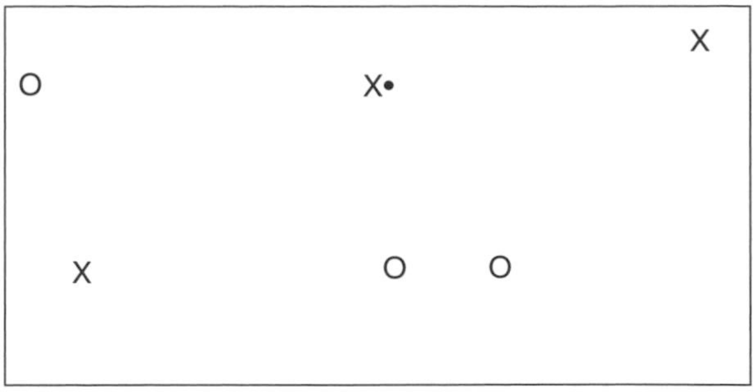

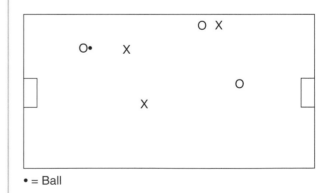

• = Ball

FIGURE 4.3

PRACTICE TASK

Setup
Partner practice of pass and control or setting up when 5 to 10 yards/meters apart

Goals
· One touch to control and set up.
· Firm and accurate passing with outsides of both feet.

Cues
· Passing
  – Face the direction you are passing.
  – Keep nonkicking foot next to the ball.
  – Use the outside of the foot and point the toe inward.
  – Strike the ball through its center.
· Receiving
  – Get in line with the ball as it comes.
  – Use one touch with the outside of the foot to set yourself up for the next pass.

GAME 2

Setup
3v3 in 30 by 20 yards/meters, narrow goal, no goalkeeper (see figure 4.4)

Goals
· Quick control and setup.
· Firm and accurate passing with inside or outside of foot as appropriate.
· Heads up for vision.
· Score in small goal.

Conditions
· Maximum of three touches before passing (depending on abilities of students).
· Head-height rule.

• = Ball

FIGURE 4.4

Tactical Problem
Attacking the goal

Lesson Focus
Shooting

Objectives
Learn the three principles of good shooting:
- Shoot on sight.
- Hit the target.
- Keep the shot low.

GAME 1

Setup
6v6 on small field of 30 by 30 yards/meters with large goals (8 yards/meters) (see figure 4.5)

Goals
- Shoot when possible.
- Hit the target (the whole goal).

Questions

Q: *What should you do when you're this close to the goal?*
A: Shoot.

Q: *Why should you shoot?*
A: Because if you don't shoot you won't score!

Q: *Where should you aim when you shoot?*
A: At the whole goal so you can force the goalkeeper to make a save.

Q: *Should you aim high or low?*
A: Low.

Q: *Why should you shoot low?*
A: It's harder for the goalkeeper to go down to make a save.

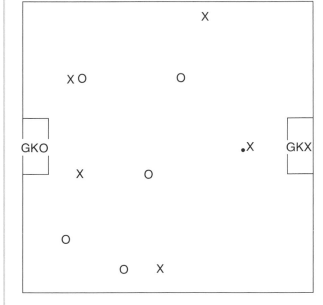

• = Ball   GK = Goalkeeper

FIGURE 4.5

PRACTICE TASK

Setup
Partner practice (see figure 4.6) with static or moving ball (with goalkeepers if groups of three are needed)

Goals
- Shoot ball between two posts or cones.
- Keep all shots below waist height.

Cues
- Take a long step to the ball.
- Keep the nonkicking foot next to the ball.
- Use the instep (or laces).
- Keep head and toe down.

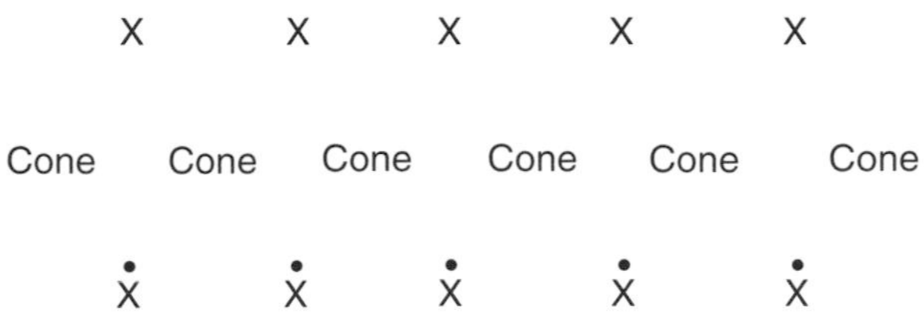

FIGURE 4.6

GAME 2

Setup
Repeat game 1.

Goals
- Specific number of shots, depending on ability.
- Specific number of on-target shots.

Lesson 5

Tactical Problem
Attacking the goal

Lesson Focus
Use target player to create shooting opportunities

Objective
Target player to lay (pass) the ball off for a shot by supporting player (see practice task).

GAME 1

Setup
6v6 in 50 by 40 yards/meters, full-size goals (see figure 4.7)

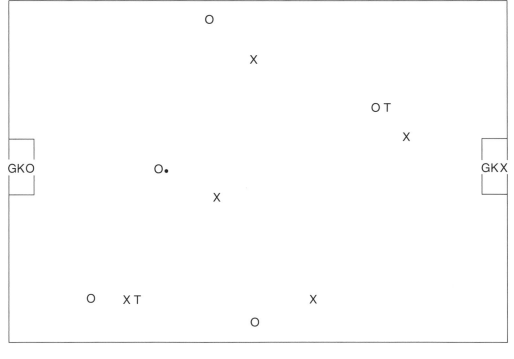

• = Ball   GK = Goalkeeper   T = Target player

FIGURE 4.7

Goal

Get an early pass to target player, then move to support the target player.

Conditions

- One target player per team (OT, XT).
- One defender marking target player.

Questions

Q: What should other players do when their own target player has the ball?
A: Provide support.

Q: Where is a good place to support?
A: In a position to receive a pass and shoot.

PRACTICE TASK

Setup

Shooting from target player lay off (pass) (see figure 4.8); one goalkeeper, one collector, one target player, three or four shooters

Goals

- Accurate pass to target.
- Firm lay off by target player (to the side).
- Clean strike of moving ball by shooter.
- Specific number of shots on-target.

Cues

- Shooter
  - Firmly pass to the target.
  - Run to the side of the target to receive the return pass.
  - Shoot the moving ball immediately.
- Target player
  - Firmly pass to the side.

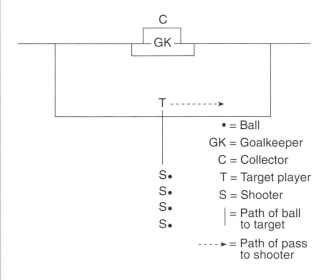

FIGURE 4.8

- • = Ball
- GK = Goalkeeper
- C = Collector
- T = Target player
- S = Shooter
- | = Path of ball to target
- ----➤ = Path of pass to shooter

GAME 2

Setup

6v6 in 50 by 40 yards/meters, full goal (see figure 4.9)

Goals

- Shield or lay off by target player.
- Support for target player.
- Specific number of shots on goal per team.

Conditions

- Play with one target player (rotate).
- Target player cannot turn with ball.
- Goals scored from a lay off by the target player count double.

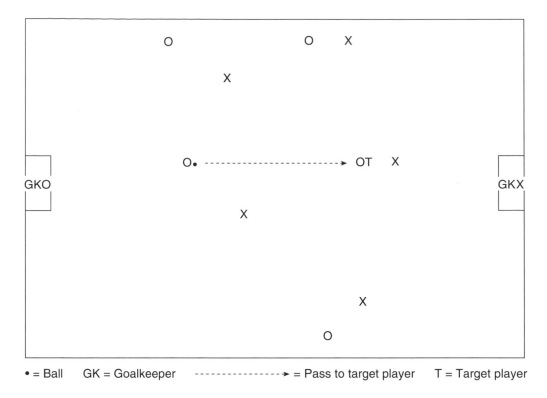

• = Ball   GK = Goalkeeper   ---------------→ = Pass to target player   T = Target player

FIGURE 4.9

Lesson 6   Level I

Tactical Problem
Restarting play

Lesson Focus
Throw-in

Objective
Quick use of correctly taken throw-in to move attack forward.

GAME 1

Setup
6v6 in 60 by 30 yards/meters, full goal (see figure 4.10), narrow field so ball goes out of play often and players take many throw-ins

Goal
Take quick throw-ins.

Question
> Q: *How can you quickly get the ball into play on a throw-in?*
> A: Player O1 throws to nearest player (O2), who passes it back to O1.

PRACTICE TASK 1

Setup
Partner practice, throw, control, return

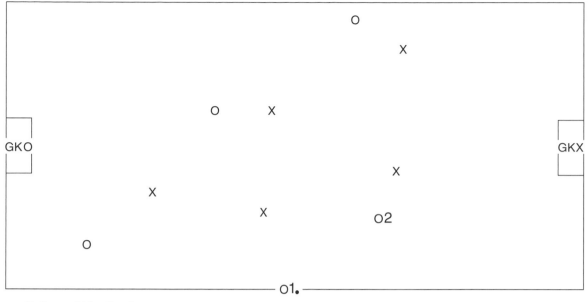

• = Ball   GK = Goalkeeper

FIGURE 4.10

Cues

- Thrower
  - Use two hands.
  - Take the ball behind the head.
  - Keep two feet on the ground at all times.
  - Throw to the receiver's feet and move onto the field.
- Receiver
  - Control and return the ball to the thrower.

PRACTICE TASK 2

Setup

2v1 (defender O) in 30 by 10 yards/meters (see figure 4.11)

Conditions

- Attack starts with throw-in at 10-yard/meter line.
- Support player (X2) must get free to receive return pass.

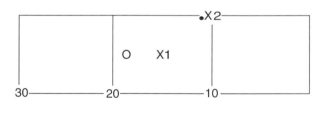

FIGURE 4.11

Goals

- Receiver (X1) of throw-in turns with ball or passes ball back to teammate (X2).
- X1 and X2 get ball to 30-yard/meter line under control by 2v1.

Cues

- Thrower (X2)
  - Use two hands.
  - Take the ball behind the head.
  - Keep two feet on the ground at all times.
  - Throw to the receiver's feet and move onto the field.
- Receiver (X1)
  - Control and return the ball to the thrower.

GAME 2

Repeat game 1.

Lesson 7

Tactical Problem
Restarting play

Lesson Focus
Attacking at corner kicks, the short corner

Objective
Using corners to create scoring opportunities.

GAME 1

Setup
6v6 in 40 by 50 yards/meters, full goal, referee calls many corners (see figure 4.12)

Goal
Be aware of the corner kick as a chance to score.

Question

Q: *How can you use a corner to score?*
A: Get the ball into the center.

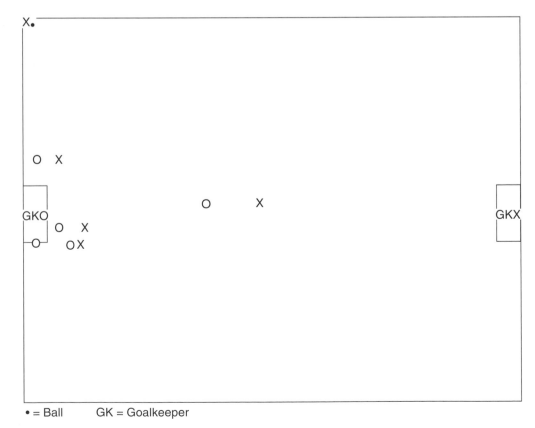

• = Ball   GK = Goalkeeper

FIGURE 4.12

PRACTICE TASK

Setup
Team practice, unopposed (no goalkeeper), short corners (see figure 4.13)

Goal
Use short corners to attack goal.

Cues
- Short corner.
- Two (X5, X6) attackers go to corner.
- X5 quickly passes to X6.
- X6 dribbles closer to the goal before passing or shooting.

GAME 2

Repeat game 1.

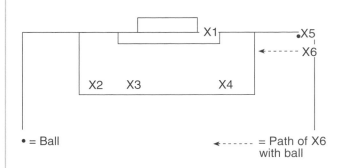

• = Ball

◀------ = Path of X6 with ball

FIGURE 4.13

Level II

At level II, students again focus on the tactical problems of maintaining possession of the ball and attacking the goal, but they progress to defending the goal and defending space. The focus of maintaining possession now shifts from solutions for players who have the ball to contributions of teammates without the ball. This early focus on off-the-ball movement is critical because soccer players spend much more time without the ball, and they should spend this time in productive movement. As in all invasion games, players need to learn when and where they should move to help their team keep possession of the ball.

After paying additional attention to attacking the goal, students focus on defending space and the goal. It is appropriate to shift the focus to defense because students will understand that they must solve defensive problems for their team to succeed. Modified games at level II enable students to see the value in marking or guarding opponents and in having the goalkeeper properly positioned to receive the ball when it comes. Brief attention to the goalkeeper's distribution of the ball allows the game to develop its complexity by the end of level II. Distribution at this level is rolling or throwing the ball, which is more appropriate than kicking in small-sided games.

It is important for players to learn to pay attention to those without the ball for potential plays.

Tactical Problem
Maintaining possession of the ball

Lesson Focus
Supporting the ball carrier

Objective
Students being positioned to receive a pass.

GAME 1

Setup
3v3 in 30 by 20 yards/meters, narrow goal
(see figure 4.14)

Goals
- Accurately pass with insides and outsides of feet.
- Players move into position to receive a pass.
- Player with the ball looks for support.

Conditions
- Three touches (each player has two touches to receive the ball and one to pass or shoot).
- Head-height rule.

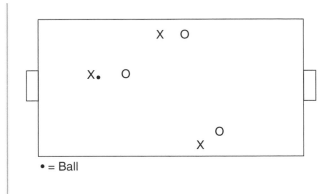

• = Ball

FIGURE 4.14

Questions

Q: How can players without the ball help a player who has the ball?
A: Be in a position to receive a pass.

Q: Where should supporting players go?
A: Away from defenders into open space.

Q: Any open space?
A: Anywhere you can receive a pass—into a passing lane (this could be behind a teammate with the ball if necessary).

PRACTICE TASK

Setup
2v1 in 20 by 10 yards/meters, pass and support (see figure 4.15), two attackers (X and S). On the signal the defender (O) attacks the ball, the supporter (S) moves to one side, and the attacker (X) draws the defender and passes. Play for six passes or until O wins the ball.

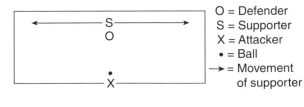

O = Defender
S = Supporter
X = Attacker
• = Ball
→ = Movement of supporter

FIGURE 4.15

Goals

- Supporting player moves to a good position.
- Attacker (X) waits for defender (O) to close in before passing.
- Three repetitions and rotate.

Cues

- Defender attacks the ball on the signal.
- Supporter moves quickly to the side.
- Attacker passes as defender advances.

GAME 2

Repeat game 1.

Lesson 9 ⌒ Level II

Tactical Problem

Maintaining possession of the ball

Lesson Focus

Supporting the ball carrier

Objective

Constant support for player with the ball.

GAME 1

Setup

4v4 (min) or 6v6 (max) in 40 by 30 yards/meters, full or narrow goal (see figure 4.16)

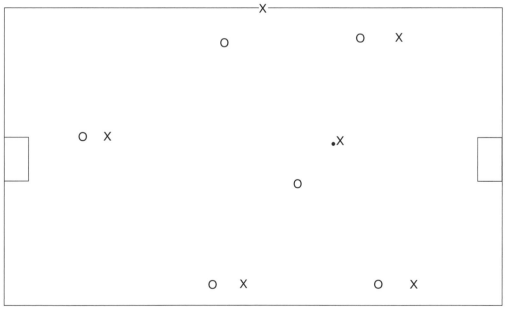

• = Ball

FIGURE 4.16

Goals

- Be in a position to receive a pass.
- Be aware that ball carrier needs support to be able to pass.

Conditions

- Three touches (depending on abilities).
- Head-height rule.

Questions

Q: *How can players without the ball help a player who has the ball?*
A: Be in position to receive a pass.

Q: *Where should supporting players go?*
A: Away from defenders and into a passing lane.

PRACTICE TASK 1

Setup

3v1 (passive defender) in 10 by 10 yards/meters, unopposed possession (see figure 4.17)

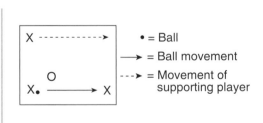

FIGURE 4.17

Goals

- Be aware of best location for support.
- Provide two options for ball carrier.

Cues

- As the ball is passed, X2 moves to support the player who will give the next pass (X1).
- Move quickly and call for the ball.

PRACTICE TASK 2

Setup

3v1 (active defender) in 10 by 10 yards/meters, possession (see figure 4.18), rotate defender at 10 passes or when ball goes out of grid

FIGURE 4.18

Goals

- Ten consecutive passes with ball in grid.
- Provide two options for ball carrier.
- Use maximum possible angle of support.

Condition

Defender must attack the ball.

Cues

- Move to support the passer (don't get stuck with defender between you and the ball).
- Move quickly and call.
- Passer waits for the defender to come to you before passing.
- Use firm passes.

GAME 2

Setup
Repeat game 1.

Goals
- Ball carrier always has two open receivers.
- Support quickly and call for the ball.

Lesson 10

Tactical Problem
Attacking the goal

Lesson Focus
Turning with the ball

Objective
Quick turns while in possession of the ball.

GAME 1

Setup
1v1 in 20 by 10 yards/meters, two feeders (F) (see figure 4.19), if O wins the ball from X, she becomes the attacker

Goal
Receive pass from feeder and turn to pass to other feeder.

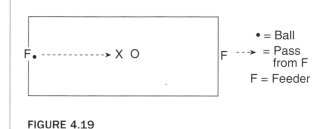

FIGURE 4.19

Questions

Q: *What does the attacker need to do in this situation?*
A: Turn quickly.

Q: *How can the attacker turn past the defender?*
A: Flick with the outside of the foot and move forward onto the ball.

PRACTICE TASK

Setup
In partners 10 yards/meters apart, receive pass and turn

Cues
- Receive and turn in one move.
- Push the ball with the outside of the foot.
- Clock analogy (receive the ball from 12:00 and push it to 4:00 or 8:00).

GAME 2

Setup
3v3 in 20 by 20 yards/meters, two feeders (see figure 4.20)

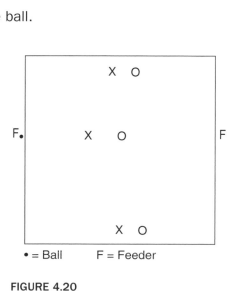

FIGURE 4.20

Goals
- Receive pass from feeder.
- Work as a team to pass to other feeder.
- Each pass to feeder earns 1 point.

Condition
Cannot return a pass to the feeder who gave the pass.

Lesson 11 Level II

Tactical Problem
Attacking the goal

Lesson Focus
Shooting

Objectives
- Receive ball and execute quick shot on-target.
- Follow the shot for rebound.

GAME 1

Setup
Shooting derby, 2v2 in 30 by 20 yards/meters (see figure 4.21), with two feeders, one goalkeeper, and one collector (eight players total) and a full goal. Switch every eight trials.

Goal
Use one touch to control, then shoot on-target.

Question

Q: *If you receive the ball this close to the goal, what should you do?*
A: Turn and shoot.

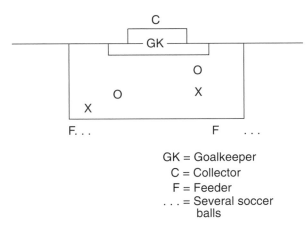

GK = Goalkeeper
C = Collector
F = Feeder
. . . = Several soccer balls

FIGURE 4.21

PRACTICE TASK

Setup
Pressure shooting in penalty area (see figure 4.22), with three shooters (alternating every three shots), two feeders, one goalkeeper, and two collectors. Switch every eight trials.

Goal
Specific number of shots on-target.

Cue
Set up for shot with one touch to right or left (left if pass is from left feeder, right if pass comes from right feeder).

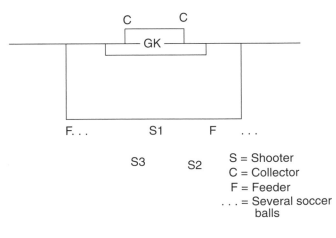

S = Shooter
C = Collector
F = Feeder
. . . = Several soccer balls

FIGURE 4.22

GAME 2

Setup
4v4 in 30 by 20 yards/meters, full goal

Goals
- Even number of shots from 10 and 20 yards/meters.
- Specific number of shots on-target.

Lesson 12

Tactical Problem
Defending space

Lesson Focus
Marking (guarding) and pressuring the ball

Objective
Understanding the need to mark players and to pressure the ball to defend space.

GAME 1

Setup
4v4 in 40 by 30 yards/meters, full goal

Goals
- Defenders are in position between opponent and own goal.
- Defenders are in position so they can see opponent and ball.

Condition
Mark (or guard) an opposing player.

Questions

Q: How can you make it hard for opponents to receive the ball?
A: Mark (or guard) them.

Q: Where should you stand to mark them?
A: Between your opponent and your goal.

Q: As the ball nears your opponent, what should you do?
A: Get closer to your opponent.

Q: As your opponent nears your goal, what should you do?
A: Again, get closer to your opponent.

PRACTICE TASK

Setup
1v1 plus two feeders in 20 by 10 yards/meters (see figure 4.23)

Goals
- Prevent opponent from turning.
- Keep appropriate distance.
- Use appropriate stance.

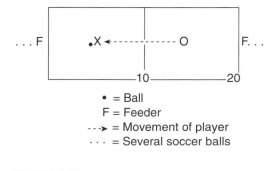

• = Ball
F = Feeder
--→ = Movement of player
· · · = Several soccer balls

FIGURE 4.23

Conditions
- Feeders at 0 and 20 yards/meters.
- Alternate feeds.

Cues
- Close down opponent quickly.
- Stop one arm's length away.
- Get low.
- Use staggered stance.
- Wait for opponent to try to turn.
- Don't dive into the tackle.

GAME 2

Setup
Repeat game 1.

Goals
- Close space between you and opponent as ball is played.
- Prevent opponent from turning.

Lesson 13 Level II

Tactical Problem
Defending the goal

Lesson Focus
Goalkeeping, positioning

Objective
Goalkeeper positioned to narrow the angle.

GAME 1

Setup
2v2 in 20 by 20 yards/meters, full goal with one goalkeeper per team (see figure 4.24)

Goal
Give attacker as little target to shoot at as possible.

Condition
Goalkeeper cannot come past the 10-yard/meter line.

Question
Q: *How can the goalkeeper give the attacker less area to shoot at?*
A: Move out or sideways to narrow the angle.

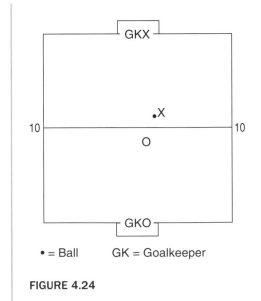

• = Ball   GK = Goalkeeper

FIGURE 4.24

PRACTICE TASK

Setup

Goalkeeper versus goalkeeper (1v1) in 20 by 20 yards/meters, full goal (see figure 4.25)

Goals

- Goalkeeper moves to narrow the angle.
- Goalkeeper moves side to side and off the line.

Conditions

- Start dribble from 0 yards each time.
- Shoot from a different point outside 10 yards/meters each time.

Cues

- Goalkeeper comes off the goal line toward the ball.
- Stay low.

GAME 2

Setup

4v4 in 40 by 30 yards/meters, full goal, rotate goalkeepers

Goals

- Goalkeeper moves to narrow the angle.
- Goalkeeper moves side to side and off the line.

• = Ball   GK = Goalkeeper

FIGURE 4.25

Lesson 14 Level II

Tactical Problem

Defending the goal

Lesson Focus

Goalkeeping, gathering the ball

Objectives

- Get body behind ball.
- Bring ball into chest.

GAME 1

Setup

Goalkeeper versus goalkeeper (1v1) in 20 by 10 yards/meters

Goal

Get in line with oncoming shot.

Condition

Cooperative shots at half pace.

Questions

Q: *Where should the goalkeeper be positioned to stop the ball?*
A: In line with the ball.

Q: *What is the best way to securely hold the ball?*
A: Cradled into the chest.

PRACTICE TASK

Setup
Partner practice (hand feeds at low, medium, and high heights)

Goals
- Get the body behind the ball (in line with the shot).
- Take ball into chest.

Condition
Make partner move as he improves.

Cues
- Get in line with the oncoming shot.
- Take the ball into the chest.
- Cradle the ball.
- Protect the ball.

GAME 2

Setup
2v2 in 20 by 20 yards/meters, full goal plus goalkeepers

Goals
- Goalkeepers narrow the angle.
- Put body behind ball.
- Take ball into chest.

Level III

Level III builds directly on level II, further investigating the tactical problems of attacking the goal and defending space. We increase tactical complexity with creating space in attack and winning the ball. We investigate additional methods of restarting play, specifically, using restarts to score. Since we are increasing tactical complexity at level III, skill requirements also increase. We assume that students have learned the material covered in levels I and II and therefore have some degree of technical competence accompanying their developing understanding. Though technical and tactical competencies develop at different rates for different students, level III is likely suitable for upper middle school or beginning high school students.

Introducing an offensive target player at level III shows students how to create shooting opportunities as a team. An emphasis on one-touch passing enables them to more effectively create space for chances at shooting. Having introduced the target player, we can investigate solutions to prevent this target player from turning with the ball and attacking the space between her and the goal. At level III, the game looks more developed both offensively and defensively.

Level III introduces free kicks, of which there are two types:

- The direct free kick is awarded for most offenses, including pushing, tripping, and using hands on the ball. The player taking the free kick may shoot directly at goal.
- The indirect free kick is awarded for offenses such as unsporting conduct or obstruction (of an opponent when the ball is not playable). The ball must be touched by two players before a goal can be scored.

Learning how to create space and form an attack are important to achieving a goal.

Lesson 15 Level III

Tactical Problem
Maintaining possession of the ball

Lesson Focus
Supporting the ball carrier

Objective
Provide support so passer can split the defense (i.e., pass the ball between two defenders).

GAME 1

Setup
2v2 to target player in 30 by 20 yards/meters, with two target players (OT and XT) along the end line (a total of 3v3) (see figure 4.26)

Goal
Get ball to target player (who can move along the end line).

Conditions
  · Three touches.
  · Head-height rule.

Question

Q: *How can the target player help teammates find him?*
A: Constantly move sideways along the end line to support teammates.

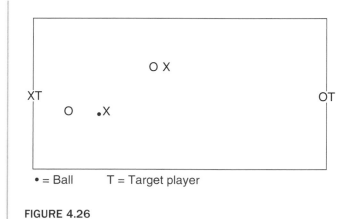

• = Ball   T = Target player

FIGURE 4.26

PRACTICE TASK

Setup

4v2 (defenders) possession game in 20 by 20 yards/meters (see figure 4.27)

Goals

- Make 10 consecutive passes (splitting defenders with a pass counts as two passes).
- Give angle of support so passer can split defense.

Condition

Defenders must attack the ball.

Cues

- Passer splits the defenders.
- Supporters position themselves so passer can split the defenders.

GAME 2

Setup

6v6 in 50 by 40 yards/meters, full goal

Goal

Split defenders with pass to put teammate in scoring position.

Condition

Head-height rule.

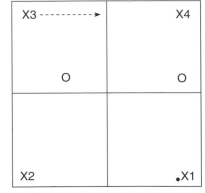

• = Ball

------➤ = Movement of supporting player (X3) so passer (X1) can split defenders

FIGURE 4.27

Lesson 16

Level III

Tactical Problem

Attacking the goal

Lesson Focus

Penetration using a target player

Objective

Use target player for early penetration.

GAME 1

Setup

4v4 in 30 by 20 yards/meters, full goal (see figure 4.28)

Goals

- Get ball to target player quickly with an accurate pass.
- Target player holds ball and threatens goal.

Condition

Each team must leave a target player in opponent's half and a central defender in own half.

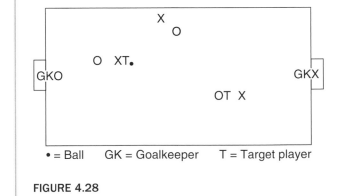

• = Ball   GK = Goalkeeper   T = Target player

FIGURE 4.28

Question

Q: What can the target player do when she receives the ball?
A: Hold (keep possession of the ball), turn, or lay off.

PRACTICE TASK

Setup

2v1 to goal (plus one goalkeeper) in 20 by 10 yards/meters (see figure 4.29). Start with feed to target player by support player and switch roles every four trials.

Goal

Target player to hold, shield and turn, or lay off (short sideways pass) to a teammate.

Cues

· Target player
- Hold.
- Turn and shoot.
- Look for support.
- Follow shot for rebound.
· Support player
- Support target player.

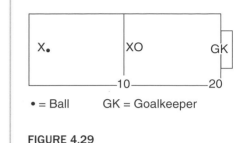

• = Ball   GK = Goalkeeper

FIGURE 4.29

GAME 2

Setup

Repeat game 1.

Goal

Target player to hold and turn or hold and lay off to supporting players.

Lesson 17

Level III

Tactical Problem

Creating space in attack

Lesson Focus

One-touch (or first-time) passing

Objective

Using a first-time pass to create space (a first-time pass is one given immediately without using any touches to control the ball).

GAME 1

Setup

2v2 plus two players per team at outside corners in 20 by 20 yards/meters for total of 4v4 (see figure 4.30)

Goals

· Possession.
· Ten passes.

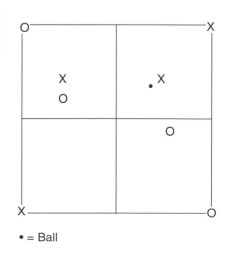

• = Ball

FIGURE 4.30

Conditions

- Four players in grid can only use first-time pass. Outside players can move 10 yards/meters along each line.
- Inside players cannot tackle outside players.

Question

Q: *What does the first-time pass enable you to do?*
A: Move the ball quickly.

PRACTICE TASK

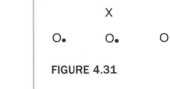

FIGURE 4.31

Setup

3v1 pressure pass using two balls (see figure 4.31) with first-time passes (alternate balls)

Goal

Accurate redirection of ball by a first-time pass to the player without a ball.

Cues

- Decide early where the ball has to go.
- Redirect the ball with the inside or outside of the foot.

GAME 2

Setup

4v4 in 40 by 30 yards/meters, small goals, no goalkeeper

Condition

Two players per team must play one touch (designate one of these players as target player), then rotate.

Goals

- Speed of ball movement.
- Speed of support.

Lesson 18   Level III

Tactical Problem
Creating space in attack

Lesson Focus
One-touch passing

Objective
Use a first-time pass to beat a defender (one-two play).

GAME 1

Setup

2v1 to target player (T) in 30 by 10 yards/meters (see figure 4.32). Start with feed to defender (O) at 20 yards/meters; defender gives first-time pass back and moves forward.

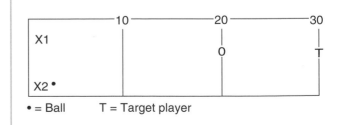

FIGURE 4.32

Goal

As a team, X1 and X2 must get ball to target player.

Condition

Defender must go to the ball.

Question

Q: *How can two players help each other beat one defender?*
A: Use a give-and-go or one-two play.

PRACTICE TASK

Setup

2v2 with passive defenders on 10 and 30 yards/meters in 40 by 10 yards/meters (see figure 4.33)

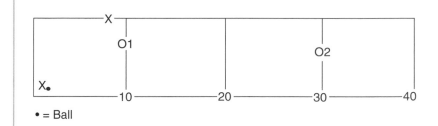

• = Ball

FIGURE 4.33

Conditions

- Defenders must go to the ball.
- Each defender can only advance a maximum of 10 yards/meters.
- Attackers must beat each defender with a give-and-go play.
- O1 stops once beaten. O2 moves only when ball crosses the 20.

Cues

- Supporter
  - Position yourself ahead of the ball.
  - Return the pass (first time) behind the defender.
- Ball carrier
  - Draw the defender toward you.
  - Give (pass) and go (for return).

GAME 2

Setup

Repeat game 1.

Goal

Appropriate timing of give-and-go play.

GAME 3

Setup

4v4 in 40 by 30 yards/meters, small goals, no goalkeeper

Goal

Use give-and-go play at appropriate times to beat opponents.

Conditions

- Two players per team play one touch and then rotate.
- Extra goal awarded for a give-and-go play that beats an opponent.

Tactical Problem
Winning the ball

Lesson Focus
Containment and tackle

Objectives
- Stay on feet.
- Make a solid tackle.

GAME 1

Setup
3v3 in 30 by 20 yards/meters, no goal (see figure 4.34)

Goal
Control ball and get ball to 30-yard/meter line.

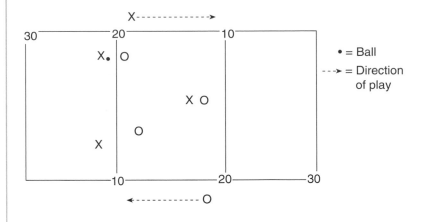

FIGURE 4.34

Condition
Take on your opponent (try to dribble around her) before passing.

Question

Q: How can you slow an attacker and win the ball?
A: Channel (i.e., guide the opponent in a particular direction) and tackle.

PRACTICE TASK 1

Setup
1v1 in 20 by 10 yards/meters. Defender (O) passes ball to attacker (X) and advances to close him down. X tries to dribble around O to the 20-yard/meter line (see figure 4.35).

Goal
Channel and tackle.

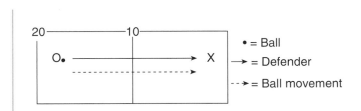

FIGURE 4.35

Conditions
- Defender feeds from 20 yards/meters.
- Can move to close down attacker when ball crosses 10 yards/meters.

Cues
- Close quickly to about 6 feet (2 meters).
- Staggered stance in front and to one side of the opponent.
- Channel the attacker to his weak side (i.e., to his left if player is right-footed).
- Stay on your feet and wait for the attacker to move (to go around you).
- Get your foot in for solid tackle (or poke the ball out of play).

PRACTICE TASK 2

Setup
1v1 block tackle practice (standing). On count of three both players use inside of the same foot to make a solid tackle on the ball.

Goal
Firm tackle.

GAME 2

Repeat game 1.

Lesson 20 Level III

Tactical Problem
Restarting play

Lesson Focus
Near-post corner

Objective
Use near-post corner to create scoring opportunities.

GAME 1

Setup
6v6 in 40 by 50 yards/meters, full goal, referee calls many corners

Condition
Place a(n) (offensive) player on near (front) post for each corner.

Goal
Awareness of corner as a chance to score.

Question

Q: *How can the near-post corner be effective?*
A: The near-post player can redirect the ball for incoming attackers.

PRACTICE TASK

Setup
Team practice, unopposed, at near-post corner (see figure 4.36)

Goal
Use near-post corner to score.

Cues
- Corner taker (X1) aims for head of near-post player (X2).
- Near-post player (X2) redirects ball back and out with head or foot (a flick).
- Attackers (X3, X4, and X5) run to meet the flick.

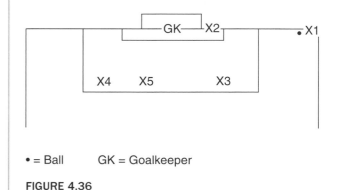

• = Ball   GK = Goalkeeper

FIGURE 4.36

GAME 2

Repeat game 1.

Lesson 21 Level III

Tactical Problem
Restarting play

Lesson Focus
Attacking with free kicks

Objective
Use free kicks to score.

GAME 1

Setup

6v6 in 60 by 40 yards/meters, full goal, referee calls many free kicks while players are in a variety of positions on the field

Goal

Awareness of free kicks as scoring opportunities.

Question

Q: *How can you use a free kick to threaten the goal?*
A: Shoot, pass, or cross depending on position of free kick.

PRACTICE TASK

Setup

Team practice, opposed, direct or indirect free kicks from a variety of angles, three teams working at each goal. All free kicks are from outside the penalty area (see figure 4.37).

Goal

Attack from free kick using different strategies (including shot, chip, and cross) depending on angle and type of kick.

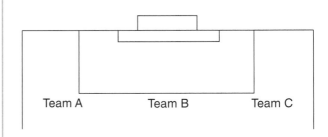

Team A Team B Team C

FIGURE 4.37

Cues

- Shooting, hit the target.
- Pass to shoot, pass the ball into the shooter's path.
- Cross to the center of the goal area.

GAME 2

Repeat game 1.

Level IV

At the beginning of level IV, students will revisit maintaining possession of the ball because they are able to investigate this tactical problem in a larger playing area. Solutions to the problem include controlling the ball with the thigh and chest and long passing. A focus on using the overlapping run to create space provides additional width in attack, which students must now use effectively. Solutions to the problem of using this space include dribbling, crossing the ball, and heading toward goal. These skills are used in bigger playing spaces, making level IV more suitable for high school students with some soccer experience and ability.

The offensive focus on crossing and heading necessitates further attention to the defensive problems this focus creates. These problems are defending space in the penalty area and winning the ball from offensive opponents in wide positions. Solutions include clearing the ball and making sliding tackles.

Maintaining possession of the ball is an important skill to hone.

Lesson 22 Level IV

Tactical Problem
Maintaining possession of the ball

Lesson Focus
Long passing

Objective
Use long pass to keep possession and switch play.

GAME 1

Setup
6v6 in 60 by 40 yards/meters, full goal

Goal
Use long pass to switch defense to attack quickly.

Condition
One target player per team (rotate).

Questions

Q: *How can you use the space on the field?*
A: Stay spread out.

Q: *How can a long pass help you?*
A: It reaches teammates who are away from the ball and helps you quickly move from defense to attack.

PRACTICE TASK

Setup

Long pass, partner practice, static and rolling balls

Goal

Distance and accuracy of a pass above head height.

Cues

· Take a long step to the ball.
· Keep the nonkicking foot next to the ball.
· Place the kicking foot under the ball.
· Contact the ball with top of the foot (laces of the shoe).
· Lean back as you follow through.

GAME 2

Repeat game 1.

Lesson 23   Level IV

Tactical Problem
Maintaining possession of the ball

Lesson Focus
Receiving the long pass

Objective
Control and set up the ball with feet, thigh, and chest.

GAME 1

Setup
4v4 throw and control game in 50 by 40 yards/meters, no goals

Condition
Throw and control (player 1 throws to player 2, who controls the ball with any part of the body and then picks it up and throws it to another player on his team—in this way players progress down the field).

Goal
Control ball and stop it on the goal line.

Question

Q: *What must you do to succeed in receiving a long pass?*
A: Receive and control the ball from the air.

PRACTICE TASK

Setup
Partner practice, hand feeding to feet, thigh, chest

Goals
- Bring ball down to feet quickly.
- Kill the bounce and set up for next move to right, left, or front.

Cues
- Foot
  - Kill the bounce with the inside or outside of the foot.
  - Drag the foot across the ball to kill the bounce.
- Thigh
  - Bring the thigh up to the ball.
  - Withdraw the thigh on impact.
  - Kill the bounce when the ball falls.
- Chest
  - Bring the chest out to the ball.
  - Withdraw the chest on impact.
  - Kill the bounce when the ball falls.

GAME 2

Setup
4v4 in 60 by 40 yards/meters, no goals

Goal
Control ball and stop it on the goal line.

Conditions
- Target players (rotate).
- Maximum of 10-yard/meter dribble.

Lesson 24   Level IV

Tactical Problem
Maintaining possession of the ball

Lesson Focus
Combining short and long passing

Objective
Use combination of short and long passes to maintain possession.

GAME 1

Setup
6v6 possession game in 60 by 40 yards/meters, no goal (see figure 4.38)

Goal
Control ball and stop it on goal line.

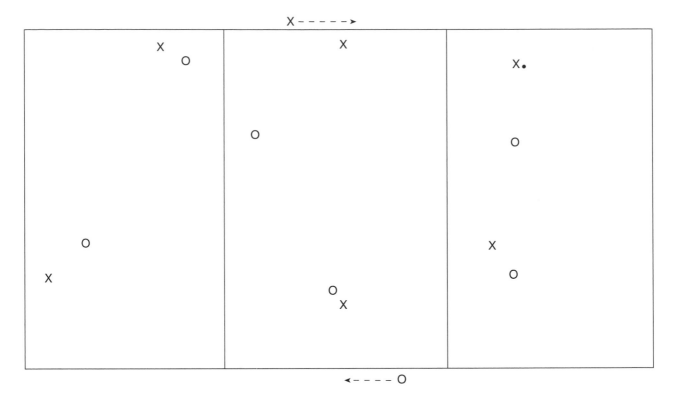

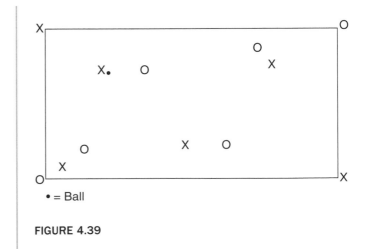

• = Ball   – – – ➤ = Movement of player

FIGURE 4.38

Conditions
- Three touches.
- Restricted areas.
- Two forwards, two players midfield, two defenders.

Questions

Q: *Is it best to use long or short passes or a combination of both?*
A: Combination.

Q: *What do short passes do to the defenders?*
A: Bring them in toward the ball.

Q: *Leaving space for what?*
A: Longer passes to space behind the defenders.

PRACTICE TASK

Setup

4v4 possession game plus two outside corner players per team in 30 by 20 yards/meters for a total of 6v6 (see figure 4.39)

• = Ball

FIGURE 4.39

Goals

- Combine short and long passes to keep ball.
- Use short passes to draw opponents.
- Follow with long pass to open up the game.

Conditions

- Corner players can move 10 yards/meters along each sideline.
- Inside players cannot tackle players at outside corners.

Cue

Short, short, short (passes to draw in opponents), long (pass to the space that has been created).

GAME 2

Setup

6v6 in 60 by 40 yards/meters, full goals, no restrictions

Goal

Combine short and long passes to maintain possession and to move the ball into a scoring position.

Lesson 25 — Level IV

Tactical Problem

Creating space in attack

Lesson Focus

Overlapping run

Objective

Use overlapping runs to create space at the flanks (overlapping is made by a supporting player around the side of a teammate with the ball, usually at the side of the field).

GAME 1

Setup

6v6 in 30 by 50 yards/meters, short and wide, full goal

Goal

Awareness of need to use width to best advantage in attack.

Questions

Q: *Where is the most space on the field?*
A: In wide areas.

Q: *How can you use this space?*
A: Get players into wide areas to receive a pass.

Q: *What can wide players do when they get the ball?*
A: Cross the ball into the center.

Setup

Overlap and cross drill (see figure 4.40). Passer (X) passes to target player (T); X overlaps, receives return pass from T, and crosses the ball. Nonpasser (Y) and target player (T) run to center of goal to meet the cross.

Variation

Y overlaps, receives pass from T, and crosses. X passes to T, X and T run to center of goal.

Goals

· Speed of overlap run.
· Timing of pass to runner.

Condition

Static defenders (O) at first, then change to active defenders (O).

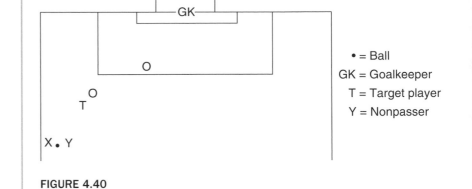

• = Ball
GK = Goalkeeper
T = Target player
Y = Nonpasser

FIGURE 4.40

Cues

· X passes to T and runs wide around T (overlapping run down the sideline).
· T receives and passes the ball back into X's path.
· Y sprints to center of goal area.

GAME 2

Setup

Repeat game 1.

Goal

Use overlapping run in game situation.

Condition

If you pass to the wing you must follow the pass to overlap the receiver.

Lesson 26   Level IV

Tactical Problem
Using space in attack

Lesson Focus
Using width in attack

Objectives
· Awareness of areas of field best suited to dribbling.
· Acquisition of dribbling skills.

GAME 1

Setup

6v6 in 50 by 50 yards/meters, short and wide, full goal

Goal

Awareness of the areas of the field that contain the most space in attack (i.e., the flanks or wings).

Question

Q: *Other than make a cross, what do wide players have space to do?*
A: Run at and around defenders, dribble.

PRACTICE TASK 1

Setup

Play in threes, continuous dribbling relay

Goals

- Control with insides and outsides of both feet.
- Pace and change of pace.

Cues

- Push or stroke the ball.
- Keep the ball close.

PRACTICE TASK 2

Setup

Repeat task 1 with cone for defender

Goals

- Beat the defender (i.e., the cone) with the ball.
- Perform push and run, fake shot and push, step over and push.

Cues

- Push and run.
- Fake the shot and push (the ball around the cone with the outside of the foot).
- Accelerate.

GAME 2

Setup

Repeat game 1.

Condition

Mark or guard 1v1.

Goal

Attack the space behind your opponent whenever possible.

Lesson 27 — Level IV

Tactical Problem
Using space in attack

Lesson Focus
Using width in attack

Objective
Beating a defender with the dribble.

GAME 1

Setup
2v2 to opposite goal line in 30 by 20 yards/meters

Goal
Awareness of need to move forward when teammates are marked and of the necessity of getting past an opposing defender while keeping the ball under control.

Condition
Mark or guard 1v1.

Questions

Q: *If there is space behind your opponent, what can you do?*
A: Go around her.

Q: *How?*
A: Dribble, push the ball past, and accelerate.

PRACTICE TASK 1

Setup
1v3 in 30 by 10 yards/meters, static defenders on 10, 20, and 30 yards/meters (see figure 4.41)

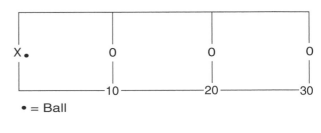

• = Ball

FIGURE 4.41

Goals
· Beat each defender in turn and cross the 30-yard/meter line with ball under control.
· If tackled, retrieve ball and continue to next defender.
· Use push and run, feint shot and push, step over and push.

Condition
Defenders cannot move. Defenders must give the ball back to the attacker if they win a tackle.

Cues
· Push and run.
· Feint and push.
· Accelerate.

PRACTICE TASK 2

Setup
Extend practice task 1.

Condition
Defenders can only move along their lines.

GAME 2

Setup
4v4 in 40 by 30 yards/meters, small goals (no goalkeeper)

Goal
Beat opponents in 1v1 game situation.

Conditions
- Mark 1v1.
- Attempt to beat an opponent before passing.

Lesson 28

Tactical Problem
Using space in attack

Lesson Focus
Using width in attack

Objective
Deliver an accurate cross after the dribble.

GAME 1

Setup
4v3 (including goalkeeper) in 20 by 40 yards/meters, short and wide, one feeder (F) feeds to any X (see figure 4.42)

Goals
- Attack to score from a cross.
- Be aware of necessity of a good cross.
- Defense to bring the ball under control to the 20-yard/meter line.

Question

Q: If you have a chance to deliver a cross, where should you aim?
A: Toward the center of the goal but away from the goalkeeper.

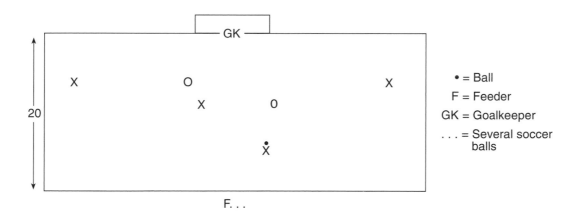

FIGURE 4.42

PRACTICE TASK

Setup

Continuous crossing drill in 60 by 50 yards/meters, two full goals (see figure 4.43). Crossers (X) dribble and cross away from goalkeeper. Goalkeeper collects and feeds X waiting at side of goal, X proceeds down the side of the field to cross the ball. After making a cross, X moves to side of goal and waits for next feed from goalkeeper. Numbers in this practice can vary; figure 4.43 shows an eight-player drill rotating counterclockwise. Crosses come from right.

Goals

· Flighted ball from the wings.
· Ball crossed away from goalkeeper.

Cues

· Move down the field quickly.
· Cross the ball away from the goalkeeper.

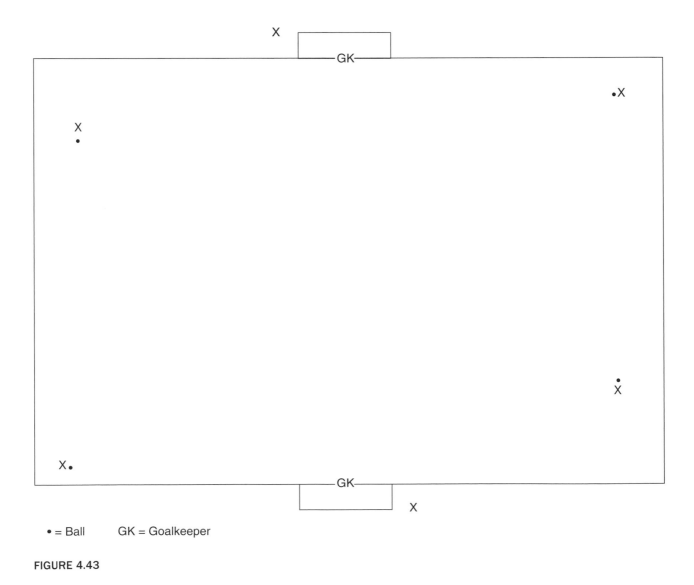

• = Ball   GK = Goalkeeper

FIGURE 4.43

GAME 2

Setup
6v6 in 60 by 50 yards/meters (plus one coach and one feeder per team). Alternate feeds for each team. Feeder must feed to either right or left winger.

Goal
Maximize use of width of field.

Conditions
- Each team has two permanent wingers.
- Feeders give alternate feeds to each team and must feed to winger.

Lesson 29

Tactical Problem
Using space in attack

Lesson Focus
Using width in attack

Objective
Score with the head.

GAME 1

Setup
Heading game, 3v3 in 30 by 20 yards/ meters, small goal

Goals
- Score with head.
- Become aware of need to use head to change the direction of the ball.

Conditions
- Throw, head, throw, head (thrown ball must be headed to another teammate and caught).
- Game includes only throwing, heading, and catching (progress is made up the field in this way).
- Must head ball into goal to score.

Questions
Q: *When might you be able to score with your head?*
A: From a cross.

Q: *Where should you head the ball to?*
A: At the goal and down.

Q: *Why head it down?*
A: To make it harder for the goalkeeper to make a save.

PRACTICE TASK 1

Setup
Threes static practice (see figure 4.44) with one header (X) and two feeders (O). Each feeder has a ball. Alternate feeds and head back to feeder.

O•   X   •O

FIGURE 4.44

Goals

- Use correct contact point (hairline).
- Use body for momentum.
- Head down to a receiver.

Cues

- Get behind the ball.
- Contact the ball on the hairline.
- Use the trunk of the body for momentum.
- Head the ball down.

PRACTICE TASK 2

Setup

Threes right-angle practice (see figure 4.45) with one header (X) and two feeders (O) and only one ball per group

Goal

Change direction with header.

Cues

- Get behind the ball.
- Head across the ball's line of flight to change its direction.
- Contact the ball on the hairline.
- Use the trunk of the body for momentum.
- Head the ball down.

X   •O

O

FIGURE 4.45

GAME 2

Setup

6v6 in 60 by 40 yards/meters, full goals

Goals

- Score with head.
- Understand value of using full width of field.

Conditions

- Two permanent wingers per team.
- Can only score with head.
- Can pick up and hand feed inside 10 yards/meters if necessary because of low-quality crosses.

Lesson 30   Level IV

Tactical Problem
Defending space

Lesson Focus
Clearing the ball

Objective
Clear the ball from danger using height, width, length.

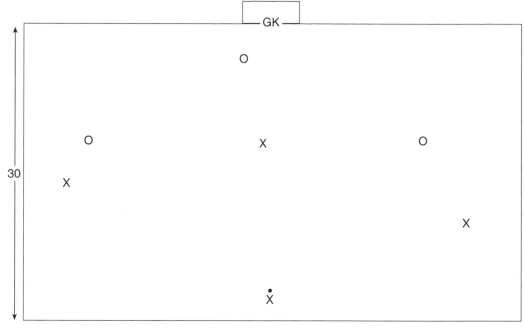

• = Ball   GK = Goalkeeper

FIGURE 4.46

GAME 1

Setup
4v4 (three defenders plus goalkeeper), attack versus defense in 30 by 50 yards/ meters (see figure 4.46)

Goals
- Attack and score.
- Defenders keep ball away from goal.

Conditions
- Attack ends with a goal or with the ball out of play at the end of the field.
- Restart attack at 30 yards/meters.
- Throw in as normal for ball out at sideline.

Questions

Q: If a cross comes in what should you do?
A: Clear it.

Q: Where should you clear to?
A: High, wide, and long, in that order.

Q: Why is the order important?
A: High gives you time to get under the ball again. Wide moves the ball away from the goal to the side. Long adds distance between you and the goal.

PRACTICE TASK

Setup

Clearances practice (see figure 4.47) with high-thrown (for accuracy) feeds to feet or head of each defender (O), with one feeder (F from wing). Defender clears ball and goes to back of line to wait for next feed. Also include one collector behind the goal.

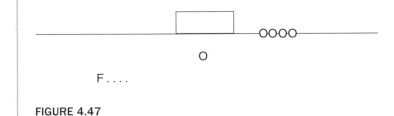

FIGURE 4.47

Goals

- Each defender clears with height, width, length.
- Clears ball out of play at nearest point if necessary (back over feeder's head is ideal).

Cues

- Accelerate to meet the ball.
- Clear as high, wide, and long as possible.
- Clear away from, not across, the goal.

GAME 2

Repeat game 1.

Lesson 31 Level IV

Tactical Problem
Winning the ball

Lesson Focus
Slide tackle

Objective
Ability to tackle at a stretch using poke and slide tackles.

GAME 1

Setup
All-in tackling in 20 by 20 yards/meters

Goal
Tackle at a stretch with poke or block.

Conditions
Knock out other balls but keep your own. Once your ball is out, go to adjoining 20- by 20-yard/meter grid and start again.

Questions

Q: If you cannot stay on your feet to tackle what must you do?
A: Go down on the ground to tackle, but make sure you win the ball.

Q: How should you go down?
A: Slide.

PRACTICE TASK

Setup

1v1 slide tackle practice in 20 by 10 yards/meters (see figure 4.48)

Goals

- Use correct position and technique for slide tackle.
- Defender makes slide tackle inside 20 yards/meters.

Conditions

- Both defender (O) and attacker (X) start at 0 yards.
- O can only tackle after X starts to run with ball at medium speed.

Cues

- Get close to the ball carrier.
- Fold under the leg nearest to your opponent as you slide.
- Knock the ball with your other leg (left leg in figure 4.48).

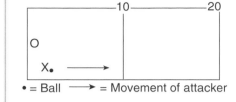

• = Ball   ⟶ = Movement of attacker

FIGURE 4.48

GAME 2

Setup

5v5 in 60 by 40 yards/meters, full goal with goalkeeper

Condition

Head-height rule.

Goals

- Mark, channel the opponent, and tackle using the most appropriate technique.
- Use slide tackle as a last resort.

Level V

By the time students reach level V, the game is tactically complex and approaching its mature form. There is more large-field play, and solutions to tactical problems require more advanced movements and teamwork. For example, additional solutions for creating space include the crossover play for either a shot or a cross. Additional use of space includes adding depth to the attack by appropriately timing supporting runs toward the goal.

Defending space also becomes more complex, with students learning how to cover each other and how to recover to provide depth in defense. Because attacking players are shooting more effectively at this level, goalkeeping should develop to include diving to make saves and distributing the ball over greater distances. Level V culminates with further investigation of offensive and defensive aspects of restarting play.

Level V represents content for advanced soccer players and might be most appropriate for an elective class of experienced players. The atmosphere in this type of class might resemble that of a coaching environment.

Once ready, students can utilize all they have learned by practicing in large fields of play.

Lesson 32 Level V

Tactical Problem
Using space in attack

Lesson Focus
Using depth in attack

Objective
Understanding the value and use of support from behind.

GAME 1

Setup
4v4 in 40 by 30 yards/meters, full goal

Goal
See value of supporting from a defensive position.

Conditions
 • Target player on each team.
 • Players cannot turn with the ball.

Question
  Q: *What options are available to the target player when he receives the ball?*
  A: Pass to the side, pass back.

PRACTICE TASK 1

Setup
3v1 in 30 by 20 yards/meters (see figure 4.49)

Goals
- Get ball to 30 yards/meters.
- Target player controls and shields the ball, passes to either teammate (X), and runs forward or diagonally for the return pass.

Conditions
- Start with feed to feet of target player (T) at 15 yards/meters.
- Use only three touches (two touches to control the ball, one to pass) in order to speed up the game.
- Defender (O) must go to the ball.

Cues
- Target player looks for support at the side and behind.
- One supporter is to the side and one is behind.

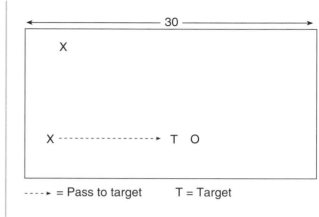

---> = Pass to target   T = Target

FIGURE 4.49

PRACTICE TASK 2

Setup
4v2 in 40 by 30 yards/meters, extension of practice task 1

Goals
- Get ball to 40 yards/meters.
- Target player controls and shields the ball, passes to a teammate, and runs forward or diagonally for the return pass.

Conditions
- Start with feed to feet of target player (T) at 20 yards/meters.
- Three touches.
- Defenders must go to the ball.

GAME 2

Repeat game 1.

Lesson 33   Level V

Tactical Problem
Using space in attack

Lesson Focus
Using depth in attack

Objective
Make well-timed attacking runs to the penalty area.

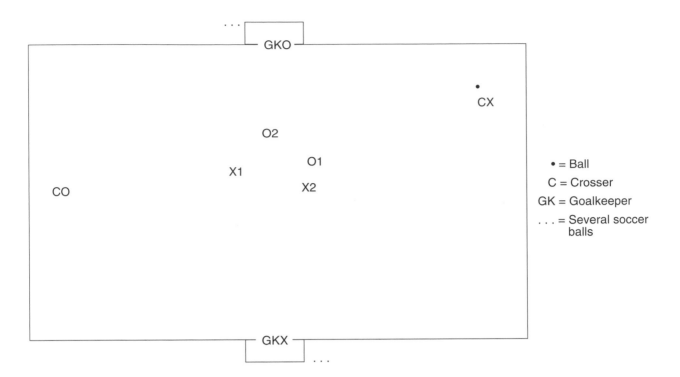

FIGURE 4.50

GAME 1

Setup
Eights, 2v2 plus two crossers (CO and CX) and two goalkeepers in 30 by 50 yards/ meters, short and wide (see figure 4.50)

Goal
Understand that a static attacker is easier to mark than a moving one.

Conditions
· Goalkeeper must feed a crosser (who is unopposed).
· Crosser serves ball toward opposing goal.

Questions
Q: *Where should you (X1 and X2) be located as the ball is crossed: level with, behind, or in front of the ball?*
A: Behind the ball.

Q: *Why?*
A: So you can move forward onto the cross.

PRACTICE TASK

Setup
In pairs (see figure 4.51), the striker feeds the winger, the winger crosses, and the striker finishes. Switch roles.

Goals

- Time the run so striker moves onto the cross.
- Score with head or foot.

Cues

- Striker holds the run and stays behind the ball.
- Striker waits for the cross and moves onto it.
- Winger crosses away from the goalkeeper.

GAME 2

Setup

4v4 in 40 by 50 yards/meters, full goal

Goal

Well-timed runs to meet crosses.

Condition

Three touches in central 20 yards/meters (middle of field).

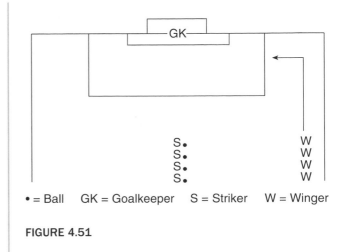

• = Ball   GK = Goalkeeper   S = Striker   W = Winger

FIGURE 4.51

Lesson 34 Level V

Tactical Problem
Creating space in attack

Lesson Focus
Crossover play

Objective
Use crossover play to create space.

GAME 1

Setup
3v3 possession game in 20 by 20 yards/meters

Goal
Awareness of need to create space in a confined area.

Condition
No pass over 10 yards/meters.

Question

Q: *How can you create space in a confined area?*
A: Short passes, crossover.

PRACTICE TASK 1

Setup
Free dribbling in 30 by 20 yards/meters with crossovers, one ball per two players

Goal

Introduce crossover play by allowing players to exchange possession by using a crossover with any player.

Cues

- Passer leaves ball for receiver.
- Communicate with "leave it" or "mine" or call your name.

PRACTICE TASK 2

Situation drill, crossovers leading to shot and cross (see figure 4.52)

Goal

Awareness of situations in which crossover play is most useful.

Cues

- Receive and shoot
  - Passer (X1) leaves ball for receiver (X2).
  - Communicate with "leave it" or "mine."
  - X2 receives and shoots.
- Receive and cross
  - Drill begins with ball in a wide position.
  - Passer (X2) leaves ball for receiver (X1).
  - Communicate "leave it" or "mine" or call your name.
  - X1 receives and crosses.
  - X2 continues toward goal to meet the cross.

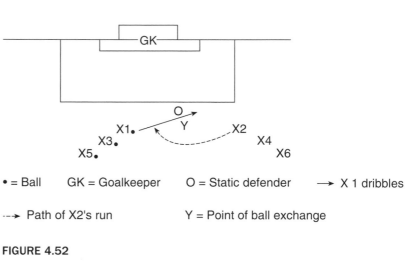

• = Ball   GK = Goalkeeper   O = Static defender   ⟶ X 1 dribbles

--➤ Path of X2's run   Y = Point of ball exchange

FIGURE 4.52

GAME 2

Setup

6v6 in 50 by 40 yards/meters, full goal

Goal

Use crossover play to create space and chance to score.

Condition

Must perform one crossover play in attacking half before approaching goal in each attack.

Lesson 35   Level V

Tactical Problem

Defending space

Lesson Focus

Delaying the attack

Objectives

- Understand that the first role of the individual defender is to delay the attack, keeping the ball in front of him, to give teammates time to recover.
- Delay and channel.

GAME 1

Setup
3v3 (including goalkeeper) in 30 by 20 yards/meters (see figure 4.53) with one full goal, attack versus defense

Goal
Create uneven numbers.

Condition
Head-height rule.

Questions

Q: *What should you do if you have fewer defenders than your opponents have attackers?*

A: Delay the attack to give teammates time to recover.

Q: *How can you delay your opponents?*

A: Use channeling to make the opponent go where you decide.

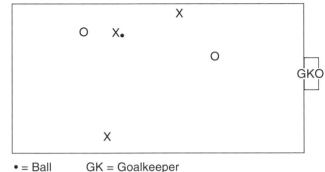

• = Ball   GK = Goalkeeper

FIGURE 4.53

PRACTICE TASK

Setup
2v1 in 30 by 10 yards/meters, no goal (see figure 4.54)

Goals
- Close space quickly.
- Don't dive in for a tackle; stay on feet.
- Channel path of ball between your opponents to delay the attack (also known as jockeying).
- Challenge for ball at appropriate moment.

• = Ball

FIGURE 4.54

Condition
Attackers must control ball and get it to end line.

Cues for Defenders
- Close the space.
- Position to force the sideways pass.
- Move across and back; slide and drop back.

GAME 2

Setup
3v3 in 30 by 20 yards/meters, two small goals (no goalkeeper)

Goals
- Close space quickly.
- Don't dive; stay on feet.
- Channel path of ball.
- Challenge for ball at appropriate moment.

Condition
Head-height rule.

Tactical Problem
Defending space

Lesson Focus
Making recovery runs

Objective
Make appropriate recovery runs to get between ball and goal and to cover first defender.

GAME 1

Setup
2v2 in 30 by 10 yards/meters

Goals
 • Both teams get ball to end line.
 • Understand need to cover teammate.

Condition
Head-height rule.

Questions
 Q: What should forward players do if one teammate is trying to delay an attack?
 A: Recover to help defensively.

 Q: Where should the recovering defenders recover to?
 A: Behind the first defender.

PRACTICE TASK

Setup
2v1 plus one retreating defender in 30 by 10 yards/meters (see figure 4.55)

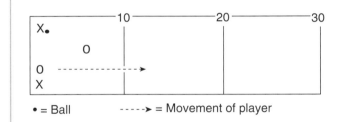

• = Ball   -----▶ = Movement of player

FIGURE 4.55

Goals
 • Defenders work as a pair to stop attackers from reaching the end line, tandem defense.
 • One defender goes to the ball, the other covers and stays with the opponent.

Conditions
 • Retreating defender cannot move until attackers start.
 • Retreating defender must get goal side (i.e., behind) of first defender before challenging for the ball.

Cues
 • First defender delays the attack.
 • Recovering defender recovers quickly, moving behind teammate.
 • Take your own opponent.
 • Cover your teammate.
 • Communicate.

GAME 2

Setup

4v4 in 40 by 30 yards/meters, full goal with goalkeeper

Goals

- Defend in numbers.
- Get goal side.
- Cover for first defender.
- Communicate.

Condition

Head-height rule.

Lesson 37

Tactical Problem

Defending the goal

Lesson Focus

Goalkeeping, diving to save

Objectives

- When and how to dive to tip a ball around or over the goal.
- Saving in 1v1 situations.

GAME 1

Setup

2v2 in 20 by 10 yards/meters, full goal plus goalkeeper (see figure 4.56)

Goals

- Shoot on sight.
- Hit target to force a save.

Question

Q: *What are a goalkeeper's priorities in saving a shot?*
A: Hold the ball if possible; tip the ball out of play if necessary. Do not give up rebounds.

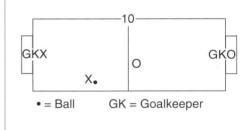

FIGURE 4.56

PRACTICE TASK

Setup

Goalkeeper versus goalkeeper (1v1) in 20 by 10 yards/meters, two full goals

Goals

- Tip ball around goal if you cannot hold it.
- If diving, take off from foot nearest ball.
- In 1v1, smother ball at attacker's feet.

Condition

If you take the ball across the 10-yard/meter line, you must go around the goalkeeper; otherwise shoot from outside the 10-yard line.

- Hold or tip the ball out of play.
- Take off on the foot nearest to the ball when diving.

GAME 2

Repeat game 1.

Lesson 38 Level V

Tactical Problem
Defending the goal

Lesson Focus
Goalkeeping, distributing the ball

Objective
Quick, accurate, efficient distribution.

GAME 1

Setup
4v2 (three defenders plus one goalkeeper versus two attackers) in penalty area (approximately 20 by 40 yards/meters (see figure 4.57)

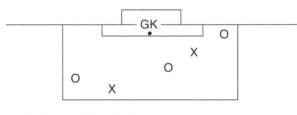

• = Ball   GK = Goalkeeper

FIGURE 4.57

Goals
- Defenders move away from goalkeeper to provide an outlet for the goalkeeper.
- Goalkeeper uses effective distribution to get the ball away from the goal.
- Attackers win ball and shoot.

Conditions
- Attacker feeds ball to goalkeeper from 20 yards/meters.
- Goalkeeper cannot kick the ball out.

Questions
Q: Whom should the goalkeeper give the ball to?
A: The first available player.

Q: How should the goalkeeper give the ball?
A: He should roll it if possible.

Q: Why is rolling best?
A: It gets the ball to the ground quickly. It is easier to receive and control a rolling ball than a bouncing ball.

PRACTICE TASK

Setup
Partner practice, rolling, overarm throws

Goal

Quick, accurate distribution so receiver can easily control ball.

Cues

- Roll the ball firm and flat.
- Keep the arm straight during overarm throws for increased distance.
- Use a bent-arm throw for speed.

GAME 2

Repeat game 1.

Lesson 39 — Level V

Tactical Problem
Restarting play

Lesson Focus
Attacking with corner kicks to the far-post

Objective
Use far-post corners to create scoring opportunities.

GAME 1

Setup

6v6 in 40 by 50 yards/meters, full goal, referee randomly calls many corners

Goal

Awareness of corner as a chance to score.

Question

Q: What is the advantage of a far-post corner?
A: Ball moves away from defense.

PRACTICE TASK

Setup

Team practice, unopposed, at far-post corners (see figure 4.58)

Goal

Use far-post corners to score.

Cues

- Corner taker crosses away from the goalkeeper to the far-post area.
- All players at the edge of penalty area attack the far-post area when the kick is taken.

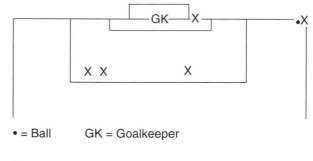

• = Ball   GK = Goalkeeper

FIGURE 4.58

GAME 2

Repeat game 1.

Tactical Problem
Restarting play

Lesson Focus
Defending corner kicks

Objective
Prevent scoring at corners.

GAME 1

Setup
6v6 in 40 by 50 yards/meters, full goal, referee randomly calls many corners

Goal
Awareness of need to defend against corners.

Question

Q: How can you effectively defend corners?
A: Mark opponents and clear the ball.

PRACTICE TASK

Setup
Team practice, opposed (see figure 4.59)

Goal
Appropriate marking and positioning of defenders for near-post, far-post, and short corners.

Cues
· Mark an opponent.
· Be the first to meet the ball when it is crossed.
· Clear the ball high, wide, and long.

GAME 2

Repeat game 1.

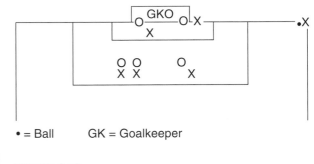

• = Ball　　GK = Goalkeeper

FIGURE 4.59

Tactical Problem
Restarting play

Lesson Focus
Defending free kicks

Objectives
· Efficiently defending free kicks.
· Setting a wall.

GAME 1

Setup

6v6 in 60 by 50 yards/meters, full goal, referee calls many free kicks

Goal

Efficient defensive setup

Question

Q: *How can you successfully defend a free kick?*
A: Mark opponents or set a wall.

PRACTICE TASK

Setup

Team practice, opposed, with direct or indirect free kicks from variety of angles. The attacking team decides from where to take each free kick and whether the kick is direct or indirect.

Goals

- Correct marking.
- Setting of two-, three-, four-, and five-player walls (five players if free kick is central, two if it is wide, three or four if it is in between).

Cues

- Set the wall quickly.
- Tallest players form the outside of the wall.
- Mark opponents if you are not in the wall.
- Line up the outside of the wall with the near post so that the wall covers half the goal (see figure 4.60).

• = Ball   GK = Goalkeeper

FIGURE 4.60

GAME 2

Repeat game 1.

Summary

This chapter has covered the five levels of tactical complexity for teaching soccer. You may choose to base an instructional unit on one particular level. For example, with novice players you would focus on lessons for level I. We recommend focusing a unit on one level of tactical complexity because doing so enables your students to develop both their offensive and defensive performance as they progress in their understanding of the game.

Nevertheless, you may choose to develop your students' understanding of one specific tactical problem during a unit. In this case you could select the material related to the tactical problem from across the five levels of tactical complexity. Whichever approach you choose, base your instruction on developing tactical awareness and an understanding of the game of soccer and not simply on performing isolated kicking, trapping, and heading skills.

You can use many, if not most, of the lessons in this chapter with other invasion games such as floor or field hockey, team handball, and ultimate Frisbee. Although we have not included specific chapters for these games in this book, they are similar to soccer in tactical complexity.

Their tactical problems are the same as those in soccer even though the solutions may use different on-the-ball skills. You will see this in the next chapter, which is on basketball.

By following levels of tactical complexity you help your students progressively increase their understanding and performance. The levels we presented in this chapter are comprehensive, and though games might break down because of inadequate skill execution, student performance will improve with increased understanding of what to do in game situations.

CHAPTER 5

Basketball

As an invasion game, basketball shares many of the tactics found in soccer. In this chapter we apply several strategies from chapter 4 to games and practices specific to basketball. Once you have taught the similar tactics in soccer and basketball, it should be easy for you to apply these tactics to other invasion games such as ultimate Frisbee, floor hockey, and team handball.

Our recommended lesson format for basketball follows the game, practice, game sequence outlined in chapter 2. If you are thinking, *I don't have enough baskets for teaching these lessons,* you are not alone. Some practitioners we have worked with have (a) bolted extra hoops on the wall, (b) rotated teams onto a court, (c) rotated players into a game, (d) assigned four teams (of 2 or 3 students) to one basket or two teams to each side of a basket, (e) used stations that alternate game play and practice, (f) played on half-courts, (g) assigned extra students responsibilities such as coaching, scoring, officiating, and serving as team trainer, and (h) used targets painted on the wall such as those used in WallTar (Stevens and Collier 2001).

As in the soccer chapter, we assume that you will use balls of appropriate size and weight to facilitate game play and skill development and to foster success. The sizes of the teams used in the conditioned games depend on what tactics and skills you want to emphasize. For example, a 1v1 game forces students to dribble to get away from or around their defenders, while a 3v3 game has more opportunities for passing, setting screens, and using a give-and-go. You can assign players or teams a court or basket at the beginning of a unit and they can remain there for most game and practice activities. Assigning baskets or courts eliminates reorganizing and helps your lessons run smoothly.

We present the tactical framework and levels of tactical complexity for basketball in tables 5.1 and 5.2. We briefly describe each level before outlining its associated lessons.

Guide the students through the information they need, such as deciding what size ball is appropriate.

Table 5.1 Tactical Problems, Movements, and Skills in Basketball

Tactical problems	Off-the-ball movements	On-the-ball skills
SCORING		
Maintaining possession of the ball	• Support the ball carrier • Fake and replace	• Triple threat • Passing—chest, bounce, overhead • Catching—target hand, jump stop • Pivot, jab step, drop, step, dribble, ball fake, juke, offensive rebound
Attacking the basket	• Post play	• Jump shot, set shot • Layup, power layup • Follow the shot
Creating space to attack	• Clear-out • Pick away • Fast break • V-cut, L-cut	• Skip pass • Baseball pass
Using space in attack	• Set a screen • Pick-and-roll • Give-and-go	• Give-and-go
PREVENTING SCORING		
Defending space	• Jump-ball alignment, free-throw alignment, full-court press	
Defending the basket area (key)	• Boxing out • Zone defense • Match-up defense • Player to player	• Rebound, outlet pass
Winning the ball	• Defense off the ball	• Defense on the ball
RESTARTING PLAY		
• Jump ball—offensive and defensive • Sideline throw-in—offensive and defensive • End line throw-in—offensive and defensive • End line throw-in—following a score off a press		

Table 5.2 Levels of Tactical Complexity for Basketball

Tactical problems	I	II	III	IV
SCORING				
Maintaining possession of the ball	• Triple threat • Ball fake • Jukes • Appropriate passes	• Support		
Attacking the basket	• Shooting (3-8 ft, or 1-2.4 m) • Dribbling	• Give-and-go	• Lay-up	• Offensive plays against zone

(continued)

Table 5.2 (continued)

Tactical problems	I	II	III	IV
SCORING				
Creating space to attack	· Dribbling to reposition · V-cut, L-cut	· Screen on ball	· Pick off the ball	· Fast break · Clear-out
Using space in attack		· Outlet pass	· Pick and roll · Transition	
PREVENTING SCORING				
Defending space		· Defending against screen		· Offensive and defensive free throws
Defending the basket (key)				· Zone defense
Winning the ball		· Defense on ball and off · Boxing out		· Zone defense on and off ball
RESTARTING GAME				
Jump ball			· Offensive · Defensive	
Inbound pass			· Inbound sideline plays	· Inbound end-line plays
Foul shot		· Long pass · Pick away · Baseline movement		· Inbound plays off press

Level I

We suggest that students at level I focus on offense. Defensive qualities are important, but if introduced too soon defense may prohibit the development of offensive skills, especially if peers play defense aggressively. Introduce defense after students have developed some proficiency with on-the-ball skills. Rather than eliminate defense, control defensive play by instituting three levels of involvement:

1. Cooperative defense, in which the defensive player stays 2 arm's lengths away from the opponent, is relatively passive. At times the defensive player even coaches the opponent.

2. Active defense, in which the defensive player stays about 1 arm's length away from the opponent and has active hands and feet but makes no attempt to intercept the ball.

3. Competitive defense, in which the defensive player assumes the appropriate position depending on whether the opponent has the ball and attempts to intercept the ball.

One of our local practitioners refers to these defensive levels as *cold, warm,* and *hot.* She assigns defensive levels according to each student's ability. Doing so has helped her challenge more skilled players while providing successful and equally challenging experiences for novice players.

One way to teach students how to play offensively is to assign specific defensive levels that will provide a challenging experience.

Lesson 1 ⊙

Tactical Problem
Attacking the basket

Lesson Focus
Shooting within the zone, which is 3 to 8 feet (1-2.4 meters) from the basket

Objective
Receive pass, square the body to basket, and shoot accurately.

GAME 1

Setup
3v3, half-court, 5-minute scoring game

Goal
Score as often as possible.

Conditions
- Complete three consecutive passes before shooting.
- Score 1 point for each shot attempted, 2 points for each basket made.
- All restarts begin at half-court.
- No dribbling.

Questions

Q: *What was the goal of your game?*
A: Score as many points as possible.

Q: *From where on the court did you score most of your points?*
A: Close to the basket.

Q: *Why is it better to shoot near the basket rather than far from the basket?*
A: More likely to score—higher percentage shot.

Q: *What else can you do to increase your chances of scoring?*
A: Use good shooting form. Use the backboard as a target.

PRACTICE TASK

Setup

All players shoot three shots from each of the five spots marked around the basket (3-8 feet (1-2.4 meters) away). Partner rebounds ball and passes accurately to teammate. Shooter provides target hands, squares up, and shoots.

Goal

Score on 2 of 3 shots at each spot.

Cues

Shooting—square up, remember BEEF:
 Base firm.
 Elbow under ball.
 Extend arm.
 Follow through toward target (square above rim on backboard).

GAME 2

Setup

3v3, half-court, 5-minute scoring game

Goal

Score as many field goals as possible.

Lesson 2 Level I

Tactical Problem
Maintaining possession of the ball

Lesson Focus
Create passing lanes by using on-the-ball skill execution and off-the-ball movement

Objectives
 • Present target hand to show passer where to pass.
 • Receive ball in triple-threat position.
 • Perform a ball fake before passing.
 • Make a lead pass just ahead of the target hand.

GAME 1

Setup
3v3, half-court, possession game

Goal
Complete three passes before shooting.

Conditions
- Score 1 point for each successful pass and 2 points for a basket.
- No dribbling.
- All restarts occur at half-court.

Questions

Q: What was the goal of your game?
A: Complete three passes before shooting.

Q: When you were passing, what did you do to keep the defense from stealing the ball?
A: Used arms and body to protect the ball; used ball fakes and jukes to throw off the opponent.

Q: Did you use any signals to let your teammates know you wanted to receive the pass?
A: Held hand up or out to let passer know where to pass the ball.

PRACTICE TASK

Setup
Use 3v3 practice passing and moving from point to wing, baseline, and high and low posts (no passes between post positions). Mark positions with tape, poly spots, and so forth (see figure 5.1). Player passes and then moves to another position. The player receiving the ball must (1) present a target for the passer, (2) receive the ball in a triple-threat position and jump stop, (3) give a ball fake or juke (fake and jukes are also known as feints—body movements to fool opponents) before passing, and (4) perform a quick, accurate lead pass to her partner. Use cooperative to active defense and switch from offense to defense after 10 passes or 2 minutes. Continue as time allows.

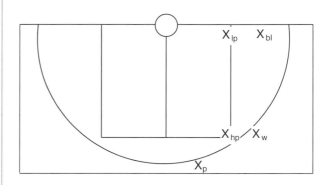

bl = Baseline
w = Wing
p = Point
lp = Low post
hp = High post

FIGURE 5.1

Goals
- Present target hand to passer.
- Receive ball in triple-threat position.
- Perform a ball fake or juke before passing.
- Make a lead pass ahead of the target hand.

Cues
- Target hand (receiver).
- Triple threat (passer)—ball at the hip, knees bent, elbows out.
- Fake a pass, make a pass (passer).

GAME 2

Setup

3v3, half-court, possession game

Goal

Complete three passes before shooting.

Conditions
- Score 1 point for each successful pass and 2 points for a basket.
- No dribbling.
- All restarts occur at half-court.
- Maintain possession by providing a target for the passer, receiving the ball in a triple threat, and using a ball fake.

Lesson 3 Level I

Tactical Problem

Maintaining possession of the ball

Lesson Focus

Creating passing lanes while off the ball

Objective

Off-the-ball player uses quick cut or fake-and-replace movements to get open to receive a pass.

GAME 1

Setup

3v3, half-court, possession game

Goal

Complete three consecutive passes on three consecutive possessions.

Conditions
- Complete at least three passes before shooting.
- Score 1 point for three consecutive passes, 2 points for a basket.

Questions

Q: *What was the goal of the game?*
A: Complete three consecutive passes and shoot.

Q: *What did you have to do to get three consecutive passes?*
A: Move to an open space and get away from the defense.

Q: *How were you able to get away from your defender?*
A: By using cuts and fakes.

PRACTICE TASK 1

Setup

Players start at one of the five offensive positions (see figure 5.1) in a 3v3 gamelike practice task with cooperative to active defense. The ball starts at the top of the key, with the point guard slapping the ball, signaling teammates to cut away from their defenders and then move back (first to get open for a pass, or to move toward the basket). The player receiving the pass does the same thing, slapping the ball and passing to an open teammate. Switch from offense to defense after 10 passes or 2 minutes. Continue as time allows.

Goal
Use quick jab steps and fake movements to create a passing lane and receive a pass.

Conditions
- Provide a target for receiving the ball.
- Receive the ball in triple threat.
- Use a ball fake before passing.

PRACTICE TASK 2

Setup
Repeat practice task 1 but allow players to shoot when in the zone (3-8 feet, or 1-2.4 meters, from the basket).

Goal
Use quick jab steps and fake-and-replace movements to create a passing lane and receive a pass.

Cues
- Quick cuts.
- Target hands.
- Fake a pass, make a pass.

GAME 2

Setup
3v3, half-court, possession

Goal
Complete three consecutive passes on three consecutive possessions.

Conditions
- Complete at least three passes before shooting.
- Score 1 point for three consecutive passes, 2 points for a basket, and 5 points for three consecutive passes on three consecutive possessions.

Lesson 4   Level I

Tactical Problem
Maintaining possession of the ball

Lesson Focus
Decision making before passing

Objectives
- Determine the appropriate situations for using overhead, bounce (using one or two hands), and chest passes during game play.
- Perform passes accurately and appropriately during game play.

GAME 1

Setup
3v3, half-court, possession game

Goal
Complete three consecutive passes on three consecutive possessions.

Conditions
- Complete at least three passes before shooting.
- Score 1 point for three consecutive passes, 2 points for a basket, and 10 points for three consecutive passes on three consecutive possessions. (Ask students to be aware of the types of passes they use during game play.)

Questions

Q: *What was the goal of the game?*
A: Complete three consecutive passes on three consecutive possessions.

Q: *What types of passes did you use during your game?*
A: Overhead, bounce, and chest passes.

Q: *Why did you use all these types of passes?*
A: To throw the ball long, to get around a defender, or to throw a hard or quick pass.

PRACTICE TASK

Setup
Players start at one of the five offensive positions (see figure 5.1) in a 3v3 gamelike practice task with cooperative to active defense (same as previous lesson). Ball starts at the top of the key, with the point guard slapping the ball to signal teammates to cut away from their defenders and then to cut back (first to get open for a pass, or move toward the basket). The pass must be a skip pass, that is, a long pass that goes over or past one teammate and on to another. The player receiving the pass does the same thing until 10 consecutive overhead passes have been completed. Repeat this task for the bounce pass, using active defense to create the need for the bounce pass, but this time pass to adjacent players. Finally, players repeat this task for the chest pass, using cooperative to active defense, and pass to teammates as they cut away from their defenders.

Goal
10 consecutive passes during each passing rotation.

GAME 2

Setup
3v3, half-court, possession game

Goal
Complete three consecutive passes on three consecutive possessions.

Conditions
- Complete at least three passes before shooting.
- Score 1 point for three consecutive passes, 2 points for a basket, and 10 points for three consecutive passes on three consecutive possessions.

Extension
Defense scores 2 points for each steal and 1 point if they tip or touch the ball.

Tactical Problem
Attacking the basket

Lesson Focus
Identifying an open lane to the basket and dribbling to drive and shoot

Objective
Use a power dribble to drive and score.

GAME 1

Setup
3v3, half-court game

Goal
Score as often as possible.

Condition
No dribbling except to drive to the basket.

Questions

Q: *When you receive the ball, what are your three options?*
A: Shoot, pass, dribble.

Q: *When should you dribble?*
A: To drive to the basket.

Q: *When you have the ball and an open lane to the basket, what should you do?*
A: Drive quickly toward the basket and shoot.

PRACTICE TASK 1

Setup
Partners, one ball per pair. The player with the ball must use a ball fake, make a juke or jab step, and drive to the basket and then jump stop and shoot while partner is a cooperative defender.

Goals
  · Make strong dribble and drive toward the basket.
  · Demonstrate good form while performing jump stop and shot.
  · Use square on backboard to aim and shoot.

Cues
  · Ball down, eyes up.
  · Two-foot jump stop.
  · Shoot for the square.

Question

Q: *How does the dribble change when someone is guarding you?*
A: You keep the ball closer to your body and keep your body between the defender and the ball.

PRACTICE TASK 2

Setup
Use 1v1, one ball per pair. Start at foul line. Check ball and get in a triple-threat position.

Goal
Score in 15 seconds or less.

GAME 2

Setup
3v3, half-court game

Goal
Shoot as often as possible using a dribble and drive.

Conditions
- No dribbling except to drive to the basket.
- Can only score from a drive to the basket.

Lesson 6

Tactical Problem
Using space in the attack

Lesson Focus
Use the dribble for repositioning to make a pass

Objectives
- Use proper dribbling technique.
- Position body between defensive player and the ball.
- Identify the need for repositioning to create passing lanes.

GAME 1

Setup
3v3, half-court game

Goal
Score without dribbling.

Conditions
- Three consecutive passes before shooting.
- Players may dribble when needed.
- Active defense on the ball and competitive defense off the ball (no contact).

Questions

Q: Why was it difficult to score without dribbling?
A: Teammates were covered.

Q: What can players with the ball do when teammates are covered?
A: Dribble to reposition until off-the-ball players are able to cut and create passing lanes.

Q: What can players off the ball do to open passing lanes?
A: Use feints, jukes, and cuts.

PRACTICE TASK

Setup
Use 2v2 dribble reposition drill with a passive to active defense. Player with ball starts from the point position and dribbles to find an open pass to her teammate. Off-the-ball player uses various cuts to get open and receive a pass from the on-the-ball player. The extra players are coaches. One watches the defenders and makes sure they position appropriately and safely and do not make contact with the ball or ball carrier; the

other watches the offense to see if they use jabs, jukes, cuts, and so on to effectively reposition themselves to create open passing lanes. Players can shoot when open. Switch roles after three shot attempts.

Goal

Dribble to reposition (on-the-ball player) and create a passing lane (off-the-ball player).

Cues

- Quick cuts.
- Dribble with body between defender and ball.
- Watch belly button of offensive player attempting fake.
- Read and anticipate.

GAME 2

Setup

3v3, half-court, possession game

Goal

Dribble only when there are no open passing lanes and off-the-ball players need to create passing lanes.

Conditions

- No dribbling except to drive to the basket or to reposition to make a pass.
- Active defense on the ball and competitive defense off the ball (no contact).

Level II

We recommend reviewing level I content, the triple threat, the ball fake, and so forth, allowing students to refine and integrate these skills as they practice and play the game. You may need to repeat or extend one or two specific lessons from level I to improve your students' skill or tactical understanding.

Level II focuses on preventing scoring, specifically by winning the ball and defending space. If games break down because the defense is too active, you may want to restrain the defensive players by assigning degrees of intensity (passive, active, or competitive). Have students focus on their form and their positioning relative to the ball, the basket, and other defensive players.

Two lessons in this level are on attacking the basket. Unlike the individual skills covered in level I, the offensive skills here involve other team members and require teamwork. You may find that this is a good time to talk about the meaning of being a member of a team and the importance of working together.

Students must learn how to prevent the other team from scoring.

Tactical Problem
Creating space to attack

Lesson Focus
Creating passing lanes in the zone

Objective
Use cuts (L-cut or V-cut) to elude a defender and get open for a shot.

GAME 1

Setup
3v3, half-court game

Goal
Get open to receive a pass in the zone.

Conditions
· Shoot only from the zone (3-8 feet, or 1-2.4 meters, around the basket).
· Score 1 point for attempting a shot and 2 points for making a basket.

Questions

Q: *What was the goal of the game?*
A: To get open to receive a pass in the zone.

Q: *How do you do that?*
A: Move fast, use a fake or juke, run one way and then change directions really fast.

Q: *What do you need to consider before making a cut?*
A: The position of the ball and of the defenders.

PRACTICE TASK

Setup
Use 2v1 with one active defender and two offensive players. Ball begins at the point position and passer waits until defender is guarding her before passing. Then when she sees her teammate fake or juke, she ball fakes and times the pass to the open receiver. The receiver cuts toward his defender and then away with target hands up to communicate where the passer should pass the ball. The defender stays between the passer and receiver, using active defense about an arm's length away. After the receiver catches a pass three times, all players rotate positions. Groups of three can rotate on and off the court and serve as coaches when on the sidelines.

Goals
· Off-the-ball player uses quick cuts to elude the defender and get open in the zone.
· Off-the-ball player shows target hands.
· On-the-ball player uses a ball fake and anticipates when and where to pass.

GAME 2

Setup
3v3, half-court game

Goal
Off-the-ball players get open in the zone.

Lesson 8 Level II

Tactical Problem
Attacking the basket

Lesson Focus
Using the give-and-go to score

Objectives
- Fake, pass, and cut to the basket.
- Time and throw a lead pass back to the cutter.
- Shoot off the pass.

GAME 1

Setup
3v3, half-court game

Goal
Off-the-ball players get open in the zone.

Conditions
- Must complete at least two passes before shooting.
- All shots must be made within 3 to 5 feet (1-1.5 meters) of the basket.

Questions
Q: Off-the-ball players, how were you able to get open in the zone?
A: Pass and cut or fake or juke away from the basket and then move quickly toward the basket.

Q: What did you do to keep the defender from getting between you and the ball?
A: Used a strong juke or jab step, crossover step, or quick move toward the basket.

Q: What did you need to consider before driving to the basket?
A: The position of the ball and of the other defenders.

PRACTICE TASK

Setup
Use 2v2 with active defenders and one ball. Two players serve as coaches. Each offensive player practices give-and-go three times and then rotates into the coaching role. Move to other side of basket and repeat; practice give-and-go three times first with cooperative and then with active defense.

Goal
Score off a give-and-go.

Cues
- Pass and cut.
- Use the target hand.
- Keep the defender behind you.

Question

Q: What did you do to complete the give-and-go when there was competitive defense?
A: Used more fakes, dribbled to create passing lanes, and got open to support the player with the ball.

Cues

- Make quick cuts.
- Present target hands.
- Anticipate when and where to pass.

GAME 2

Setup
Repeat game 1.

Goal
Score off a give-and-go.

Condition
Earn 1 extra point if give-and-go is used to score.

Lesson 9 ⊙   Level II

Tactical Problem
Creating space to attack

Lesson Focus
Setting a pick to create space

Objectives

- Set a pick on the opponent defending the on-the-ball player.
- On-the-ball player fakes or jukes and drives off the pick and shoots.

GAME 1

Setup
3v3, half-court game

Goal
Get on-the-ball player open so he can shoot.

Conditions

- Different team member restarts play on each possession.
- Earn 1 point for hitting the rim and 2 for getting the ball through the hoop.
- Players call their own fouls.

Questions

Q: How were you able to get the on-the-ball player open to shoot?
A: Perform a pick.

Q: What is a good body position for the player setting a pick?
A: Wide base, bent knees, arms across body for self-protection.

Q: What is the best way for the player with the ball to use the screen?
A: Fake and then brush off the screen to create an open space to drive to the basket or shoot.

PRACTICE TASK

Setup

Use 2v1, active defense, one ball. The off-the-ball offensive player executes a pick and the on-the-ball offensive player uses the pick to move to open space and score. The defense is active, supporting yet challenging the opponents. After the shot, another 2v1 group moves onto the court and runs the same drill. When on the sidelines, players each pick a player on the court to coach and give feedback to when the play ends. One coach watches to see if the pick is set correctly, one watches to see if the offensive player uses screen correctly, and the third watches the defense to ensure it is at an appropriate level.

Goal

Successfully execute a screen three times in a row.

Cues

- Stand firm, straddle feet.
- Hands across the trunk (girls high, boys low), ready to take a charge.
- Shooter–fake, cross step, and drive or shoot.

GAME 2

Setup

Repeat game 1.

Lesson 10 — Level II

Tactical Problem
Creating space to attack

Lesson Focus
Getting open in the zone

Objective
Off-the-ball player uses picks to get open in the zone.

GAME 1

Setup

3v3, half-court game

Goal

Off-the-ball players get open in the zone.

Conditions

- No dribbling.
- Active to competitive defense on off-the-ball players.
- Shoot only in the zone.
- Score 1 point for hitting the rim and 2 points for making a basket.

Questions

Q: Off-the-ball players, how were you able to get open in the zone?
A: By setting a pick on a teammate's defensive player to free the teammate up.

Q: How did you determine where to set the pick?
A: Considered the positions of the ball and of the defensive players.

Q: What should you do while your teammate is approaching to set a pick on your defender?
A: Fake or juke the defender away from the pick or basket.

PRACTICE TASK

Setup

Use 3v2, with two cooperative defensive players covering off-the-ball players and one coach observing the timing and form of the pick. The ball starts at the guard position, and the point passes to the wing and moves to pick the defender of the third offensive player, who is positioned near the baseline. Once the pick is set, the third offensive player cuts into the zone, receives a pass from the wing, and shoots. Rotate after three trials and continue until all players have had three chances to set a pick away from the ball. Players can repeat the drill with active or competitive defense.

Goals

· Determine the best location for the pick.
· Set a strong pick.
· Set defender up for the pick and then brush off the pick and into the zone.
· Shoot off the pass.

GAME 2

Setup

3v3, half-court game

Goal

Off-the-ball players use picks to get open in the zone.

Conditions

· No dribbling.
· Active to competitive defense on off-the-ball players.
· Shoot only in the zone.
· Earn 1 point for receiving a pass in the zone, 1 point for hitting the rim, and 2 points for making a basket (see figure 5.2).

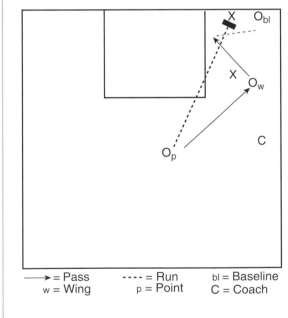

→ = Pass	---- = Run	bl = Baseline
w = Wing	p = Point	C = Coach

FIGURE 5.2

Tactical Problem

Winning the ball

Lesson Focus

Defensive positioning when off the ball

Objectives

- Demonstrate proper defensive positioning, placing the body between the defender and the basket and keeping the ball-side hand between the defender and the ball.
- Watch the ball.
- Maintain active feet and hands.

GAME 1

Setup

3v3, half-court game

Goal

Keep opponent from scoring.

Conditions

- Use competitive defense to guard opposing player.
- No dribbling.
- Complete at least three passes before shooting.
- Defensive team scores 1 point if offensive team does not complete three passes.
- No violations or fouls.

Questions

Q: *What did you do to keep the opposing team from scoring?*

A: Closely guarded and rebounded so they wouldn't get a second shot.

Q: *What defensive positions or actions interfered with the offense the most and kept your opponent from scoring?*

A: Keeping your body between the opponent and the goal, positioning your ball-side hand between the ball and the opponent, maintaining a ready position (medium body posture, weight forward, ready to move), keeping hands and feet active.

PRACTICE TASK

Setup

With a partner, players practice off-the-ball defensive positioning (partners can also coach each other). Players can dribble, but as soon as they pick up the dribble, the defensive player moves closer and has active hands and feet.

Goal

Either steal the ball without fouling or cause a turnover.

Cues

- Keep your body between the opponent and the goal.
- Stay in the ready position.
- Maintain active hands and feet.
- Watch the ball.

GAME 2

Repeat game 1.

Tactical Problem
Winning the ball

Lesson Focus
On-the-ball defense

Objectives
- Use body angle to force movement away from the basket. (Note: similar to channeling in soccer.)
- Use ball-side hand to deny a passing lane to off-the-ball players.

GAME 1

Setup
3v3, half-court game

Goal
Prevent on-the-ball player from passing.

Conditions
- No dribbling.
- At least three consecutive passes before shooting.
- Defensive team receives 1 point for turnovers and 2 points for steals (without fouling).

Question

Q: *How did you prevent the on-the-ball player from passing?*
A: Overplayed to limit potential passing lanes, closely guarded the player with the ball, and used hands to block potential passing lanes.

PRACTICE TASK

Setup
Use 2v2, active to competitive defense, the player with the ball starts at the point position and attempts to pass to her teammate. The defensive player assumes defensive posture and attempts to prevent the pass for 5 seconds (defender can count "one Mississippi, two Mississippi," and so on). The two players waiting off the court coach and then rotate into the drill after the offensive team has had three possessions. The offensive team becomes the defense and the defensive team rotates off the court to coach.

Goal
Either steal the ball without fouling or cause a turnover.

Cues
- Position body to block passing lanes.
- Use hands to block passing lanes.
- See the ball.
- Anticipate.

GAME 2

Repeat game 1.

Allowing students to group themselves into varying levels of skill-based groups allows for a positive experience.

Level III

The lessons at level III continue to increase in tactical complexity. The game forms involve 4v4 situations emphasizing player-to-player defense and offense. Tactics such as creating space and using space in attack require greater skill and tactical understanding. We introduce jump balls for starting and restarting play. Lessons at level III may require more space than those at levels I and II.

As with level II, you may want to review the content from previous levels. You may find that some students are not ready for level III. If this is a problem, consider grouping students by abilities so that advanced players have an opportunity to improve and less-advanced players can continue to refine basic skills and tactical knowledge. When using the tactical approach, grouping by ability is easy because you can assign teams to individual courts or half-courts and each team can work on independent tasks or tactical problems.

Our experiences with grouping have been mostly positive. Discretion is the key to successful grouping by ability. A teacher at a local high school assigns levels to different courts: a high school court, a college court, and a pro court. She directs the students to accordingly assign themselves to a court. In many cases, self-selection by students is better than assignment by teachers. Of course, certain classes and students will need your guidance to attain effective groupings.

Tactical Problem
Restarting play

Lesson Focus
Inbound (sideline) pass

Objective
Pick away from the ball to create space for an inbound pass when restarting play.

GAME 1

Setup
3v3, half-court game

Goal
Score within three passes.

Conditions
- Restart play from sidelines on all violations and fouls.
- Inbound pass counts as one pass.
- If no shot is attempted within three passes, the offensive team has made a turnover and the ball must be taken out at the sideline.
- Player inbounding the ball must remain stationary until ball is passed.
- Active defense.
- No dribbling.

Questions

Q: *What did your team do to score within three passes?*
A: Got open and created space near the ball.

Q: *What did your team do to get open and create space, particularly during inbound plays?*
A: Faked and cut to the ball and picked teammates' defenders so teammates could get away and come to the ball.

Q: *If the ball is on the sideline at about midcourt, how should your team set picks to create space for the inbound pass?*
A: Spread out, pick away to create space toward the ball, and cut toward the ball.

PRACTICE TASK

Setup
Teams create an inbound play that provides two different options (using two different players) for allowing a shot within three passes

GAME 2

Repeat game 1.

Note
Allow teams to show their inbound plays during closure.

Tactical Problem
Attacking the basket

Lesson Focus
Jump shot

Objective
Use a jump shot to shoot over the defense when shooting within 12 feet (4 meters) of the basket.

GAME 1

Setup
3v3, half-court game

Goal
Score on three consecutive possessions.

Conditions
- All shots must be taken from within 12 feet (4 meters) of the basket.
- Off-the-ball defense is cooperative to active and on-the-ball defense is active to competitive.
- Defensive team receives 2 points for blocking a shot (no contact).
- Offensive team receives 1 point for hitting the rim and 2 points for making a field goal.

Question

Q: *What were some things you did to score when closely guarded?*
A: Used fakes and jukes and used a jump shot.

PRACTICE TASK

Setup
Arrange five or six spots around the perimeter of the basket, keeping within 6 to 12 feet (2-4 meters). Players pair up and play 1v1, beginning with cooperative defense. The defender passes the ball to the offensive player; plays defense, turns, and follows the shot to the basket; retrieves the ball; and again passes the ball to the offensive player. Players rotate after 3 to 5 shots and repeat the drill with active and then competitive defense.

Goal
Score on three consecutive possessions.

Cues
- Receive pass in triple threat.
- Square shoulders to the basket.
- Jump straight up.
- Shoot at peak of jump.

GAME 2

Repeat game 1.

Tactical Problem
Winning the ball

Lesson Focus
Defensive positioning following a shot to regain possession of the ball

Objectives
- Box out the opposing player at release of the shot.
- Rebound the ball and make outlet pass.

GAME 1

Setup
3v3, half-court game

Goals
- Prevent offensive team from scoring.
- If offense shoots, do not allow a second shot.

Conditions
- No dribbling.
- At least three consecutive passes before shooting.
- Defensive team receives 1 point for winning or rebounding the ball after only one shot.

Questions

Q: *What was the goal of the game?*
A: To prevent scoring and prevent a second shot.

Q: *What did you do to prevent a second shot?*
A: Rebounded the first shot.

Q: *How did you position yourself to get the rebound?*
A: Moved between the defensive player and the basket.

PRACTICE TASK

Setup
Use 2v2, plus one shooter and one outlet. O3 shoots the ball (see figure 5.3). On the release, X1 and X2 turn and box out offensive players. X3 moves right or left, depending on which side of the basket the rebound occurs. The player rebounding the ball turns and passes to the outlet, X3. Repeat three times and then rotate.

Goal
Successfully rebound the ball and make outlet pass three times in a row.

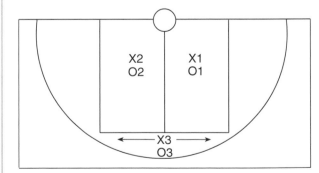

——→ = Movement of player

FIGURE 5.3

GAME 2

Setup
Repeat game 1.

Condition
Defensive team gets 1 point for successful rebound and outlet pass.

Lesson 16

Tactical Problem
Defending space

Lesson Focus
Player-to-player defense

Objectives
- Call picks and screens.
- Move around picks and screens.
- Stay with player.

GAME 1

Setup
4v4, half-court

Goals
- Defensive team uses player-to-player competitive defense to keep opponent from scoring.
- Offensive team uses picks to score and to create passing lanes in the attack.

Conditions
- Call your own fouls.
- Dribble only to drive to the basket.

Questions

Q: *What are the advantages of player-to-player defense?*
A: All players are closely guarded, which increases chances to win the ball, and all defensive members know their responsibilities.

Q: *What are the disadvantages?*
A: Defense can get spread out too far away from the basket, and it's difficult to match players of equal abilities.

Q: *How can you help your teammates while in player-to-player defense?*
A: Let them know when a pick is being set and pick up the offensive player threatening to score.

Q: *What should you do when you're picked or screened?*
A: Move around the pick so you can stay with your player.

PRACTICE TASK 1

Setup
Players review and practice on- and off-the-ball defensive positions in 3v3

PRACTICE TASK 2

Setup
Use 3v3, two coaches, one ball, competitive defense. Offensive players execute on-the-ball screens. Defensive players being screened must fight around the screen and stay with their opponents. Coaches evaluate defenders' abilities to get around the screen.

Goal
Keep opponent from getting an open shot.

PRACTICE TASK 3

Setup
Use 3v3, two coaches, one ball, competitive defense. Offensive players execute off-the-ball screens. Defensive players that are screened must fight around the screen and stay with their opponents. Coaches evaluate defenders' abilities to get around the screen.

Goal
Keep opponent from getting an open shot.

Cues
- Call "screen left" or "screen right."
- Fight around the screen.
- Stay between your player and the basket.

GAME 2

Setup
Combine practice tasks two and three. Rotate coaches into the game after 2 minutes.

Goal
Keep offensive team from scoring for 30 seconds.

Lesson 17 Level III

Tactical Problem
Using space in the attack

Lesson Focus
Offense against player-to-player defense

Objective
Use picks or screens to free on- and off-the-ball players to create support and scoring opportunities.

GAME 1

Setup
4v4, half-court

Goals
- Defense plays competitive player-to-player defense.
- Offense scores as many points possible.

Conditions
- Different team member restarts play on each possession.
- Players call their own fouls; 30-second offensive clock (must shoot within 30 seconds).
- Defensive team gets 3 points if offensive team does not get a shot off within 30 seconds.

Question
Q: *What did you do to score against the player-to-player defense?*
A: Set picks or screens to free teammates, used cuts to get away from defenders, and moved the ball quickly and accurately.

PRACTICE TASK 1

Setup
Practice a teacher-designed offensive play. Play offense against a player-to-player defense, 4v4, active defense, one ball, full or half-court.

Goal
Score three times in a row using offensive play.

PRACTICE TASK 2

Setup
Teams create and practice their own offensive plays against player-to-player defense. Each team of four creates an offensive play and practices it against the opponent (other four players). Use active defense.

Goal
Score three times in a row using offensive play.

Cues
- Anticipate ball and player movements.
- Identify opportunities to get a player open.

GAME 2

Repeat game 1.

Condition
Team scores an extra point when it executes a play successfully.

Lesson 18 Level III

Tactical Problem
Winning the ball and using space in the attack

Lesson Focus
Transitioning from defense to offense

Objectives
- Rebound and outlet.
- Set up offense as quickly as possible.

GAME 1

Setup

4v4, half-court

Goals

- Defense uses outlet pass after rebounding ball.
- Offense scores as many points as possible.

Conditions

- Remember to box out and use outlet pass on a defensive rebound.
- Players call their own fouls; 30-second offensive clock.
- Defensive team gets 1 point for successful rebound and outlet pass.

Questions

Q: Why should you make an outlet pass after rebounding the ball?
A: To get the ball out of the key and away from opponents and to get the ball down the floor faster.

Q: Which player should get the outlet pass?
A: A player who is not involved in the rebound and is on the same side of key where the ball rebounds.

Q: Where and how should the outlet player go to receive the outlet pass?
A: To the sideline nearest the player rebounding the ball; move quickly to create a passing lane.

PRACTICE TASK 1

Setup

Use 4v4, with one shooter and one outlet, O4 shoots ball (see figure 5.4). On the release, X1, X2, and X3 turn and box out offensive players. X4 moves right or left, depending on where the rebound occurs. The player rebounding the ball turns and passes to the outlet, X4. Repeat three times and then rotate.

Goal

Successfully complete three consecutive outlet passes.

Cues

- Rebound.
- Protect the ball.
- Pivot away from the basket.

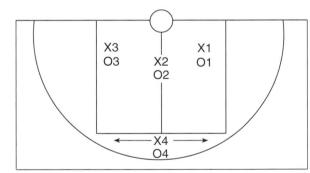

⟶ = Movement of player

FIGURE 5.4

PRACTICE TASK 2

Setup

Extend practice task 1. After outlet pass, point guard or off guard moves toward center court to create a passing lane. The next available player fills the outside lane, opposite the rebound. Trailing players move down the court as quickly as possible and assume offensive positions.

Goal

After rebounding the ball, use no more than five passes to score.

Cues

- Get and go.
- Quickly move down the court.
- Stay wide and spread out to maintain passing lanes.

GAME 2

Setup

Repeat game 1.

Level IV

Lessons in level IV require 5v5 game play. The first few lessons emphasize starting and restarting play in the full court. Students may remain in half-court games unless the tactical problem dictates a full court, such as when learning the fast break. When using a full court, try rotating teams on and off the court. Allowing only one shot at the basket can also make games move more quickly and can optimize playing time for all students. Consider using the curriculum model in *Complete Guide to Sport Education* (Siedentop, Hastie, and van der Mars 2004), which advocates using students to coach, officiate, record statistics, keep score, act as trainers, and fulfill other responsibilities of team management. Following this model will help you maintain high levels of student involvement while exposing your students to other aspects of sport participation.

A primary tactic addressed in level IV involves defending the basket, specifically, using 2-1-2 zone defense and defensive alignment during a free throw. For the offensive side, we introduce scoring tactics that use space in the attack, including offensive plays to use against a 2-1-2 zone defense, offensive alignments to use during a free throw, and a fast break. Of course, a number of other zone defenses or offensive alignments can be addressed at level IV.

Students should learn to play defensively.

Tactical Problem
Winning the ball

Lesson Focus
Positioning to gain possession of a jump ball

Objectives
- Match with a player on the circle.
- Position for offensive jump balls.
- Position for defensive jump balls.

GAME 1

Setup
4v4, half-court

Goal
Gain possession of the ball off the jump ball.

Conditions
- After every basket use a jump ball to restart play.
- Players rotate so that each participates in the jump ball.
- Team gaining possession of the jump ball continues offensive play until it scores or until the other team wins the ball.

Questions

Q: *What did you and your teammates do to win the jump ball?*
A: Matched up with opponents on the circle for the jump ball.

Q: *If you thought your team would win the jump ball, how did you line up on the circle?*
A: Close to the basket so we could turn and score.

Q: *If you thought your team would lose the jump ball, how did you line up on the circle?*
A: Between the offense and the basket so we could defend the goal.

PRACTICE TASK 1

Setup
Practice the jump ball. Players match up according to height. Use four players per group and one ball and one circle. Two players jump, another player tosses, and the other coaches. Do three jumps before rotating. Rotate through all players twice, allowing six jumps each. Jumping players try to tip the ball to the coach.

Goal
Win 3 of 6 jump balls.

Cues
- Match up.
- Knees bent.
- Jump when tosser releases the ball.

PRACTICE TASK 2

Setup
Practice offensive and defensive jump balls, 3v3 with one tosser, one coach, one ball, one circle, and one basket. Play jump ball until one team scores or the other team wins the ball. Rotate after each jump ball.

Goal
Win the jump ball and score.

Cues
- Match up.
- Anticipate offensive or defensive jump balls.
- React.
- Transition quickly.

GAME 2

Repeat game 1.

Lesson 20 — Level IV

Tactical Problem
Winning the ball

Lesson Focus
Rebounding from the foul lane

Objective
Position offensively and defensively for free throws.

GAME 1

Setup
5v5, full court

Goal
Win rebounds on foul shots.

Condition
Free throws awarded for all fouls and violations.

Questions

Q: *How should the offensive team line up on a free throw?*
A: Between the defensive players on the sidelines of the key, with one player at half-court to defend against a potential fast break.

Q: *How should the defensive team line up on a free throw?*
A: Begin with a player on the block next to the basket, then position one player on the other side of the offensive player, with one player close to the shooter, ready to block out.

PRACTICE TASK

Setup

Offensive and defensive teams alternate free throws. Practice defensive positioning after the ball release and practice making outlet passes, as in a fast break. If the offensive team gets the rebound, continue play until the offense scores or until the defense wins the ball.

Goals

- Defensive team gets all rebounds off the free throws.
- Offensive team regains possession of missed free throws.

Cues

- Step in at ball release.
- Step in quickly and firmly hold position.
- Keep body against opponent.

GAME 2

Repeat game 1.

Lesson 21   Level IV

Tactical Problem

Using space in the attack and attacking the basket

Lesson Focus

Outlet pass and fast break

Objectives

- Execute pivot and outlet pass from rebound.
- Move ball down the floor using wide formation.
- Score from a break.

GAME 1

Setup

5v5, full court

Goal

Defense uses outlet pass after rebounding the ball and scores before opponent sets up.

Conditions

- Players call their own fouls; 30-second offensive clock.
- Defensive team gets 1 point for successful rebound and outlet pass and 3 points for scoring off the break (within 8 seconds of the rebound).

Questions

Q: *After the rebound, what did you do to get the ball down the floor quickly?*
A: Used fast, accurate passes and quickly created open passing lanes down the court.

Q: *What was the best way to create these passing lanes?*
A: By moving down the court, spreading out, and using the whole court.

PRACTICE TASK

Setup

Use 5v5, with one shooter (05) and one outlet (X5) (see figure 5.5). On the ball release, X1, X2, X3, and X4 turn and box out offensive players. X5 moves right or left, depending on which side of the basket the rebound occurs. The player rebounding the ball turns and passes to the outlet, X5. Then the point guard or off guard moves up the court and toward the center court in order to create a passing lane. The next available player fills the outside lane, opposite the rebound. Trailing players move down the court as quickly as possible and assume offensive positions. Repeat the task three times and then rotate.

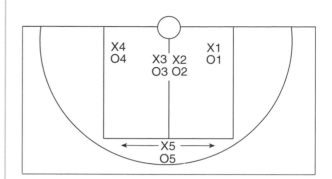

——→ = Movement of player

FIGURE 5.5

Goal

Score off three consecutive fast breaks.

Cues

- Anticipate.
- Move quickly to support.
- Support down the court, toward the basket.
- Stay wide.

GAME 2

Repeat game 1.

Lesson 22 Level IV

Tactical Problem

Attacking the basket and creating space to attack

Lesson Focus

Layup and clear out

Objective

Use a "clear out" to create space for a teammate to drive to the basket and score using a layup.

GAME 1

Setup

5v5, half-court

Goal

Score off the dribble.

Conditions

- Restart at half-court.
- After one scoring attempt, defense goes on offense and offense rotates out while a new team of five rotates in at half-court and plays defense.
- Use player-to-player defense.
- Offensive team must score off the dribble.
- Earn 1 point for hitting the rim and 2 points for making a field goal.

Questions

Q: *What did off-the-ball players do to allow the on-the-ball player to score off the dribble?*

A: Cleared the lane so that the on-the-ball player could drive to the basket.

Q: *What type of shot was used to score?*

A: A layup.

PRACTICE TASK 1

Setup

Players pair up and play 1v1, using cooperative defense. The offensive player starts at the three-point line with the ball, fakes or jukes, and drives to the basket. Players use right hands when shooting from the right side of the basket and left hands when shooting from the left side of the basket. Rotate after each drive and begin the drive from different areas of the three-point line. Increase the intensity of the defense to active and then to competitive as play improves.

Goal

Score on three consecutive possessions.

Cues

- Fake, use crossover step, dribble, and drive.
- Take off from left, then shoot right (right side of basket).
- Take off from right, then shoot left (left side of basket).

PRACTICE TASK 2

Setup

Add players to the game (3v3, 4v4, or 5v5). Begin with cooperative defense. Allow teams to devise different methods of clearing and distracting defenders. Teams can also design plays. Encourage teams to work on reading defense and encourage the on-the-ball player to anticipate cuts and picks.

Goal

Score on three consecutive possessions.

Cues

- Fake toward the basket and then cut away.
- Create space in which the driving player can lay off (in case defender stops the drive).

GAME 2

Repeat game 1.

Tactical Problem
Restarting play

Lesson Focus
Inbound pass from offensive end line

Objective
Run a set play to achieve inbound pass.

GAME 1

Setup
5v5, full court

Goal
Score within 10 seconds of inbounding the ball from the end line.

Conditions
- No dribbling except to drive to the basket.
- Use a 2-1-2 defense to defend space around the basket.
- Restart play from the end line.

Question
Q: *What did your team do to score within 10 seconds of the inbound pass?*
A: Passed quickly, moved quickly, and set up screens and picks to create open passing lanes.

PRACTICE TASK 1

Setup
At the end line, practice a teacher-designed play against a 2-1-2 defense. Play 5v5 with active defense on a half-court.

Goal
Score three times in a row against a 2-1-2 defense.

PRACTICE TASK 2

Setup
Teams create and practice their own end-line plays against 2-1-2 defense. Each team of five creates an offensive play and then practices it against the opponent. Use active defense.

Goal
Score three times in a row against a 2-1-2 defense.

Cues
- Know your role.
- Execute your role.
- Timing is everything.

GAME 2

Repeat game 1.

Condition
Team scores an extra point when it successfully executes a play.

Lesson 24 Level IV

Tactical Problem
Defending space

Lesson Focus
2-1-2 zone defense

Objectives
- Team executes a 2-1-2 zone defense.
- Individual players execute proper defensive positioning when on and off the ball.

GAME 1

Setup
5v5, full court

Goal
Use a 2-1-2 defense to keep opponent from scoring.

Conditions
- No dribbling in the front court.
- Must complete at least three passes to different players before attempting a shot.

Questions

Q: *Where did the offensive team take most of its shots?*
A: Outside the key area.

Q: *Was the zone defense easier or harder to play than the player-to-player defense?*
A: Easier, because we didn't have to move as much and it was easier to keep offense away from the basket and to get rebounds because we were closer to the basket.

Q: *What were disadvantages of the zone defense as compared with the one-on-one defense?*
A: We couldn't always get to the ball, it was hard to defend long-range shooters and hard to play when two players were in our zone, and we couldn't see all offensive players at once.

PRACTICE TASK 1

Setup
Practice a 2-1-2 zone shift with one team playing defense and the other team standing around the perimeter. The offensive team passes the ball quickly around the perimeter, allowing the defensive players to practice positioning and covering opponents inside their areas of the zone. Practice talking to each other, communicating the positions of offensive players.

Goal

Give the offensive team no open shots within 15 feet (5 meters) of the basket.

PRACTICE TASK 2

Setup

Repeat task 1 but focus on positioning for on-the-ball and off-the-ball defense, picking up or escorting players as they pass through your area of the zone, and knowing when not to pick up an offensive player (e.g., not guarding players too far from the basket to be shooting threats).

Goal

Know positions of off-the-ball players at all times.

Cues

- Talk.
- Anticipate.
- Play aggressive on-the-ball defense.
- Cover players in your zone.

GAME 2

Repeat game 1.

Lesson 25 Level IV

Tactical Problem

Creating and using space in the attack

Lesson Focus

Offense against a 2-1-2 defense

Objectives

- Run offensive plays against a 2-1-2 defense.
- Identify strengths and weaknesses of a 2-1-2 defense.

GAME 1

Setup

5v5, full court

Goals

- Defense uses a 2-1-2 defense to defend space around the basket.
- Offense scores off the 2-1-2 defense.

Conditions

- No dribbling in the front court.
- Complete at least three passes to different players before attempting a shot.

Question

Q: *What did you do to score off the 2-1-2 zone defense?*
A: Moved the ball quickly; drew one or more defenders to create passing lanes, and used screens to create shooting opportunities.

PRACTICE TASK 1

Setup

Practice a teacher-designed offensive play against a 2-1-2 defense. Play 5v5 with active defense on a full court or half-court.

Goal

Score three times in a row against a 2-1-2 defense.

Cues

- Move the ball quickly.
- Use lots of off-the-ball movement.
- Pick or screen.

PRACTICE TASK 2

Setup

Teams create and practice their own offensive plays against a 2-1-2 defense. Each team of five creates an offensive play and then practices it against an opponent. Use active defense.

Goal

Score three times in a row against a 2-1-2 defense.

Cues

- Pass quickly.
- Cut quickly.
- Support.
- Screen.

GAME 2

Repeat game 1.

Condition

Team scores an extra point when it executes a play as planned and scores a basket off the play.

Summary

In this chapter, we have provided four levels of lessons. The lessons do not encompass the full range of teaching possibilities, and you can develop many other lessons and sequences. We hope we have given you a starting point for developing your own sequence of lessons at four or even more levels, depending on the time you have available and the abilities of your students or players.

Let students play at a level in which they are comfortable. Impose only those conditions that they are ready to handle. If you or your students become frustrated, stand back and assess the situation. Talk to your students. They need to understand how to modify games so everyone can play and be successful. Remember, it is not participation but *success* that increases the likelihood of your students' future involvement in basketball. So sound the buzzer and let the games begin!

CHAPTER 6

Lacrosse

Kath Howarth

State University of New York
Cortland, New York

This chapter continues to explore a tactical approach to the teaching of invasion games, focusing on lacrosse. Lacrosse creates some interesting challenges for the teacher. First, the adult game has a distinct form for men and another for women. Second, lacrosse requires a stick and therefore fostering early success in the game can be a little more challenging for the teacher. Lacrosse is an exciting and unusual game in which students run fast while using basic skills of catching and throwing. The use of space behind the goal is unique and creates special problems for the defense. With careful planning and the use of modified equipment, a generic form of lacrosse can be introduced to coed classes with the understanding that as students begin to enjoy the game, they may want to learn the specific skills and tactics of women's and men's lacrosse in club or varsity teams.

The facilities and equipment needed for this introduction to lacrosse include the following:

- Either a large indoor space with a high roof or a space outdoors.
- Modified equipment including beginner sticks or short-handled youth sticks.
- One soft ball per student, either normal size or slightly larger than a lacrosse ball (the latter is provided with beginner sticks).
- Several small goals, preferably enough for small-sided games of 3 to 7 players per side, with safe space to play in behind each goal.
- At least one full-size set of goal posts (more if possible) to show how the goal affects the placement of attack and defense players around the goal and goalie. Shooting nets, which cover the center of the goal but have open edges, are good for creating a challenge to scoring goals. Marking a centerline and a fan in front of the goal circle is desirable.
- Markers for extra goal circles, such as spots, rubber lines, and so on.
- A variety of balls, such as small foam balls and handballs, that can be used for throwing and catching games that remove the technical frustrations of using sticks in exploring some tactical situations.

Sticks can be shortened to a length appropriate for your students' level.

All lessons in this chapter start with a game, though you may need to insert some simple warm-up activities using the stick and ball to allow for extra individual practice. It is likely that older students will be familiar with some aspects of lacrosse, and frustrations may vary for individual students as you introduce the game problems. Allow some games to be played without sticks so that the flow of the games can be felt without the technical problems sometimes posed by the sticks. Many lessons in this chapter have a diagram to help you visualize the field of play and players' positions. Not every players' stick position has been shown, only the key players' stick positions (such as the player with the ball and the next player to receive) were included.

Safety is a priority, especially when implements are used in invasion games. For lacrosse to be played safely by a coed class, the authentic ball cannot be used. Authentic sticks, particularly the men's sticks, are also unsafe unless the safety precautions required for the adult sport are followed. Teachers need to follow school district rulings about eye protection and mouth guards. Only a noncontact form of lacrosse should be introduced in physical education. This form does not reduce, but rather enhances, the fun of the game at a beginning level.

We present tactical problems, movements, and skills in lacrosse in table 6.1. A detailed outline of the levels of complexity for each tactical problem appears in table 6.2. Some concepts will take more time to develop than others, particularly because of the associated stick skills that must be acquired. Lessons may need to be repeated and extended to allow students time to develop confidence in the requisite techniques. In this chapter, we briefly describe each level before listing its lessons.

Table 6.1 Tactical Problems, Movements, and Skills in Lacrosse

Tactical problems	Off-the-ball movements	On-the-ball skills
SCORING		
Maintaining possession of the ball	• Supporting the ball carrier	• Protecting the ball • Safe passing and catching • Picking up the ground ball
Maintaining possession of the ball	• Supporting the ball carrier	• Protecting the ball • Safe passing and catching • Picking up the ground ball
Attacking the goal	• Cutting and replacing • Passing patterns	• Shoot, feed, turn, roll, dodge
Creating space in attack	• Clearing patterns • Transition overlaps • Picks • Trail, V-cut • Settled attack • Fast break	• Passing—long, short, back, feed, swing
Using space in attack	• Give-and-go • Timing cuts • Using width and depth • Pick and roll	• Cradling either hand at top • Driving and drawing
PREVENTING SCORING		
Defending space	• Marking, pressure, denial, covering the passing lane • Interception, sliding	• Clearing the ball away from goal
Defending the goal	• Goalkeeping • Player-to-player defense • Zone defense	• Goalkeeper—receiving, clearing the ball • Intercepting, clearing the ball • Picking up loose ball
Winning the ball	• Double team • Positioning	• Blocking the ball, ground ball control

(continued)

Tactical problems	Off-the-ball movements	On-the-ball skills
RESTARTING PLAY		
Draw or face-off	• Positioning	• Taking the draw or face-off
Free position	• Positioning	• Passing, running, shooting
Off-side/out of bounds	• Positioning	• Passing, running, shooting

Table 6.1 *(continued)*

Table 6.2 Levels of Tactical Complexity for Lacrosse

Tactical problems	I	II	III	IV
SCORING				
Maintaining possession of the ball	• Safe pass • Safe catch • Pick up loose ball • Signaling	• Support the ball carrier • Change hands when running • Variety of passing	• Use of trail • Change hands to pass	• Variety of cradling and passing under pressure
Attacking the goal	• Shooting	• Shooting • Cutting, rolling, dodging	• Feed the cutter	• Variety of shots • Fakes • Passing patterns • Plays
Creating space in attack	• Triangle shape in attack • Dodging	• V-cut	• Fast break • Cutting and replacing • Overlaps • Clearing	• Settled attack • Picks • Transition to attack
Using space in attack		• Give-and-go • Timing the cut	• Width and depth	• Swinging play in attack • Creating overlaps
PREVENTING SCORING				
Defending space		• Marking the ball carrier • Intercepting	• Covering the passing lane • Sliding	• Backing up • Team defense
Defending the goal		• Ball, player, goal position	• Team defense • Player-to-player defense	• Player-to-player defense • Zone defense • Communication
Winning the ball	• Ground ball pickup	• Block the pass • Intercept		• Double team

Teaching Sport Concepts and Skills

Tactical problems	I	II	III	IV
RESTARTING PLAY				
Draw or face-off	• Positioning	• Support ball carrier	• Specific roles for restarts, free positions, and so on	• Use draw or face-off to start
Free position	• Signaling			
Off-side or out of bounds				

Level I

The most important goals at level I are maintaining possession and protecting the ball. Lacrosse is fun because during play there are usually lots of opportunities to score. Thus attacking the goal is also a priority. Since passing and catching with the lacrosse stick present particular problems, lessons for level I focus on developing safe passing and catching skills, especially those related to accuracy and to creating open passing lanes. Games in level I can be started simply with a pass rather than with the more difficult draw or face-off starts used in the women's and men's competitions. In fact, the shape of some of the modified beginner sticks can hinder these starting techniques. When play goes out of bounds, the nearest player can bring the ball on onto the field, or the ball can change possession. Emphasis on defense is low in level I because the game needs to flow and the technical problems of passing and catching are sufficient handicaps at first. However, there is good reason to emphasize what the defender can do when the ball is in the air or on the ground, since the skill of catching can be practiced in defense as intercepting. Also, picking up the ball is an important part of the beginner game, whether it is done on offense to maintain possession or on defense to win the ball and regain possession. Success when in possession of the ball is the key to motivation in the early stages of lacrosse.

© PhotoDisc

A focus on learning to catch and pass properly will later help students to enjoy the fast pace of the game.

Tactical Problem
Maintaining possession of the ball

Lesson Focus
Passing, signaling, receiving, and controlling the ball

Objectives
- Protect the ball.
- Signal for and control the ball.
- Pass quickly and accurately.

GAME 1

Setup
1 + 1 + 1 (see figure 6.1)

Goals
- Keep the ball in the air or in the stick.
- Score by successfully passing the ball among the three players.

Conditions
- Stay in restricted area.
- Five passes without a miss equals one point.

Questions

Q: *What was the goal of your game?*
A: To keep the ball safe.

Q: *How did you score?*
A: By successfully passing the ball between each of us.

Q: *What did you have to do when the ball was missed and was on the ground?*
A: Scoop it up.

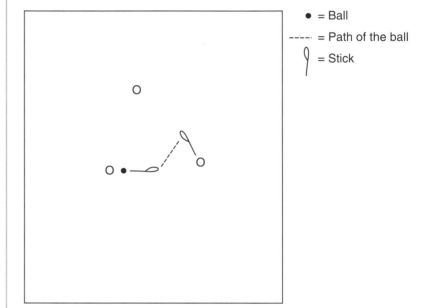

- = Ball
- - - - = Path of the ball
= Stick

FIGURE 6.1

PRACTICE TASK 1

Setup
In the triad, throw the ball to the right and left of players

Goals
- Catch the ball safely.
- Pass accurately to the side of the player signaling for ball.
- Lead the catcher by sending the ball away from his body.

Cues
- Catching
  - Present a target by reaching out to the ball and opening the face of the stick to the ball.
  - Point your feet and the stick in the same direction.
  - Cushion the ball as it enters the stick.
  - Take both hands to your nondominant side to catch or try to change hand position.

- Throwing
  - Throw side-on to target, taking the head of your stick back and pointing the bottom of your stick toward your target (partner's stick).
  - Make a high overarm throw with your top hand and pull your bottom hand in as your top hand moves toward the target.

PRACTICE TASK 2

Alone, practice picking up a ground ball

Goal

Pick up the ball smoothly and continue running.

Cues

- Point the head of the stick at the ball.
- Lower the stick to your bottom-hand side and push firmly with your bottom hand through the pickup.
- Place your foot on the opposite side level with the ball.
- Raise the stick quickly to maintain control and to prepare to pass or shoot.

GAME 2

Setup

2v1 using a hoop as a goal (see figure 6.2)

Goals

- Score as many goals as possible in the set amount of time.
- Pass accurately to your partner and away from the defender.

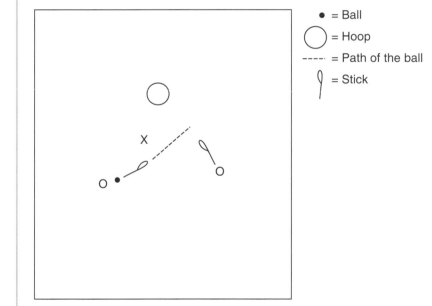

Conditions

- Score 1 point for every goal and an extra point for three passes made without interception by the defender and without dropping the ball.
- Defender must stay a stick's length away from the hoop.
- Only one person can go for the ground ball (the nearest person).

FIGURE 6.2

Questions

Q: *Why was this game harder than the first?*
A: Because there was a defender and we had to score as many goals as possible in a set time.

Q: *How did you keep the ball?*
A: By keeping passes short and accurate.

Q: *What difference did the defenders make?*
A: They made us move in order to pass and catch safely.

Tactical Problem

Maintaining possession of the ball

Lesson Focus

Passing from the nondominant side, signaling, receiving and controlling the ball

Objectives

- Protect the ball.
- Signal for and control the ball.
- Pass quickly and accurately from both sides of the body.

GAME 1

Setup

2v1 (see figure 6.3)

Goals

- Keep the ball in the air or in the stick.
- Score by successfully passing the ball between you and your partner four times.

Conditions

- Stay in restricted area.
- Use cool defense (defender stays one arm's length away).

Questions

Q: *What was the goal of your game?*

A: To keep the ball safe and away from the defender.

Q: *How did you score?*

A: By passing the ball between us four times.

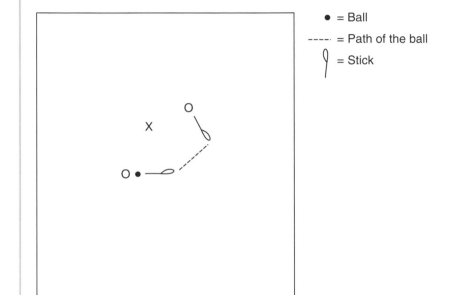

● = Ball

----- = Path of the ball

◗ = Stick

FIGURE 6.3

PRACTICE TASK

Setup

In a triad, throw the ball from your right or left side depending on where the defender stands (throw from the free side)

Goals

- Pass accurately from your free side (the side away from the defender) to the player signaling for the ball.
- Catch the ball safely.
- Signal for the pass.
- Get to the ball first when it's on the ground.

Cues

- Throwing
  - When throwing from your dominant side, step with your opposite foot toward the target, move the head of your stick back and point the bottom of your stick toward the target (partner's stick), perform a high overarm throw with your top hand, and pull your bottom hand in as your top hand moves toward the target.
  - From your nondominant side try a shovel pass. Swing the stick across your body, drop the head of the stick down, and shovel the ball toward the receiver (like when you shovel snow).
- Catching
  - Signal by reaching out to the ball and opening the face of your stick to the ball.
  - Point your feet and stick in the direction the thrower is moving so that you are not blocked by the defender.
  - Cushion the ball as it enters the stick.
  - Take both hands to your nondominant side to catch or try to change hand position.
  - React quickly after a missed pass. When there is a ground ball, the first person to the ball gets possession.

GAME 2

Setup

3v3 keep-away (no goals), played with sticks or with no implement depending on the skills of the students (see figure 6.4)

Goals

- Score as many goals as possible in the set amount of time.
- Pass accurately to your team and away from the defenders.

Conditions

- Score 1 point for every three successful passes made without an interception by the defender or without dropping the ball.
- Defender must stay a stick's length away from opponent.

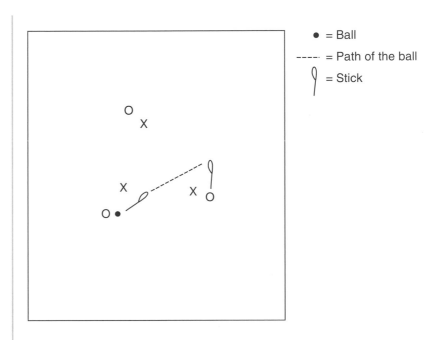

● = Ball

---- = Path of the ball

= Stick

FIGURE 6.4

Questions

Q: *Why was this game harder than the first?*
A: Because there was a defender and we had to score as many goals as possible in a set time.

Q: *How did you keep the ball?*
A: By keeping passes short and accurate and away from the defender.

Q: *What difference did the defenders make?*
A: They made us move in order to pass and catch safely. We had to pass from and to the free side.

Tactical Problem
Creating space in attack

Lesson Focus
Creating passing lanes

Objectives
- Move to open space.
- Make safe passes.

GAME 1

Setup
Use 1v1 with a feeder (three players total) behind a marker and with a goal (hoop or line). See figure 6.5.

Goal
Get open, receive the pass, and go to the goal.

Condition
Feeder cannot move over line until pass has been made.

Questions
Q: *How did you get open?*
A: Moved and signaled into open space away from the defender.

Q: *How did the feeder know when to pass the ball?*
A: There was an open space (passing lane) between the feeder and the receiver's stick. The receiver watched and made eye contact with the feeder.

PRACTICE TASK

Setup
In a triad, throw the ball to the receiver's stick as the receiver signals and moves away from a stationary defender. Increase the defender's role from stationary to moving as the attack becomes more successful (see figure 6.6).

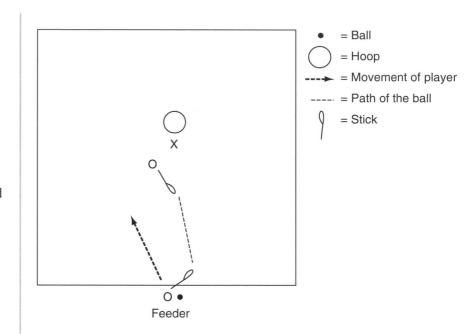

●	= Ball
◯	= Hoop
---▶	= Movement of player
----	= Path of the ball
⌇	= Stick

FIGURE 6.5

●	= Ball
----	= Path of the ball
⌇	= Stick

FIGURE 6.6

Goals

- Pass accurately to the free side of the player signaling for the ball.
- Lead the attack away from the defense by passing ahead of her outstretched stick.
- Signal for the pass and catch the ball safely.

Cues

- Dodging
  - Use a sudden fake or sharp sprint to get into open space.
  - Lead with the stick held out as a target.
- Catching
  - Signal by reaching out and opening the face of the stick to the ball.
  - Keep the stick as still as possible to give a good target.

GAME 2

Setup

3v3 keep-away (no goals)

Goals

- Score as many points as possible in the set amount of time.
- Pass accurately to your team and away from the defender.

Conditions

- Score 3 points for three successful passes made without an interception by the defender and without dropping the ball.
- Score 2 points if one pass was dropped within the three completed possessions.
- Score 1 point if two passes were dropped within the three completed possessions.
- Defender must stay a stick's length away from the opponent.

Questions

Q: *Why was this game harder than the first?*
A: Because there was a defender and we had to score as many goals as possible in a set time.

Q: *How did you score the most points?*
A: By passing and catching accurately without dropping the ball or losing possession.

Q: *What did the defenders make you do?*
A: They filled the space between us and made us dodge and move quicker in order to pass and catch safely.

Q: *What is a passing lane?*
A: An open space between the player with the ball and the receiver.

Lesson 4 Level I

Tactical Problem
Attacking the goal

Lesson Focus
Shooting

Objectives

- Shoot with control.
- Cut, control, and shoot on target.

GAME 1

Setup

Use 1v1 with a feeder (three players total) behind a marker and with a goal (e.g., street hockey or real lacrosse goal with the center area marked with pinnies to represent a goalie). See figure 6.7.

Goal

Get open, receive the pass, and shoot.

Conditions

- Feeder cannot move over line until pass has been made.
- Static defense.

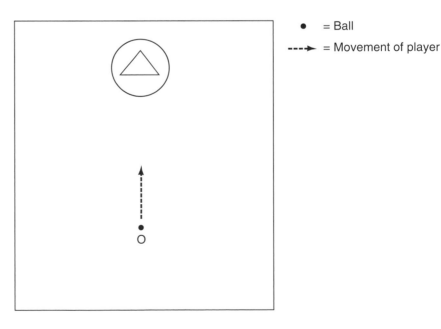

● = Ball
---▶ = Movement of player
----· = Path of the ball
❩ = Stick

FIGURE 6.7

Questions

Q: When did you shoot?
A: When in front of the goal because this position gave the most space to aim at.

Q: Where did you aim the ball?
A: Into the corners and angled downward.

PRACTICE TASK

Setup

Individual practice. Each player has a ball (see figure 6.8). Make sure there are lots of targets.

Goals

- Run toward the goal or target and bounce the ball into the corners of the goal.
- Shoot from the optimal position in front of the goal.

Cues

- Maintain speed through the shot.
- Follow through to make the ball go downward.
- Practice in pairs and receive the ball from a partner then run to the goal to score.

● = Ball
---▶ = Movement of player

FIGURE 6.8

Teaching Sport Concepts and Skills

GAME 2

Setup
3v3 with one goal and with a cone at the other end of the space to mark the start the game (see figure 6.9)

Goals
- Score as many times as possible.
- Keep the shooting space open and ready for the shooter to move into in order to receive the ball.

Conditions
- The three attackers become defenders after scoring.
- Start the game from the cone after each goal.
- Pass at least once before taking a shot.
- No defender is allowed to stand in front of goal.

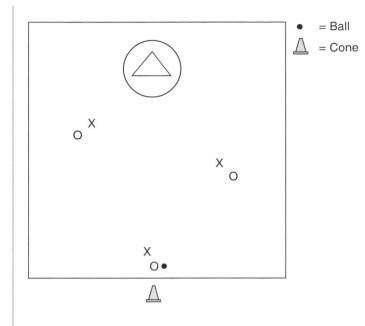

FIGURE 6.9

Questions

Q: *What was the primary aim for the attacking team?*
A: To get a player in front of goal and ready to take a shot.

Q: *How did you do this?*
A: By keeping that space open so someone could dodge or cut away from her defender into that space and receive the ball.

Q: *What was hard about this game?*
A: Timing the move to receive and shoot the ball from the best spot in front of goal and keeping the space open for the person to run into and score.

Lesson 5 — Level I

Tactical Problem
Creating space in attack

Lesson Focus
Giving passing options for the ball carrier

Objectives
- Use the attack triangle.
- Create passing lanes.

GAME 1

Setup
3v3 keep-away with no goal (see figure 6.10)

Goal
Offer options for the ball carrier by forming a triangle shape in attack.

Condition

Change possession of the ball after five successful passes. (Five passes is one point—keep score.)

Questions

Q: *Why is a triangle important for your game?*

A: It gives the ball carrier two different directions in which to pass the ball.

Q: *What else do you have to think about when you are helping your teammate make a safe pass?*

A: Opening up space for the pass by creating a passing lane between me and the ball.

Q: *In which direction should the ball carrier pass, if possible?*

A: Away from her defender and into the open space.

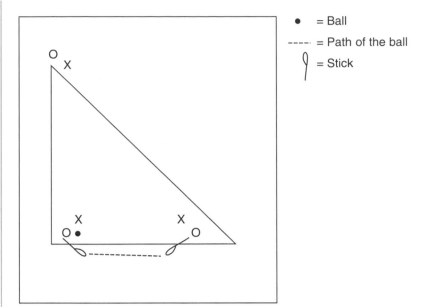

● = Ball

---- = Path of the ball

⊽ = Stick

FIGURE 6.10

PRACTICE TASK

Setup

Play in threes. The defender marks the receiver (from front or behind). The receiver moves suddenly away from the defender to signal and receive the ball (see figure 6.11). The pie shape on the diagram represents the free side of the player who is moving to receive the ball.

Goals

- Create space by dodging away from a defender.
- Create space by moving with the ball away from the defender.

Cues

- The receiver makes the move very sudden.
- The receiver leads with the open stick.
- The receiver fakes if necessary.
- Defender marks the thrower (front or side).
- Receiver moves in the direction in which the thrower is open (thrower's free side).
- Thrower only passes to the receiver if there is no defender between them (there is a passing lane).

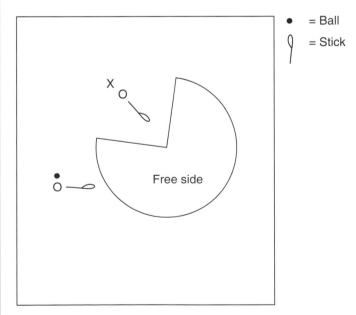

● = Ball

⊽ = Stick

Free side

FIGURE 6.11

Setup

3v3 with one goal and one hoop (see figure 6.9)

Goals

- Score as many goals as possible.
- Keep the triangle shape while on offense and help the ball carrier by creating passing lanes and open spaces.
- The defense scores by regaining possession and taking the ball to the hoop.

Conditions

- The three attackers become defenders after 5 minutes of play, at which time scoring starts over.
- Start the game from the hoop after each goal is scored.
- Pass at least once before taking a shot.
- No defender is allowed to stand in front of the goal.
- Defending team can score by taking the ball away from the offense and putting it in the hoop.

Questions

Q: *What was the primary aim for the attacking team?*
A: To score.

Q: *How did you score?*
A: By keeping space open and giving options to the passer by using a triangle shape in offense.

Q: *How else did you create space?*
A: By opening up passing lanes among teammates and taking the ball away from the defender to pass.

Q: *What is a passing lane?*
A: The open space between the ball and the receiver (free of defense players).

Q: *What do you do to create that space?*
A: Use dodging and fakes and move the stick away from the defender to pass or to signal for the pass.

Lesson 6 — Level I

Tactical Problem

Attacking the goal

Lesson Focus

Using the space behind the goal

Objectives

- Feed the ball to a cutter.
- Use the player behind the goal as a safety.

GAME 1

Setup

3v3 with one goal (see figure 6.12)

Goal

Offer options behind goal for the ball carrier by forming a triangle shape in attack.

Conditions

- One attacker must always be behind the goal.
- Change possession after a goal has been scored.
- The ball must be passed at least once to the person behind the goal.

Questions

Q: *Why is a triangle important for your game?*

A: It gives the ball carrier two different directions in which to pass the ball.

Q: *What is the point of the player behind the goal?*

A: He can feed the ball to players who are in positions to score.

Q: *Anything else?*

A: He can be a safety receiver because his defender will probably not mark him as closely behind the goal.

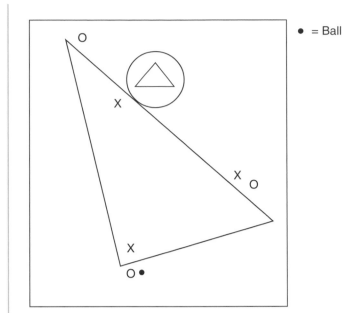

● = Ball

FIGURE 6.12

PRACTICE TASK

Setup

Play in threes. The defender marks the receiver at the start. The receiver moves suddenly away from the defender and toward the goal to signal and receive the ball from the feeder, who stands behind and to the side of the goal (see figure 6.13).

Goal

Feed the cutter at the right moment so that she can score.

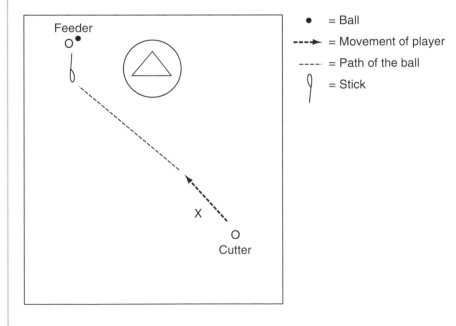

● = Ball

----➤ = Movement of player

----- = Path of the ball

〿 = Stick

FIGURE 6.13

Cues

- Cutter
  - Make the move very sudden.
  - Lead with the open stick.
  - Fake if necessary.
- Feeder
  - Make the pass flat and direct.
  - Time the pass so that the receiver is in the best shooting position.

GAME 2

Setup

3v3 with one goal and one hoop at the opposite end of the playing area.

Goals

- Offense scores in the goal as many times as possible.
- Offense keeps triangle shape and helps the ball carrier by creating passing lanes and open spaces.
- Defense scores by regaining possession and taking the ball to the hoop.

Conditions

- Start the game from behind the goal.
- There must be an attack player behind the goal all the times.
- The three attackers become defenders after 5 minutes of play, at which time scoring starts over.
- Pass at least once before taking a shot.

Questions

Q: What was the primary aim for the attacking team?
A: To score.

Q: How did you do this?
A: By keeping space open and giving options to the passer by using a triangle shape in offense.

Q: What was the role of the player behind the goal?
A: To be a feeder and a safety receiver.

Q: What important skills does that player need?
A: Accurate passing and good timing.

Level II

At level II the major focus is still on maintaining possession and scoring. However, lessons start looking at simple tactical concepts for defending the player and the goal. As students become more successful in scoring, you will need to study the roles of offensive players who are off the ball, particularly because play can continue behind the goal. Thus using and creating space in lacrosse have an added dimension around the goal. As the defense improves, attack players have to help each other more by considering when and where to move. Students need to develop attacking skills such as changing hands on the stick and to develop a variety of passing options. Attackers also need to work on scoring goals when less time and space are available.

Attacking skills such as different hand placements and passes must be learned.

Lesson 7

Tactical Problem
Maintaining possession

Lesson Focus
Supporting the ball carrier

Objectives
- Help a teammate under pressure.
- Pass under pressure.

GAME 1

Setup
3v3 in a square area

Goals
- Offer options for the ball carrier by creating passing lanes.
- Score by making four successful passes.

Conditions
- Change possession after four passes.
- The ball must be passed at least once to each person.

Questions

Q: *How can you support your teammates?*
A: Signal clearly with the stick away from the defense and change position so that the defender is kept busy.

Q: *What can the ball carrier do to maintain possession when under pressure from the defender?*
A: Pull the stick away from the defender and keep feet moving while looking for help.

PRACTICE TASK

Setup

Play in threes. The defender marks the ball carrier, who is trying to move toward the goal (a hoop). The offense tries to dodge past the defense, and the second offense moves to help the ball carrier (see figure 6.14).

Goal

Support the offense.

Cues

- Receiver
  - Move very clearly and early.
  - Lead with the open stick to the side away from the defender in order to create a passing lane.
  - Change position when the ball carrier changes stick position in order to keep the passing lane open.
- Passer
  - Keep head up and look for help.
  - Pass only if the offense has opened a clear passing lane.
  - Keep the stick and ball away from the defense.
  - Keep feet moving.

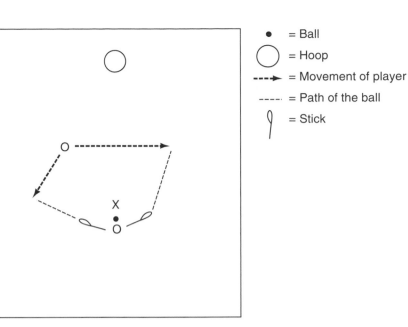

• = Ball
◯ = Hoop
---▶ = Movement of player
---- = Path of the ball
⌇ = Stick

FIGURE 6.14

GAME 2

Setup

4v3 with one goal and a hoop for the defense to take the ball to when they regain possession (see figure 6.15)

Goals

- Offense scores in the goal as many times as possible.
- Offense keeps the triangle shape and helps the ball carrier by moving and creating passing lanes and open spaces.
- Defense scores by regaining possession and taking the ball to the hoop.

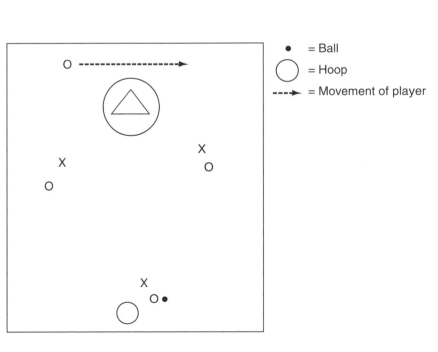

• = Ball
◯ = Hoop
---▶ = Movement of player

FIGURE 6.15

Conditions

- Start the game from behind the goal.
- There must be an unmarked attack player behind the goal at all times, and each player fills this role in turn.
- The three attackers become defenders after 5 minutes of play, at which time scoring starts over.
- Pass at least once before taking a shot.

Questions

Q: *How did you score?*

A: By keeping the shooting space open and giving options to the passer by using a triangle shape in offense.

Q: *What was the role of the player behind the goal?*

A: To support a player under pressure by being a safety receiver.

Q: *What important skills does that player need?*

A: Accurate passing and good timing.

Lesson 8 — Level II

Tactical Problem

Defending space

Lesson Focus

Marking an opponent off the ball and pressuring the opponent with the ball

Objectives

- Pressure the pass.
- Be ready to intercept the ball.

GAME 1

Setup

3v3 with one goal for the offense and a line to which the defense can take the ball to safety (see figure 6.16)

Goals

- Prevent scoring.
- Keep your opponent from receiving the ball.

Conditions

- No body contact.
- No stick checking.
- Score 1 point for intercepting a ball, getting a ground ball, or taking a ball to safety.

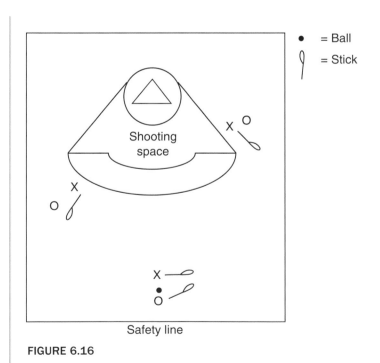

FIGURE 6.16

Questions

Q: What do you do when your opponent has the ball?

A: Stay between him and the goal and follow his stick with my stick.

Q: What do you do in defense when your opponent does not have the ball?

A: Stop her from receiving a pass either by marking her and forcing the pass to go elsewhere or by intercepting the pass.

PRACTICE TASK 1

Setup

Play in pairs with one ball. The attacker runs down a line or a channel of space with the ball. The defender tries to position himself so that the attacker is forced to stay on one side of the line or channel (this may be the attacker's weak side or the area away from the middle of the field or the goal). See figure 6.17.

Goals

- Defender controls the attacker's movement through body positioning.
- Defender reduces the options for the attacker.

Cues

- Mirror the attacker's movement and stick position.
- Go hip to hip.

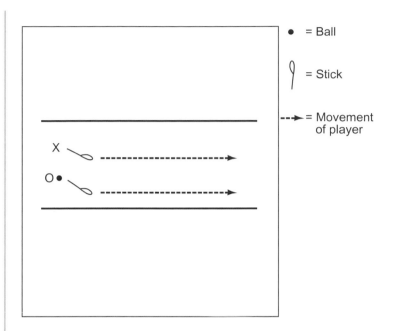

FIGURE 6.17

PRACTICE TASK 2

Setup

Play in threes with one ball. Two attackers pass the ball to and fro. The defender starts at right angles to and 2 yards/meters away from the attack (see figure 6.18). As the passes are made, the defender times a fast run to try to intercept the ball. If she intercepts, she passes the ball back and tries again with the other attacker. Players change roles after five tries.

Goals

- Time the run to the preparation movement of the passer.
- Keep running once the ball is in your stick.

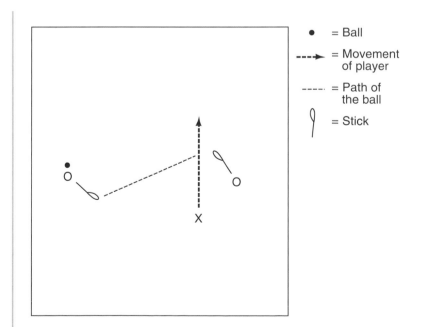

FIGURE 6.18

Cues

- Stretch the stick out, watch the passer carefully, and accelerate.
- Keep the stick still and don't try to knock the ball down.

GAME 2

Setup

3v3 with one goal for the offense and a line to which the defense can take the ball to safety

Goals

- Prevent offense from entering the shooting area to score.
- Keep your opponent from receiving the ball.

Conditions

- No body contact.
- No stick checking.
- Score one point for intercepting, getting a ground ball, or taking the ball to the safety line.

Questions

Q: *How do you decide where to force your offense to move with the ball?*
A: Force the offense away from the shooting area, and make offensive players move their sticks to their weak (nondominant) sides.

Q: *Where on the field is it safest to go for an interception?*
A: Away from the scoring area and away from the center of the field.

Q: *If your opponent has the ball, where should you be and why?*
A: Between him and the goal to slow him down and force him away from a shooting position.

Lesson 9 Level II

Tactical Problem
Winning the ball

Lesson Focus
Regaining possession of a loose ball and gaining possession in transition

Objectives

- Win the draw or face-off.
- Win the ground ball.

GAME 1

Setup

3v3 keep-away with no goals

Goals

- Reduce the number of passes the opposition can make.
- Regain possession of the ball.

Condition

No body or stick contact.

Questions

Q: What do you do to regain possession of the ball?
A: Intercept or be the first on the ball when it goes on the ground.

Q: How can you make it harder for your opponents to pass?
A: Mark them closely both on and off the ball.

Q: What should you do when you lose the ball?
A: Quickly try to get it back and become a defender.

PRACTICE TASK 1

Setup

Play in threes with one ball (see figure 6.19). O1 rolls the ball between O2 and O3, who both try to get to the ball, pick it up, and gain possession (first player there gets the ball). The winner passes the ball to O1.

Goals

- Get to the ball first.
- Pick up the ball and keep moving.

Cues

- Move quickly.
- Lower the head of the stick and push it strongly under the ball to scoop the ball up.
- If the ball is moving away too fast, quickly stop it and then scoop it up.

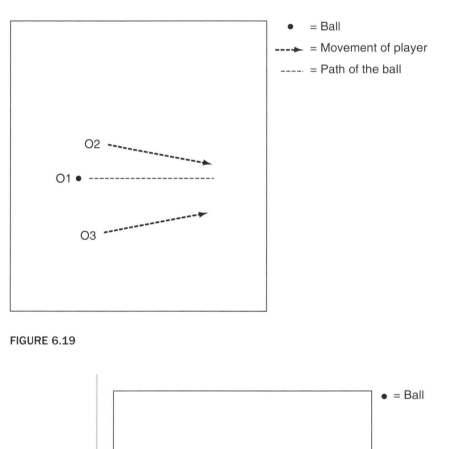

FIGURE 6.19

PRACTICE TASK 2

Setup

Play in threes with one ball (see figure 6.20). Set up the draw (rather than the face-off since the draw gets the ball into the air). One player acts as the official and places the ball between the backs of the other players' sticks. The other two players draw and try to get the ball toward their wings.

Goal

Win the ball either by moving it toward your goal or by catching it.

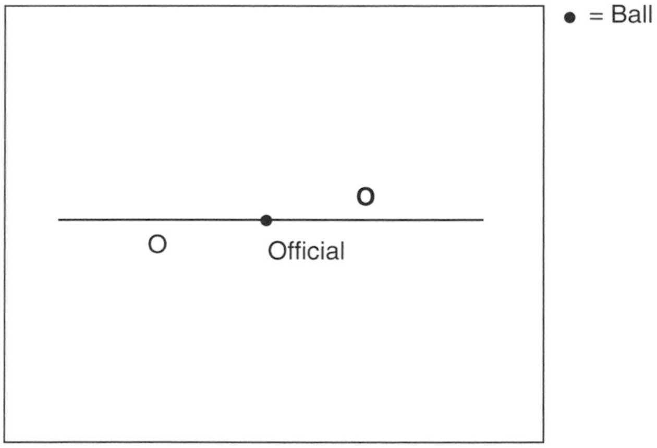

FIGURE 6.20

The two O's in the center represent the two players who take the draw (in the women's game) or the two midfielders who take the face-off (in the men's game). Until this happens, they are both in offense. Once the game begins they become offense or defense depending on whose team won the draw or face-off.

Cues

- Bend your knees and stay balanced to hold the ball between the backs of the sticks.
- Listen for the whistle (official can say "whistle").
- Pull the stick quickly up and away.
- Try different pressures and speeds to control the ball.

GAME 2

Setup

3v3 with a line for a goal plus three extra players (one is the official and the other two are extra defenders guarding their own goal line (see figure 6.21)

Goals

- Win the draw and score by carrying (not throwing) the ball over the goal line.
- Regain possession by being first on any ground ball or by intercepting a pass.

Conditions

- No body contact.
- No stick checking.

Questions

Q: *When is your first chance to win the ball?*
A: At the draw.

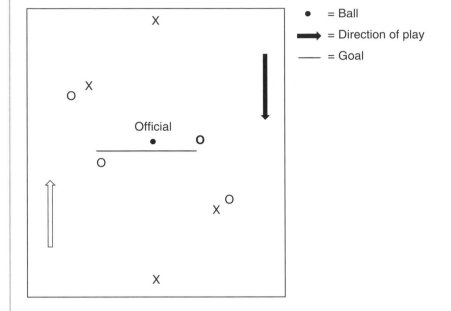

FIGURE 6.21

The two O's in the center represent the two players who take the draw (in the women's game) or the two midfielders who take the face-off (in the men's game). Until this happens, they are both in offense. Once the game begins they become offense or defense depending on whose team won the draw or face-off.

Q: *Are there other opportunities to win the ball?*
A: Yes, if the ball goes on the ground and if there is a bad pass that we can intercept.

Q: *What happens if the ball goes out of bounds?*
A: The game stops and one of the teams is given the ball.

Lesson 10   Level II

Tactical Problem
Creating space in attack

Lesson Focus
Making space in order to get free to receive the pass

Objective
Use a V-cut.

GAME 1

Setup
1v1 with a feeder (three players total) and with a hoop or goal or line (see figure 6.22)

Goal
Get free to receive the ball and go to the goal.

Condition
The original feeder cannot continue in the game unless it is to receive the ball from the defense if the defense gains possession.

Questions
> Q: *How can you create space for yourself to get free from your defender?*
>
> A: Move in one direction and then quickly move in another.

> Q: *Where do you want the ball to be passed?*
>
> A: Into the space where I am moving away from my defender.

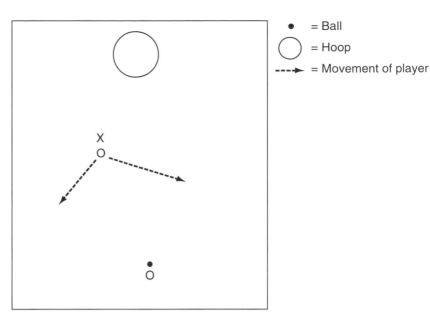

FIGURE 6.22

PRACTICE TASK

Setup
Play in threes. Practice the V-cut, with the final move being toward the ball (see figures 6.23 and 6.24).

Goal
Create space in which to receive the ball.

Cues
- Receiver
  - Make the move very sudden and partially signal with the stick to make the defender follow.
  - Cut forward with a stronger signal into the space you create.
  - Once you are successful, try other directions for the V-cut.
  - Always receive the ball while moving away from the defender.
- Passer
  - Pass only if the offense has opened a clear passing lane and given a convincing signal.

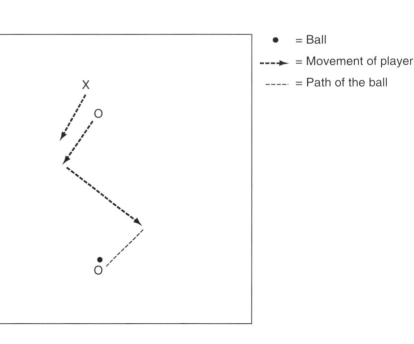

FIGURE 6.23

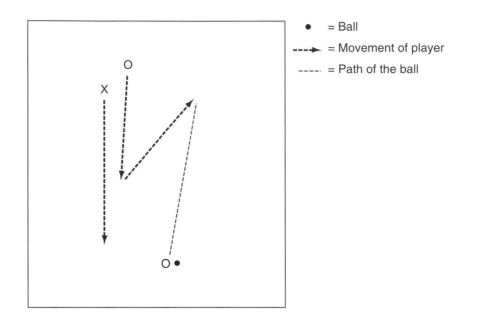

= Ball

----→ = Movement of player

---- = Path of the ball

FIGURE 6.24

GAME 2

Setup
5v5 game with two goals (see figure 6.25)

Goal
Help your team by creating space and cutting to the ball.

Conditions
- Start the game from the goal line.
- There must be at least three passes before your team can score.

Questions
Q: *What was the primary aim for the attacking team?*
A: To score.

Q: *How did you do this?*
A: By cutting and recutting to open up spaces.

Q: *Which cut is the hardest to mark?*
A: The one that goes upfield toward the ball.

Q: *Why is that hard?*
A: Because at first the V-cut takes the defender toward her goal, which leaves the space between the passer and the ball uncovered.

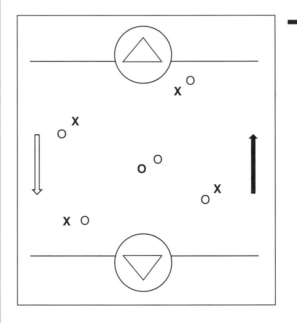

→ = Direction of play

FIGURE 6.25

The two O's in the center represent the two players who take the draw (in the women's game) or the two midfielders who take the face-off (in the men's game). Until this happens, they are both in offense. Once the game begins they become offense or defense depending on whose team won the draw or face-off.

Tactical Problem
Creating space in attack

Lesson Focus
Creating and using space with the pass

Objective
Use a give-and-go.

GAME 1

Setup
2v2 with a hoop or goal or line (see figure 6.26)

Goal
Pass to your teammate, move to receive the ball, and go to the goal.

Conditions
- The ball must be passed twice before the goal is scored.
- The O that starts the play with the ball is the only player who can score.

Questions
Q: *How can you open up space to free yourself?*
A: By passing the ball to another player.

Q: *What does the defense do?*
A: Move and look toward the ball.

PRACTICE TASK

Setup
Play in fours. Practice the give-and-go with cool (almost stationary) defense (see figure 6.27).

Goal
Create a space in which to receive the ball by deflecting the defender's attention from your space.

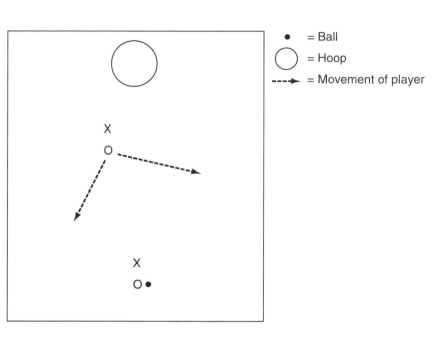

● = Ball
◯ = Hoop
----▶ = Movement of player

FIGURE 6.26

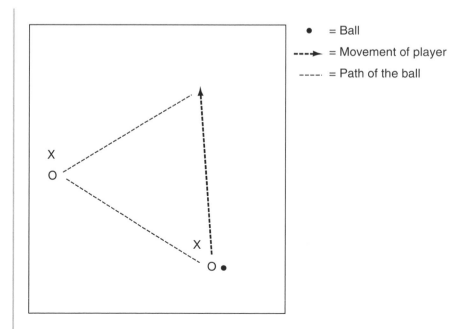

● = Ball
----▶ = Movement of player
----- = Path of the ball

FIGURE 6.27

Cues

- Passer
  - Send the ball out to the receiver on the wing.
  - When the defender looks after the ball, cut behind him and move again to receive the ball.
- Receiver
  - Control the ball quickly and keep your head up to see the runner moving for the give-and-go.

GAME 2

Setup

Use 4v4 with two goals (or hoops) at both ends of the field. (Having two options for scoring at each end keeps the game wide). See figure 6.28.

Goal

Help your team by creating space using the give-and-go midfield.

Conditions

- Start the game from the goal line.
- There must be at least three passes before your team can score.

Questions

Q: *What was the primary aim for the attacking team?*
A: To create space and score.

Q: *How did you do this?*
A: By opening up space with give-and-go moves.

Q: *How did this help you?*
A: The ball moves across the field and makes the defensive players move their focus. It gives us a chance to move and lose our defenders midfield.

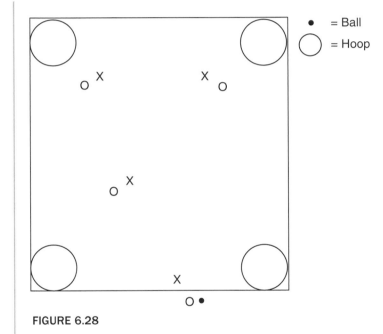

FIGURE 6.28

Lesson 12 Level II

Tactical Problem

Defending the goal

Lesson Focus

Preventing offense from entering the goal area with or without the ball

Objective

Defend opponents on goal-side and ball-side when both on and off the ball.

GAME 1

Setup
3v3 with a goal

Goal
Prevent offense from moving into the shooting area.

Conditions
- Defense starts with 10 points.
- Defense loses a point for every goal scored against them.
- Defense wins a point for every interception or other possession gained.

Questions

Q: *How can you keep your opponent from scoring?*
A: By preventing them from getting into a scoring position.

Q: *What does the defense need to do?*
A: Place themselves between offensive players and the goal area and closely mark the offensive player with the ball.

PRACTICE TASK

Setup
Play in threes. With a hoop or cone as a goal, practice correct goal-side and ball-side defensive positioning (see figure 6.29).

Goals
- Force your attacker away from the dangerous shooting area by positioning yourself goal-side.
- Move ball-side to make a pass as difficult as possible.

Cues
- Place your feet within the angle made by drawing lines from the goal to your player and from the player to the ball. Standing in this angle is standing in the goal-side, ball-side position.
- Try to see the ball as well as your opponent. As your player moves from one side to another, change your position so that you are always covering his line to the goal.
- Use your stick to reach into the passing lane if possible.

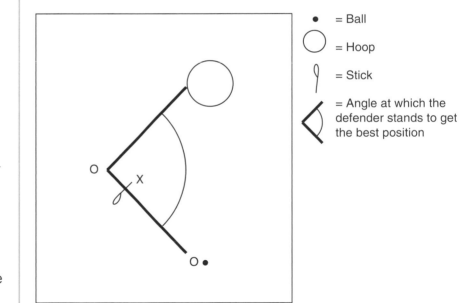

= Ball

= Hoop

= Stick

= Angle at which the defender stands to get the best position

FIGURE 6.29

GAME 2

Setup

3v3 with one goal (see figure 6.30)

Goal

Keep the offense from scoring a goal.

Conditions

- Start the ball at different points (e.g., from the center, from behind goal, and so on).
- Play short, intense games (e.g., 5 minutes) to see if the defense can be successful.

Questions

Q: *What was the primary aim for the defending team?*
A: To keep the offense out of the scoring area.

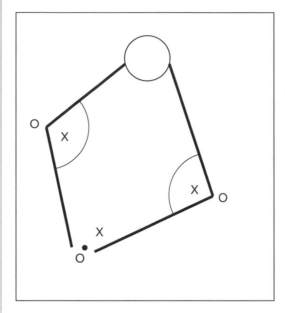

• = Ball

◯ = Hoop

⟨ = Angle at which the defender stands to get the best position

FIGURE 6.30

Q: *How did you do this?*
A: By marking the opponent goal-side and ball-side whenever possible.

Q: *How did doing this help you?*
A: The offensive players always had a defender between them and their goal, and so they had to make passes away from the target area.

Level III

Level III develops general offense and defense tactics into more team-oriented concepts. As the numbers of players on teams increase, so does the need to anticipate future plays two or three moves ahead. Working on offense may mean having more, equal, or fewer numbers than your opponents, depending on the situation. Using a fast break or creating width and depth of support for the person with the ball demands an awareness of several options by off-the-ball offensive players. Similarly, defensive players begin working together to cover a free offensive player or begin working as a unit in a zone. In level III the tactical use of a free position or a turnover after a foul is added to the repertoire of solutions for restarting the game. At this level the roles of different players can be explored as can the importance of transitioning from offense to defense.

Team-oriented plays require players to think ahead.

Lesson 13 Level III

Tactical Problem
Maintaining possession

Lesson Focus
Protecting the ball

Objective
Change hands to protect the ball.

GAME 1

Setup
3v3 within a square area marked by cones

Goal
Protect the ball and keep possession.

Conditions
- A successful pass to each player (minimum of three passes, but could include more) scores a point.
- Defense cannot touch a stick or person.

Questions
Q: How can you keep the ball safe?
A: Keep the stick and ball away from the defense.

Q: How do you do that?
A: Pull the stick to the side that is away from the defender and run away from the defender.

PRACTICE TASK

Setup
Play in twos. Player in possession practices taking the ball away from the defender's stick by moving his own stick away and changing his top hand to the side the stick is moved to (i.e., top hand on the left of the body is the left hand).

Goal
Change hands smoothly and keep control of the stick.

Cue
Slide the bottom hand up to switch hands so that the stick remains under control.

GAME 2

Setup
3v3 in a square area marked by cones

Goal
Protect the ball by switching hands.

Conditions
- Score by keeping the ball for at least three successful passes.
- Score one extra point by switching hands to protect the ball.

Questions
Q: *How did you keep possession?*
A: By changing hands and taking the ball away from the defender.

Q: *What do you now need to learn?*
A: How to make an overarm pass from the nondominant side.

Lesson 14   Level III

Tactical Problem
Maintaining possession

Lesson Focus
Variety in passing

Objectives
- Change hands to pass.
- Pass to a trail player.

GAME 1

Setup
3v3 within a rectangular area, with goals marked by cones at each end

Goal
Protect the ball and keep possession.

Conditions
- Must change hands to protect the ball.
- Score points for changing hands and for carrying the ball through the goals marked by cones.

Questions

Q: *How can you keep the ball safe?*
A: Keep the stick and ball away from the defense.

Q: *What about passing the ball? How do you pass safely?*
A: Pass the ball from the side away from the defender.

Q: *Which passes can be used?*
A: The overarm from each side and the shovel pass from the nondominant side.

PRACTICE TASK 1

Setup

Play in threes. Practice passing the ball from the nondominant side after changing hands. Have a static defender stand on the dominant side (see figure 6.31).

Goals

· Change hands smoothly and keep control of the stick.
· Pass away from the defender.

Cues

· Slide the bottom hand up to switch hands so that the stick is under control.
· Step onto the opposite foot to throw.
· Begin with short passes.

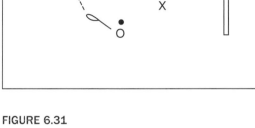

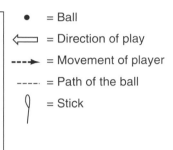
= Ball
= Direction of play
= Movement of player
= Path of the ball
= Stick

FIGURE 6.31

PRACTICE TASK 2

Setup

Play in threes. Practice passing the ball to a person behind you (a trail player) while there is a defender in front of you (see figure 6.32).

Goal

Use the player behind you as a safety or for changing the point of attack.

Cue

Use a shovel pass to speed up the pass (which will be short) and to protect the stick from the defender.

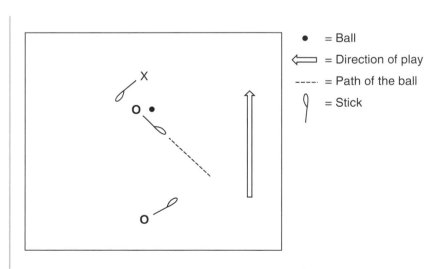

= Ball
= Direction of play
= Path of the ball
= Stick

FIGURE 6.32

GAME 2

Setup
Use 3v3 in a large square area marked by cones. If possible, place a goal in the middle of the area (see figure 6.33).

Goal
Protect the ball by switching hands to pass and by using the trail player.

Condition
Keep the ball for at least three successful passes before scoring in the goal.

Questions

Q: *How did you keep possession?*
A: By changing hands, passing from the side away from the defender, and using the trail player.

Q: *How will you know there is a trail player?*
A: The trail player will call.

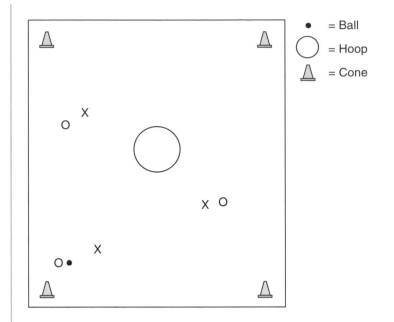

● = Ball
◯ = Hoop
⌂ = Cone

FIGURE 6.33

Lesson 15   Level III

Tactical Problem
Defending space

Lesson Focus
Covering the most dangerous spaces

Objectives
· Cover the passing lanes.
· Move over to cover the most dangerous players.

GAME 1

Setup
3v2 within a rectangular area with a goal at one end

Goal
Defend the most dangerous spaces.

Condition
Offense must make three passes before shooting at the goal.

Questions

Q: *Where are the most dangerous spaces?*
A: In front of the goal and between the ball and my opponent.

Q: *How do you defend these spaces?*
A: Mark goal-side and ball-side.

Q: What happened when offensive players got past their defenders?
A: They ran to the goal and scored.

Q: How can a defender cope with this?
A: Leave your own opposing players and go to the offensive player with the ball.

PRACTICE TASK

Setup
Play in threes. The free attacker with the ball runs toward a goal (cone or hoop). The defender decides when to leave the second attacker to prevent the free attacker from scoring (see figure 6.34).

Goal
Slide when you still have time to take on the new attacker, but do not allow an easy pass to your other opponent, who would then have an open goal.

Cues
- Keep your stick high to cover the passing lane.
- Move diagonally but be ready to switch directions and stay with the new attacker.
- Use quick and balanced footwork.

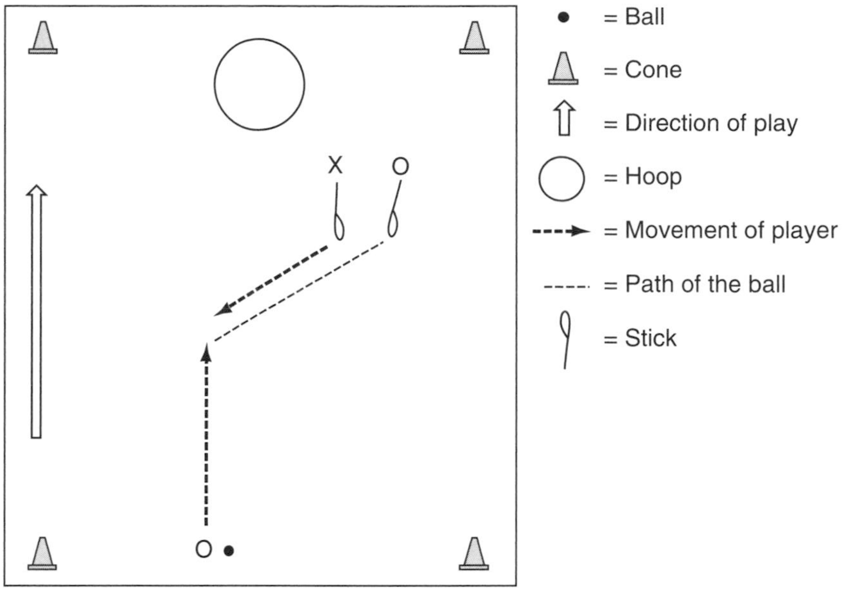

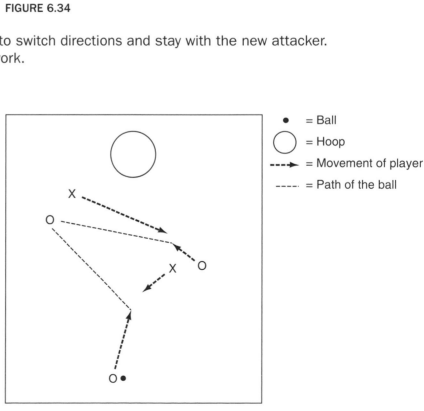

FIGURE 6.34

• = Ball
△ = Cone
⇧ = Direction of play
◯ = Hoop
---▶ = Movement of player
----- = Path of the ball
⅄ = Stick

GAME 2

Setup
3v2 in a large square area marked by cones, one goal (see figure 6.35)

Goals
- Keep your player from attacking the goal.
- Be ready to take on any player who is free and moving toward goal with the ball.

Condition
Start the game with the free player holding the ball at the far end from the goal.

FIGURE 6.35

• = Ball
◯ = Hoop
---▶ = Movement of player
----- = Path of the ball

Q: *How did you defend space?*
A: By making sure my opponent did not get into a shooting area.

Q: *What other job did you have as a defender?*
A: To watch for any other player who was free and moving into a danger area.

Q: *Why did you decide to slide onto that player?*
A: She was more dangerous than my player. That is, she had the ball, was free, and was going toward the goal.

Lesson 16 Level III

Tactical Problem
Attacking the goal and creating space

Lesson Focus
Working as a team to score

Objectives
· Feed a cutter to give the optimum shot.
· Cut and replace.

GAME 1

Setup
Use 5v5 with a goal at each end. If possible, mark a fan in front of the goal circle as is done for women's games (see figure 6.36).

Note
This game may be played without sticks by using a ball such as a handball. Doing so removes the frustration of not being able to control the passing well enough to achieve teamwork.

Goal
Work as a team to create chances to score.

Condition
No player can stand in the fan or run into the goal circle.

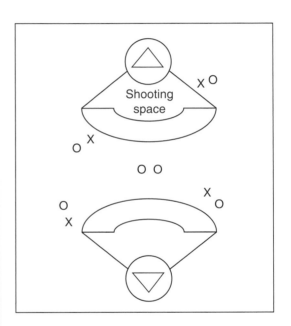

FIGURE 6.36

The two O's in the center represent the two players who take the draw (in the women's game) or the two midfielders who take the face-off (in the men's game). Until this happens, they are both in offense. Once the game begins they become offense or defense depending on whose team won the draw or face-off.

Questions

Q: *Why is standing in the fan not allowed?*
A: Because it is dangerous and you take up the best shooting space for the attack.

Q: *How can you work as a team to create scoring chances?*
A: Give the player with the ball good space to run into for scoring. Keep moving to give passing options in case the player needs to pass.

Q: *What can you do to help your teammate with the ball?*
A: Be a trail or a cutter or be mobile to keep my defender from being able to go to the player with the ball.

PRACTICE TASK

Setup

Play in fives (with one ball). One player stands behind the goal and acts as a feeder. Two attackers, each with a defender, practice cutting into the scoring area (the fan) to receive the ball and score (see figure 6.37).

Goals

- Work as a team so that the feeder can pass to a cutter in the best position to score.
- Cutters work out who is in the best place to cut to the ball.
- The other cutter replaces and balances the game.

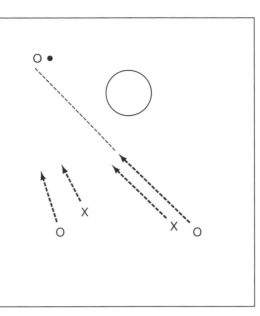

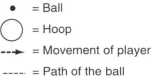

- • = Ball
- ◯ = Hoop
- --➤ = Movement of player
- ----- = Path of the ball

FIGURE 6.37

Cues

- Cutters who are diagonally opposite the feeder are in a good position because their defenders will find it hard to see both the ball and them.
- Feeder must wait for best cut and then make flat and direct pass.

GAME 2

Setup

5v5 with one goal

Note

This game can also be played without sticks until the players gain more confidence.

Goal

Work as a team to score a goal.

Conditions

- Start the game at the far end from the goal.
- Try to score quickly.
- If the first run fails, take the ball behind the goal for safety and try to send cutters through.

Questions

Q: How did you work as a team to attack the goal and score?
A: We kept the shooting area open and made good decisions about when and where to move.

Q: What jobs did you have as an attacker?
A: I could be the cutter, the trail, the free player with the ball, the feeder behind the goal, or the helper on either side of the player with the ball.

Q: How did you create space to help the teammate with the ball?

A: I cut into a scoring position. I kept my defender away from my teammate and the shooting area by making myself dangerous. I used the space behind my teammate and let her know I was trailing.

Lesson 17

Tactical Problem
Creating space in attack

Lesson Focus
Fast break

Objective
Overlap with a free player and create space that is hard to defend.

GAME 1

Setup
Use 4v3 with a goal at one end. If possible, mark a fan in front of the goal circle as is done in women's games (see figure 6.38).

Note
This game may be played without sticks by using a ball such as a handball. Doing so removes the frustration of not being able to control the passing well enough to achieve the goal.

Goal
Work as a team to take advantage of an extra player in the attack.

Condition
No player can stand in the fan or run into the goal circle.

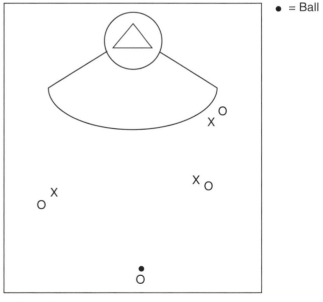

● = Ball

FIGURE 6.38

Questions

Q: *If you are the free player with the ball, what should you do?*

A: Look toward the goal and score if possible.

Q: *What if you are too far away from the goal to score? Should you pass?*

A: No, because then you lose the extra attack by passing to a marked player.

Q: *What should you do instead?*

A: Run toward the goal until a defender has to move over to defend me and then look for the next free player.

PRACTICE TASK

Setup

Play in fives, with three attackers and two defenders. Use one goal. O1 is free with the ball, O2 and X2 are next in line toward the goal, and O3 and X3 are nearest to the goal (see figure 6.39).

Goals

- Work as a team so that the player with the ball drives to the goal and forces X2 to move toward him (to slide).
- O1 passes to O2 once O2 is free.
- O2 forces X3 to slide and then passes to O3, who scores the goal.

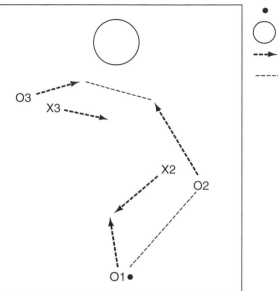

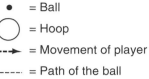

- • = Ball
- ◯ = Hoop
- - - ▸ = Movement of player
- - - - - = Path of the ball

FIGURE 6.39

Cues

- Follow the three D's: Drive, Draw, and Dunk.
- Drive toward goal looking to score.
- Use your movement to draw a defender over to you to stop your progress.
- Dunk (pass) the ball to the new free player.
- Time the pass so that it occurs before the defender can block but after the defender has decided to slide.

GAME 2

Setup

5v5 with one goal

Note

This game can be played without sticks until the players feel confident enough to try sticks.

Goal

Work as a team to score a goal.

Conditions

- Start the game at the far end from the goal.
- Try to score quickly by recognizing the fast break.
- If the first run fails, take the ball behind the goal for safety, settle the attack around the goal, and try to send cutters through.

Questions

Q: *How did you work as a team to attack the goal and score?*
A: By driving toward the goal to get away from my opponent and to create a fast break.

Q: What do you do as the free attacker with the ball?

A: The three D's: Drive, Draw, and Dunk.

Q: How did you help the teammate who had the ball?

A: I kept my defender away from her by pulling out to the side and making myself dangerous. When my opponent left me to slide over to her, I signaled for the ball.

Lesson 18 Level III

Tactical Problem
Using space in attack

Lesson Focus
Width and depth of attack in transition from defense to offense

Objective
Connect and overlap in the midfield.

GAME 1

Setup

Use 5v5 with a goal at each end. If possible, mark a fan in front of the goal circle as is done in women's games. Begin the game in a diamond shape, or a 1-3-1 formation (see figure 6.40).

Note

This game may be played without sticks by using a ball such as a handball. Doing so removes the frustration of not being able to control the passing well enough to achieve the goal.

Goal

Work as a team to use all available space in attack.

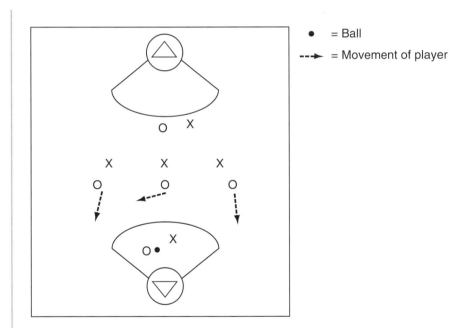

FIGURE 6.40

Condition

No player can stand in the fan or run into the goal circle.

Questions

Q: *If one of your teammates suddenly gets the ball from the opposition, what should you do?*

A: Quickly help them.

Q: *Where are good places to help?*

A: Along the sides of the field or from behind the goal.

Q: *Why are these good spaces?*

A: Because they are safe and open, and opponents are more likely to use spaces nearer to the goal.

PRACTICE TASK

Setup

Play in fives. One player starts with the ball on the ground near the goal the team is defending. Three players set up in midfield: two on the wing and one in the center. One player waits near the goal the team is attacking (see figure 6.41).

Goals

- Work as a team so that the player who picks up the ball has passing options across the whole width of the field.
- The player who passes the ball continues behind the ball carrier as a trail to create depth in attack.

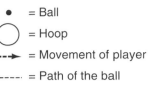

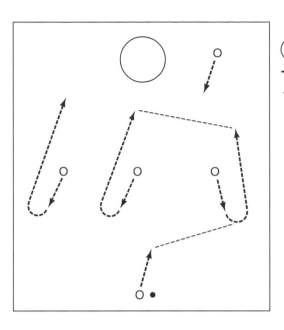

FIGURE 6.41

Cues

- Watch the direction of the pickup, which indicates where the player will look first.
- Start to move early and if you do not receive the ball, move to support the ball carrier at the side.
- Follow the game so that there is width and depth of support.
- Use entire field.

GAME 2

Setup

5v5 with two goals

Note

This game can be played without sticks until the players feel confident enough to try sticks.

Goal

Work as a team to use all the space on the field.

Conditions

- Toss for first possession, which starts at the defending goal.
- Restart the game at the goal where the previous goal was scored.

Questions

Q: How did you work as a team to use space, attack the goal, and score?
A: By making sure that we had players on each wing to create width and also in front of and behind the ball to create depth.

Q: What did you do as the attacker with the ball?
A: Looked up quickly to see where my team was on the field.

Q: How did you help the teammate who had the ball?
A: Used a space different from the rest of my team to help provide lots of options.

Having more players on the field increases the level of difficulty and options for play.

Level IV

Games at level IV are typically larger, and the overall pattern and detail of the game are more developed. Greater skill is required to meet the greater options available in level IV. For example, players begin using a long but risky pass from wing to wing. Shooting is harder because the defense is stronger at defending the goal. Using full-size goals is important at this stage. The offensive players learn some simple plays that occur in a settled attack around the goal so that if their first run fails they can still confuse and outmaneuver the defense. The defense needs to clear the ball, using the goalie as the first-line attack (a player can be designated to take this role, since it is unlikely that there will be a goalie in your games). Students can practice simple plays for opening up attack positions in front of the goal and can consider their different roles as offense near the goal, offense in the midfield, and defense near the goal in terms of risks, responsibilities, and required skills.

Lesson 19   Level IV

Tactical Problem
Creating space in attack

Lesson Focus
Passing patterns

Objective
Clear the ball from the goal to the attacking end.

GAME 1

Setup

Use 5v5 with a goal at each end of the field. If possible, mark a fan in front of the goal circle as is done in women's games. Play the game in a diamond shape, or a 1-3-1 formation (see figure 6.42).

Note

This game may be played without sticks by using a ball such as a handball. Doing so removes the frustration of not being able to control the passing well enough to achieve the goal.

Goal

Work as a team to clear the ball from the goal into attack.

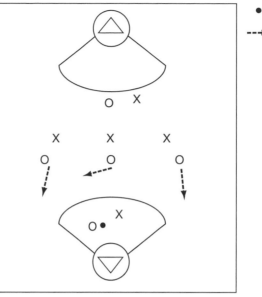

FIGURE 6.42

Condition

A player starts the game by passing the ball from inside the goal circle.

Questions

Q: *Where is the safest place to clear the ball to?*
A: Out to the wing away from the shooting area.

Q: *Where should players move in order to help?*
A: Out to the sides of the field away from their opponents.

Q: *What should the attackers do as they see the ball being cleared to the sides of the field?*
A: Get ready to meet the ball and then take it to the goal.

PRACTICE TASK

Setup

Play in fours with a goalkeeper in the goal with the ball. The three players act as defense, with two playing on the wings and one playing in the center. More defensive players wait their turn to play behind the goal. (see figure 6.43).

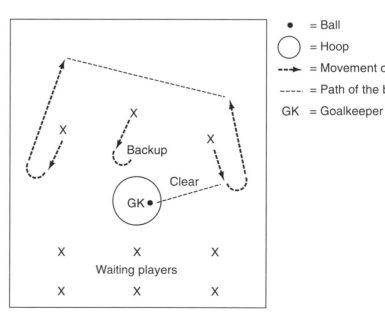

FIGURE 6.43

Goal

Work as a team so that the goalie has a safe clear and so that the player who receives the ball has backup and a player to pass to.

Cues

- Defenders cut away from goal and lead to the outside of the field with their sticks.
- Players not receiving the pass roll around and support the ball carrier from the side and from behind.

GAME 2

Setup

6v6 game with two goals

Note

This game can be played without sticks until the players feel confident enough to try with sticks.

Goal

Work as a team to clear the ball up the field to the attack.

Conditions

- The game starts when a player in one of the goal circles clears the ball.
- The player in the goal circle then moves out and becomes a field player for the rest of the game.
- No player should remain in the goal.

Questions

Q: How did you work as a team to create space to clear the ball?
A: Players moved to the outside of the field to create width.

Q: What did you do if you were not used by the goalie?
A: I looked to see where my team was and either dropped back as the safety player or cut again to receive the next pass.

Q: What did the attack players do to help the team?
A: They cut toward the person bringing the ball up the field to give her lots of options.

Q: What happened then?
A: They took the ball toward the goal to score.

Q: What patterns did your team make?
A: A basic diamond that widened at the wings and narrowed at the goals.

Lesson 20 Level IV

Tactical Problem
Defending space and winning the ball

Lesson Focus
Team defense

Objective
Back up a defender and double-team.

GAME 1

Setup

Use 6v6 with a goal at each end of the field. If possible, mark a fan in front of the goal circle as is done in women's games. Play the game in a diamond shape, or a 1-3-1 formation (see figure 6.44).

Goal

Work as a team to defend space and win the ball.

Conditions

· A player starts the game by passing the ball from inside the goal circle.
· No player can remain in the fan without an opponent.

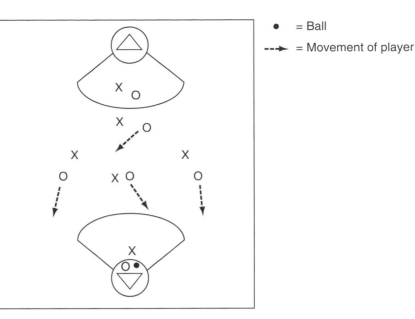

 = Ball

---▶ = Movement of player

FIGURE 6.44

Questions

Q: *What should your team do when a player with the ball gets past one of your players?*
A: Help out by sliding.

Q: *Can you provide help before a player has gotten past a defender?*
A: We can double-team the ball carrier.

Q: *Where should you try to be, relative to the ball, to be able to double-team?*
A: Between the goal and the ball carrier and behind my defender.

PRACTICE TASK

Setup

Play in threes. There is one attacker with the ball and one defender marking goal-side. The second defender calls to the first defender, who guides the attacker into the double-team (see figure 6.45).

Goal

Work as a team so that the attacker is guided into the second defender and has no forward passing lane.

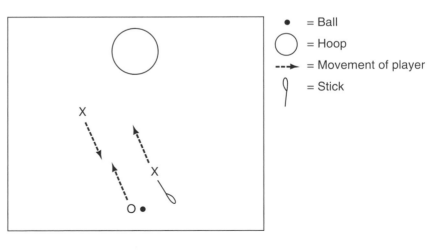

 = Ball

◯ = Hoop

---▶ = Movement of player

⑨ = Stick

FIGURE 6.45

Cues

· First defender uses body as a barrier (no contact) to force the attacker in the direction of the second defender.
· Second defender verbally communicates that he is there as the double-team helper.

GAME 2

Setup
6v6 game with two goals

Goal
Work as a team to back up each other when playing defense, using the slide and the double-team.

Conditions
- The game starts with a clear by a player in a goal circle.
- The player in the goal circle then moves out and becomes an extra field player for the rest of the game.
- No player should remain in the goal.

Questions

Q: *How did you work as a team to give support and backup?*
A: We had defenders behind us to slide or to double-team.

Q: *When is a double-team most likely to happen?*
A: When the attacker nears a shooting opportunity and when the attack is in a smaller area (e.g., around the goal).

Q: *What key elements make team defense work well?*
A: Positioning and communicating with the defender marking the ball carrier.

Lesson 21 — Level IV

Tactical Problem
Creating space in attack

Lesson Focus
Balance in team attack

Objective
Settled attack.

GAME 1

Setup
Use 5v5 with a goal. If possible, mark a fan in front of the goal circle as is done in women's games (see figure 6.46).

Goal
Work as a team around the goal in order to score.

Conditions
- A player starts the game by passing the ball from behind the goal.
- No player can remain in the fan without an opponent.

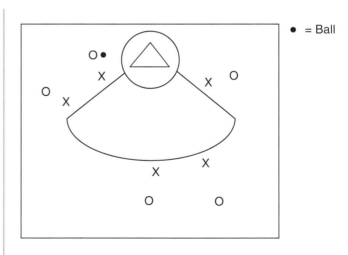

 = Ball

FIGURE 6.46

Questions

Q: What should your team do when a player has the ball behind the goal?
A: Cut into the shooting area to receive and shoot.

Q: What do the other players do as the cutter goes through?
A: Keep the shooting area open by staying out of it, move to fill the space left by the cutter and balance the attack, or help the feeder by offering another passing option on the outside of the shooting area.

Q: If an open cutter does not emerge, what can you do?
A: Pass the ball around the outside of the circle and wait for another cutter or go in with the ball.

PRACTICE TASK

Setup

Play in fives. One attacker stands behind the goal with the ball and all other attackers circle the goal (see figure 6.47).

Goal

Work as a team to keep the ball moving among the attack players.

Cues

- Keep the ball moving as quickly as possible.
- Keep the circle big to make it harder for defenders to cover the space.
- Keep changing the direction of the pass.

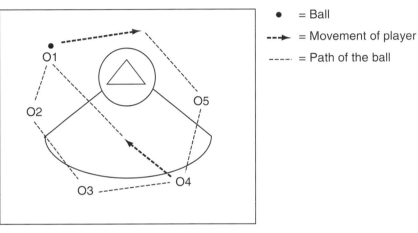

● = Ball

---▶ = Movement of player

----· = Path of the ball

FIGURE 6.47

Extension

Play in fives. If the settled attack is working, add cutters.

Goal

Work as a team to pass the ball around the circle and to feed into a cutter who is in a position to shoot.

Cue

The player opposite the ball is in a strong position to cut since it is hard for the defender to see both that player and the ball.

GAME 2

Setup

5v5 game with two goals

Goal

Work as a team to play settled attack.

Conditions
- The game starts with a clear by a player in a goal circle.
- The ball must go behind the attacking team's goal once before the team can settle around the goal and try to score.

Questions

Q: How did you work as a team to score a goal?
A: We balanced ourselves around and behind the goal.

Q: Why is doing this helpful for the offense?
A: It creates space in the shooting area and gives a lot of options for passing and cutting.

Q: What key elements help the offense succeed?
A: Keeping the offense balanced when cutters go through and keeping the ball moving so that it's hard for the defenders to watch both the ball and their opponents.

Lesson 22   Level IV

Tactical Problem
Defending the goal

Lesson Focus
Defending dangerous shooting spaces

Objective
Play a team defense.

GAME 1

Setup
Use 5v5 with a goal. If possible, mark a fan in front of the goal circle as is done in women's games.

Goal
Work as a team around the goal in order to defend the goal.

Conditions
- A player starts the game by passing the ball from behind the goal.
- No player can remain in the fan without an opponent.

Questions

Q: What should you do as the defense when a player has the ball behind the goal?
A: Position to see the ball and the opponent and hold our sticks high to cover space.

Q: What does the defender of the feeder do?
A: Wait level with the goal in case the feeder tries to circle to score.

Q: How can you hinder passing into the shooting area?
A: Hold our sticks up and toward the shooting area and follow our player through the shooting area, staying between him and the ball.

PRACTICE TASK

Setup

Use 3v3 with a goal. One attack player starts with the ball behind the goal (see figure 6.48).

Goal

Work as a team to keep the ball from being passed or taken into the shooting area.

Cues

- Position yourself so that you can see the ball and your player.
- Keep your stick high to cover any passes made into the danger area.
- Communicate where the ball is, who is marking the ball carrier, when there is a cutter, and so on.

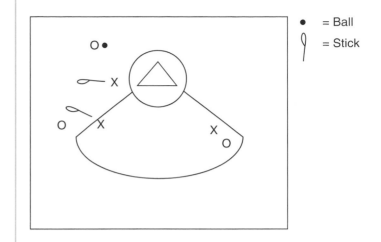

●	= Ball
⎧	= Stick

FIGURE 6.48

GAME 2

Setup

5v5 game with one goal (see figure 6.49)

Goal

Work as a team to defend the goal.

Conditions

- The game starts at the centerline.
- The offense must take the ball behind the goal once before scoring.

Questions

Q: *How did you work as a team to defend the goal?*
A: We positioned ourselves so that we could see the ball and our opponents.

Q: *How did you help each other?*
A: We talked to each other.

Q: *What did you tell your teammates?*
A: Where the ball was, who was marking the ball carrier, and whether there was a cutter or a free player.

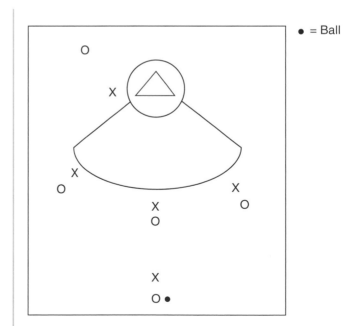

●	= Ball

FIGURE 6.49

Tactical Problem
Restarting the game

Lesson Focus
Using the restart to the team's advantage

Objectives
· Take the draw.
· Take a free position.

GAME 1

Setup
Use 7v7 with two goals (see figure 6.50). If possible, mark a fan in front of the goal circle as is done in women's games.

Goal
Take advantage of a possession from a restart.

Conditions
· The game starts with a center draw.
· If the game goes out of bounds or there is a foul, a free position is given to restart play.

Questions
Q: *What should your team do when the centers are taking the draw?*
A: We should try to get into good positions to catch the ball.

Q: *Who are the major players at this moment?*
A: The midfielders on the wings. The centers also have to control the draw.

PRACTICE TASK

Setup
Play in sevens. Two players take the draw while two midfielders (and their defenders) wait on the wings to receive the draw. One person acts as the official and sets up the draw (see figure 6.51).

Goal
Work as a team to get possession of the draw.

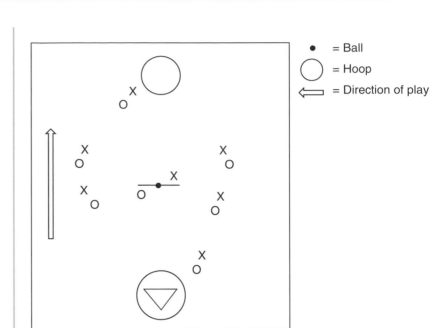

FIGURE 6.50

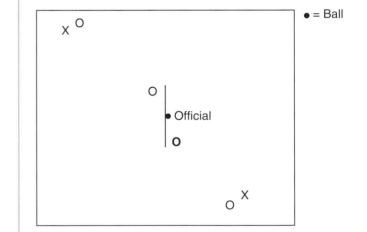

FIGURE 6.51

The two O's in the center represent the two players who take the draw (in the women's game) or the two midfielders who take the face-off (in the men's game). Until this happens, they are both in offense. Once the game begins they become offense or defense depending on whose team won the draw or face-off.

Cues

- Try to hold your stick still until the whistle.
- Practice a draw with your left hand at the top and a draw with your right hand at the top.
- During the draw, try to catch the ball yourself as well as to get it to your attacker.

GAME 2

Setup

7v7 game with two goals

Goals

- Work as a team to win the draw and get early possession.
- Help when the game is restarted (e.g., for an infringement, a play out of bounds, and so on).

Condition

Teams score an extra point for getting possession at the draw.

Questions

Q: How did your team get the draw?
A: We balanced ourselves around the circle according to where we thought the ball would go.

Q: Who are important players in winning the draw?
A: The wingers and the center players.

Q: What can they do to be ready?
A: Hold their sticks high and have their feet ready with with weight forward to take quick action toward the ball.

Q: What should you do at any restart?
A: Look around, see who can help the player with the ball, and see if the team is spaced to give width and depth to support.

Lesson 24 Level IV

Tactical Problem
Creating space in attack

Lesson Focus
Using plays to create space in front of goal

Objective
Use picks.

GAME 1

Setup
Use 5v5 with one goal. If possible, mark a fan in front of the goal circle as is done in women's games (see figure 6.52).

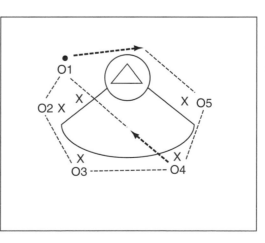

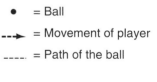

FIGURE 6.52

Goal

Create space in front of the goal for a shot.

Condition

No player can remain in the fan without an opponent.

Questions

> Q: *What should your team do to create space?*
> A: Make an open space in front of the goal.

> Q: *How do you do that?*
> A: Draw our defenders away and create a settled attack around the goal.

PRACTICE TASK

Setup

Play in fours, and pick opposite (like an off-ball screen/pick in basketball). The feeder behind the goal receives the ball from O1, who is on the same side of the goal area. O1 moves across the front of the goal as if cutting for the ball. When the cut is not used, O1 picks the defender (X) of O3, who then cuts to receive the feed (O2) from behind the goal (see figure 6.53).

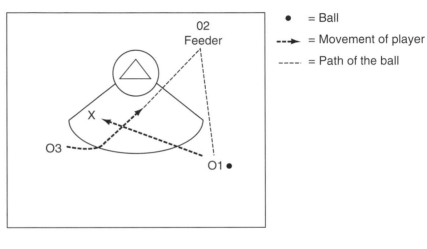

● = Ball
--→ = Movement of player
---- = Path of the ball

FIGURE 6.53

Goal

Work as a team to create space for shooting using a pick.

Cues

- Move safely into the pick.
- Keep the stick close to the body.
- Make the first cut convincing.
- O2 signals clearly to receive and shoot.

GAME 2

Setup

7v7 game with two goals

Goal

Work as a team to score using a pick.

Condition

Teams score an extra point for using the pick in front of the goal.

Questions

> Q: *How did your team create space in front of the goal?*
> A: We used picks.

Q: What is important about using picks?

A: Making them safe (i.e., performing them in view of the defender, using a controlled run, and correctly timing the move away from the pick when receiving the ball).

Summary

The levels of tactical complexity covered in this chapter should help you present lacrosse to students in coed physical education classes so that they experience both the fun and challenges of a unique sport that uses an implement to catch the ball.

Remember that at any time lacrosse sticks can be put aside so that students can try out tactical problems free from technical constraints. Where necessary, take extra time to establish confidence in stick handling through small games and game-like practices rather than pushing toward a larger game. If the tactical insights gained through more familiar games such as soccer and basketball are included in the introduction to lacrosse, student confidence to try something new will grow as they see that all team games have many similar concepts. Lacrosse can then be taught as a game with familiar tactical concepts but presenting unique challenges such as the use of a stick to catch and maintain possession of the ball and the use of space behind the goal.

Although at the competitive level there are different sports for men and women, the basic tactical concepts for lacrosse remain the same. Use of the specific equipment and rules required for either game would be inappropriate for the majority of students participating in your physical education classes. However, their interest and motivation to continue playing recreationally or competitively can be developed through careful presentation of levels of tactical complexity and, of course, through your assessment of the level of your students' abilities and experience.

CHAPTER 7

Rugby

Rugby will be unfamiliar to many of you, yet once you are introduced to the game you will find it fast paced and action packed. This chapter introduces the game to you as teachers so that you can teach it to your students. In fact, this chapter was requested by one of our recent student teachers, who had taught a rugby unit in a middle school. Upon hearing our plans for this book, she said, "Please tell me you're including a chapter on rugby!"

Rugby has some similarities with American football, particularly the shape of the ball and the method of scoring. In fact, American football developed from rugby. Rugby was first played in 1823 at Rugby School (hence the name of the game) in England when, during a soccer (football) game, it is said that a boy named William Webb Ellis picked up the ball and ran with it. The game became known as rugby football and grew in popularity as rules developed to distinguish it from soccer. The full name of the game is rugby union and its rules are governed internationally by the International Rugby Board. In the mid- to late 19th century a slightly different version of the game emerged, which in 1893 became known as *rugby league*. Rugby league became a professional game while rugby union was played only by amateurs until the 1990s, when it too became a professional game. Rugby union and rugby league are distinguished by the number of players on a team (15 in rugby union and 13 in rugby league) and by the restart rules. This chapter focuses only on rugby union.

The rules of rugby might confuse teachers and students who are new to the game, so we introduce rules in stages and only when they are needed to shape the developing game. However, to give you a general picture of the game and to distinguish rugby from American football (for the American reader), we first overview some key rules:

- A regulation game of rugby uses 15 players per team, but for this chapter we provide instructional content for a maximum of 7 players per side and we use a noncontact tag rugby (RFU, 2003) version of the game that is similar to the flag football played in the United States (in fact, flag belts can easily be used in this rugby version).
- The ball must be passed backward or sideways. This rule sometimes causes problems in early learning since it seems difficult to progress if the ball cannot be passed forward. This rule can make for interesting problem-solving experiences for students.
- A fumbled pass that goes forward and hits the ground is a knock-on, which results in a restart being awarded to the opposing team.
- A try is scored when the ball is placed on the ground behind the try line (think of a touchdown in American football that has to be placed, not thrown or dropped, onto the ground in the end zone).
- Players can only support and assist teammates from behind (i.e., blocking is not permitted as it is in American football).
- In tag rugby, players must stay on their feet. If a player in possession of the ball goes down to the ground (even when scoring a try) or if a player dives to retrieve a ball, a free pass is awarded to the nonoffending team.
- After having his tag pulled, the player with the ball has been tagged and must pass within 3 seconds and three strides. The tagger must call "tag" (so the player with the ball knows that he has been tagged) and return the tag to its owner before either player can resume involvement in the game.
- When a tag is made, the players from both teams must return to their respective sides of the ball before resuming involvement in the game.
- The player with the ball cannot shield the flag and should always carry the ball in two hands.
- Players may not kick the ball in tag rugby.

The scope and sequence of the lessons on rugby are broken down tactically in tables 7.1 and 7.2. From a tactical perspective, rugby is very much a possession game. It is all about keeping and advancing the ball to score. This focus is clearly reflected in the framework shown in table 7.1 and in the tactical levels in table 7.2, where much of the content involves ball possession. Early lessons shape the game, introducing primary rules, and students need to learn the importance of moving forward with the ball, passing, and supporting the ball carrier so that when a tag is made the player in possession has a teammate to pass to. With some simple restarts, the game of tag rugby starts to take shape at level I. At level II players learn how to defend space, though the savvy games player at the secondary level will no doubt understand the need for 1v1 coverage at an earlier stage (i.e., they may cover instinctively at level I). With improved defense, students should begin to learn ways to create space and penetrate defense, such as by using the dummy (fake) pass. The game continues to take shape at level II with more sophisticated restarts and with the introduction of a one-player scrum and then a three-player scrum (don't worry, scrums are explained and illustrated later in the chapter). Introducing the scrum requires body-to-body contact so some safety precautions will be necessary.

Assuming that students develop the ability to defend space and tag the ball carrier, instruction at level III should focus on more sophisticated ways of creating space to penetrate and score. Two-player moves such as the loop and the scissors are challenging, requiring on-the-ball skill and off-the-ball movement by both players. Level III also adds the line-out as a way of restarting if the ball goes out of bounds.

Table 7.1 Tactical Problems, Movements, and Skills in Rugby

Tactical problems	Off-the-ball movements	On-the-ball skills
SCORING (OFFENSE)		
Maintaining possession of the ball	• Support—running with the ball carrier	• Running with the ball • Passing
Advancing the ball		• Drawing a defender • Running forward in possession • Scoring a try
Creating and using space to penetrate and score	• Dummy passes • Looping moves • Scissors moves	• Looping moves • Scissors moves
PREVENTING SCORING (DEFENSE)		
Defending space	• 1v1 coverage • Making the tag	
RESTARTING PLAY		
• In-field restarts • Out-of-bounds restarts		• Free pass • Tap back • One-player scrum • Three-player scrum • Line-out

Table 7.2 Levels of Tactical Complexity for Rugby

Tactical problems	I 4v4	II 4v4 to 7v7	III 7v7
SCORING (OFFENSE)			
Maintaining possession of the ball	• Running with the ball • Passing • Supporting—running with the ball carrier		
Advancing the ball	• Running forward in possession • Drawing a defender • Scoring a try		
Creating and using space to penetrate and score		• Dummy passes	• Looping moves • Scissors moves
PREVENTING SCORING (DEFENSE)			
Defending space	• Making the tag	• 1v1 coverage	
RESTARTING PLAY			
	• Free pass • Tap back	• One-player scrum • Three-player scrum	• Line-out

Level I

Level I lessons provide a simple introduction to the game of rugby. In lesson 1, students play a simple possession game with several extensions so that a modified game of rugby can take place in subsequent lessons. The remaining level I lessons focus on moving the ball forward as a team and scoring.

Lesson 1   Level I

Tactical Problem
Playing the game and maintaining possession of the ball

Lesson Focus
Team organization and shaping the game

Objective
Understand game rules and basic passing.

GAME 1

Setup
4v4 possession game in 30 by 20 yards/meters (see figure 7.1)

Goal

Keep the ball away from the other team.

Conditions

- Players can run and pass in any direction, but they must stop and pass to a teammate when their tag is pulled off by an opponent.
- The tagger must return the tag to its owner before either player can resume involvement in the game.
- A dropped ball goes to the other team.
- If the ball goes out of bounds (including if the ball carrier puts a foot on the line), the other team gets a free pass to restart from where the ball went out.
- At any restart, opposing players must be 5 yards/meters back.

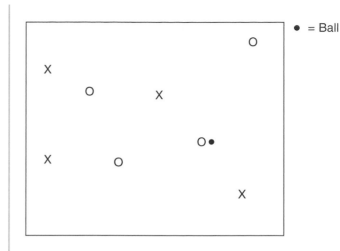

FIGURE 7.1

Questions

Q: What must you do in this game?
A: Keep the ball.

Q: How can your team keep the ball?
A: Run and pass.

Extensions

Introduce the game extensions one at a time to allow the game to gradually take shape. Introducing these extensions will take time and may even require another lesson (depending on your available time) as players adjust to each new rule:

- Play 4v4 across a line (now we add direction to the game but still allow the ball to be passed in any direction—see figure 7.2). Cross the line while carrying the ball to score.
- Do not pass the ball forward and allow players to support and assist the ball carrier only from behind (i.e., do not permit blocking as seen in American football).
- Score a try by placing the ball down behind the line.

Questions

Q: If you cannot pass the ball forward, how do you get it to the other end of the field?
A: By running forward with the ball.

Q: Where do your teammates need to be to help you?
A: Behind or to the side.

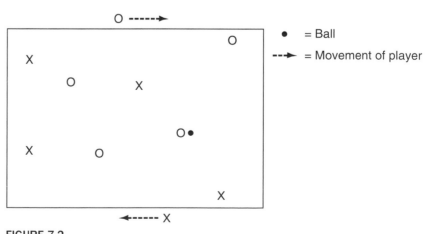

FIGURE 7.2

Tactical Problem
Maintaining possession and advancing the ball

Lesson Focus
Running forward, passing backward, and scoring a try

Objectives
- Score a try by placing the ball down.
- Run forward and accelerate when in possession of the ball.
- Look behind and pass to teammates.

GAME 1

Setup
4v4 in 30 by 20 yards/ meters (see figure 7.3)

Goal
Move the ball forward to score a try.

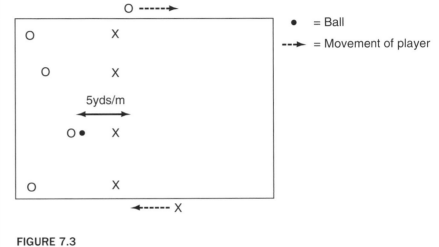

= Ball

= Movement of player

FIGURE 7.3

Conditions
- Score a try by placing the ball down behind the line.
- Ball cannot be passed forward.
- Ball carrier must stop and pass to a teammate when her tag is pulled off by an opponent.
- Tagger must return the tag to its owner before either player can resume involvement in the game.
- A dropped ball goes to the other team for a free pass (restart from where the ball was dropped).
- At any restart, opposing players (X's in figure 7.3) must be 5 yards/meters back from the horizontal line along which the ball is positioned. (Note that this is not the same as being 5 yards/meters from the ball. In a game played with 15 players per side on a full-size field, this distance would be 10 yards/meters, and you can increase to this distance if your players need more space.)
- Restart an out-of-bounds ball with a free pass.
- Players can only support and assist teammates with the ball from behind (i.e., no blocking).

Note
These conditions are the basic conditions for all games from this point on. To avoid repetition, we will refer to them as game conditions.

Questions
Q: *How do you score a try?*
A: By placing the ball down with pressure (not dropping the ball) behind the line.

Q: If you cannot pass the ball forward, how do you get it to the other end of the field?
A: By running forward with the ball.

Q: Where do your teammates need to be to help you?
A: Behind or to the side.

PRACTICE TASK

Setup

In teams, practice running single file and scoring a try (see figure 7.4). O1, O2, O3, and O4 run forward at the same pace, with the ball beginning at O4. O4 places the ball down and moves to the side, slowing so that the rest of the team can pass. O3 picks up the ball and runs on before placing the ball down, moving to the side, and slowing.

Goal

Use downward pressure to correctly score a try.

Cues

· Place the ball down.
· Pick up and accelerate.

Extension

Instead of placing the ball down, the ball carrier turns and passes to the next player in line.

Cues

· Hold the ball with two hands across the seams (see figure 7.5).
· Turn to look at the receiver.
· Pass underhand (for a quicker release than overhand) and aim for the receiver's chest.
· Accelerate when you receive the ball.

GAME 2

Setup

Repeat game 1.

Goals

· Use correct technique to score a try.
· Support from behind the ball carrier.
· Run forward and pass accurately.

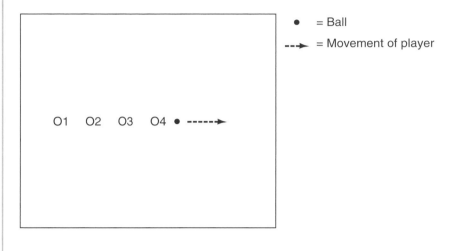

● = Ball
--→ = Movement of player

O1　O2　O3　O4 ● -----→

FIGURE 7.4

© Tim McGrew/Hot Shots

FIGURE 7.5

Tactical Problem
Maintaining possession and advancing the ball

Lesson Focus
Running forward, passing sideways or backward, and providing support

Objectives
- Ball carrier runs forward and accelerates.
- Teammates support the ball carrier by positioning to the side and slightly behind.

GAME 1

Setup
4v4 in 30 by 20 yards/meters (see figure 7.3)

Goal
Move the ball forward to score a try.

Conditions
Game conditions

Questions

Q: Where are the most effective locations for supporting teammates to help the passer?
A: Behind and to the side.

Q: Why is being to the side important?
A: So a team does not pass the ball too far backward.

Q: So as the ball carrier runs forward, what do the teammates have to do?
A: Run with the ball carrier.

PRACTICE TASK

Setup
In teams, practice running in a staggered line and passing (see figure 7.6). O1, O2, O3, and O4 run forward at same pace, and O1 begins with the ball. With O2 off her shoulder, O1 passes to O2, who accelerates to get ahead of O3 before passing. O3 accelerates and passes to O4. Switch the middle players and restart.

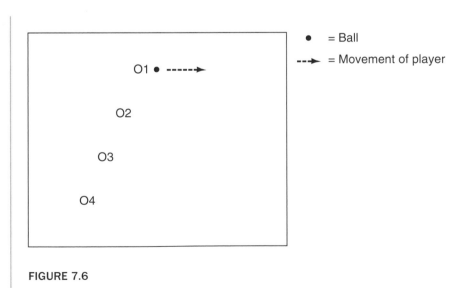

FIGURE 7.6

Cues

- Accelerate when you receive.
- Slow after you pass.
- Swing the arms across the body (see figure 7.7).
- Aim in front of the receiver's chest.

Extension

Pass down the line and back. O4 sends the ball back to O3 after receiving and the practice ends with O1 scoring a try.

GAME 2

Setup
Repeat game 1.

FIGURE 7.7

Goal
Move the ball forward to score a try and support teammates in possession of the ball.

Lesson 4

Tactical Problem
Advancing the ball

Lesson Focus
Drawing a defender

Objective
Draw the defender to the ball carrier before passing.

GAME 1

Setup
4v4 in 30 by 20 yards/meters (see figure 7.3)

Goal
Find ways to beat defenders with a pass.

Conditions
Game conditions

Questions

Q: *How can you beat a defender by passing?*
A: By running at the defender.

Q: *When should you pass?*
A: When you get close to the defender (but not so close the pass will be intercepted).

Q: *What do you need from your teammates?*
A: Support (i.e., someone to pass to).

PRACTICE TASK

Setup
In teams of four, play 2v1v1 in 20 by 10 yards/meters (see figure 7.8).

Goal
O1 and O2 combine to beat O3 and O4 by passing.

Conditions
- O3 can only move forward when O1 starts to move.
- When beaten by the pass, O3 cannot recover (i.e., O3 is out of the game).
- O4 can only move once O3 has been beaten.

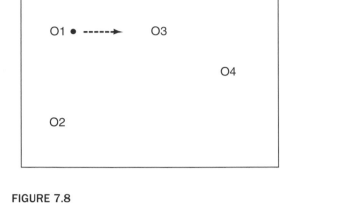

FIGURE 7.8

Cues
- O1 runs at O3 while O2 supports.
- O1 times the pass as O3 advances (when O3 is about 1 yard/meter, away).
- O2 runs at O4 while O1 supports, and then O2 passes back to O1.

Note
Defenders (O3 and O4) might start intercepting the pass since they know it is coming. At this point O1 and O2 could fake a pass (i.e., make the passing motion without actually passing). A fake is called a dummy pass and is formally taught at level II, but do not be surprised if some of the more savvy games players begin using the dummy pass now, and do not discourage its use.

GAME 2

Repeat game 1.

Goals
- Beat defenders with passes where possible.
- Run at defenders and commit them to the tag.

Lesson 5 | Level I

Tactical Problem
Restarting play

Lesson Focus
Restarting play with a tap back to simulate the scrum restart (introduced later)

Objectives
- Restart play using a tap back involving two players.
- Advance the ball quickly from the restart.

GAME 1

Setup
4v4 in 30 by 20 yards/meters (see figure 7.3)

Goals
- Score.
- Retain possession and move forward after restarts.

Conditions
Game conditions

Question
Q: *How can you restart and make good use of the space ahead of you?*

A: Get the ball into the space as quickly as possible.

PRACTICE TASK

Setup
In pairs, practice the tap back (see figure 7.9), getting the ball to a player who will then pass it out to teammates (see figure 7.10).

Goals
- Use quick passes and movements.
- Player O4 receives the ball before the gain line (i.e., before running past player O1).

Note
This practice enables you to start building understanding of basic positions in the game. The player receiving the tap back (player O2 in figure 7.10) is called the scrum half, while the player receiving the pass (player O3) is known as the fly half. Player O4 is the center. Knowing these positions is important when you start developing the seven-a-side version of the game at the next level.

Cues
- Player O1 places foot on the ball and rolls it back.
- Scrum half (O2) gets the line moving with a pass ahead of the fly half (O3).

GAME 2

Setup
Repeat game 1.

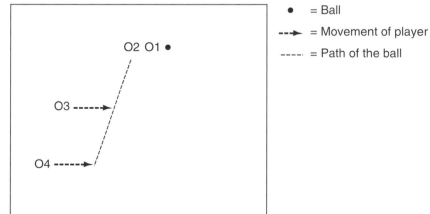

FIGURE 7.9

- ● = Ball
- --→ = Movement of player
- ----- = Path of the ball

O2 O1 ●

O3 ----→

O4 ----→

FIGURE 7.10

Goal
Effectively restart and move the ball to space.

Note
The tap back is now the restart when any rule infractions occur, when the ball goes out of bounds (taken from inside the sideline), and when a team scores (taken from the center of the field).

Level II

Well done! You have introduced your students to a basic game of rugby with rules that are easily understood and implemented. Though you have only taught five lessons, bear in mind that this is a new game for most students and learning it may take time. You may need to spread one lesson over two classes (depending on the length of the class) to help students gain sufficient understanding. Nevertheless, the content of level I should enable your students to play and officiate their own games, leaving you free to instruct and provide feedback as needed.

Lessons in level II focus first on defending space, which in turn requires more creativity by attacking players if they are to penetrate and score. We then address restarts, specifically by introducing the scrummage, or scrum for short. In the full (15-sided) version of rugby there are eight players in a scrum. However, in the seven-sided game there are only three: two props on the outside and a hooker in the middle. These players (three from each team) bind together (see figures 7.11 and 7.12) and lean against each other until the ball is put into the middle of the scrum by the scrum half (see figure 7.13). Each player in the scrum places her head to the left of the opposite player's head so that she leans against the opposite player with her right shoulder contacting her opponent's (as shown with just two players in figure 7.14). Once the scrum is set, the ball is put in and the two sets of players push against each other. The hooker uses his foot to hook the ball and push it through the back of the scrum for the scrum half to pick up and begin the attack.

FIGURE 7.11

FIGURE 7.12

FIGURE 7.13

FIGURE 7.14

A scrum is used to restart the game following a rule infraction, with the put-in awarded to the team that did not break the rule. Scrums can also be used to restart when the ball goes out of bounds, with the put-in awarded to the team that did not cause the ball to go out. The advantage of putting the ball into the scrum is one of positioning. The ball is always put in from the left of the put-in team's scrum, and the hooker can hook the ball more easily with the right foot when the ball comes from the left side. There is also an advantage in timing in that, with more advanced thinking, the hooker can signal with the left hand when she wants the ball to be put in and so will know when to raise her foot.

Important rules regarding the scrum are that (a) the ball must be rolled down the midline between the two sets of players and (b) the hooker cannot raise his foot until the ball enters the middle of the scrum. Violating either of these rules results in a free kick to the other team. A free kick is taken by one player who puts the ball down at the place of the infraction, taps it with her foot, picks it up, and begins play. Lastly, if the ball is not hooked between the legs of the scrummaging players (the ball sometimes rebounds off players' legs and back out of the tunnel), the scrum is retaken with the put-in staying with the same team.

Some important safety concerns arise from the scrum, particularly of a scrum collapsing when players push against each other. A collapse might lead to injury, but you can decrease the likelihood of a collapsed scrum by teaching players to keep their shoulders higher than their hips and by allowing players to lean against each other and support the hooker only when the ball is put in. The scrum then becomes a contest between the two hookers.

Lesson 6 Level II

Tactical Problem
Defending space

Lesson Focus
1v1 coverage

Objective
Cover each offensive player by a marking defender.

GAME 1

Setup
4v4 in 30 by 20 yards/meters (see figure 7.3)

Goal
Match up players at every restart.

Conditions
Game conditions

Question

> Q: *What is the best way to defend your space when the other team has the ball?*
> A: 1v1. Match up across the field with the other team so they cannot get through easily.

GAME 2

Setup
4v4 in 30 by 20 yards/meters (see figure 7.3)

Note
The game continues with the same conditions. Encourage players to match up with opponents, particularly at restarts, to ensure 1v1 coverage that will make penetration by the offensive team more difficult. This lesson does not include a skill practice since defending space is best practiced within the game, but you might need to freeze play at times to illustrate where you are or are not seeing effective one-on-one coverage. The extended game play can also serve to review previously learned content and to emphasize that improved defense requires more creativity from the offensive team (the focus of lesson 7).

Tactical Problem
Creating space to penetrate

Lesson Focus
Dummy passes

Objectives
Beat a defender with either a pass or a dummy pass.

GAME 1

Setup
4v4 in 30 by 20 yards/meters (see figure 7.3)

Goal
Find ways to beat defenders.

Conditions
Game conditions

Questions

> *Q: Now that the defense is better, how can you beat defenders?*
> A: With a pass.

> *Q: What can you do if defenders try to intercept your passes?*
> A: Fake the pass and keep the ball.

PRACTICE TASK

Setup
In teams of four, play 2v1v1 in 20 by 10 yards/meters (see figure 7.8).

Goal
O1 and O2 combine to beat O3 and O4 with passes or with dummy passes if O3 and O4 try to intercept.

Conditions
· O3 can only move forward when O1 starts to move.
· When beaten, O3 cannot recover (i.e., O3 is out of the game).
· O4 can only move once O3 has been beaten.
· Rotate attackers and defenders every two repetitions.

Cues
· O1 runs at O3 while O2 supports.
· O1 times the pass as O3 advances (about 1 yard/meter, away).
· If O3 moves to intercept, show and go.
· Go on and beat O4.

GAME 2

Setup
Repeat game 1.

Goals
· Beat defenders with passes or dummy passes.
· Run at defenders and commit them to the tag.

Tactical Problem
Restarting play

Lesson Focus
One-player scrum

Objective
Use correct binding technique against an opponent.

GAME 1

Setup
4v4 in 30 by 20 yards/meters (see figure 7.3)

Goal
Restart with heel back and one-on-one coverage.

Conditions
Game conditions

Question

Q: *Does anyone know of another way players restart the game in rugby?*

A: With a scrum. (Note that this response is a bit optimistic as it is unlikely that any of the students will have watched rugby. Still, some students may have seen rugby and may answer, "Players pile up and fight for the ball," which is what a scrum looks like to the uninitiated. You will probably have to provide the term scrum.)

PRACTICE TASKS

Setup
- 1v1 scrum. Practice binding and leaning against an opponent (see figure 7.14).
- 1v1 scrum with the ball put in and heeled back (see figure 7.15). Players work cooperatively, alternating put-ins.

Extension
Competitive repetitions where the other team's hooker also tries to hook the ball.

Goals
- Each player demonstrates strong scrummaging position.
- Ball is put in down the middle, heeled back, and retrieved behind the scrum.

Cues
- Binding—place your right shoulder against the right shoulder of your opponent.
- Place your head below your opponent's arm.

FIGURE 7.15

© Tim McGrew/Hot Shots

- Keep your shoulders above your hips.
- Keep your knees bent, back straight.
- Scrum half puts the ball in straight and moves to the back of the scrum.

Note

The scrummaging position of the player on the left in figure 7.14 is better than that of the player on the right (who is the taller of the two). The player on the left is in a stronger position, with hips lower than the shoulders and a straighter back.

GAME 2

Setup

Repeat game 1 using one-player scrum for all restarts

Condition

Scrummaging players can only lean, not push.

Goal

Appropriately use one-player scrum to restart and initiate the attack.

Note

The 1v1 scrum is the first step in introducing formal restarts and it has implications for the tagging feature of tag rugby. You need to stipulate that players can only be tagged in open play (i.e., tags cannot be pulled in scrums, or later, in line-outs).

Lesson 9 — Level II

Tactical Problem
Restarting play

Lesson Focus
Three-player scrum

Objective
Use correct binding technique with teammates and against opponents.

GAME 1

Setup

4v4 in 30 by 20 yards/meters (see figure 7.3)

Goal

Restart with 1v1 scrum and one-on-one coverage.

Conditions

Game conditions with 1v1 scrum to restart.

Questions

Q: *If we increase the number of players on each team to seven, we need to increase the size of the scrum to how many?*
A: Three. (Students may or may not know this answer, so you might have to provide it.)

Q: *How can the three players in each team's scrum work to win the ball?*
A: Together.

Q: *How?*
A: Designate one player to hook the ball and two players to support the hooker.

Note

Here you can introduce the positions of the two props (who prop up the hooker on either side) and the importance of these players binding together to function as a unit.

PRACTICE TASKS

Setup

- 3v3 scrum. Practice binding together as a unit (see figures 7.11 and 7.12) and leaning against opponents (see figure 7.13).
- 3v3 scrum with ball put in and hooked back. Players work cooperatively, alternating put-ins between teams, and only the possession team's hooker hooks the ball.

Extension

Competitive repetitions in which the other team's hooker also tries to heel the ball.

Goals

- Each player demonstrates a strong scrummaging position.
- Players use correct binding and head placement within the scrum.
- Ball is put in down the middle, heeled back, and retrieved behind the scrum.

Cues

- Bind around the waist (see figure 7.12), with the hooker's arms over those of the props.
- Place right shoulder to the right shoulder of the opponent (heads to the left).
- Keep head below opponent's arm.
- Keep shoulders above hips.
- Keep knees bent and back straight.
- Scrum half puts the ball in straight and moves to the back of the scrum.

Note

Both of the two players closest to the camera in figure 7.13 have reasonable scrummaging positions, with their knees bent, backs straight, and shoulders above their hips. The player on the left has a slightly stronger position, as his legs are farther back.

GAME 2

Setup

7v7 in 50 by 30 yards/ meters, using a three-player scrum for all restarts (see figure 7.16)

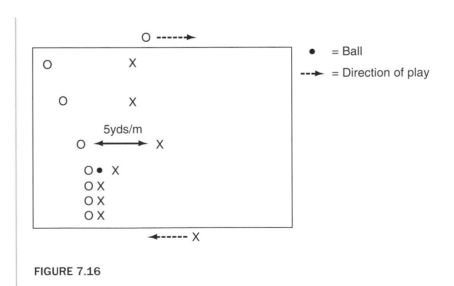

FIGURE 7.16

Note

The progression to a 7v7 game requires reorganization. The simplest way to accomplish this transition is to combine teams of four into teams of eight. Doing so leaves one player per team off the field. This player can act as a referee (giving two referees per game) or coach (giving one coach per team). Using teams of eight also keeps skill practice at four players per group, which is a number students will have become accustomed to by now.

Conditions
- Game conditions with three-player scrum for all restarts.
- Scrummaging players can only lean, not push.

Goal

Appropriately use three-player scrum to restart and initiate the attack.

Note

This lesson requires additional time and should be spread over two sessions so that students can learn the intricacies of binding together and against the opposing scrum. In addition, players should have the opportunity to experience all positions in the scrum (which is also known as the "forwards") and in the "backs" (the players outside the scrum). The individual positions within the backs are known as the scrum half (the player who puts in and receives from the scrum), the fly half (the player who receives the outlet pass from the scrum half), the center (the player next in the line), and the winger (the player on the end, with the most space to run).

Level III

At this point your students have come a long way. They are able to play a 7v7 game with appropriate restarts and they understand basic positions. However, they will find it increasingly difficult to penetrate the opposition in the 7v7 game because there are more players on the field and therefore there is less space available for offense (even though the field is now slightly bigger than in the 4v4 game previously played). Greater creativity in attacking is called for and attack becomes the focus of the early lessons in level III, with players (particularly the backs) learning to work together to create and use space to penetrate and score. Learning the scissors and loop moves will be easy for students who have played American football because of their similarities with the reverse moves sometimes performed by wide receivers. Again, these moves are more complex and you might need an extra lesson to progress from unopposed performance to game play.

Further attending to the appropriate restart for the out-of-bounds ball completes the 7-a-side version of tag rugby. A line-out is illustrated in figures 7.17 and 7.18. The team that did not move the ball out of bounds gets the throw-in, which is usually taken by the hooker. The opposing hooker stands just inside the sideline and does not rejoin the game until after the throw, leaving two players (the two props) to contest the line-out. The goal is to catch the ball and pass it to the scrum half, who then distributes it to the backs. Remember that at restarts the opposing backs must be 5 yards/meters (10 yards/meters on a full-size field) away from the horizontal line on which the ball lies. The same rule applies to line-outs and you can increase the distance to give more space to the attacking team if necessary.

FIGURE 7.17

FIGURE 7.18

Teaching Sport Concepts and Skills

Tactical Problem
Creating space to penetrate

Lesson Focus
Drawing the defender and using dummy passes in a 7v7 game

Objective
Run at defenders and beat them with a pass or dummy during open 7v7 play.

GAME 1

Setup
7v7 in 50 by 30 yards/meters, using a three-player scrum for all restarts (see figure 7.16)

Goal
Penetrate the opponent's backs.

Conditions
Game conditions with a 3v3 scrum to restart.

Questions

Q: *If spaces are tight and it is difficult to get through the defense, what tactics have we previously learned that will help?*

A: Drawing the defenders and passing or using a dummy pass.

Q: *Which of the opposition's players should you run at? (Another way of asking this is, "Where is the most space to attack?")*

A: The outside player (the winger).

PRACTICE TASK

Setup
4v4 in 30 by 30 yards/meters or in half of the game field (see figure 7.19), restarting with free passes or tap backs

Goal
Attack the outside player, where there is the most space to exploit.

Cues
· Run diagonally at the outside player.
· Draw (the defender) and pass or dummy pass.

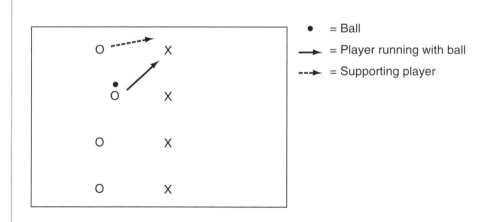

• = Ball

⟶ = Player running with ball

⤏ = Supporting player

FIGURE 7.19

GAME 2

Repeat game 1.

Tactical Problem
Creating space to penetrate

Lesson Focus
Switching the direction of play with a scissors move

Objective
Employ a scissors move in practice and game play (see Practice Task).

GAME 1

Setup
7v7 in 50 by 30 yards/meters, using a three-player scrum for all restarts (see figure 7.16)

Goal
Penetrate the opponent's backs.

Conditions
Game conditions with a 3v3 scrum to restart.

Question

Q: *If spaces are tight and you run out of space on the outside of the field, what can you do?*

A: Switch play. (This can be done with a scissors move.)

PRACTICE TASK

Setup
Unopposed four-player practice (see figure 7.20). O1 runs at the outside player, O2 cuts inside and behind O1, O1 passes to O2 so that O1 is shielding the ball from the defender, O2 continues the movement by passing to O3, who passes to O4, who scores in the corner. Rotate the middle players every two repetitions.

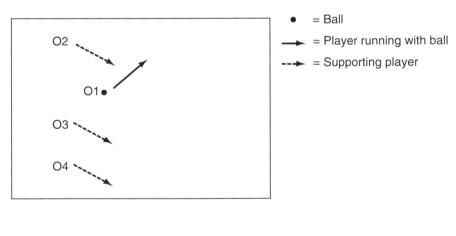

•	= Ball
→	= Player running with ball
⇢	= Supporting player

FIGURE 7.20

Goal
Perform one scissors move while moving the ball from one end of the practice area to the other (the move needs about 30 yards/meters, of space).

Note
Practicing the scissors move is best done at walking speed until students understand the pattern.

Cues

- Ball carrier (O1)
  - Run diagonally at outside player.
  - Give the pass so that you shield the ball with your body.
- Player O2
  - Call "inside" and cut in.
  - Receive the ball and move diagonally to link up with O3.
- Players O3 and O4
  - Support O2 and be prepared to execute another scissors if necessary.

Extension

4v4 in 30 by 30 yards/meters or in half of the game field (see figure 7.19), restarting with free passes or tap backs.

Goal

Attack the outside player and use scissors to change the direction of play.

Cues

- Run diagonally at the outside player.
- Draw the defender and execute scissors where possible.

Note

As defenders begin to anticipate the scissors, offense may use the dummy scissors where instead of passing, the ball carrier fakes the pass and continues running.

GAME 2

Repeat game 1.

Lesson 12 Level III

Tactical Problem

Creating space to penetrate

Lesson Focus

Creating a player-up situation by using a loop move

Objective

Employ a loop move in practice and game play (see Practice Task).

GAME 1

Setup

7v7 in 50 by 30 yards/meters, using a three-player scrum for all restarts (see figure 7.16)

Goal

Penetrate the opponent's backs.

Conditions

Game conditions with a 3v3 scrum to restart.

Question

Q: If you are the ball carrier, how can you create space after you have passed the ball?
A: Loop around the player you just passed to.

PRACTICE TASK

Setup

Unopposed four-player practice (see figure 7.21). O1 runs forward and passes to O3. O1 loops around O3 to receive a pass before linking with O4. Rotate the middle players every two repetitions.

Goal

Perform one loop move while moving the ball from one end of the practice area to the other (the move needs about 30 yards/meters, of space).

Note

The loop can be performed in the outside areas of the field (i.e., by looping around the outside player, perhaps O2 in this case, and exploiting any available space on the wing). Again, this move is best practiced at walking speed until students understand the pattern.

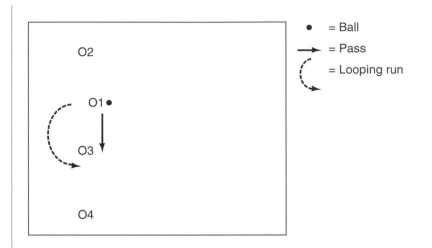

FIGURE 7.21

Cues

- Ball carrier (O1)
  - Run at opposite player.
  - Pass to O3 and loop around.
- Player O3
  - Receive pass and wait.
  - Return pass to O1.
- Player O4
  - Support O1 and be prepared to receive (passive role in this one until next repetition).
  - Next repetition starts with O4.

Extension

4v4 in 30 by 30 yards/meters) or in half of the game field (see figure 7.19), restarting with free passes or tap backs.

Goal

Use loop move to penetrate.

Cue

Loop and rejoin the attack.

Note

Though figure 7.21 shows player O1 looping around one teammate (in this case player O3), O1 can always loop around both players to the outside and receive a pass from O4 at the end of the line. Encourage such creativity.

GAME 2

Repeat game 1.

Tactical Problem
Restarting play

Lesson Focus
Restarting play from out of bounds using a two-player line-out

Objective
Employ a line-out to restart play in practice and game play (see figures 7.17 and 7.18).

GAME 1

Setup
7v7 in 50 by 30 yards/meters, using a three-player scrum for all restarts (see figure 7.16)

Goal
Review scrum restart.

Conditions
Game conditions with a 3v3 scrum to restart.

Question

> Q: *How do invasion games usually restart after the ball goes out of bounds?*
> A: The ball is thrown in (the same happens in rugby).

PRACTICE TASK

Setup
In pairs, practice throwing and catching for the line-out. Partners stand 5 to 7 yards/meters apart and use a straight throw so that the receiver must jump to catch the ball above the head.

Goals
  · Straight throw at jumping height.
  · Throw underhand (two hands) or overhand (one hand).

Cues
  · Throw straight.
  · Throw at jumping height.
  · Catch and turn 90 degrees while still in the air (for a pass to scrum half, see extension).

Extension
  · Unopposed practice in groups of four. The hooker throws and the props jump to catch and pass to the scrum half. Rotate positions.
  · Opposed practice (4v4) with contested line-outs.

GAME 2

Setup
7v7 in 50 by 30 yards/meters, using scrum and line-out restarts as appropriate

Goal
Use both scrums and line-outs to restart the game and initiate attacks.

Summary

The 13 lessons in this chapter are designed to give you and your students a basic understanding of rugby. Remember that we have limited the content to a 7-a-side, noncontact version of the game, so there is a lot involved in the full game that was not included. Nevertheless, tag rugby provides a safe, skillful, fast, and exciting game for students to play, and it makes for a rewarding teaching experience as well. Good luck!

CHAPTER 8

Volleyball

A tactical games approach is a problem-solving approach that places students at the center of deciding *what* to do (tactical awareness), *how* to do it (skill execution), *when* to do it (timing), *where* to do it (space), and *when* (risk). For students to think tactically, they must ask, "What should I do in this situation?" When you focus on getting students to think tactically, you move away from simply saying, "Do this." As the teacher, you design a situation (a set of playing conditions) that highlights the game problem you want students to solve. Placing students in these situations emphasizes the decision making and social dynamics of sport-related games.

To help students begin solving the problem of setting up to attack in volleyball, you could place them in a 3v3 game on a modified court (narrower and shorter with a lower net). Initiate the game with a free toss (used as the serve) and have teams alternate serves on every point. The goal of this game is for players to contain the first pass on their side of the court. The situation and conditions help teams of students identify what movements and skills are needed to contain the ball in order to set up for an attack.

There are two basic types of game knowledge. First is *about-game knowledge,* which includes the rules and procedures that make games work, such as ways of starting and restarting play and the locations of boundaries. Second is *in-game knowledge,* which includes the skills and movements related to a specific game. Table 8.1 accounts for both types of knowledge as it presents our framework of the tactical problems of volleyball and their required off-the-ball movements and on-the-ball skills.

Let's take a closer look at the fundamental offensive tactic of any volleyball game, the pass-set-attack. Setting up to attack involves the on-the-ball skills of forearm and overhead passing and attacking. The relevant off-the-ball movements, which are often overlooked, involve opening up (establishing an unobstructed space), transitioning (establishing a new position), supporting (backing up teammates), and pursuing (following and saving the ball to continue play). A player who does not receive the serve needs to support teammates, be ready to pursue

Teachers must incorporate instruction with hands-on learning.

Table 8.1 Tactical Problems, Movements, and Skills in Volleyball

Tactical problems	Off-the-ball movements	On-the-ball skills
SCORING (OFFENSE)		
Setting up to attack	• Base • Open up • Support • Pursuit • Transition	• Forearm pass – Free ball – Serve receive • Overhead pass – Set
Winning the point	• Transition – To attack – To base	• Attack – Hit or spike – Down ball – Dink or tip – Roll shot • Serve – Underhand – Overhand
Attacking as a team	• Serve receive • Free ball • Cover • Transition • Communication	• Pass-set-attack combinations
PREVENTING SCORING (DEFENSE)		
Defending space on own court	• Base • Open up • Pursuit	
Defending against an attack	• Base • Read • Adjust • Transition	• Dig • Solo block
Defending as a team	• Base – Floor defense – Up defense – Back defense • Communication	

a difficult pass, and transition for the next play. If taught, these off-the-ball movements optimize students' tactical awareness and thus improve overall game play. You also need to consider what about-game knowledge is developmentally necessary, such as knowing how to rotate and knowing boundaries and the rules of starting and restarting play. You should also teach appropriate terminology such as base, free ball, and serve receive. These terms can be viewed as tactical concepts to assist your students' understanding.

As in chapters 4 through 7, lessons cycle through number of players (i.e., 2v2, 3v3, 4v4), questions and answers, practice, and game. Games should be modified (i.e., lower net, smaller court) to represent the advanced form and exaggerated (e.g., contain the first contact on one side of the net or a two-contact rule) to present students with tactical problems (Thorpe, Bunker, and Almond 1986).

Basic Triad Formation

Using a basic triad formation in volleyball provides you with many options for situated learning. Figure 8.1 shows the triad for practicing setting. The triad involves a minimum of three players fulfilling three roles described as initiator, performer, and follow-through player (Griffin 1994). The initiator starts the drill with a skill or simulated skill such as a toss or serve. The initiator provides the game tempo for the practice in order to assist the performer's trial intensity. The performer is the primary player and focus of the practice. The follow-through player could act either as the target who stops and retrieves the ball or as a performer who executes the next logical skill or movement. In figure 8.1 the initiator is labeled with a T (tosser), the performer with an S (setter), and the follow-through player with an H (hitter).

The power of the triad formation is that it is gamelike. You can conduct it on a volleyball court using the net and simulating the flow of volleyball games. It has sequences such as toss and pass to target; toss and set to target; serve and pass (serve and receive) to target; or pass, set, and hit (or spike). For example, practicing forearm passing in this format makes students aware of where to set up to attack. You can adapt the triad formation to meet the contextual needs of your students, facilities, and equipment. The following are suggestions for working in the triad formation:

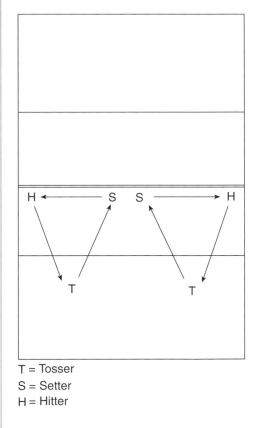

T = Tosser
S = Setter
H = Hitter

FIGURE 8.1

- *Use more than three students.* The triad does not necessarily use *only* three students. Adding another performer, collector, or feeder can help the flow of practice when you have limited space (e.g., few courts), limited equipment (e.g., few balls and nets), and large numbers of students. Including more players is especially useful when students are novice players because, as you know, the ball does not always go where they want it to go. Using extra players can decrease the time required for ball retrieval and maintain the flow of the activity.

- *Organize the triad by teams,* depending on the type of drill and the size of the class. If you have teams of 6 to 8 players, it is easy to divide these teams for triad work. You should also be able to have 2 to 3 small groups working on one regular volleyball net and court.

- *Have a two-ball minimum rule.* The two-ball rule allows the practice to run smoothly. The target player should have one ball ready to go and bounce that ball to the feeder or tosser to help the practice run smoothly. Using a bounce pass is a built-in safety feature because it allows sufficient time for the tosser to react and catch the ball.

- *Modify the formation.* If students are unable to toss the ball over the net, modify the drill by having the tosser duck under the net and toss the ball from the net to the back row. This modification still uses a gamelike triad but may be more developmentally appropriate for your students.

When structuring net games, be mindful of the court dimensions, available equipment, and number of students. Modifications simplify and slow the game, providing students the opportunity to think tactically (i.e., problem solve). Remember that small-sided volleyball games played in reduced court areas with a lower net and a larger, softer ball use the same regulations, solutions, and skills as the full game.

Teaching Volleyball

Volleyball is a difficult game for novice players for the simple reason that if students cannot hit the ball in the right direction, at the right angle, and with the correct amount of force, a game cannot take place. Instead your students will experience endless frustration by their inability to keep the ball in play individually and as a team. Here are several suggestions for increasing the likelihood of successful, modified game play:

- *Initiate games from a free ball.* Teaching the serve to novice students is not necessary for maximizing game play in small-sided games. When working with novice players or beginning a unit, the free ball (i.e., an easy, rainbow toss over the net) facilitates game play for your students. Remember that receiving the serve is one of the most difficult skills of the game. Beginning games with a free toss will structure your students for success and enable them to focus on solving the tactical problems of volleyball.

- *Encourage a no-ace or cooperative-serve rule.* After you introduce the serve you should establish a no-ace rule, which makes receiving the serve easier for a while.

- *Teach students how to toss.* Take the time to teach your students how to toss and provide them with practice. Insist that they toss with two hands (overhead if necessary) and with no spin. A one-handed spinning toss is difficult to receive and decreases the likelihood of the ball being returned. View tossing as an essential skill in volleyball, as students need to be able to initiate games and practices.

- *Add volleyball courts by using badminton courts.* Use badminton courts (nets and lines) to maximize your use of facilities and equipment and to allow for more game play and practice.

- *Practice variations.* Here are several ways you can vary tasks:
  - Vary number of passers
  - Vary initial starting point for serving or receiving
  - Vary flight of ball
  - Vary speed of ball
  - Vary sides of court used (one or two sides)
  - Vary serve
  - Vary areas of the court to serve to or receive in
  - Vary players involved (add hitters, blockers, and diggers)

Levels of Tactical Complexity

You should never teach tactics that exceed the abilities of your students and you should always promote safety and success. Table 8.2 presents the levels of tactical complexity that you can use to develop your students' tactical awareness. You can view these levels as the possible scope and sequence for teaching volleyball in your physical education program.

The following principles can guide you in developing appropriate lesson progressions. We encourage developmentally appropriate practice, which means that you adjust the situated learning both across grade levels and within each class:

Table 8.2 Levels of Tactical Complexity for Volleyball

Tactical problems	I	II	III	IV	V
SCORING (OFFENSE)					

Setting up to attack	• Pass
	  – Forearm
	  – Set
	• Open up
	• Base
		• Transition
		• Pursue and save
					• Play sets

Winning the point	• Down ball and spike
	• Transition
		• Down ball and spike	• Serve	• Spike
				  – Crosscourt
				  – Line
				  – Roll
				  – Tip	

Attacking as a team			• Serve receive (3v3)	• Serve receive (6v6)	• 1 Attack coverage
PREVENTING SCORING (DEFENSE)					
Defending space on your own court		• Free ball • Base • Open up			
Defending against an attack			• Dig	• Block – Solo	
Defending as a team					• Floor position • Double block

- Move students from cooperative to competitive situations. In cooperative play (i.e., maintaining a rally), students work with a partner or team toward a goal. In competitive play (e.g., 3v3 volleyball game), students work in a team against an opponent. Students should explore the idea that cooperation is an essential component of good competition. This idea speaks to the social and behavioral dynamics (e.g., teamwork, good sporting behavior, fair play, game etiquette) of sport-related games.

- Move from simple to complex. By doing so you provide students with the opportunity for early success, which we believe leads students to perceive competence. Teachers should continually ask what the learners need to know to challenge their knowledge and improve their game performance. This notion cuts across skills and movements within each game as well as across tactical problems.

- Move from smaller (2v2 or 3v3) to larger (4v4 or 6v6) games. Including fewer players increases overall game involvement and slows the pace of the game, which makes it easier for students to experience the problems and play the game.

Level I

Lessons in level I set students up to play the simplest form of volleyball and encourage them to understand the principles of ball placement and court positioning. These principles lay the groundwork for solving the tactical problems of setting up for attack and winning the point. The on-the-ball skills include the basic forearm (free ball) and overhead (set) pass and the attack (down ball and hit or spike). Off-the-ball movements include returning to base position, opening up, and transitioning. Note that the early lessons progress slowly to match the complexity of volleyball skills, moving from the concept of containing the ball on your side of the court to setting up using the forearm pass to attack (down ball and spike). We have found that students are motivated by learning to attack. This motivation makes teaching skills such as the set easier. This notion builds on the assumption of the tactical approach that students learn best if they know what to do before they understand how to do it.

Forearm passing is a fundamental skill for volleyball.

Lesson 1 💿

Tactical Problem
Setting up to attack

Lesson Focus
Base positions and containing the ball on your court

Objective
Make initial pass high and in the middle of the court (playable ball).

GAME 1

Setup
3v3

Goal
Set up to attack the ball.

Conditions
- Make court narrow and short, set up as seen in figure 8.2.
- Initiate game from a playable toss (free ball).
- Alternate free ball after each rally.
- Have a serving team.

Notes
- Easy toss is a two-hand soccer throw-in (rainbow toss).
- Base position is a player's home, or recovery, position during a game.

Questions
Q: What did you do to contain the ball on your side of the court?
A: Controlled the ball and hit it high.

Q: How did you accomplish this?
A: With an overhead or forearm pass. (Note that the novice might not know the terms but will possibly say, "like this," while showing you the actions.)

Q. Which way is best for receiving the serve?
A. Using the forearms.

Q: Where is a safe place to pass?
A: Into the middle of the court.

PRACTICE TASK

Setup
Forearm pass, triad

Goals
- Pass a playable ball, one that is high and in the middle of the court, so that another player can hit it.
- Focus on medium body posture and flat platform.

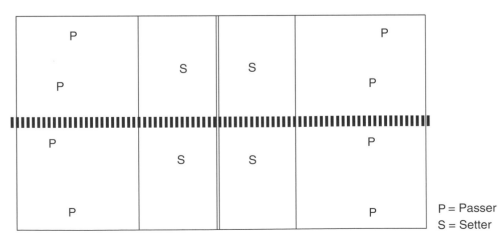

P = Passer
S = Setter

FIGURE 8.2

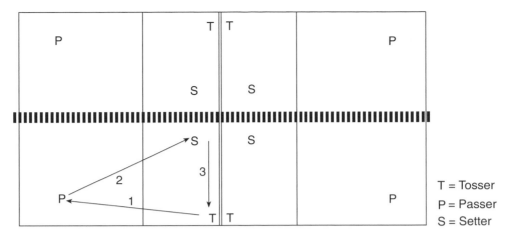

FIGURE 8.3

Conditions
- Do three trials before rotating.
- Tosser prompts by hitting the side of the ball and then gives a playable toss to the passer, who passes the ball to the target (setter).
- Setter catches the ball and then bounces it back to the tosser (see figure 8.3).

Cues
- Medium body posture.
- Feet to the ball.
- Belly button to target.
- Thumbs together, flat platform (i.e., forearms level).

GAME 2

Setup
3v3

Goals
- Attempt a forearm pass as the first contact on your side of the net.
- Earn 1 point for select and attempt (i.e., for trying the forearm pass, even if the result is not playable).

Lesson 2   Level I

Tactical Problem
Setting up to attack

Lesson Focus
Learning base position and containing the ball on your court using the forearm pass

Objective
Select the forearm pass and execute a playable ball in the middle of your court.

GAME 1

Setup
3v3

Goal

Set up to attack the ball.

Conditions

- Make court narrow and short.
- Initiate game from a playable toss (free ball).
- Alternate free ball after each rally.
- Rotate serving team (see figure 8.2).

Notes

- Easy toss is two-handed soccer throw-in (rainbow toss).
- Base position is a player's home, or recovery, position during a game.

Questions

Q: What did you do to set up a playable ball on your side of the court?
A: Hit the ball high to the middle of the court using the forearm pass.

Q: How do you perform the forearm pass?
A: Use medium body posture and a flat platform and point your belly button at the target.

Q: Why should you use the forearm pass?
A: The flat platform has a larger, flatter surface that makes it easier to block the ball (i.e., to receive).

PRACTICE TASK

Setup

Forearm pass practice, triad

Goals

- Perform three trials or two playable balls before rotation.
- Hit a playable ball, one that is high and in the middle of the court, so another player can hit the ball.
- Focus on medium body posture and pointing the belly button to the target.

Conditions

- Tosser prompts by hitting the side of the ball and then gives a playable toss to the passer, who passes the ball to the target (setter).
- Setter catches the ball and bounces it back to the tosser (see figure 8.3).

Extension

Move passer to other positions in the back row.

Cues

- Medium body posture.
- Feet to the ball.
- Flat platform.
- Belly button to target.

GAME 2

Setup

3v3

Goals

- Use a forearm pass as first contact on your side of the net.
- Earn 1 point if the first pass is a playable forearm pass.

Tactical Problem
Setting up to attack

Lesson Focus
Learning base position and containing the ball on your court using the forearm pass

Objective
Call first ball and execute a playable forearm free pass to the middle of your court.

GAME 1

Setup
3v3

Goal
Set up to attack the ball.

Conditions
- Make court narrow and short.
- Initiate game from a playable toss (free ball).
- Alternate free ball after each rally.
- Rotate serving team (see figure 8.2).

Notes
- Easy toss is two-handed soccer throw-in (rainbow toss).
- Base position is a player's home, or recovery, position during a game.

Questions

Q: *How do you know it is your ball to play?*
A: By watching the path of the ball during the serve (toss).

Q: *What do you do to be sure you get the ball? So you perform the forearm pass?*
A: Move my feet to align with the path of the ball and call the ball "mine."

PRACTICE TASK

Setup
Forearm pass practice, triad

Goals
- Complete three trials before rotation.
- Pass a playable ball, one that is high and in the middle of the court, so another player can hit the ball.
- Move feet to the ball and call the ball ("mine").

Conditions
- Tosser prompts by hitting the side of the ball and then gives a playable toss that forces the passer to move his feet (e.g., two steps side to side or up or back).
- Passer calls ball.
- Target (setter) catches the ball and bounces it back to the tosser (see figure 8.3).

Cues
- Medium body posture.
- Feet to the ball.
- Flat platform.
- Belly button to target.
- Call "mine."

GAME 2

Setup
3v3

Goals
- Call ball and select and execute the forearm pass as the first contact on your side of the net.
- Earn 1 point if the passer calls the first ball and executes a playable forearm pass.

Lesson 4 Level I

Tactical Problem
Winning the point

Lesson Focus
Attacking the ball

Objective
Select and execute a down ball (i.e., a standing spike) or spike (with a jump).

Note
Again, in this lesson we shift from setting up to attack to the attack itself, a skill that we might be introducing earlier than you are accustomed to when teaching volleyball. Our reason for this is motivational in that students get a lot out of learning to attack and once they are able to attack they see greater value in quality setting as you work backward from the spike (or down ball).

GAME 1

Setup
3v3

Goals
- Set up to attack.
- Earn 1 point when team has two hits on its side.

Conditions
- Make court narrow and short.
- Initiate game from a playable toss (free ball).
- Alternate free ball after each rally.
- Rotate serving team (see figure 8.2).
- Use up to three hits.

Note
Easy toss is two-handed soccer throw-in (rainbow toss).

Questions
Q: *What are you setting up to do when you get two hits on your side?*
A: To attack.

Q: *How do you attack in volleyball?*
A: With a hit, spike, or down ball.

Q: *How does an attack help you win the point?*
A: It's hard to return.

PRACTICE TASK

Setup
Toss to attack, use triad

Goals
- Hitter performs 3 to 5 trials.
- Tosser tosses a high ball (1 yard/meter high, near the spiking line) for hitter to attack.

Conditions
- Organize on two courts (two teams of three players).
- Tosser (setter) tosses a high ball near the spiking line for the hitter to attack (see figure 8.4). The toss should simulate a set rainbow toss.
- Hitter selects to hit a down ball or a spike.
- Feeder keeps the balls from becoming a danger in the field of play and gives the balls, one at a time, to the tosser.
- Collector scoops up the balls after the hit and rolls them to the feeder.

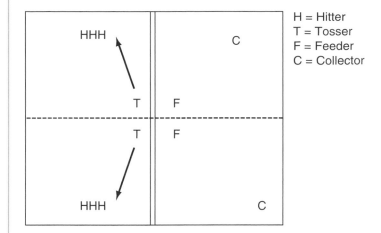

H = Hitter
T = Tosser
F = Feeder
C = Collector

FIGURE 8.4

Note
For safety during hitting practice, have two teams work together on the same side of the court and be sure that all teams hit the same way.

Cues
- Down ball (i.e., a hit without the jump)
  - Feet to the ball.
  - Throw hands high.
  - Swing fast.
- Hitting (with a jump)
  - Feet to the ball.
  - Jump.
  - Throw hands high.
  - Swing fast.

GAME 2

Setup
3v3

Goals
- Set up to attack to win the point.
- Earn 1 point when team attempts to attack the ball.

Tactical Problem
Setting up to attack

Lesson Focus
Setting up to overhead pass (set) the ball

Objective
Select and execute an overhead pass from a playable forearm pass.

GAME 1

Setup
3v3

Goals
- Use a forearm pass as the first contact on your side of the net.
- Earn 1 point by attempting to attack the ball.

Conditions
- Make court narrow and short.
- Initiate game from a playable toss (free ball).
- Alternate free ball after each rally.
- Rotate serving team (see figure 8.2).
- Use up to three hits.

Note
Easy toss is two-handed soccer throw-in (rainbow toss).

Questions
Q: What is the purpose of the second hit?
A: To set up a player to attack.

Q: Where should you set up the player to attack?
A: Close to the net (about 1 yard/meter away) by using a high, rainbow ball.

Q: How should you set up the player?
A: With the overhead pass or set.

PRACTICE TASK

In triads—toss; overhead pass (set); catch.

Goal
Player performs 3 of 5 trials successfully and then rotates.

Conditions
- Passer prompts by hitting (slapping) the side of the ball and then tosses a playable forearm pass to the setter.
- Setter sets the ball to the target (target hitter) (see figure 8.5).

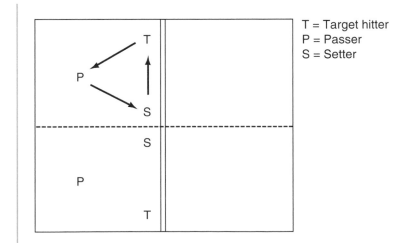

T = Target hitter
P = Passer
S = Setter

FIGURE 8.5

Cues
- Medium posture.
- Hands high (at forehead).
- Volleyball-shaped hands.
- Square to target.
- Finish like Superman (extend arms and legs).

GAME 2

Setup
3v3

Goals
- Select and attempt to set up for an attack by using the overhead pass (set).
- Earn 1 point if there are two hits on your side.

Lesson 6

Tactical Problem
Setting up to attack

Lesson Focus
Setter moving (opening up) into position to set up

Objectives
Open up to set.

GAME 1

Setup
3v3

Goals
- Select and attempt to set up for an attack using the overhead pass (set).
- Earn 1 point if the there are two hits on your side.

Conditions
- Make court narrow and short.
- Initiate game from a playable toss (free ball).
- Alternate free ball after each rally.
- Rotate serving team (see figure 8.2).
- Use up to three hits.

Note
Easy toss is two-handed soccer throw-in (rainbow toss).

Questions
Q: What direction does the setter face when the ball is on the other side of the net?
A: She faces the net.

Q: What does the setter need to do once the ball is on her side of the net?
A: Turn to see the ball.

Q: How does the setter do this?
A: Pivot, turn, and call "here."

PRACTICE TASK 1

Setup
Practice opening up and setting, use triad

Goals
- Setter opens up.
- Setter makes 3 or 4 sets to target hitter.
- Setter performs a good set, which is a rainbow ball (1 yard/meter high and 1 yard/meter off the net).

Conditions
- Tosser prompts by hitting (slapping) the side of the ball and then gives a playable toss (simulates a good forearm pass) to the setter, who sets the ball to the hitter.
- Setter is in ready position at the net.
- When the ball is hit, setter opens up and sets the ball to the hitter, who catches it and bounces it back to the tosser (see figure 8.6).

Cues for Opening Up
- Ready position at the net.
- Medium to high posture.
- Hands high for block.
- Pivot (turn) to the passers.
- Call "here."
- See the passer play the ball.
- Adjust to set the ball (happy feet).

Cues for Setting
- Medium posture.
- Hands high (at forehead).
- Volleyball-shaped hands.
- Square to target.
- Finish like Superman (extend arms and legs).

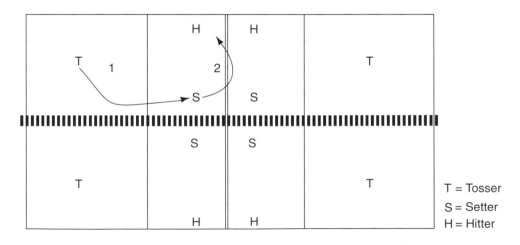

FIGURE 8.6

T = Tosser
S = Setter
H = Hitter

PRACTICE TASK 2

Setup
Extend previous drill (only if students are ready for the challenge)

Goals
- Setter opens up.
- Setter makes 3 or 4 good sets to the hitter.
- Setter performs a good set, which is a rainbow ball (1 yard/meter).

Conditions
- Target (hitter) prompts by hitting (slapping) the side of the ball and then gives a playable toss (free ball) to the passer, who passes to the setter.
- Setter is in ready position at the net.
- When the ball is hit, the setter opens up and sets the ball to the hitter, who catches it and starts again (see figure 8.7).

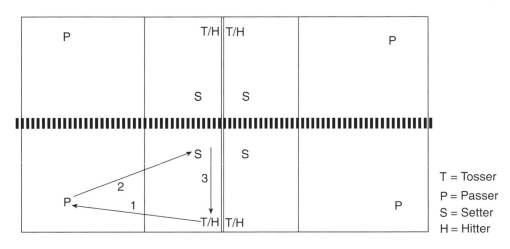

T = Tosser
P = Passer
S = Setter
H = Hitter

FIGURE 8.7

GAME 2

Setup
3v3

Goals
- Select and execute skills to set up the pass-set-attack on your side of the net.
- Earn 1 point for an attempt at pass-set-attack.

Lesson 7 Level I

Tactical Problem
Winning the point

Lesson Focus
Transitioning to attack

Objective
Successful transition by passer to hitter.

GAME 1

Setup
3v3

Goals
- Set up to attack.
- Earn 1 point when team attempts to set up to pass-set-attack.

Conditions
- Make court narrow and short.
- Initiate game from a playable toss (free ball).
- Alternate free ball after each rally.
- Rotate serving team (see figure 8.2).
- Use up to three hits.

Note
Easy toss is two-handed soccer throw-in (rainbow toss).

Questions

Q: *Where should you be while waiting for the ball?*
A: In base position, ready to move.

Q: *How do you get ready to attack (spike or hit) the ball?*
A: Move to where the set is going and transition.

PRACTICE TASK

Setup
Passer practices transitioning to attack, use triad

Goals
- Passer–hitter performs 3 to 5 trials.
- Passer–hitter passes and then transitions to attack (hit).

Conditions
- Organize on courts A and B (two teams of three players). See figure 8.8.
- Tosser tosses a free ball to the passer–hitter, and the passer uses the forearm pass to get the ball to the setter.
- Setter catches the ball and tosses a rainbow set (1 yard/meter high and 1 yard/meter off the net).
- As setter catches, passer–hitter transitions to hitter for the attack.
- After hitter attacks the ball, he returns to the passing line.

Note
For safety during hitting practice, have two teams work together on the same side of the court and have all teams hit one way.

Cues
- Hitting
  - Feet to the ball.
  - Jump.
  - Throw hands high.
  - Swing fast.
- Transitioning
  - Establish new position.

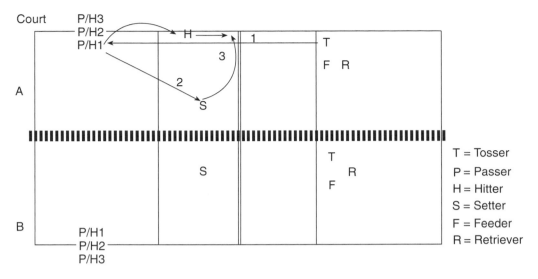

Court

A

B

P/H3
P/H2
P/H1

H

3

2

S

1

T

F R

T

F

R

S

P/H1
P/H2
P/H3

T = Tosser
P = Passer
H = Hitter
S = Setter
F = Feeder
R = Retriever

FIGURE 8.8

GAME 2

Setup
3v3

Goals
· Set up to attack.
· Earn 1 point for getting two hits on a side and 2 points for executing a pass-set-attack.

Level II

Having introduced volleyball in its most basic tactical form, you can further students' understanding at level II. Begin level II by using a few of the lessons from level I as review. Have students continue to solve the tactical problem of setting up to attack and winning the point by focusing more on the on-the-ball skill of hitting (spiking) and on the off-the-ball movement of transitioning (establishing a new position). Also get your students to solve the problem of how to pursue and save a ball in order to keep the rally going for their teams.

Introduce the problem of defending space on your court, which involves the off-the-ball movements of base and adjust. Tactical problems at level II include defending space against a free ball in order to set up to attack. Doing this involves understanding many off-the-ball movements such as base positioning, pursuing, and transitioning. Continue to initiate play with a free toss.

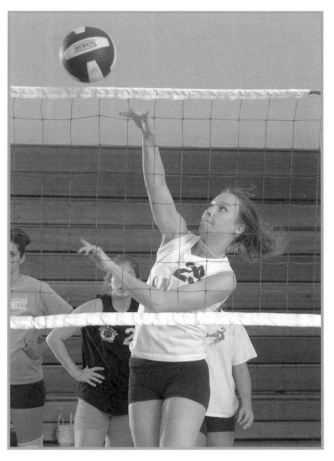

Honed spiking skills require students to learn how to defend their side of the net.

Lesson 8

Tactical Problem
Setting up to attack

Lesson Focus
Reviewing setting up to attack

Objectives
· Select and execute the forearm pass and the opening up by the setter.
· Increase the difficulty of practice.

GAME 1

Setup
3v3

Goals
· Set up to attack.
· Earn 1 point by attempting to use two hits (contacts) on a side.

Conditions

- Make court narrow and short.
- Initiate game from a playable toss (free ball).
- Alternate free ball after each rally.
- Rotate serving team (see figure 8.2).
- Use up to three hits.

Note

Easy toss is two-handed soccer throw-in (rainbow toss).

Questions

Q: *What are you setting up to do?*
A: Attack and win a point.

Q: *Where should the first pass go?*
A: High in the air and into the middle of the court.

Q: *Who should play the second ball?*
A: The setter (a person close to the net).

PRACTICE TASK

Setup

Practice setting up to attack, use triad

Goals

- Perform 2 to 3 trials or two playable balls before rotating.
- Set up a playable ball, one that is high and in the middle of the court, so another player can hit the ball.
- Focus on medium posture, feet to ball, flat platform, belly button to target, calling the ball.

Conditions

- Tosser stands behind the 10-yard/meter line and tosses a free ball to the passer.
- Tosser moves passer up and back and laterally.
- Passer uses forearm pass to get the ball to the setter.
- Setter catches the ball (see figure 8.9).
- Tosser can also move the ball from side to side and up and back to increase difficulty for the passer.

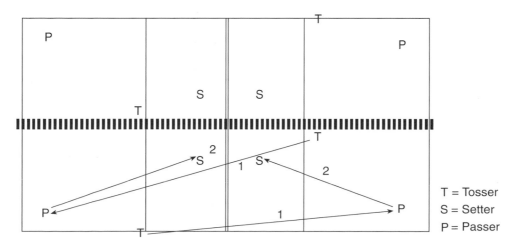

FIGURE 8.9

Cue
Review lessons from level I.

GAME 2

Setup
3v3

Goal
Earn 1 point by making two hits (contacts) on a side.

Lesson 9 Level II

Tactical Problem
Setting up to attack

Lesson Focus
Pursuing and saving

Objective
Successfully pursue and save a ball off the court and make it playable.

GAME 1

Setup
3v3

Goal
Earn 1 point by making two hits (contacts) on a side.

Conditions
- Make court narrow and short.
- Initiate game from a playable toss (free ball).
- Alternate free ball after each rally.
- Rotate serving team (see figure 8.2).
- Use up to three hits.

Note
Easy toss is two-handed soccer throw-in (rainbow toss).

Questions

Q: When can you save a ball that is not in the court but is still in the air?
A: When the first or second passes stay in playable territory but go outside the boundaries of the court.

Q: What do you do when your teammate passes the ball into playable territory but off of the court?
A: Chase it.

Q: How do you do this?
A: Run forward quickly.

Q: What skill do you use to make the save?
A: The reverse forearm pass.

PRACTICE TASK

Setup
Practice pursuing and saving, use triad

Goals
- Pursue and save the ball for 3 of 5 trials.
- Use two hits to send the ball over the net in order to reinforce moving as a system.

Conditions
- Tosser tosses a high, playable ball out of bounds for passers to pursue and save.
- After toss, the tosser returns to setter base to play setter role (see figure 8.10).

Cues
- Individual
  - Use medium posture.
  - Run toward the ball.
  - Run with hands apart.
  - Use reverse forearm pass.
  - Get back to the court.
  - Keep platform parallel to the ground.
  - Pass a high, playable ball.
- Team
  - Move as a system.
  - Use contact player as the point.
  - All players shift.

GAME 2

Setup
3v3

Goals
- Pursue and save a ball to the middle of the court.
- Play a continuous rally.

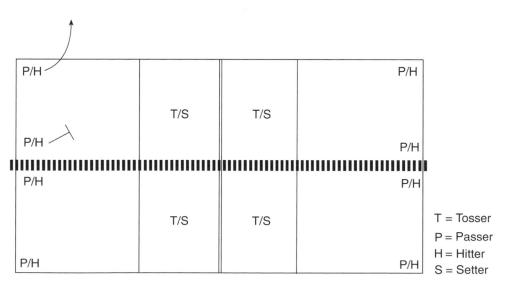

FIGURE 8.10

Tactical Problem
Winning the point

Lesson Focus
Transitioning to attack

Objective
Passer successfully transitions to hitter.

GAME 1

Setup
3v3

Goals
- Set up to attack.
- Earn 1 point by attempting to pass-set-attack.

Conditions
- Make court narrow and short.
- Initiate game from a playable toss (free ball).
- Alternate free ball after each rally.
- Rotate serving team (see figure 8.2).
- Use up to three hits.

Note
Easy toss is two-handed soccer throw-in (rainbow toss).

Questions
Q: *Where should you be while waiting for the ball?*
A: In base position, ready to move.

Q: *How do you get ready to attack (spike or hit) the ball?*
A: Move to where the set is going and transition.

PRACTICE TASK

Setup
Passer practices transitioning to attack, use triad

Goals
- Passer–hitter executes 3 to 5 trials.
- Passer–hitter passes and then transitions to attack (hit).

Conditions
- Organize on courts A and B (two teams of three players).
- Tosser tosses a free ball to the passer–hitter.
- Passer uses forearm pass to get the ball to the setter.
- Setter catches the ball and tosses a rainbow set (1 yard/meter high and 1 yard/meter off the net).
- As setter catches, passer–hitter transitions to hitter for attack.
- After hitter attacks the ball, he returns to the passing line (see figure 8.8).

Note
For safety during hitting practice, have two teams work together on the same side of the court and have all teams hit one way.

Cues
- Hitting
  - Feet to the ball.
  - Jump.
  - Throw hands high.
  - Swing fast.
- Transitioning
  - Establish new position.

GAME 2

Setup
3v3

Goals
- Set up to attack.
- Earn 1 point for making two hits on a side and 2 points for executing a pass-set-hit.

Lesson 11 Level II

Tactical Problem
Winning the point

Lesson Focus
Approaching for attack (spike approach)

Objective
Hitter successfully transitions off the net and approaches.

GAME 1

Setup
3v3

Goals
- Select and execute an attack (pass-set-hit).
- Earn 1 point by attempting to attack (down ball, hit or spike).

Conditions
- Make court narrow and short.
- Initiate game from a playable toss (free ball).
- Alternate free ball after each rally.
- Rotate serving team.
- Use up to three hits.

Notes
- Easy toss is two-handed soccer throw-in (rainbow toss).
- You can change the size of the court to meet students' needs.
- Arrange players in positions of passer, setter, and hitter as shown in figure 8.11.

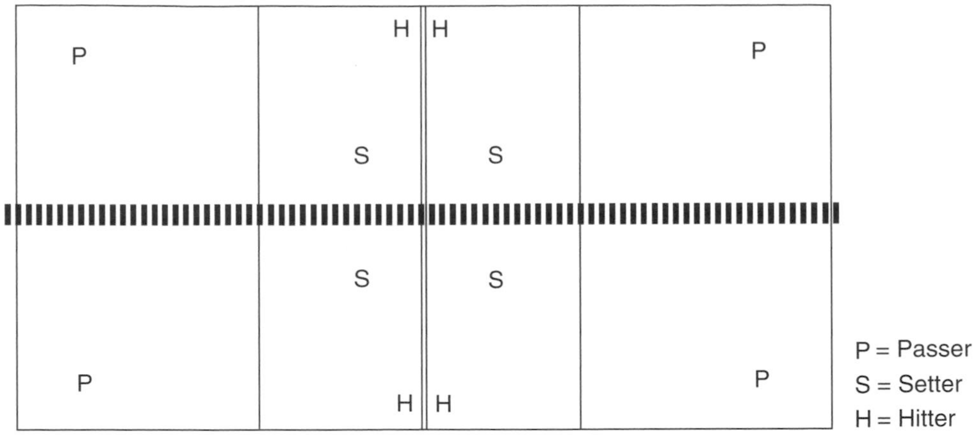

P = Passer
S = Setter
H = Hitter

FIGURE 8.11

Questions

Q: Where is the front hitter's base position?
A: Facing the net to see how play develops on the opponent's side and to block a bad pass.

Q: What should the hitter do when the ball crosses the net?
A: Transition and move off the net.

Q: How does the hitter approach to attack?
A: Run to the ball and approach.

PRACTICE TASK

Practice approaching to attack

Goal
Hitter performs 3 of 5 trials and then rotates.

Conditions
- Two teams practice together (teams A and B).
- Setter slaps the ball (to prompt the hitter to move back from the net) and tosses a high, outside set after the hitter has transitioned off the net.
- Hitter approaches to attack (hit or spike) the ball (see figure 8.12).

Extensions
- Teams continue hitting practice by switching sides in order to experience hitting from both the left and right front positions.
- Teams hit from behind the 10-yard/meter line, with setter tossing a high set at the 10-foot line to allow hitters to swing fast and through without hitting the net.

Cues
- Feet to the ball.
- Jump.
- Throw hands high.
- Swing fast.
- Heel of open hand strikes ball.
- Wrist snap.

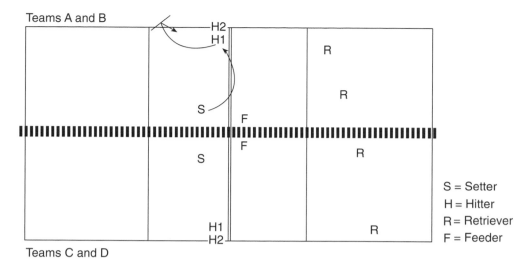

Teams A and B

Teams C and D

S = Setter
H = Hitter
R = Retriever
F = Feeder

FIGURE 8.12

GAME 2

Setup
3v3

Goals
- Select and execute an attack (pass-set-hit).
- Earn 1 point when your team sets up and attacks (down ball, hit or spike).

Lesson 12

Tactical Problem
Winning the point

Lesson Focus
Setting to attack

Objectives
- Execute hittable set and successful transition off the approach to attack (hit or spike).
- Set a hittable ball that is high and 0.5 to 1 yard/meter off the net (rainbow set).

GAME 1

Setup
3v3

Goals
- Use forearm pass as first contact.
- Hitter transitions off the net.
- Earn 1 point by attempting to attack (hit or spike).

Conditions

- Make court narrow and short.
- Initiate game from a playable toss (free ball).
- Alternate free ball after each rally.
- Rotate serving team.
- Use up to three hits.

Note

Easy toss is two-handed soccer throw-in (rainbow toss).

Questions

Q: Where should the setter set the ball?
A: He should set it 0.5 to 1 yard/meter off the net.

Q: How should the hitter get ready to hit?
A: Transition off the net.

Q: When should the hitter approach?
A: When the ball is at its apex (highest point).

PRACTICE TASK

Setup

Practice setting and hitting

Goal

Execute pass and hit successfully for three trials before rotating.

Conditions

- Use two teams and three balls.
- Tosser slaps ball (prompts) so that the setter and hitter make off-the-ball movements (open up, transition).
- Tosser tosses ball to setter, using a good forearm pass.
- Setter sets (forearm or overhead pass) and hitter hits a down ball or spikes (see figure 8.13).

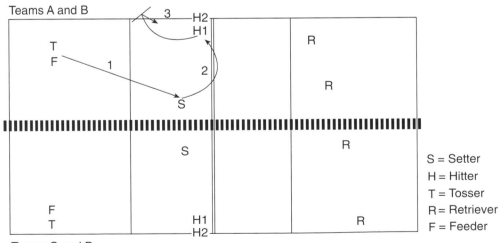

S = Setter
H = Hitter
T = Tosser
R = Retriever
F = Feeder

FIGURE 8.13

GAME 2

Setup
3v3

Goal
Earn 1 point for two hits and 2 points for a successful attack.

Lesson 13 ⊙

Tactical Problem
Defending space on your court

Lesson Focus
Defending against a free ball, using base positions, and opening up

Objective
Successfully defend space on your court.

GAME 1

Setup
3v3

Goals
- Start in base positions.
- Use forearm pass as first contact.
- Setter opens up.
- Two hits (contacts) earn a point.

Conditions
- Make court narrow and short.
- Initiate game from a playable toss (free ball).
- Alternate free ball after each rally.
- Rotate serving team.
- Use up to three hits on a side.
- Setter is in a ready position.

Note
Easy toss is two-handed soccer throw-in (rainbow toss).

Questions

Q: *What do you do when a free ball comes over the net?*
A: Move to play the ball in your area.

Q: *What does the setter do?*
A: Opens up.

Q: *What does the hitter do?*
A: Transitions off the net.

Q: *What does the passer do?*
A: Splits the court, balances the court, and plays in the middle of the court.

PRACTICE TASK

Setup

Practice defending against a free ball

Goal

The team performs three trials successfully, moving correctly as a team, and then rotates positions.

Conditions

- Use two teams and three balls.
- Passer for team A is tosser for team B.
- Tosser slaps ball and prompts to be ready.
- Setter, hitter, and passer call "free" and make appropriate off-the-ball movements.
- Setter opens up and calls "here."
- Hitter transitions off the net.
- Passer balances the court by playing in the middle back.
- Tosser tosses the ball (a free ball).
- Passer, setter, and hitter attempt a pass-set-hit (see figure 8.14).

GAME 2

Setup

3v3

Goals

- Defend space in your court against a free ball.
- Earn 1 point for calling "free."

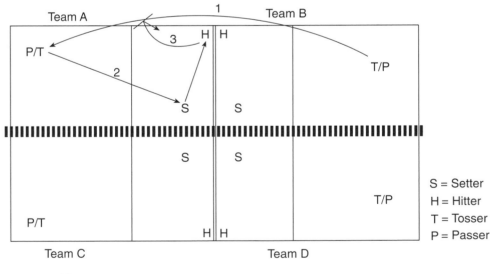

FIGURE 8.14

Level III

It is time to introduce the serve (underhand or no-ace overhead). Students should begin to understand the difference between receiving a free ball and receiving a serve. Introduce them to a basic serve-receive formation. You may also introduce the dig, which is a type of forearm pass for receiving balls that are attacked (hit or spiked). At level III you should challenge your students with more complicated gamelike practices (skill and movement combinations) to increase their action profile. Feel free to play 3v3 or move to 4v4 as larger teams become necessary for meeting the developmental needs of your students. Remind your students that if they are not doing something (playing the ball, moving to base, transitioning, or adjusting), they are doing something wrong. Volleyball is a moving game!

A solid serve is necessary to keep the game active.

Lesson 14 Level III

Tactical Problem
Attacking as a team

Lesson Focus
Using two players to receive a serve

Objectives
Team serve-receive, forearm pass, and support.

GAME 1

Setup
3v3

Goal
Earn 1 point by making two hits (contacts) on a side.

Conditions
- Use narrow court.
- Initiate game from a playable toss (free ball).
- Alternate free balls and rotate before your team gives each free ball.
- Use up to three hits on a side.
- Setter is in a ready position.

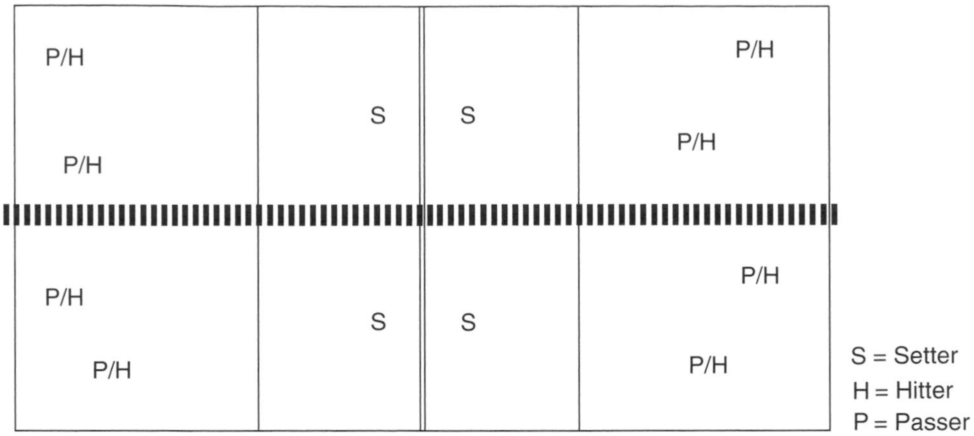

P/H

S   S

P/H

P/H   P/H

P/H

S   S

P/H

P/H   P/H

S = Setter
H = Hitter
P = Passer

FIGURE 8.15

Note

Arrange players in positions of passer, setter, and hitter as shown in figure 8.15.

Questions

> Q: *What do players do to serve-receive as a team?*
> A: Organize, play a position, and set up in a formation.

> Q: *How do you serve-receive as a team?*
> A: Call the ball, open up, and support.

PRACTICE TASK

Setup

Two players practice the serve-receive.

Goal

Perform 3 of 5 trials successfully and rotate.

Conditions

- Use two teams and three balls.
- Tosser slaps the ball (prompts) and tosses a free ball or makes an easy underhand or overhead serve for passers 1 and 2 to receive.
- Setter is a target setter and catches the ball (see figure 8.16).

Cues

- On-the-ball skills
  - Block the ball with your forearms.
- Off-the-ball movements
  - Call the ball using "mine," "good," or "out."
  - Open up.
  - Support.

Note

If you can, use a full court.

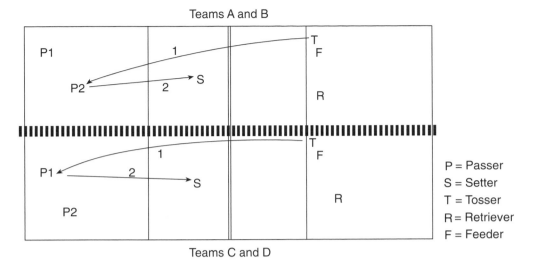

Teams A and B

P1   1

P2   2   S

T
F

R

P1   1

P2   2   S

T
F

R

P = Passer
S = Setter
T = Tosser
R = Retriever
F = Feeder

Teams C and D

FIGURE 8.16

GAME 2

Setup
3v3

Goals
- Use forearm pass as first contact.
- Nonpasser opens up or supports.
- Earn 1 point when support player calls "good" or "out" and passer calls "mine."

Lesson 15   Level III

Tactical Problem
Winning the point

Lesson Focus
Starting the point on the attack

Objective
Overhead serve.

GAME 1

Setup
3v3

Goal
Start your game with either an underhand or overhead serve.

Conditions
- Use narrow court.
- Initiate game from a no-ace serve.
- Alternate serves and rotate on serve (side-out).
- Use up to three hits on a side.
- Setter is in a ready position.

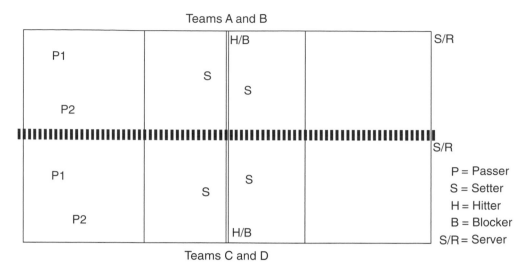

Teams A and B

Teams C and D

P = Passer
S = Setter
H = Hitter
B = Blocker
S/R = Server

FIGURE 8.17

Note

Arrange players in positions of passer, setter, and hitter as shown in figure 8.17.

Questions

Q: What serve gives you the most options?
A: The overhead serve.

Q: How do you make an overhead serve?
A: Perform a throwing action, tee up the ball, lift the ball, make firm contact, and finish to the top of the net.

PRACTICE TASK 1

Setup

Practice overhead serve.

Goal

Gradually move back to service line.

Condition

Students work in pairs, starting at the spike line and gradually moving back to the service line.

Cues

• Tee up the ball.
• Lift the ball.
• Make firm contact.
• Finish toward the top of the net.

PRACTICE TASK 2

Setup

Practice overhead serve.

Goals
- Perform three trials successfully before rotating—overhead serve to serve receive.
- Server: overhead serve over the net into back court.
- Passer: a playable ball, one that is high and in the middle of the court, so another player can hit the ball.

Conditions
- Tosser prompts by hitting the side of the ball and then executes a modified overhead serve from the spiking line.
- Passer receives the serve and passes it to the target (setter).
- Setter catches the ball and bounces it back to the tosser (see figure 8.16).
- Server gradually moves back to the service line.

Cues
- Overhead serve
  - Tee up the ball.
  - Lift the ball.
  - Make firm contact.
  - Finish to the top of the net.
- Receiving the serve
  - Use medium body posture.
  - Block the ball.
  - Point belly button to target.

GAME 2

Setup
3v3

Goal
Start game with an overhead serve.

Lesson 16

Tactical Problem
Winning the point

Lesson Focus
Starting the point on the attack

Objective
Execute overhead serve and transition into the court.

GAME 1

Setup
3v3

Goal
Force passers to move for serve receive.

Conditions

- Use a narrow court.
- Initiate game from a playable no-ace serve.
- Alternate serves and rotate on the serve (side-out).
- Use up to three hits on a side.
- Setter is in a ready position.

Note

Arrange players in positions of passer, setter, and hitter as shown in figure 8.17.

Questions

Q: *To where do you serve to get the passers to move?*
A: To open spaces.

Q: *How do you do that?*
A: Position feet and follow through.

PRACTICE TASK

Setup

Practice serving and transitioning to the court

Goal

Execute 3 of 5 trials successfully and rotate.

Conditions

- Use two teams and three balls.
- Server serves and transitions into the court to receive a free ball from the tosser (i.e., server now becomes a passer).
- Passer passes to the setter.
- Setter catches the ball and the next server begins her turn (see figure 8.18).

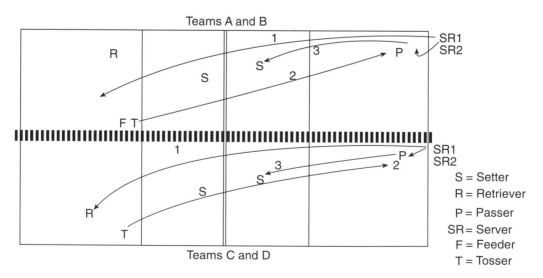

FIGURE 8.18

Cues

- Tee up the ball.
- Lift the ball.
- Make firm contact.
- Finish to the top of the net.

Note

If you can, use a full court.

GAME 2

Repeat game 1.

Lesson 17   Level III

Tactical Problem

Setting up to attack and winning the point

Lesson Focus

Combining skills and movements

Objective

Perform pass-set-hit combinations.

GAME 1

Setup

3v3

Goals

- Serve receive with two players.
- Earn 1 point with a pass, set, and attempted hit.

Conditions

- Use narrow court.
- Initiate game from a no-ace serve.
- Alternate serves and rotate on serve (side-out).
- Use up to three hits on a side.

Questions

Q: *What does a team need to do to win a point when receiving a serve?*
A: Make a forearm pass, set, transition, open up, communicate, and support.

Q: *What would make a team win more points?*
A: Being consistent, communicating, and working as a team.

PRACTICE TASK 1

Setup

Practice pass-set-hit

Goal

Pass and hit for 3 of 5 trials successfully before rotating.

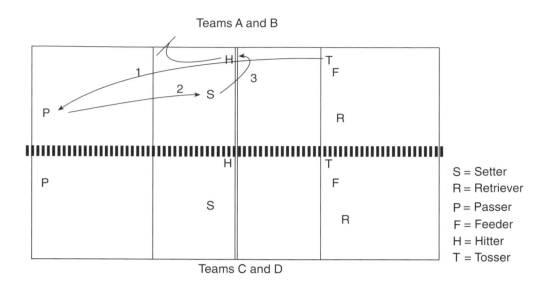

Teams A and B

Teams C and D

S = Setter
R = Retriever
P = Passer
F = Feeder
H = Hitter
T = Tosser

FIGURE 8.19

Conditions
- Use two teams and three balls.
- Tosser slaps the ball (prompts) so the setter and hitter make off-the-ball movements (open up, transition).
- Tosser tosses the ball to the passer, who uses a forearm pass to get the ball to the setter.
- Setter sets (forearm or overhead pass) and hitter hits or spikes (see figure 8.19).

Note
Tosser can also use a modified overhead serve.

PRACTICE TASK 2

Setup
Practice serving and a receive-set-hit combination.

Goal
Pass and hit successfully for 3 of 5 trials before rotating.

Conditions
- Use two teams and three balls.
- Server slaps ball (prompts) so setter and hitter make off-the-ball movements (open up, transition).
- Server tosses ball to passer, who uses forearm pass to get the ball to the setter.
- Setter sets (forearm or overhead pass) and hitter hits or spikes (see figure 8.20).

Note
Server can also use any easy underhand or overhead serve.

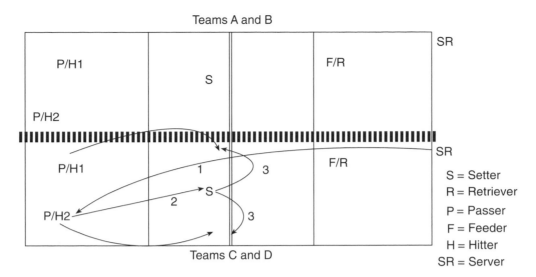

Teams A and B

SR

P/H1   S   F/R

P/H2

P/H1   1   3   F/R   SR

S

2

P/H2   3

Teams C and D

S = Setter
R = Retriever
P = Passer
F = Feeder
H = Hitter
SR = Server

FIGURE 8.20

GAME 2

Repeat game 1.

Lesson 18   Level III

Tactical Problem
Defending against an attack

Lesson Focus
Digging

Objective
Contain the dig on your court.

GAME 1

Setup
3v3

Goals
- Win a point with a downball or spike if possible.
- Be aware of the need to contain the dig on your side of the court.

Conditions
- Use a narrow court.
- Initiate game from a no-ace serve.
- Rotate on the serve (side-out).
- Use up to three hits on a side.

Note
Arrange players in positions of passer, setter, and hitter as shown in figure 8.21.

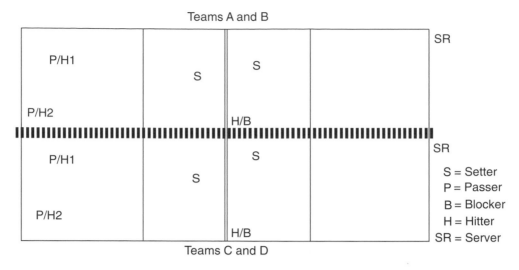

Teams A and B

SR

P/H1

S

S

P/H2

H/B

SR

P/H1

S

S

P/H2

H/B

Teams C and D

S = Setter
P = Passer
B = Blocker
H = Hitter
SR = Server

FIGURE 8.21

Questions

Q: What is your role as a player in the back row?
A: To dig the ball, keep the ball in play, and save the ball.

Q: How can you dig a spike ball and contain it on your side of the court?
A: Be low and dig to self.

Q: Why should you contain the ball on your side of the court?
A: To counterattack and to set and hit.

PRACTICE TASK

Setup
Practice digging triad

Goal
Perform 3 of 5 trials successfully and rotate.

Conditions
- Use one team and three balls.
- Tosser slaps the ball (prompts) so the digger adjusts to low posture.
- Tosser tosses or hits a down ball (mock spike) to the digger across the court.
- Digger digs ball to self (see figure 8.22).

Note
This task may not seem gamelike, but if players focus on digging to self, it will help them learn to contain the ball on their side of the court. If players can dig high to self, then the next progression is to dig to the center of the court.

Cues
- Low posture.
- J-stroke.
- Dig to the center of the court.

Note
Repeat practice, going to digger one down the line.

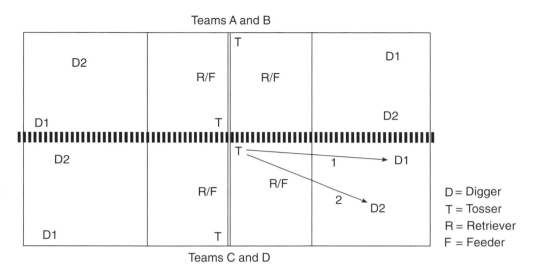

Teams A and B

Teams C and D

D = Digger
T = Tosser
R = Retriever
F = Feeder

FIGURE 8.22

GAME 2

Setup
3v3

Conditions
- Rally score.
- Regular serve.

Note
Rally score is when all side-outs earn an extra point (think of it as fast-forwarding the game).

Lesson 19   Level III

Tactical Problem
Defending against an attack

Lesson Focus
Containing a dig on your court

Objective
Dig a spiked ball.

GAME 1

Setup
3v3

Goals
- Win a point with a hit or spike when possible.
- Be aware of the need to contain the dig on your side of the court.

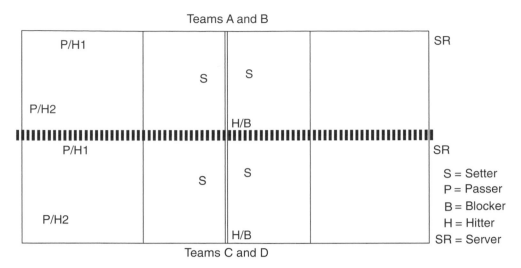

Teams A and B

Teams C and D

S = Setter
P = Passer
B = Blocker
H = Hitter
SR = Server

FIGURE 8.23

Conditions

- Use a narrow court.
- Initiate game from a no-ace serve.
- Rotate on serve (side-out).
- Use up to three hits on a side.

Note

Arrange players in positions of passer, setter, and hitter as shown in figure 8.23.

Questions

Q: *How do you get ready to dig?*
A: Watch the hitter and dig low before the hitter spikes.

Q: *How do you contain a dig on your side of the court?*
A: Be low and dig to the center of the court.

PRACTICE TASK

Setup

Dig a spike

Goal

Dig for 3 of 5 trials successfully and rotate.

Conditions

- Use two teams and three balls.
- Setter slaps ball (prompts) so hitter transitions off the net to hit.
- Setter tosses a high, outside set.
- Hitter hits or spikes ball.
- Digger adjusts to low posture.
- Digger digs to self (see figure 8.24).

GAME 2

Setup

3v3

Condition

Rally score.

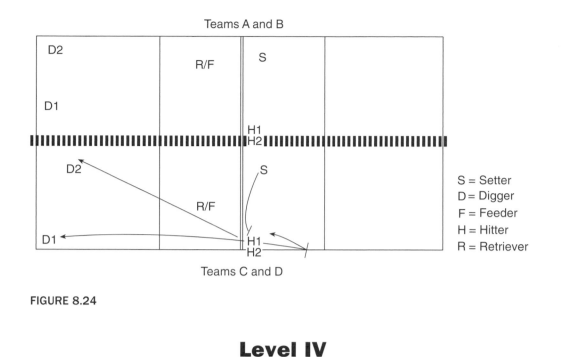

Teams A and B

S = Setter
D = Digger
F = Feeder
H = Hitter
R = Retriever

Teams C and D

FIGURE 8.24

Level IV

Tactical complexity in level IV addresses the problem of attacking as a team by increasing the number of players from 4 or 6 and by expanding the court. You should feel comfortable to play 4v4 or 6v6 if doing so meets the developmental needs of your students. Revisit the basic

Once students are ready, begin allowing more players.

problems of setting up for attack and winning the point. You may also introduce an offensive serve-receive pattern (i.e., the W). Practicing a serve-receive pattern provides students with the opportunity to problem solve opening up, transitioning, providing support, and using base positions in the advanced game form. This level allows you to introduce a specialized setter position that increases the attack possibilities to include left, right, and middle attack. We encourage you to again initiate games from a free ball to maximize game play before gradually returning to a serve.

Lesson 20 Level IV

Tactical Problem
Attacking as a team

Lesson Focus
Serve-receive as a team

Objective
Serve-receive and transition to attacks.

GAME 1

Setup
6v6

Goal
Set up to attack.

Conditions
- Full court.
- Regulation rules.
- Initiate game from a free ball from the server position.
- Rally score.

Questions

Q: *What is the best way to organize your team to receive the serve?*
A: Use the W serve-receive formation, playing positions.

Q: *How does using a serve-receive formation help your team?*
A: It helps with communication and all players know their roles.

PRACTICE TASK

Setup
Serve-receive formation using a free ball

Goal
Base player returns to a home or recovery position when the ball passes over the net.

Conditions
- Use two teams and three balls.
- Server first serves an easy ball to team A and team A sets up to attack and transitions to base (see figure 8.25).
- Server then tosses a free ball and team A sets up to attack (see figure 8.26).
- Each team has three trials at three serve-receive positions (rotations).

Team A
Team B
P/H
P
P
S
P
P/H
B
B
B
SR
F
R
B = Blocker
S = Setter
R = Retriever
P = Passer
F = Feeder
H = Hitter
SR = Server

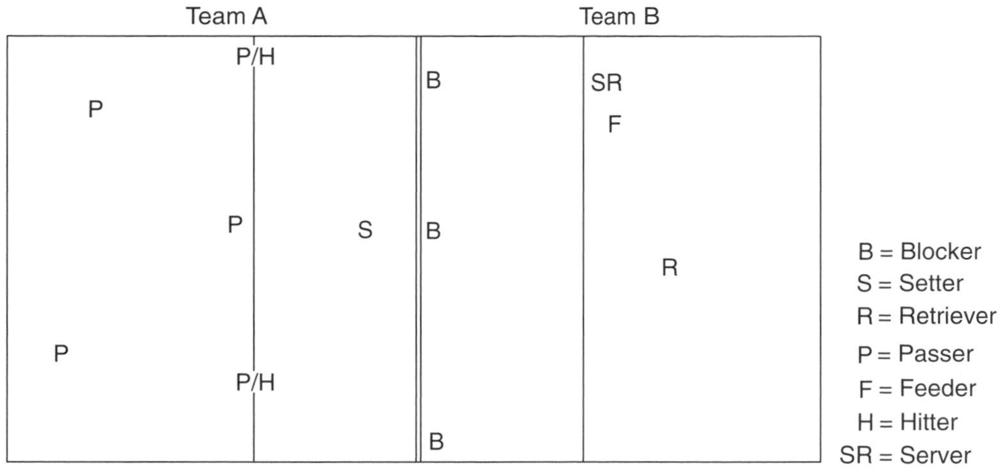

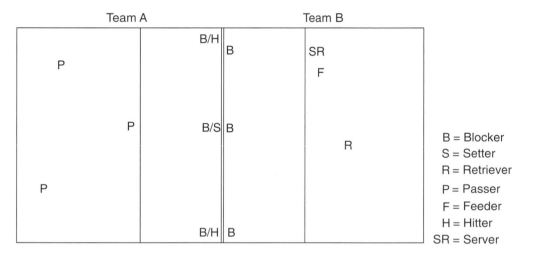

FIGURE 8.25

Team A
Team B
P
P
P
B/H
B/S
B/H
B
B
B
SR
F
R
B = Blocker
S = Setter
R = Retriever
P = Passer
F = Feeder
H = Hitter
SR = Server

FIGURE 8.26

GAME 2

Setup
6v6

Condition
Regulation game.

Lesson 21 — Level IV

Tactical Problem
Winning the point

Lesson Focus
Ball placement when spiking (e.g., crosscourt and down the line)

Objective
Use attack variations.

GAME 1

Setup
6v6

Goal
Win the point by attack.

Conditions
- Regulation court (if possible).
- Regulation rules.
- Initiate game from a free ball from the server position.
- Rally score.

Note
Teams can implement the no-ace serving rule as a variation.

Questions

Q: What do you want to do when you attack (spike) the ball to win a point?
A: Kill the ball, spiking it so that players cannot return it.

Q: What are different ways to attack?
A: Tip, down ball, spike (crosscourt, down the line, roll shot).

PRACTICE TASK

Setup
Vary attack

Goal
Hitters execute 3 of 5 trials successfully.

Conditions
- Use two teams and 3 or 4 balls.
- Tosser tosses a good pass to setter 1, then tosses a pass to setter 2.
- Setter 1 sets a high outside ball for the hitter to spike down the line or crosscourt, or to tip (see figure 8.27).

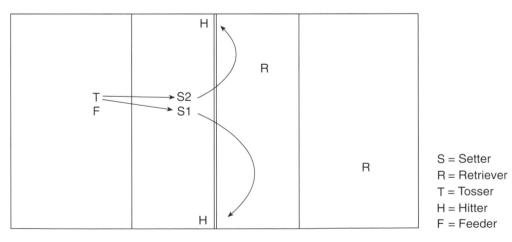

S = Setter
R = Retriever
T = Tosser
H = Hitter
F = Feeder

FIGURE 8.27

GAME 2

Setup
6v6

Condition
No-ace serve or regulation serve.

Lesson 22 Level IV

Tactical Problem
Defending against an attack

Lesson Focus
Solo block

Objective
Attempt to front the hitter and block.

GAME 1

Setup
4v4

Goal
Defend against a spike.

Conditions
 • Use a narrow court, slightly lower net, and regulation rules.
 • Initiate game from a free ball from the server position.
 • Rally score.

Questions

Q: *What is the first-line defense against an attack?*
A: Blocking.

Q: *How do you block?*
A: Put your arms up before the hit or spike.

PRACTICE TASK

Setup
Solo block against a spike

Goal
Blocker executes 3 of 5 trials and then rotates.

Conditions
 • Use two teams and 3 or 4 balls.
 • Setter tosses high, outside sets for hitter to hit or spike.
 • Blocker blocks (see figure 8.28).

Cues
 • Hold hands high.
 • Front the hitter.
 • Jump when hitter swings arm.
 • Press to center court.

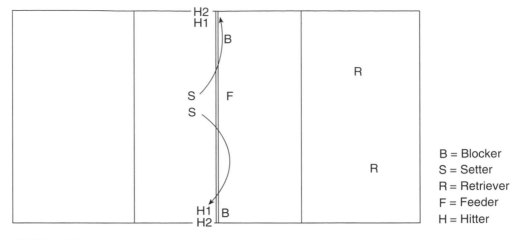

FIGURE 8.28

B = Blocker
S = Setter
R = Retriever
F = Feeder
H = Hitter

GAME 2

Setup
Two games of 4v4

Conditions
- No-ace serve.
- Rally score or regulation game.

Lesson 23 Level IV

Tactical Problem
Attacking as a team

Lesson Focus
Serve receive as a team

Objective
Serve receive and transition to attack.

GAME 1

Setup
6v6

Goal
Serve receive and set up to attack.

Conditions
- Full court.
- Regulation rules.
- No-ace serve.
- Rally score.

Question
Q: What does your team need to do to set up for an attack?
A: Serve-receive, set, hit, support teammates, and communicate.

PRACTICE TASK

Setup
Free ball wash

Goal
Earn two consecutive points.

Conditions
- Use two teams and 3 or 4 balls.
- Initiate game from a free ball.
- A wash is an attempt to earn two consecutive points. For example, team A starts by receiving a free ball. Team A wins the rally and earns the right to receive the next free ball. Team B now has the opportunity to wash out, or nullify, team A's second point. If team A wins the second point it wins the game, but if team B washes team A's second point the game begins again. If team A does not win the first point, then the game starts over with team B receiving the first free ball.

Note
Implement a game manager to toss free balls from the sideline near the net standard. As the teacher, you can manage and coach one game while the other court manages itself. Remember to switch and coach the other court after 5-7 minutes.

GAME 2

Setup
6v6

Goal
Serve-receive and set up to attack.

Conditions
- Full court.
- Regulation rules.
- No-ace serve.
- Rally score.

Level V

The problem of team defense becomes the primary focus at level V, which introduces defensive systems. You should feel free to play 4v4 or 6v6 if doing so meets the developmental needs of your students. If the students are ready, you can introduce the double block and complete the tactical levels by teaching attack coverage (players supporting their hitter if he is blocked). An additional challenge for your students is to introduce different plays for setting up to attack.

The double block can help stop a spiked ball before it reaches the floor.

Lesson 24 Level V

Tactical Problem
Setting up to attack

Lesson Focus
Play sets

Objective
Setter comes from the back row to work on play sets.

GAME 1

Setup
6v6

Goal
Set up to attack.

Conditions
- Full court.
- Regulation rules.
- Initiate game from a free ball or no-ace serve.
- Free ball toss from server position, setter plays server position.
- Rotate around setter.
- Rally score.

Questions

Q: What can teams do to vary their tactics in setting up attacks?
A: Change sets.

Q: How do you change sets?
A: Setter comes from the back row, or you can vary the set height.

PRACTICE TASK

Setup
Play sets

Goal
Execute 3 of 5 setter trials successfully and then rotate.

Conditions
- Use two teams and 3 or 4 balls.
- Tosser slaps ball (prompts) for hitters to transition off the net and for setter 1 to transition to the net.
- Tosser tosses good pass to the setter target spot.
- Setter calls and sets four, then two, and then red.
  - Four ball is a high, outside set (for left front hitter).
  - Two ball is 0.5 yard/meter high and 0.5 yard/meter out from the setter (middle hitter).
  - Red is a high ball to the back (for right front hitter).
- Hitter hits.
- Repeat for setter 2 (see figure 8.29).
- Play out each set.

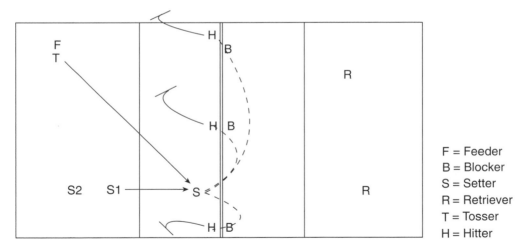

FIGURE 8.29

F = Feeder
B = Blocker
S = Setter
R = Retriever
T = Tosser
H = Hitter

GAME 2

Setup
6v6

Conditions
- No-ace serve.
- Rally score or regulation game.

Tactical Problem
Attacking as a team

Lesson Focus
Attack coverage

Objective
Play sets and attack coverage.

GAME 1

Setup
6v6

Goal
Earn 1 point with set and hit or with spike two and red.

Conditions
- Full court.
- Regulation rules.
- Initiate game from a free ball or no-ace serve.
- Free ball toss from server position, setter plays server position.
- Rotate around setter.
- Rally score.

Question

Q: *What should teams do to protect their hitter in case she gets blocked?*
A: Cover the hitter.

PRACTICE TASK

Setup
Free ball transition and attack coverage

Goal
Perform 3 of 5 trials successfully and then rotate.

Conditions
- Use two teams and 3 or 4 balls.
- Tosser slaps ball for team to call "free" and for hitter to transition off the net and setter to transition to the net.
- Passer passes free ball to target spot for setter.
- Setter calls and sets four, two, red.
- Hitter hits and team covers the hitter.

Cue
Form a funnel around the hitter.

Extension One
Base positions (see figure 8.30).

Note
Numbers represent positions in rotation.

Extension Two
Transition to attack (see figure 8.31).

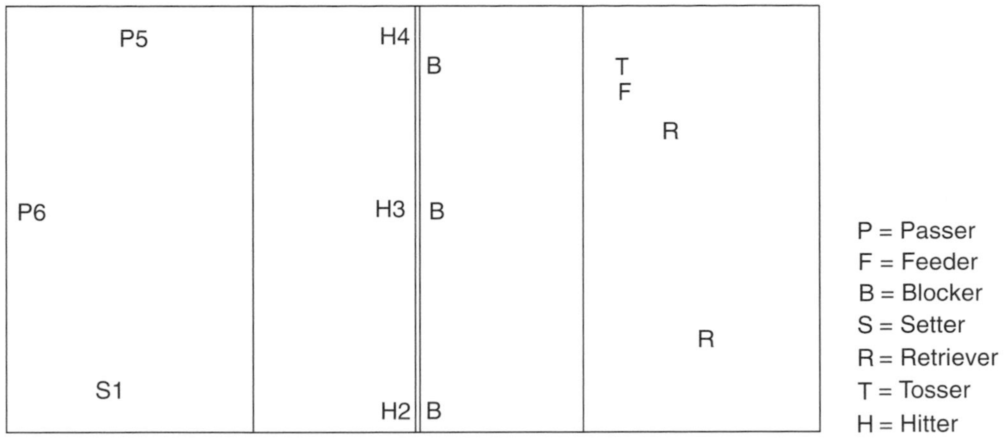

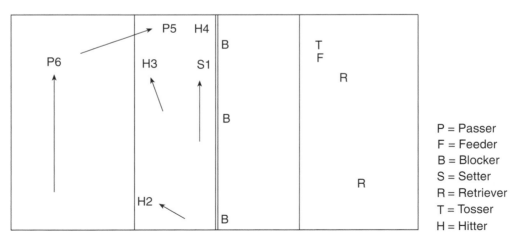

P5
H4
B
T
F
R
P6
H3
B
R
S1
H2
B
P = Passer
F = Feeder
B = Blocker
S = Setter
R = Retriever
T = Tosser
H = Hitter

FIGURE 8.30

H4
P5
B
T
F
R
B
H3
P6
S1
R
H2
B
P = Passer
F = Feeder
B = Blocker
S = Setter
R = Retriever
T = Tosser
H = Hitter

FIGURE 8.31

P5
H4
B
T
F
P6
H3
S1
R
B
R
H2
B
P = Passer
F = Feeder
B = Blocker
S = Setter
R = Retriever
T = Tosser
H = Hitter

FIGURE 8.32

Extension Three
Attack coverage if hitter four-hit or spiked (see figure 8.32).

GAME 2

Repeat game 1.

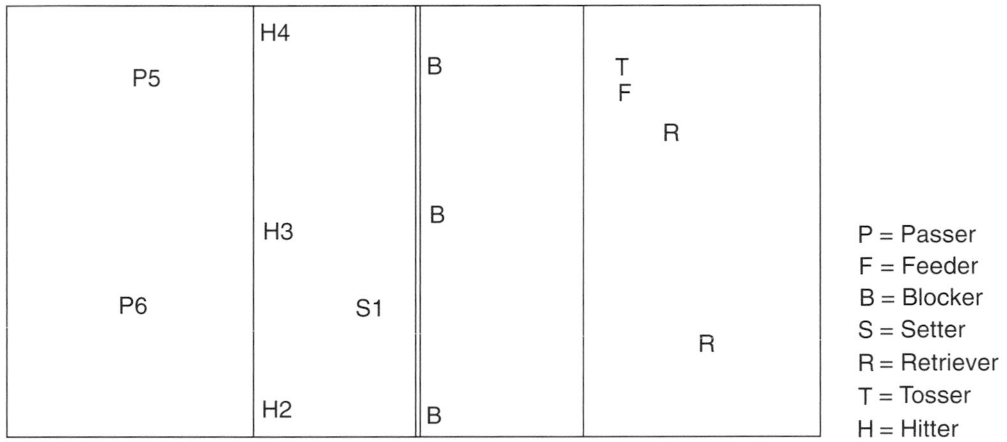

Tactical Problem
Defending as a team against an attack

Lesson Focus
Floor defense

Objective
Use floor defense against an attack.

GAME 1

Setup
6v6

Goals
  · Defend against the attack.
  · Earn 1 point with a dig-set-hit or a block.

Conditions
  · Use full court.
  · Initiate game from a free ball or no-ace serve.
  · Free ball toss from server position.

Question

  Q: *What should teams do to defend against an attack?*
  A: Organize a defense and play positions.

PRACTICE TASK

Setup
Attack defense

Goal
Perform 3 of 5 trials successfully and then rotate.

Conditions
  · Use two teams and 3 or 4 balls.
  · Tosser slaps ball (prompts) for hitter to transition off the net and setter to open up to set.
  · Tosser tosses a good pass to the setter.
  · Setter calls and sets four, two, red.
  · Hitter hits.
  · Defense plays the ball out (pass, dig-set-hit) (see figure 8.33).

Cues
  · Players
    – Start in base, read the play, adjust, make the play.
    – Use floor positions.
    – Diggers 1 and 5 cover crosscourt and line while digger 6 patrols the tip and roll shot.
    – Blockers 2 and 4 block when on the ball and cover the angle shot when off the ball.
    – Setter or blocker 3 solo or double blocks and transitions to set.

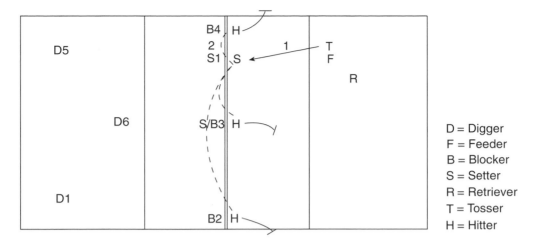

FIGURE 8.33

D = Digger
F = Feeder
B = Blocker
S = Setter
R = Retriever
T = Tosser
H = Hitter

GAME 2

Setup
6v6

Goals
· Defend against the attack.
· Earn 1 point with a dig-set-hit or a block.

Conditions
· Use full court.
· Initiate game from a free ball or no-ace serve.
· Free ball toss from server position.

Lesson 27

Tactical Problem
Attacking and defending as a team

Lesson Focus
Team tactics and communication

Objective
Successfully implement team concepts.

GAME 1

Setup
6v6

Goal
Learn team tactics.

Conditions
· Full court.
· Regulation rules.
· No-ace serve.
· Rally score.

Question

Q: *What are the goals of the game?*
A: Receiving the serve, setting up to attack, winning the point, and so on.

PRACTICE TASK

Setup
Free ball wash (refer to level IV, lesson 23 [page 252] for a description)

Goal
Earn 2 points in a row.

Condition
- Use two teams and 3 or 4 balls.
- Initiate game from a free ball.

Note
Implement a game manager to toss free balls from the sideline near the net standard. You can manage and coach one game while the other court manages itself and switch after 5 to 7 minutes.

GAME 2

Setup
6v6

Goal
Serve receive and set up to attack.

Conditions
- Full court.
- Regulation rules.
- No-ace serve.
- Rally score.

Game Extensions
An additional game to introduce to your students is *continuous volleyball* or *king* or *queen of the court.* The game uses 1-point games with either quick scoring (every point scores) or regulation volleyball scoring. You can use one or more courts, labeling one side of the court winners and the other side challengers. If a team wins, they move or stay on the winner's court. If a team loses, they try again by joining the challengers' line. The game can focus on various components of the real game:

- You can begin it from a serve, modified or no-ace serve, free ball, down ball, or spiked ball.
- You can teach other critical elements of game play such as pursuing (for a ball out of control), transitioning off the net, receiving the serve, or floor positioning for defense.
- You can help students hone skills by playing a form of triples known as *cheap shot* that moves the end line to the 10-foot (3-meter) line.
- You can regulate the offense in another modification of triples by creating rules such as only the back row can attack, the attack must go beyond the 10-foot (3-meter) line, the attack must be from the middle or back row, or any combination of these rules. This modification enables the teams to focus on specific offensive strategies.

Summary

The levels of tactical complexity and accompanying lessons in this chapter are the building blocks for your volleyball unit. We offer you lessons specifically designed to solve problems at different levels of tactical complexity, *not* units organized from the first to last lesson. For example, we encourage you to include tournament play in your units. The following are suggestions for keeping score during tournament play:

- Use goals from an earlier game.
- Increase the number of players from 3 to 4 to 6. The number of players changes the pace and momentum of the game.
- Play rally score games. Rally scores make games move faster and hold students accountable for the serve.
- Use regulation games but initiate games from a free ball or no-ace serve.
- Either score games (i.e., play to 5, 11, 15 points) or time games (i.e., play for 5, 7, 10 minutes).

We encourage you to make these materials meet the contextual needs of you, your students, your facilities, and your equipment. We view 3v3 as the basic game that forms your students' abilities to solve other aspects of volleyball. While this chapter is comprehensive, it is not exhaustive, and there are an endless number of variations and extensions for these lessons. We encourage you to design your units, mixing levels and creating your own lessons. For example, you might organize a unit primarily around level IV but include parts or variations of earlier lessons for review.

Implement the levels as a way of sequencing your games curriculum. Please do not get trapped into teaching the same lessons to each grade level or you will perpetuate the existing problem in games teaching (introducing the same skills over and over). Remember, teach the game through game!

Badminton

adminton is a game for students of all abilities. You can play it at any level and it is well-suited to teaching groups with varying abilities. Unfortunately, some students believe that badminton is a technically difficult game they cannot play. This was the case for a number of fifth graders (arguably too young to begin badminton anyway) in a class just beginning a badminton unit.

The first lesson began with a lecture on the parts of the racket, which was not stimulating and not information that these students needed or wanted to know. An introduction to the underhand serve followed because it is a necessary skill for beginning a point. Many students had difficulty performing the underhand serve, either mis-hitting the shot or missing the shuttle completely. The teacher planned to continue instruction in the underhand serve until the students reached satisfactory competence, at which point he moved to the next skill. The badminton unit ended early after two days of frustration for both teacher and students, many of whom had come to believe that they lacked the necessary skills to play the game.

The tactical approach we suggest in this chapter avoids scenarios such as this one. Students are immediately placed in modified, or conditioned, game situations. They begin a point in whichever way they find successful—even by placing the shuttle on the racket and throwing it over the net or by tossing it with the hand. The singles game is the primary focus of instruction, because it is tactically simpler than the doubles game and it ensures maximum participation. As in other chapters, the tactical complexity of the game increases as the students progress. New skills are taught after students see the necessity of having these skills for solving tactical problems in the game. Tournament play can take place at any level, but the type of game used in a tournament should not exceed the tactical complexity that students have experienced. For example, tournament play at level I should focus on the half-court singles game. We begin with alternate serving at level I. You can introduce the correct scoring and serving (i.e., score on your own service) later, preferably when students can return the shuttle well enough for rallies to take place.

Students will ideally work in pairs during badminton instruction. Doing so enables them to play singles games and practice the related tactics and skills. Using pairs also makes it easy for the teacher to later combine groups for doubles practice and competition. Play singles games on a half-court to provide a long, thin playing area that emphasizes the front and back of the court as primary spaces for attack. One court for every four participants is ideal, though these facilities may not be available to you. Where space is short there are several options:

- You can set up nets down the length of a court and, by adding some lines, create mini-courts that run across the regulation court. Though not ideal for high school students, these minicourts will give elementary and middle school students sufficient space in which to play.

- You can use spaces between courts by using string to connect net posts.

- You can rotate players on and off the court, though rotating will decrease activity time for all students and thus is not preferable.

We assume that each student will have a badminton racket and that each pair of players will have a shuttle. Students will not likely have prior badminton experience because the game is not typically taught at the elementary level due to the prohibitive length of the racket for younger learners. However, students might be familiar with some of its tactical principles through net/wall game instruction of the kind advocated in *Sport Foundations for Elementary Physical Education: A Tactical Games Approach* (2003). In particular, they might be familiar with the concept of creating space through hitting long and short. We present the framework of the tactical problems, movements, and skills in badminton in table 9.1 and the levels of tactical complexity in table 9.2.

Table 9.1 Tactical Problems, Movements, and Skills in Badminton

Tactical problems	Off-the-shuttle movements	On-the-shuttle skills
SCORING (OFFENSE)		
Setting up to attack by creating space on opponent's side of net		• Overhead clear—forehand, backhand • Overhead drop shot—forehand, backhand • High service • Underarm clear—forehand, backhand
Winning the point		• Smash • Attacking the short serve • Attacking drop shot
Attacking as a pair	• Front, back offense • Communication	
PREVENTING SCORING (DEFENSE)		
Defending space on own side of the net	• Recovery to center court—footwork	• Low service
Defending against an attack		• Returning the smash • Returning the drop shot
Defending as a pair	• Side-to-side defense • Communication	

Table 9.2 Levels of Tactical Complexity for Badminton

Tactical problems	I	II	III
SCORING (OFFENSE)			
Setting up to attack by creating space on opponent's side of net	• Clears—overhead • Drop shot—forehand	• High serve • Clears—underarm	
Winning the point		• Smash • Attacking the short serve	• Attacking drop shot
Attacking as a pair			• Front, back offense • Communication
PREVENTING SCORING (DEFENSE)			
Defending space on own side of net	• Recovery to center court—footwork	• Low serve	
Defending against an attack		• Returning the smash	• Returning the drop shot
Defending as a pair			• Side-to-side defense • Communication

Level I

At level I students focus on setting up to attack by creating space on the opposite side of the net and on defending space on their side of the net. These are the two tactical problems fundamental to badminton. Creating space is accomplished by being aware of open areas on the court. In the half-court singles game these spaces are at the back and the front of the long, narrow court. Students become aware of these spaces through appropriate teacher questioning, and then you can introduce the overhead clear and drop shot. As well as learning how to create space, students will see the need to defend space on their side of the net. As a player creates space by moving her opponent up and down the court, so her opponent will do the same. Hence space must be defended. This is where we introduce the concept of recovery.

Focusing on these two tactical problems enables the basic form of badminton to take shape. At this level students can serve underarm, overarm, or any way (even with a throw) that gets the point started. We introduce the service line in lesson 3 because students might begin to see the value of dropping a short service into the frontcourt.

We do not recommend discussing racket parts or grip. Most students will hold the racket in a way that is comfortable for them, an approximate Eastern (shake hands) grip, and so can be left alone. You can take care of grip problems early and on an individual basis by observing students and quietly correcting them. Most grip problems arise from an exaggerated Western (frying pan) grip, in which the back of the hand points to the sky when the head of the racket is parallel to the floor. To correct the grip, ask students to rotate their grip by a quarter turn either clockwise (right-handed player) or counterclockwise (left-handed player). Correcting individual grips saves students from listening to a lecture they may not need. Likewise, we do not recommend beginning with the underhand serve, which is a difficult skill for many novice players. Allow them to start the rallies by whatever means they find successful so they get to play.

At level I, students can serve any way that feels comfortable to them. Here, students have chosen to use the underarm serve.

Tactical Problem
Creating space

Lesson Focus
Half-court singles game

Objective
Keep the shuttle in play.

GAME 1

Setup
Half-court singles, using any serve (see figure 9.1)

Goal
Keep a rally going as long as possible, using overarm and underarm shots.

Questions

Q: *How do you score a point in badminton?*
A: Make the shuttle hit the floor on your opponent's side.

Q: *How can you stop your opponent from scoring?*
A: Keep the shuttle in play.

Q: *Is it easier to keep the shuttle in play with overhead or underhand shots?*
A: Overhead. (This is the case for most novices.)

PRACTICE TASK

Setup
Half-court singles

Goal
Keep a rally going as long as possible using only overhead shots.

GAME 2

Setup
Half-court singles

Goal
Be aware of what spaces can be used on other side of net.

Conditions
· Alternate service (any type).
· Score 1 point if shuttle hits floor on opponent's side of court.
· Score on every service (not only when serving).

FIGURE 9.1

Tactical Problem
Creating space

Lesson Focus
Pushing the opponent back, overhead clear

Objectives
- Understand the value of forcing opponent back.
- Push opponent back using overhead clear (forehand).

GAME 1

Setup
Half-court singles

Goals
- Be aware of what spaces can be used on the other side of net.
- Understand that it is harder to attack from the back of the court and so it is useful to push your opponent back.

Conditions
- Alternate service.
- Score 1 point if shuttle hits floor on opponent's side of court.
- Score on every service (not only when serving).

Questions

Q: *Where are the available spaces on the court?*
A: In the front and back.

Q: *Is it harder for your opponent to attack you from the front or the back?*
A: Back.

Q: *Why?*
A: Because the opponent is farther from the net.

Q: *So is it best to send your opponent to the back or to the front?*
A: Back.

Q: *Is it easier to send your opponent back by using an overhead or underhand shot?*
A: Overhead. (Use analogy of throwing for distance if necessary to explain this answer.)

GAME 1 EXTENSION

Setup
Half-court singles

Goals
- Understand that more power can be generated from overhead shots.
- Play only overhead shots.
- Push opponent back.

Condition
Use only overhead shots after the serve.

PRACTICE TASK

Setup
Half-court technique practice (cooperative)

Goal
Push opponent back.

Conditions
- Maintain forehand overhead rally.
- Hand feed if necessary.

Cues
- Get under the shuttle, using long strides.
- Line up the shuttle with the nonhitting arm.
- Break the elbow.
- Step into the shot.
- Use throwing action to contact the shuttle with the racket head.
- Snap the wrist and follow through across the body.

GAME 2

Setup
Half-court singles

Goal
Use skillful overhead clear to push opponent back in game situation.

Conditions
- Alternate service.
- Score 1 point if shuttle hits floor on opponent's side of court.
- Score on every service (not only when serving).

Lesson 3

Tactical Problem
Creating space

Lesson Focus
Pushing the opponent back, backhand overhead clear

Objective
Use backhand when necessary to push opponent back.

GAME 1

Setup
Half-court singles

Goal
Maintain rally and push opponent back.

Conditions

- Alternate service.
- Score 1 point if shuttle hits floor on opponent's side of court.
- Score on every service (not only when serving).

Question

Q: *How can you push your opponent back if the shuttle does not come to your strong (forehand) side?*

A: If possible, lean across and play a forehand anyway. Otherwise, play a backhand.

PRACTICE TASK

Setup

Half-court technique practice (cooperative)

Conditions

- Maintain a backhand rally.
- Hand feed to start if necessary.

Cues

- Move your front foot (on same side as hitting hand) toward the shuttle (to turn yourself sideways).
- Keep the elbow high.
- Contact the shuttle at its high point.
- Flick the wrist.

GAME 2

Setup

Half-court singles game, introduce underarm service

Goal

Use forehand and backhand overhead clears to push opponent to back of court.

Conditions

- Alternate service, score on every serve.
- Each point begins with underarm serve.
- Introduce service line so that players must serve beyond service line.

Lesson 4 ⊙

Level I

Tactical Problem

Creating space

Lesson Focus

Introducing the drop shot

Objective

Use drop shot to move opponent forward.

GAME 1

Setup

Half-court singles, underarm serve (if some students still cannot use underarm serve, allow a second serve by any method)

Goals

- Push opponent back with overhead clears.
- Be aware of available space at the front of the opponent's court.

Conditions

- Alternate service, score on every serve.
- Each point begins with underarm serve.
- Must serve beyond service line.

Questions

Q: *Now that you can push your opponent back, where is the space you can attack to win a point?*
A: At the front.

Q: *How do you attack this front space?*
A: Use a drop shot.

GAME 1 EXTENSION

Setup

Half-court singles

Goal

Win point by dropping shuttle into space in frontcourt.

PRACTICE TASK

Setup

Half-court technique practice. One player feeds to back of court and other player hits drop shots back.

Goals

- Land shuttle as close to net as possible.
- Land a specific number of shots inside the service line.

Cues

- Disguise by preparing as for overhead clear.
- Stiff wrist on contact.

GAME 2

Repeat game 1.

Tactical Problem
Defending space

Lesson Focus
Recovery to center court

Objective
Recover to center court between shots, using appropriate footwork.

GAME 1

Setup
Half-court singles

Goals
· Move opponent.
· Be aware of need to retain position at center court.

Questions
Q: *Where should you go between your shots?*
A: Back to the center of the court.

Q: *Why?*
A: So you can move to either the front or back of the court for your next shot.

PRACTICE TASK

Setup
Partner practice with one feeder and one hitter. Feeder has two shuttles and feeds first to the back of the hitter's court. The hitter returns and immediately recovers to center court. The feeder feeds the second shuttle to either the front or the back of the hitter's court. The hitter returns and recovers and then players rotate.

Cues
· Recover immediately after the shot.
· Use long strides to recover.
· Stay on your toes.

GAME 2

Setup
Half- or full-court singles, minitournament

Goals
· Recover to center court between shots.
· Take up position between service line and back alley.

Condition
One coach per player to encourage and reinforce movement.

Level II

Level II further develops the student's ability to create and defend space by introducing high and low service and underarm clears in the context of the tactical problem at hand. The skills are presented, again through appropriate teacher questioning, as potential solutions to the tactical problems of creating and defending space. Students at level II also can explore solutions to winning a point. Although badminton players can win points by simply moving the opponent about the court until he cannot reach a shot, winning points this way becomes less likely as the opponent's tactical awareness and skill increase. Students seek ways to win points when the opportunity arises, which makes introducing the smash appropriate. Once introduced to the smash, students will see the need to defend against it, another tactical problem that we solve. Finally, in level II students encounter the doubles game, which presents them with added tactical and technical complexities.

Learning the tactical skills necessary to win a point, and how to defend against those tactics, will help heighten the level of intensity as the students practice.

Lesson 6

Tactical Problem
Creating space

Lesson Focus
Starting the point on the attack

Objective
Use the high service to put the opponent on the defensive at the start of a point.

GAME 1

Setup
Half-court singles

Goal
Push opponent back with service.

Condition

Alternate service.

Questions

> Q: *Where is a the best place to serve to in the singles game?*
> A: To the back of your opponent's court.
>
> Q: *Why?*
> A: Because serving there will put your opponent on the defensive.

PRACTICE TASK

Setup

Half-court technique practice

Goals

- Serve high and to the opponent's backhand side.
- Land a specific number of shots in the back alley.

Condition

Alternate serving (no rallying).

Cues

- Drop shuttle.
- Flick wrist.
- Follow through.
- Land shuttle as close to baseline as possible.

Note: For students who have trouble serving, it can help to grip the racket farther down the handle.

GAME 2

Repeat game 1.

Lesson 7 Level II

Tactical Problem

Creating space

Lesson Focus

Underarm shots for maintaining depth

Objective

Use underarm (both forehand and backhand) clears to keep opponent in backcourt.

GAME 1

Setup

Half-court singles using correct serving and scoring rules (i.e., player can only score on her own service)

Goal

Be aware that it's not always possible to play overhead shots to the backcourt and so developing the underarm clear is necessary.

Condition

Use low serve to front of court.

Question

Q: If the shuttle is low, how can you get it to the back of your opponent's court?
A: Use the wrist in an underarm clear.

PRACTICE TASK

Setup

Half-court partner practice

Goals

- Use underarm shot to clear shuttle to backcourt.
- Land a specific number of shots in the back alley.

Conditions

- One player feeds to frontcourt while one hits underarm clears to back of feeder's court.
- Alternate feeds to forehand and backhand.

Cues

- Step to the shuttle (with opposite foot on forehand or same foot on backhand).
- Snap the wrist to give power.

GAME 2

Repeat game 1.

Lesson 8   Level II

Tactical Problem
Winning the point

Lesson Focus
Winning the point with a smash

Objective
Use smash to win a point.

GAME 1

Setup

Half-court singles

Goals

- Move opponent.
- Win the point.
- Be aware of the need to attack the weak clear.

Questions

Q: What is the best way to make a shot unreturnable?
A: Hit it hard and straight to the ground—use the smash.

Q: From where can you use a smash most easily?
A: From the front or middle of your court.

Q: What kinds of shots are you looking for from your opponent so you can use the smash?
A: A weak clear or a high drop shot.

PRACTICE TASK

Setup
Half-court partner practice

Goal
Shuttle hits floor as close to net as possible.

Conditions
One partner feeds high serves to midcourt and the other partner smashes.

Cues
- Prepare as for clear.
- Contact shuttle when it is high and in front of you.
- Snap wrist for power.

GAME 2

Repeat game 1, but play a competitive game.

Lesson 9 Level II

Tactical Problem
Defending against an attack

Lesson Focus
Returning the smash

Objective
Return the smash positively (i.e., do not provide a second attacking opportunity for the opponent).

GAME 1

Setup
Half-court singles game

Goals
- Win point with a smash if possible.
- Be aware of the need to return the smash without setting up an easy kill for the opponent.

Condition
Each point must start with a high serve.

Question

Q: *How can you return a smash without setting up your opponent for another smash?*
A: Play a block return or drop shot.

PRACTICE TASK

Setup
Half-court partner practice

Conditions
- One partner feeds a high serve to midcourt and the other partner smashes.
- Continue point and alternate service.

Cues
- Have feet square and racket head up to receive smash (ready position).
- Block smash, keeping a firm wrist.
- Drop shuttle into the frontcourt.

GAME 2
Repeat game 1.

Lesson 10

Tactical Problem
Defending space

Lesson Focus
Low service, doubles game

Objective
Prevent attack against the serve by keeping it low (opponents cannot hit a downward return).

GAME 1

Setup
Full-court doubles

Goals
- Be aware of potential risk of using the high serve, particularly in doubles play where the service box is shorter.
- Be aware of the potential value of a short, low serve.

Condition
Alternate serving (i.e., change on every point).

Questions

Q: Why is a high serve more risky in doubles than it is in singles?
A: The shorter service box makes a smash off the high serve more likely.

Q: What serve can you use instead?
A: A short and low serve.

Q: What is the danger associated with a short serve?
A: Hitting the net or hitting it too high and setting up an easy smash for your opponent.

PRACTICE TASK

Setup
Half-court partner practice, diagonal

Goal
Shuttle lands just on the other side of the service line, within 2 feet (0.6 meter).

Cues
- Drop the shuttle late to help disguise the serve.
- Keep the elbow (of the serving arm) tucked in.
- Serve from just below waist height to give the shuttle a flat trajectory.
- Use firm wrist.
- Stroke the shuttle.

GAME 2

Repeat game 1.

Lesson 11 Level II

Tactical Problem
Winning the point

Lesson Focus
Attacking the short serve

Objective
Punish a weak, short serve.

GAME 1

Setup
Full-court doubles game

Goal
Be aware of attacking opportunity if short serve is too high.

Condition
Each point starts with a short serve.

Question

Q: *How can you attack a short serve?*
A: Get low and hit it straight back overhead with a flick of the wrist. Look for the poor serve that goes too high.

PRACTICE TASK

Setup
Half-court partner practice, singles

Goals
- Attack the serve and put opponent on the defensive.
- Return serve flat or downward.

Conditions
One partner feeds short serves from service line and other partner attacks the serve.

Cues
- Be in ready position, weight forward, racket up.
- Punch with the arm and flick the wrist.
- Put downward (if possible) or horizontal trajectory on the return.

GAME 2

Setup

Full-court doubles game

Goal

Attack the short serve to put opponents on the defensive.

Condition

Each point starts with short serve.

Level III

Level III further shifts focus from the half-court singles game to the more tactically complex doubles game. If you have small classes or are teaching high school students, you might prefer full-court to half-court singles. While still primarily a front-and-back game, full-court singles opens up a greater use of angles in play.

Regardless of the game, students at level III can develop more technically advanced means of winning the point and defending against attack before exploring the tactical problems presented by the doubles game, specifically, attacking and defending as a pair. Students are guided to solutions involving different formations of play and then they practice these formations in game situations. The last two lessons of level III are doubles tournament play.

Once students are comfortable with the fundamentals, they can move into playing doubles, which is more tactically complex.

Tactical Problem
Winning the point

Lesson Focus
Attacking drop shot

Objective
Play an effective and fast attacking drop shot.

GAME 1

Setup
Half-court singles game

Goal
Be aware of need to play a drop shot that will reach the floor quickly.

Condition
A player cannot play two consecutive smashes.

Questions

Q: *Why is it best not to use two consecutive smashes?*
A: The opponent is probably expecting the two smashes.

Q: *If playing two smashes is not a good idea, how else can you get the shuttle to the floor quickly?*
A: Use the faster, attacking drop shot.

PRACTICE TASK

Setup
Half-court partner practice

Goals
· Achieve continual downward trajectory of drop shot.
· Land a specific number of shots inside the service line.

Condition
One partner feeds the serve high to the midcourt and the other partner plays drop shots into the frontcourt.

Cues
· Prepare as for smash.
· Contact shuttle when it is high and in front of you.
· Keep the wrist open and firm.

GAME 2

Repeat game 1.

Tactical Problem

Defending against an attack

Lesson Focus

Returning the attacking drop shot

Objective

Return the drop shot from below net height without giving an attacking opportunity to the opponent.

GAME 1

Setup

Half-court singles game

Goals

- Execute proficient drop shots.
- Be aware of need to return the drop shot in an attacking manner.

Condition

No smashes from behind the service line.

Question

Q: *How can you return the drop shot without giving an easy smash to your opponent?*
A: Use the underarm clear or touch return.

PRACTICE TASK

Setup

Half-court partner practice for keeping shuttle low to net

Goal

Use touch return to roll shuttle over net.

Condition

Both players stay inside service line, rally.

Cues

- Keep a firm wrist.
- Let shuttle hit your racket, do not move racket.

GAME 2

Repeat game 1.

Tactical Problem

Attacking as a pair

Lesson Focus

Front-and-back offense

Objective

Attack in a front-and-back formation

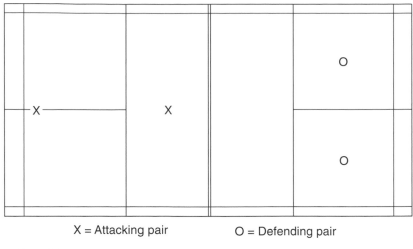

X = Attacking pair   O = Defending pair

FIGURE 9.2

GAME 1

Setup
Full-court doubles game

Goal
Recognize most effective attacking formation (front and back).

Condition
Alternate formations between front and back and side to side.

Questions

Q: What formation (front and back or side to side) gives you the best chance to attack your opponents with a smash, particularly if you are serving?
A: Front and back (see figure 9.2).

Q: Why?
A: It gives the best opportunity for making an easy smash at the front of the court, which is the best place to put the point away.

PRACTICE TASK

Setup
Full-court doubles

Goal
Keep serve low and attack the return.

Conditions
- Alternate serving on every point.
- Use low serve and follow to the net.

Cues
- Server keeps serve low and follows to the net with the racket up.
- Partner covers the middle of the backcourt to get any high, deep returns.

GAME 2

Setup
Competitive doubles game, normal rules

Goal
Attack where possible.

Condition
Regulation doubles rules.

Lesson 15 Level III

Tactical Problem
Defending as a pair

Lesson Focus
Side-to-side defense

Objective
Effectively defend against the smash (as a doubles pair).

GAME 1

Setup
Full-court doubles

Goal
Be aware that front–and–back is not an effective formation for defending against the smash.

Conditions
  · Start every point with a high serve.
  · Play front-and-back formation.

Questions

  Q: *How can you cover as much of the court as possible if you are being smashed at?*
  A: Play in side-to-side formation (see figure 9.2).

  Q: *Why is this formation best for defense?*
  A: It covers all the court and gives both players as much time as possible to see the shuttle coming toward them.

PRACTICE TASK

Setup
Full-court doubles

Goal
Move to side-to-side formation to receive smash.

Conditions
Alternate serving, must be high serve.

Cues
  · Serve high and drop back to side to side.
  · Be in ready position to defend against smash.

GAME 2

Setup
Full-court doubles, normal rules

Goal
Defending pair effectively moves to receive smash whether during a service return or during the point.

Conditions
Vary serves, regulation rules.

Lesson 16 Level III

Tactical Problem
Attacking as a pair

Lesson Focus
Review lessons and tournament play to practice attacking as a pair

Objective
Attack and communicate.

GAME 1

Setup
Full-court doubles play, rotating opponents

Goals
- Effectively attack as a pair.
- Communicate to move each other about the court.
- Move to front-and-back formation to attack.

Condition
Vary serves, high and low.

Lesson 17 Level III

Tactical Problem
Defending as a pair

Lesson Focus
Review lessons and tournament play to practice defending as a pair.

Objective
Effectively defend and communicate.

GAME 1

Setup
Full-court doubles play, rotating opponents

Goals
- Effectively defend as a pair.

- Communicate to move partner from attacking (front-and-back) to defending (side-to-side) formation.
- Cover at net for partner pushed back to receive high serve.

Condition
Vary serves, high and low.

Summary

If your students complete the three levels of tactical complexity provided in this chapter, they will have progressed from a simple to complex understanding of badminton. We recommend that you base your instructional units on one level of tactical complexity and use material from other levels to individualize your instruction as necessary.

From an offensive point of view, badminton is about setting yourself up to attack by creating space on your opponent's side of the net and then winning the point in the most effective way possible. You can easily combine these tactical problems in an instructional unit. Once they learn to solve these tactical problems, students will appreciate the need for defending space on their side of the net and defending against attacks. Presented in this way, the sequencing of instruction is logical and makes sense to students.

Understanding what to do within game situations enables players to select movements and skills for solving the tactical problems presented by the game and by the opponent. Some material in this chapter will assist your students in playing other net games, particularly tennis, which from a tactical perspective has much in common with badminton.

CHAPTER 10

Tennis

Tennis is a popular lifetime activity, and when played on public courts with moderately priced equipment, it is relatively inexpensive. You should focus on enabling your students to experience success and appreciation for tennis. Your challenge is to hook your students into the game through games!

Tennis, like badminton, is an easy game to understand tactically. Both games are played 1v1, with players having limited, alternating roles of striker and receiver. Two basic tactical conditions guide players: shot selection and court position. The premise behind a tactical approach is that students with tactical skills can play games, and these games can still be interesting, challenging, and even competitive.

Similar to the chapter on badminton (chapter 9), this chapter primarily focuses on the singles game. Singles is tactically simpler and maximizes game play. Consider the playing opportunities of four students who share a court by playing singles on half of it (i.e., play on a long and narrow court). If these four students play doubles on the same court, their opportunities to play are cut in half. We believe that doubles should be taught and played but encourage you to start your students with singles.

Your teaching challenge is to modify or arrange games so that they enable students to successfully solve the tactical problems of net games. We have developed frameworks of tactical problems, movements, and skills in tennis. Table 10.1 can help you organize the game and provide solutions to tactical problems. Table 10.2 presents the levels of tactical complexity, which assist you in matching skills and movements with student development.

Students work in pairs during most of the tennis instruction, which enables practice of tactics and skills related to a singles game. We also implement a triad formation, advocated in the volleyball chapter (chapter 8), for some practice tasks. In the triad formation you have (1) an initiator to toss or hit balls off the racket, (2) a performer to hit ground strokes, volleys, and so forth, and (3) a retriever to collect tennis balls for repeated trials. Ideally, you want one

Focus your teaching so that students can feel they have had a successful learning experience, even if they are having a frustrating time perfecting a skill.

court for every four students, but where space is short you may consider some court options suggested in the badminton chapter (chapter 9). Additional suggestions, related specifically to teaching the novice tennis player, include the following:

- Use badminton courts. We have had success using badminton courts with lower nets, and using these courts allows you to teach tennis indoors.
- Use foam tennis balls. Foam balls help increase tactical understanding and game performance early in a unit because they slow game play.
- Use racquetball rackets. Racquetball rackets help students with lower abilities master difficult techniques because they are shorter and easier to manipulate.
- Use alternatives to a regulation game. As you will read in the following lessons, we integrate 1-point games into teaching. We also use deuce games and no-ad games (4-point games) as alternatives to regulation games.

Table 10.1 Tactical Problems, Movements, and Skills in Tennis

Tactical problems	Off-the-ball movements	On-the-ball skills
SCORING (OFFENSE)		

Setting up to attack by creating space on opponent's side		• Ground stroke
		  – Forehand
		  – Backhand
		  – Crosscourt
		  – Line
		• Lob
		  – Forehand
		  – Backhand
		• Serve

Winning the point	• Footwork
	  – Approach shot
		• Volley
		  – Forehand
		  – Backhand
		  – Crosscourt
		  – Line
		• Approach shot
		• Passing shot
		• Attacking drop shot
		• Smash
		• Serve

Attacking as a pair (doubles)	• Side-to-side offense • Communication	
PREVENTING SCORING (DEFENSE)		
Defending space on own side of the net	• Recovery	

Defending against an attack		• Lob
		  – Forehand
		  – Backhand

Defending as a pair (doubles)	• Side-to-side defense • Communication	

Table 10.2   Levels of Tactical Complexity for Tennis

Tactical problems	I	II	III
SCORING (OFFENSE)			

Setting up to attack by creating space on opponent's side	• Ground stroke
	  – Forehand
	  – Backhand
	• Approach shot
	• Footwork
		• Flat serve
		• Ground stroke
		  – Crosscourt
		  – Line
		• Lob
		• Offensive
			• Passing shot
			• Attacking drop shot

Winning the point	• Volley
	  – Forehand
	  – Backhand
		• Smash
		• Volley
		  – Crosscourt
		  – Line	

Attacking as a pair		• Up-and-back forma-tion	• Both up, both back • Communication
PREVENTING SCORING (DEFENSE)			
Defending space on own side of net	• Recovery to center court	• Lob – Defensive	
Defending against an attack			• Returning the drop shot
Defending as a pair	• Up-and-back formation		• Side-to-side formation • Communication

Level I

At level I, students focus on setting up to attack by creating space on the opposite side of the net, winning the point, and defending space on their side of the net. These tactical problems provide the basics for shaping a tennis game. Creating space is accomplished by being aware of open areas on the court. When playing in a half-court singles game, these spaces are at the back and the front of a long and narrow court (a minicourt). Through teacher questioning, students become aware of these spaces and focus on the ground strokes (forehand and backhand), approach shot, and volley. As players create space by moving their opponents up and down the court, they will also see the need to defend space on their side of the court. To defend space, we introduce the off-the-ball movement of recovery. When implementing level I lessons, you can alternate service and use a bounce-hit forehand groundstroke to serve.

Tennis is a difficult game when played with regulation rackets and balls, as it often is in secondary schools. If players cannot control the ball and keep it in play, they won't have a game. With this in mind, some early lessons might need repeating to ensure the development of reliable ground strokes. You need to be able to identify sources of errors and provide corrections, particularly for unreliable ground strokes. Errors of accuracy are likely caused by a problem in the contact point. Generally, contact for the ground stroke should be made when the ball is about level with the front knee and is falling from waist height to knee height after the bounce. Lack of power might come from having a square stance upon contact. The player should step with the opposite foot on the forehand side and the same foot on the backhand side for both ground strokes and volleys.

Tennis players must learn to defend their space.

Lesson 1 Level I

Tactical Problem
Setting up to attack by creating space on the opponent's court

Lesson Focus
Awareness of court

Objective
Understand the concept of creating space.

GAME 1

Setup
No-racket game

Goal
Increase court awareness.

Note
You may have your students play either or both of the following no-racket games.

Conditions
- Short-court game (see figure 10.1)
  - Short and narrow court, toss-bounce-catch game, underhand toss.
- Half-court game (see figure 10.2)
  - Long and narrow court, toss-bounce-catch game, underhand toss.
  - Extend game by using racket.

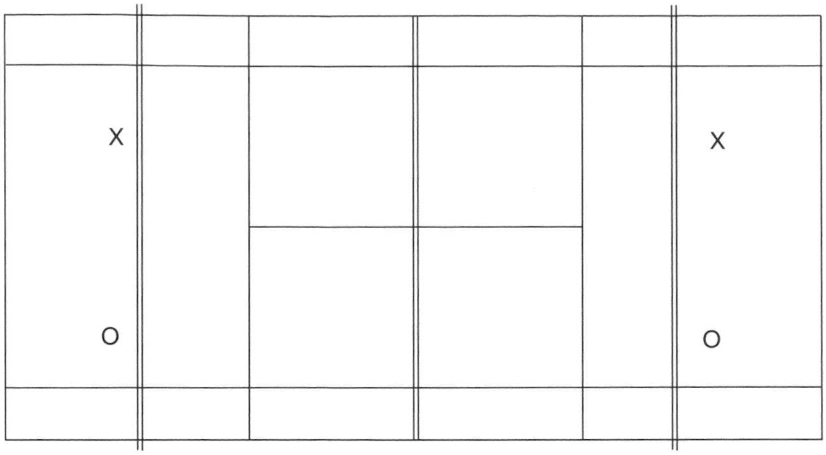

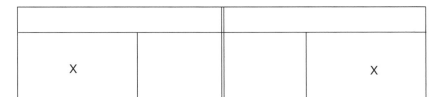

FIGURE 10.1

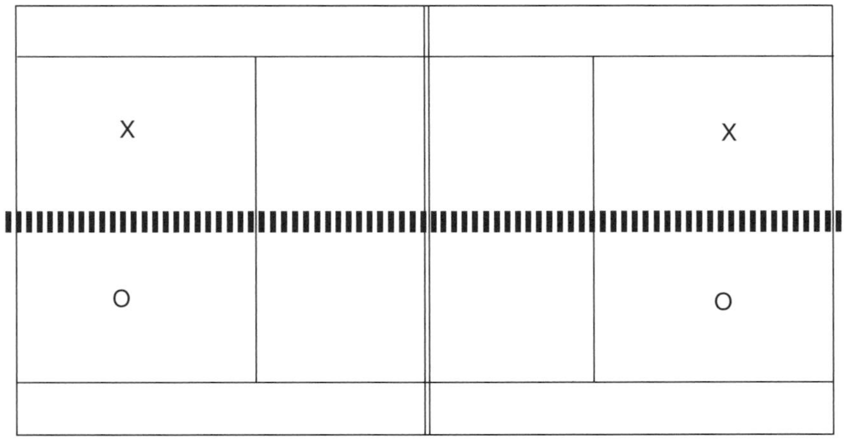

FIGURE 10.2

Questions

Q: *How do you move your opponent?*
A: Toss to an open space.

Q: *When you used a racket, which shot did you use the most?*
A: Forehand.

PRACTICE TASK

Setup
Forehand ground stroke, triad (see figure 10.3)

Goal
Perform 3 of 5 trials successfully and rotate.

Conditions
- Tosser tosses or hits ball from racket to hitter, hitter hits ground strokes, and retriever retrieves tennis balls.
- Students can say "bounce, hit," as a cue.
- Encourage the hitter to hit the ball as it falls.

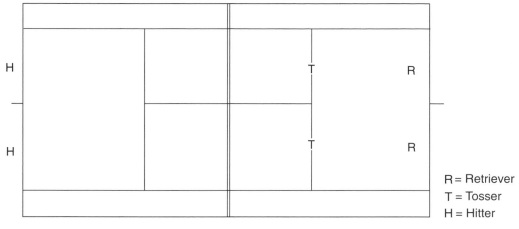

R = Retriever
T = Tosser
H = Hitter

FIGURE 10.3

Note

You can practice in pairs and use a long and narrow court if you feel your students will experience success. Although using pairs maximizes participation, we advocate working in pairs with novice players.

Cues

- Side to net.
- Racket back.
- Step and swing parallel.
- Follow through.
- Hit to space.

GAME 2

Half-court singles

Goal

Be aware of space on other side of the net.

Conditions

- Long and narrow court, bounce-hit serve
- Player with ball starts (see figure 10.2)

Lesson 2 Level I

Tactical Problem
Setting up to attack by creating space on opponent's court

Lesson Focus
Awareness of court

Objective
Create space using ground strokes.

GAME 1

Setup
Rally, short-court singles

Goal
Keep rally going for as long as possible using only ground strokes.

Conditions
· Short and narrow court, bounce-hit serve.
· Player with ball starts (see figure 10.1).

Question

Q: *What do you do to keep the rally going?*
A: Hit the ball to each other.

GAME 1 EXTENSION

Setup
Short-court singles

Goal
Be aware of space on either side of the net.

Conditions
· Short and narrow court.
· Alternate service, bounce-hit serve, 1-point games (see figure 10.1).

Questions

Q: *What did you do to win a point?*
A: Hit to an open space.

Q: *Into what spaces on your opponent's side of the net can you hit the tennis ball?*
A: Front and back and side to side.

Q: *How do you return the ball if it does not come to your forehand side?*
A: Use the backhand.

PRACTICE TASK

Setup
Backhand ground stroke, triad (see figure 10.3)

Goal
Perform 3 of 5 trials successfully and rotate.

Conditions
Tosser tosses or hits ball from racket to hitter, hitter hits ground stroke, and retriever retrieves tennis balls.

Note
You can practice in pairs and use a long and narrow court if you feel your students will experience success. Pairs maximize participation.

Cues
· Side to net.
· Racket back.
· Swing parallel.
· Follow through.

GAME 2

Setup
Half-court singles

Goal
Be aware of space on the other side of the net.

Conditions
- Long and narrow court.
- Alternate service, bounce-hit serve, 4-point games, ground strokes only (see figure 10.2).

Lesson 3

Tactical Problem
Setting up to attack by creating space on opponent's court

Lesson Focus
Understanding the value of forcing the opponent back to the baseline

Objective
Push opponent back with strong ground strokes.

GAME 1

Setup
Half-court singles

Goals
- Be aware of space on other side of the net.
- Understand that it is harder to attack from the back of the court and so it is useful to push your opponent back to the baseline.

Conditions
- Long and narrow court.
- Alternate service, bounce-hit serve, 4-point games, ground strokes only (see figure 10.2).

Questions

Q: Is it harder for your opponent to attack from the baseline or at the net?
A: From the baseline.

Q: Is it best to send your opponent to the baseline or to the net?
A: Baseline.

Q: How do you send your opponent back?
A: Play a ground stroke to the baseline.

PRACTICE TASK 1

Setup
Ground-stroke mixer, triad (see figure 10.3)

Goal
Perform 5 of 8 trials successfully and rotate.

Conditions

- Tosser tosses or hits ball from racket, mixes forehand and backhand to hitter.
- Hitter hits ground strokes and retriever retrieves tennis balls.
- Set target areas (just inside the baseline) for ball to land in.

Note

You can practice in pairs and use a long and narrow court if you feel your students will experience success. Although using pairs maximizes participation, we advocate working in pairs with novice players.

PRACTICE TASK 2

Setup

Half-court singles

Goal

Maintain rally from the baseline by using ground strokes.

Condition

Cooperation between pairs.

GAME 2

Setup

Half-court singles

Goal

Use skillful ground strokes to push opponent back in game situation.

Conditions

- Long and narrow court.
- Alternate service, bounce-hit serve, 4-point games, ground strokes only.

Lesson 4 Level I

Tactical Problem
Winning the point

Lesson Focus
Getting to the net to attack

Objective
Approach shot to net.

GAME 1

Setup

Half-court singles

Goals

- Move opponent.
- Win the point.
- Be aware of need to punish short ground strokes.

Conditions

- Play no-ad score games (4-point games).
- After serve, can play the ball before it bounces.

Questions

Q: *What did you do to a short ground stroke?*
A: Moved up to play the ball.

Q: *After you move up, is it easier to run back or keep moving toward the net?*
A: Keep moving toward the net.

Note
You can use either of the following practice tasks.

PRACTICE TASK 1

Setup
Practice approach shot (see figure 10.4)

Goals
- Perform 3 of 5 trials successfully and rotate.
- Use half-court or full court.

Conditions
- Tosser feeds a short ground stroke (hits off the racket).
- Hitter executes an approach shot and continues to net.
- Hitter then returns to the baseline to repeat practice task.
- Task can be practiced as a triad.

Cues
- Medium to low posture.
- Approach the ball.
- Racket back.
- Swing parallel and hit the ball in court.
- Move to net and get into ready position (feet set and racket head up).

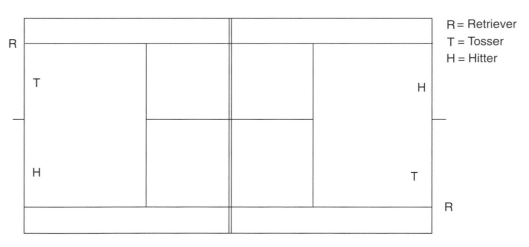

FIGURE 10.4

PRACTICE TASK 2

Setup
Half-court technique practice

Goal
Land a specific number of approach shots (3 of 5) in the backcourt.

Conditions
- One player feeds short ground strokes.
- One player hits approach shots.
- Switch roles.

GAME 2

Setup
Half-court singles

Goals
- Move opponent.
- Win the point.
- Be aware of need to punish weak ground strokes.

Conditions
- Play deuce games.
- Use long and narrow court.
- One person serves for complete deuce game.
- After serve, can play the ball before it bounces.

Lesson 5 — Level I

Tactical Problem
Winning the point

Lesson Focus
Winning the point using the volley

Objective
Use a volley to win a point.

GAME 1

Setup
Half-court singles

Goals
- Move opponent.
- Win the point.
- Be aware of need to punish weak ground strokes.

Conditions
- Play deuce games.
- One person serves for complete deuce game.
- Use long and narrow court.
- After serve, can play the ball before it bounces.

Questions

Q: What shot would you use if you keep moving toward the net?
A: Volley.

Q: What did you do to play the ball before it bounced?
A: Moved closer to the net, to the front of the court.

Note

You can use either of the following practice tasks.

PRACTICE TASK 1

Setup

Practice volley technique (see figure 10.5)

Goals

- Perform 3 of 5 trials successfully and rotate.
- Use half-court or full court.

Conditions

- One player feeds (either with a toss or off the racket).
- One player hits volley.
- Repeat three times by practicing forehand, backhand, and both.
- This task can be practiced as a triad.

Cues

- Make yourself light (weight on balls of feet).
- Use a short backswing.
- Turn side to net.
- Reach forward to hit.
- Recover to ready position.

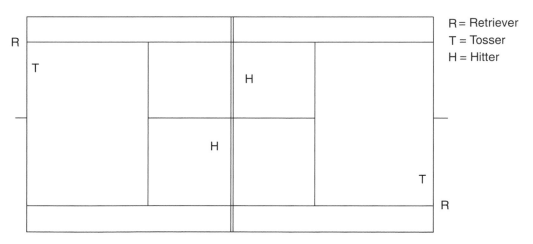

FIGURE 10.5

PRACTICE TASK 2

Setup
Half-court technique

Goal
Land a specific number of shots (3 of 5) in the backcourt.

Conditions
- One player feeds ground strokes to front court or net.
- One player hits volley (backhand and forehand).

GAME 2

Setup
Half-court singles

Goals
- Move opponent.
- Win the point.
- Be aware of need to punish weak ground strokes.

Conditions
- Play deuce games.
- One person serves for complete deuce game.
- Use long and narrow court.
- After serve, can play the ball before it bounces.

Lesson 6   Level I

Tactical Problem
Defending space on your court

Lesson Focus
Recovery to center baseline

Objective
Recover to center baseline between shots.

GAME 1

Setup
Half-court singles

Goals
- Move opponent.
- Be aware of the need to recover to center court.

Conditions
- Alternate service.
- Bounce-hit serve.
- Long and narrow court.

Question
Q: *Where should you go between your shots?*
A: Back to the center of the baseline.

PRACTICE TASK

Setup
Full-court singles minitournament

Goal
Recover to center baseline between shots.

Conditions
- One coach per player or court.
- Bounce-hit serve, no-ad scoring (4-point games).
- Change roles after each game.

GAME 2

Continue minitournament.

Level II

While level I focuses on the beginning player, level II is a step up and might be difficult for some. Level II continues to develop your students' abilities to create and defend space. You can introduce shots such as the cross-court or down-the-line ground stroke and the lob. Students should also begin serving. As in all netwall games, players can win points by moving the opponent around the court until she cannot reach the next shot. Nonetheless, this solution reaches its limits as the opponent's tactical awareness and ability improve, so at this level students will explore winning a point. After your students have practiced the volley, approach shot, and smash, their awareness for the need to defend against these attacks will increase.

The tennis serve is an important skill to hone.

Tactical Problem
Setting up to attack by creating space in opponent's court

Lesson Focus
Starting the point on the attack

Objective
Use the flat service at the start of a point.

GAME 1

Setup
Half-court singles

Goal
Get the ball in court and push opponent into backcourt with service.

Conditions
- Alternate service.
- Push opponent back.
- Use long and narrow court.

Questions

Q: *Where does the service have to land?*
A: In the service court.

Q: *Where is the best place to serve to put your opponent on the defensive?*
A: Deep into the service court.

PRACTICE TASK 1

Setup
Toss practice

Goals
- Toss accurately (or close to) racket head.
- Perform 5 of 8 trials successfully.

Conditions
- Stand along baseline with opposite toe to the line (left foot forward for right handers and right foot forward for left handers).
- Place racket butt next to front foot with racket extended in front of your body.
- Toss ball as for a serve so that it lands in or near the head of the racket on the court.

PRACTICE TASK 2

Setup
Half-court technique

Goals
- Serve deep and to opponent's backhand.
- Land a specific number (3 of 5) of serves in the back of the service court.

Condition
Alternate service (no rallying).

Cues
- Face net post.
- Place racket behind head.
- Toss up and forward.
- Reach high.
- Swing through.

GAME 2
Repeat game 1 with half-court singles.

Lesson 8   Level II

Tactical Problem
Setting up to attack by creating space in opponent's court

Lesson Focus
Variations on the ground stroke

Objective
Use crosscourt and down-the-line ground strokes.

GAME 1

Setup
Full-court singles

Goal
Be aware and vary ground strokes.

Conditions
- Two serves per person.
- Ground strokes only.
- Move opponent around court.

Questions
Q: *What do you do to move your opponent along the baseline?*
A: Vary your ground strokes.

Q: *What are the types of ground-stroke placement?*
A: Crosscourt or down the line.

PRACTICE TASK 1

Setup
Crosscourt and line practice (see figure 10.6)

Goals
- Place ground strokes crosscourt and down the line.
- Play a specific number of strokes crosscourt and down the line.

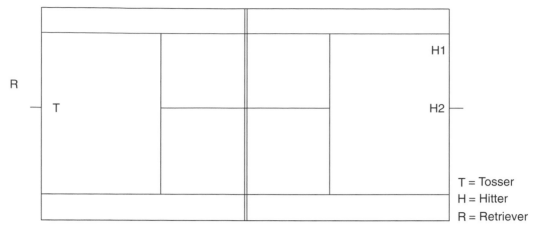

T = Tosser
H = Hitter
R = Retriever

FIGURE 10.6

Conditions
- One player feeds to other player's forehand in the corner of the baseline and other player hits crosscourt.
- Switch roles and repeat task hitting down the line.

Cues
- Step into the shot.
- Follow through to the target.

Note
This task can also be accomplished using half-court singles.

PRACTICE TASK 2

Setup
Crosscourt and line practice (see figure 10.6)

Goals
- Use crosscourt and down-the-line placement.
- Play a specific number of ground strokes crosscourt and down the line.

Conditions
- One player feeds to other player from the corner of the baseline.
- Other player starts in the middle of the court and moves to hit crosscourt.
- Switch sides of the court and switch roles.
- Repeat task, going down the line.

GAME 2

Setup
Full-court singles

Goal
Use crosscourt or down-the-line placement to move opponent.

Conditions
- Two serves per person.
- Ground strokes only.
- Move opponent around court.

Lesson 9

Tactical Problem
Winning the point

Lesson Focus
Winning the point using an approach shot and volley

Objective
Use approach shot to volley.

GAME 1

Setup
Half- or full-court singles

Goals
- Move opponent.
- Win the point.
- Be aware of need to punish short ground strokes.

Conditions
- Play no-ad score games.
- After serve, can play the ball before it bounces.

Questions
Q: What did you have to do to return a short ground stroke?
A: Move up to play the ball.

Q: After you move up, is it easier to run back or to keep moving toward the net?
A: Keep moving toward the net.

Q: What shot do you use if you keep moving toward the net?
A: Volley.

Q: Where should you place your volley?
A: In an open space or in the angles of the court to move your opponent.

PRACTICE TASK

Setup
Approach shot to volley (see figure 10.7)

Goals
- Perform 3 of 5 trials successfully and rotate.
- Use half-court or full court.

Conditions
- Tosser feeds two balls (hits off the racket).
- First ball is short ground stroke.
- Hitter executes an approach shot and continues to net for volley.
- Tosser hits another ground stroke for hitter to volley.
- This task can be practiced in pairs or in a triad.

Note
This task can be extended to include forehand and backhand of both approach shot and volley.

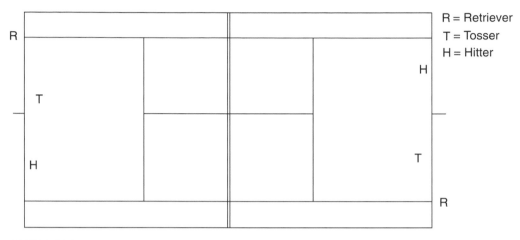

FIGURE 10.7

GAME 2

Repeat game 1 with half- or full-court singles.

Lesson 10 — Level II

Tactical Problem
Setting up to attack by creating space in opponent's court

Lesson Focus
Lob shots for maintaining depth (a logical progression if opponents are now moving to the net more frequently)

Objective
Use lob (forehand and backhand) to keep opponent back from the net.

GAME 1

Setup
Half- or full-court singles

Goal
Be aware of the need to develop lob shot.

Conditions

- Play deuce games.
- One person serves for complete deuce game.
- Push opponent back.

Question

Q: What do you do to keep the opponent back if you cannot use a ground stroke?
A: Open the face of the racket and use a lob.

PRACTICE TASK

Setup

Half-court partner lob practice (see figure 10.8)

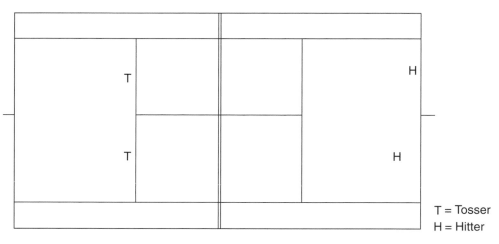

T = Tosser
H = Hitter

FIGURE 10.8

Goals

- Clear to backcourt using lob.
- Land a specific number of lobs deep to baseline (backcourt).

Conditions

- One player feeds to backcourt.
- One player hits lobs back to feeder's court.
- Switch or alternate forehand, backhand, and lobs.

Cues

- Use full backswing.
- Open the face of the racket.
- Swing low to high.
- Finish high.

GAME 2

Repeat game 1 with half- or full-court singles.

Tactical Problem
Winning the point

Lesson Focus
Winning the point using the smash

Objective
Using the smash to win a point.

GAME 1

Setup
Half- or full-court singles

Goals
- Move opponent.
- Win the point.
- Be aware of need to punish weak lob.

Conditions
- Play deuce games.
- After serve, can play the ball before it bounces.

Questions

Q: *What is the best way to make a shot unreturnable?*
A: Hit it hard and straight to the ground—use a smash.

Q: *From where on your court can you smash?*
A: From the front or middle of your court.

Q: *What kind of shot are you looking for from your opponent?*
A: For a weak lob.

Q: *Where should you place your smash?*
A: In an open space or in the angles of the court to beat your opponent.

PRACTICE TASK

Setup
Half-court partner practice

Cues
- Prepare as serve.
- Point to ball.
- Reach high, hit down.
- Finish swing after contact.

Goal
Ball hits court at angle and deep.

Conditions
One partner feeds high ground strokes to midcourt and other partner smashes.

GAME 2

Setup
Repeat game 1 with half- or full-court singles.

Condition
Competitive no-ad score game.

Lesson 12 Level II

Tactical Problem
Defending against an attack

Lesson Focus
Returning the smash

Objective
Return the smash with success (i.e., do not provide a second attacking opportunity for opponent).

GAME 1

Setup
Half- or full-court singles

Goals
- Win point with a volley or smash if possible.
- Be aware of need to return the smash without setting up an easy winner for the opponent.

Conditions
- Play no-ad score games (4 points).
- One person serves for complete game.
- Must be playable serve (no-ace rule).

Question
Q: *How can you return a volley or smash without setting up your opponent for another smash?*
A: With a defensive lob.

PRACTICE TASK

Setup
Half-court partner practice

Goals
- Perform 3 of 5 trials successfully.
- Practice both shots.

Conditions
- One player feeds with high ground stroke to midcourt and partner smashes.
- Player executes defensive lob to continue point.
- One player feeds with ground stroke and partner volleys.
- Player executes defensive lob to continue point.

Cues

- Use short backswing.
- Open the face of the racket.
- Swing low to high.
- Finish high.

GAME 2

Repeat game 1 with half- or full-court singles.

Lesson 13 Level II

Tactical Problem
Attacking as a pair

Lesson Focus
Up-and-back formation

Objective
Use up-and-back formation in doubles.

GAME 1

Setup
Full-court doubles

Goal
Use up-and-back formation.

Conditions
Flat serve, each person serves 2 points.

Questions

Q: *What are the roles and responsibilities of the back player?*
A: Serve, serve receive, hit ground strokes, and take all shots the up person does not take.

Q: *What are the roles and responsibilities of the up player?*
A: Net play and communication.

PRACTICE TASK

Setup
Full-court doubles practice

Goal
Be aware of doubles roles and responsibilities.

Conditions
- Each person serves two bounce-hit serves.
- Play points to completion.

GAME 2

Setup
Doubles

Goal
Up-and-back formation.

Conditions
- Flat serve, each person serves full game.
- No-ad scoring (4-point game).

Level III

Level III shifts from a primarily half-court singles game to a more tactically complex doubles game. Students will challenge themselves by discovering more advanced ways of winning the point and defending against attack. The final phase of level III is solving the tactical problems presented by the doubles game (attacking and defending as a pair). Once again, questions from the teacher guide students to solutions they practice in game situations.

Playing tennis doubles increases the skill challenge.

Tactical Problem
Winning the point

Lesson Focus
Attacking the short serve

Objective
Punish a weak, short serve.

GAME 1

Setup
Half- or full-court singles

Goal
Be aware of attacking opportunity if serve is short.

Conditions
- Each point starts with a short serve.
- Play deuce game.

Questions
Q: *How can you attack a short serve?*
A: With a passing shot down the line or a crosscourt shot.

Q: *What should you do after attacking a short serve?*
A: Move to the net.

PRACTICE TASK

Setup
Half-court partner practice

Cue
Same as ground stroke.

Goal
Attack the serve and put opponent on the defensive.

Conditions
- One player feeds short serves from the service line and partner attacks the serve.
- Perform a specific number of successful returns.

GAME 2

Setup
Half- or full-court singles

Goal
Be aware of attacking opportunity if serve is short.

Conditions
- Each point starts with a short serve.
- Play deuce games.

Tactical Problem
Winning the point

Lesson Focus
Attacking drop shot

Objective
Play effective, fast, attacking drop shot.

GAME 1

Setup
Half- or full-court singles

Goal
Be aware of the need to play a drop shot that reaches the ground quickly.

Conditions
- A player cannot play two consecutive volleys.
- Play deuce games.

Question

Q: What can you do besides the volley to quickly get the tennis ball to the floor?
A: Hit a faster, attacking drop shot.

PRACTICE TASK

Setup
Half-court partner practice

Goals
- Perform a fast, attacking drop shot.
- Land a specific number of shots inside the service court.

Conditions
One player feeds ground strokes to midcourt and partner plays drop shots into front court.

Cues
- Disguise the shot.
- Use open face.
- Swing high to low.

GAME 2

Setup
Half- or full-court singles

Goal
Be aware of the need to play a drop shot that reaches the ground quickly.

Conditions
- A player cannot play two consecutive volleys.
- No-ad scoring.

Tactical Problem
Defending against an attack

Lesson Focus
Returning the attacking drop shot

Objective
Return the drop shot without giving an attacking opportunity to an opponent.

GAME 1

Setup
Half- or full-court singles

Goals
· Execute proficient drop shots.
· Be aware of the need to return the drop shot in an attacking manner.

Conditions
· No volleys or smashes.
· Play deuce games.

Question

Q: *How can you return the drop shot without giving an easy volley to your opponent?*
A: With a passing shot on the run, either crosscourt or down the line.

PRACTICE TASK

Setup
Half- or full-court partner practice

Goal
Use passing shot to return.

Conditions
· In pairs, one player feeds drop shots to the other, who attempts passing shots.
· Perform 4 to 6 trials and switch roles.

Cues
· Keep ball low to the net.
· Hit the ball out of reach of opponent at net.

GAME 2

Setup
Half- or full-court singles

Goals
· Execute proficient drop shots.
· Be aware of the need to return the drop shot in an attacking manner.

Conditions
· No volleys or smashes.
· No-ad scoring.

Tactical Problem
Attacking as a pair

Lesson Focus
Side-to-side offense

Objective
Attack in a side-to-side formation.

GAME 1

Setup
Full-court doubles

Goal
Recognize most effective attacking formation (both up).

Conditions
- Vary formations among up and back and both up and both back.
- Play no-ad scoring games.

Questions

Q: *What formation (both up, both back, or up and back) gives you the best chance to attack your opponents with a volley or a smash, particularly if you are serving?*
A: Both up.

Q: *When do you get into a both up?*
A: When the back player (in the up-and-back formation) receives a short ball and plays an approach shot.

PRACTICE TASK

Setup
Full-court doubles

Cues
- Server keeps serve wide and follows into the net with racket up.
- Partner sets up at the net, protecting the alley.

Goal
Keep serve low and attack the return.

Conditions
- Alternate service on every point.
- Serve and follow to the net.

GAME 2

Setup
Competitive doubles

Goal
Attack where possible (both up).

Condition
Regulation game.

Tactical Problem
Attacking as a pair when serving

Lesson Focus
Setting up a winning volley (the poach)

Objective
Attack in a two-up formation.

GAME 1

Setup
Full-court doubles

Goal
Set up a winning volley.

Conditions
- Use two-up or up-and-back formation.
- Play no-ad scoring games.

Questions

Q: *What type of serve sets up a volley for your partner?*
A: A wide, deep serve.

Q: *What is the responsibility of the player at the net?*
A: To poach to hit a winning volley.

Q: *How do you do this?*
A: Anticipate, be ready, use footwork, hold racket up, and volley into the space.

PRACTICE TASK

Setup
Full-court doubles

Goal
Hit a winning volley.

Conditions
- Team A serves to team B for 6 to 8 serves.
- Serve wide.
- Set up net player to poach and switch roles.

GAME 2

Setup
Competitive doubles

Goal
Attack where possible.

Condition
Regulation game.

Tactical Problem
Defending as a pair against a serve

Lesson Focus
Serve-receive tactics

Objective
Effectively defend against the serve in doubles.

GAME 1

Setup
Full-court doubles

Goal
Focus on serve-receive tactics.

Condition
Two serves per person.

Question

Q: *What are the possible serve-receive tactics in doubles?*
A: · Return the ball to the feet of the advancing server.
  · Pass to the net player.
  · Lob to the net player.
  · Hit crosscourt, angled toward the server.

PRACTICE TASK

Setup
Full-court doubles

Goal
Attempt each serve-receive tactic.

Conditions
  · Doubles team A alternates serves to doubles team B.
  · Rotate after 6 to 8 serves.
  · Do not play points to completion.

GAME 2

Setup
Full-court doubles

Goal
Focus on serve-receive tactics.

Summary

We advocate tournament play to challenge your students' tactical awareness and problem solving. You can arrange scoring in tournaments by tactical problems, game forms, or ability groups. We provide three illustrations to guide you. First, if the focus of your unit was to solve the tactical problem of setting up to attack, you may limit tournament play to using ground strokes (i.e., forehand, backhand, crosscourt, down the line). Second, you can choose the game form used throughout the tournament, such as half-court singles, no-ad scoring, or deuce games. Third, students can self-select into ability groups (e.g., rookie, recreation, and all-pro leagues).

Team tennis is another tournament option. Ideally team tennis involves teams of four to eight players. Each team organizes players to play both singles and doubles matches. Each contest is a set of six games using no-ad scoring. We encourage you to modify team tennis to meet your needs. For example, you might have each team seed themselves for singles play so each player will play against the corresponding seed from another team.

This chapter has provided you with a scheme for teaching tennis using a tactical approach. We want you to make these lessons yours! This may mean modifying the content provided. The following are ways you can modify lessons and units:

- Use court rotations. If you have limited court space you can rotate students on and off half-court singles, full-court singles, and doubles games.

- Use stations. They can provide a great change of pace, focusing on specific skills and movements as well as on tournament play.

- Use student choice. Students may choose to focus on either singles or doubles. You can accomplish this by mixing singles or doubles practice throughout the unit while still focusing on tactical problems.

- Use coaches or statisticians. If you have few courts, you may want to involve students in these types of roles. Collecting statistics (e.g., winners and errors) can be helpful when assessing game performance.

Remember to focus on a limited number of tactical problems in your unit. In other words, do a few things well and work to keep the game in tennis!

CHAPTER 11

Softball

Softball is generally taught in upper elementary through high school curricula. At the secondary level, softball tends to be the last unit of the school year and often serves as more of a recreational activity than a series of instructional lessons. This is perhaps as much because of the nature of the game as the nature of the teacher at the end of a school year. As a game, softball does not lend itself to an instructional setting. The 10v10 game provides few opportunities for students to field or hit and run. Further, the best players tend to dominate key positions (i.e., shortstop, pitcher, first base), with outfield positions filled with four or more players who can't or won't even run to a ball, let alone field it.

The tactical approach promotes small-sided (i.e., 3v3, 4v4) conditioned games that allow students to focus on a specific situation and its required tactics, whether for fielding or batting and running. Not only do small-sided games foster student involvement, but they also highlight what players should do and how to do it. Dividing the class into three or four small-sided games allows the teacher to individualize instruction, as the focus of each game can vary to match the students participating. Students with less experience can focus on fundamental skills and tactical problems. More experienced students can focus on complex skills and tactical problems that they are likely to encounter as a function of their abilities.

Small-sided games require no more room than the regulation softball or baseball diamond and are best arranged in an open field. We have found the cloverleaf arrangement to be the most efficient for managing three or four small-sided games of softball. First, lay out four playing areas in a cloverleaf shape, with the home plate areas at the center (see figure 11.1). Stagger the playing areas to prevent overthrows from endangering players on adjacent fields. The center should include an area (safety zone) large enough for students to safely stand in as they wait their turns to bat. Safety rules are necessary and should define areas where students must stand

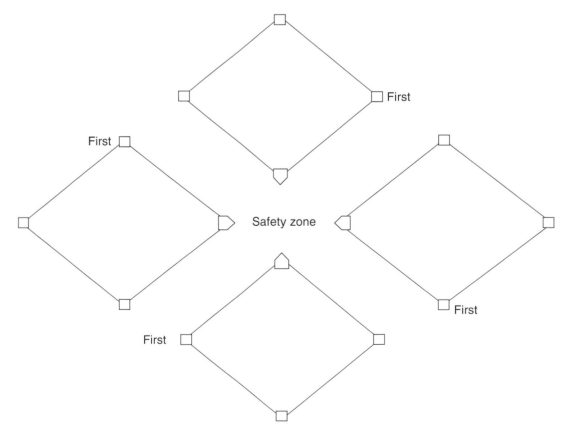

FIGURE 11.1 The cloverleaf arrangement is efficient for managing multiple games of softball.

while others are batting and what batters should do with the bat after they hit the ball.

You can divide students into teams of 6, 8, 10, or 12 for small-sided games of 3v3, 4v4, 5v5, or 6v6 on each field. We have found it best to assign students to teams and fields for an entire unit, eliminating the need for organizing teams and fields daily. At the minimum, each team and field should have three softballs and one bat. If possible, at least half of the students should have gloves.

We present the framework of tactical problems, situations, movements, and associated skills in softball in table 11.1 and the levels of tactical complexity in table 11.2. The lessons that follow serve only as examples and are not intended to encompass every detail of a lesson or every lesson of a unit.

Table 11.1 Tactical Problems, Movements, and Skills in Softball

Tactical problems	Off-the-ball movements	On-the-ball skills
SCORING (OUTS, RUNNERS)		
• Getting on base – 0-2 outs, no runners – 0-2 outs, runner on second – 0-2 outs, runner on second or third		• Hitting to left side • Grounders between left infielders • Line drives over left, center infield
• Moving the runner – 0-2 outs, runner on first – 0-2 outs, runner on second – 0-2 outs, runner on second or third	• Delaying the throw • Leading off to draw throw	• Hitting to the right side • Hitting between right infielders • Line drives over right, center of infield
– 0-1 out, runner on first – 0-1 out, runner on second – 0-1 out, runner on second and third		• Sacrifice fly
– 0-2 outs, runners on first and second – 2 outs, bases loaded		• Hitting to outfield • Line drives between gaps
• Advancing to next base – From home to first		• Step and drive • Running past first • Rounding first
– From first to second – From second to third – From third to home	• Delaying the throw	• Take-off or starting position • Sliding – Pop-up slide – Hook slide – Head first • Rounding second, third
• On a fly ball		• Tagging up

(continued)

Table 11.1 *(continued)*

Tactical problems	Movements	Associated skills
PREVENTING SCORING (OUTS, RUNNERS, BALL PLACEMENT)		
• Defending bases on throw from outfield		• Base coverage
– 0-1 out, runner on first, line drive or fly		• Throwing from outfield – To a cutoff – To a base
– 0-1 out, numerous situations where runner not forced to advance to next base		
– 0-2 outs, runner caught between bases		• Rundowns
• Defending space as a team – 0 outs, no runners – 0-2 outs, pull hitter – 0-2 outs, right-handed batter	• Positioning – Starting (base positions) – Shift for pull hitter – Shift for right-handed hitter	
• Communicating	• Calling the ball • Informing fielding player of situation • Signaling number of outs	

Table 11.2 Levels of Tactical Complexity for Softball

Tactical problems	I	II	III	IV
SCORING				
Getting on base	• Kick or hit grounders to infield • 0-2 outs, no runner	• Ball placement to get on first	• Hit grounders left, center, right • Hit line drives • 0-2 outs, runner on second or third	• Hit between infield and outfield positions
Moving the runner		• Sacrifice fly • Moving runner from first to second	• Hitting behind the runner • 0-2 outs, runner on first	• Drawing a throw to advance lead runner • Runners on first and third
Advancing to next base	• Run through first • Rounding first	• Running from first to second • Tagging up	• Running from first to third • Breaking up double play	• Slide, hook slide

(continued)

Tactical problems	I	II	III	IV
PREVENTING SCORING				
Defending space by infield, outfield position	• Fielding grounders • Fielding fly balls • 0-2 outs, no runner	• Throwing to a base from outfield • Throwing to a relay • 0-2 outs, runner on first or second • 0-1 out, runner on third	• Cutoff plays • 0-2 outs, ball hit to outfield with one or more runners on base	
Defending bases	• Base coverage on force play at first	• Cutting lead runner	• Second to first double play • Rundowns	• Third to first double play
Defending space as a team	• Positioning straight away • Backups	• Shift for left, right hand		• Positioning outfield to prevent run from scoring
COMMUNICATING				
Communication between players	• Call the ball • Signal number of outs		• Inform teammate of play	

Level I

You can use kickball, tee ball, or softball to introduce tactics in level I. We have found kickball appropriate for sixth graders, as many have not developed adequate skills in softball or baseball. This lack of skill development tends to prohibit students from fully exploring many fundamental tactical problems. If you use kickball to present level I in sixth grade, you may want to use tee ball or softball in seventh grade to review this level. Another option is to use lessons from level I to teach kickball in fifth grade and tee ball in sixth grade, and then use some lessons from levels I and II to introduce slow-pitch softball in seventh grade. Don't be afraid to use batting tees at any level. In our college softball classes, many students use batting tees during practices and games.

Tactics at level I focus on situations such as when there are 0 to 2 outs, no runners on base, and a grounder is hit to the infield or when there are 0 to 2 outs, a runner on first, and a grounder or line drive is hit to the outfield. The tactics for preventing scoring in these situations include defending space by infield position, defending space by outfield position, and defending bases, specifically first and second. The tactics for scoring include getting on base and advancing to the next base, specifically from first to second base.

By the end of the level I, students should know the infield and outfield positions as well as the boundaries and features of the playing area. By solving tactical problems, students will understand what to do at infield and outfield positions when there are no runners or there is a runner on first, and they will know how to cover first and second base on a force play. Students at level I review catching skills as they field grounders, line drives, and fly balls, and they also review and refine throwing skills.

In level I, students review and refine the offensive skills of kicking (in kickball) or batting as they solve tactical problems related to getting on base when there are 0 to 2 outs and no runners. The need to place the ball to the left side of the infield motivates students to work on accuracy and placement. The need to hit and run refines kicking and batting because hitting and running require a fluid motion from the follow-through of the swing to the drive step toward first base. Base running is also a focus of level I, and conditioned games and practices help students understand when to run past, or round, first base as well as how to advance quickly and safely to second base.

Although support play is not the specific focus of any lesson in level I, you can incorporate calling for the ball, signaling the number of outs, and backing up when teaching other elements of game play. As students are ready or as teachable moments arise, you can introduce or reinforce tactical problems through pinpointing critical aspects of a skill, movement, or play.

In this chapter we use the term *practice situation* rather than *practice task*. In softball and baseball the situation (e.g., no outs, runner on first and 1 out, runners on first and second, ground ball to shortstop) is the essence of the game and it prompts players about what to do, whether they are a fielder, batter, or base runner.

Students in level I will review catching skills.

Lesson 1

Tactical Problem
Defending space by infield position

Lesson Focus
Situation is 0 outs, no runners on base, grounder to left side of infield

Objectives
- Field grounders from third base and shortstop positions.
- Make an accurate throw to first base.

GAME 1

Setup
0 runners on base, 0 outs

Goals
- Defensive team gets runner out at first.
- Offensive team gets to first before throw.

Conditions

- Number of players is 3v3 minimum, 6v6 maximum, with 0 runners on base and 0 outs.
- Batter (or kicker) must hit (or kick) a ground ball to the left side of the infield (ground ball is any ball that hits the ground before reaching an infielder, pitcher excluded).
- Player scores a run by reaching first base safely.
- Whether safe or out, the runner returns to the dugout area.
- Inning is over after 3 runs or 3 outs, whichever comes first.

Questions

Q: *What was the goal of the game for the offensive team?*
A: Get to first before the throw.

Q: *What was the goal of the game for the defensive team?*
A: Get the runner out at first.

Q: *Today we are focusing on the defensive team's performance. How were you able to get the runner out at first?*
A: Move your feet to the ball, watch the ball into your glove, catch the ball, and throw it to first. Keep your feet moving toward first base.

PRACTICE SITUATION

Setup

Three players in the field (minimum) playing shortstop, third base, and first base and three players hitting (the battery—pitcher, catcher, batter). Extra players serve as pitcher and catcher. From a batting tee (or from a ball rolled from the pitcher's mound), the hitter (or kicker) hits (or kicks) a grounder to the left side of the infield and then runs hard and fast to first. After fielding three balls from each position (third base and shortstop), players rotate to first base or into the battery. The fielding player always calls the ball and the nonfielding player always backs up the fielding player.

Goals

- Successfully field three balls in a row at third base and at shortstop.
- Throw batter out 5 of 6 times.

Cues

- Feet to the ball.
- Watch it in.
- Catch and cover.
- Recover to throw.

GAME 2

Repeat game 1.

Tactical Problems
Defending space by infield position; defending first base

Lesson Focus
Situation is 0 outs, no runners on base, grounder to right infield

Objectives
- Field grounders from second and first base.
- Make an accurate throw to first base.

GAME 1

Setup
0 runners on base, 0 outs

Goals
- Defensive team gets runner out at first.
- Offensive team gets to first before throw.

Conditions
- Play 3v3 minimum, 6v6 maximum.
- Hitter (kicker) must hit (kick) a ground ball to right side of the infield.
- Player scores a run by safely reaching first base.
- Whether safe or out, the runner returns to the dugout area.
- Inning is over after 3 runs or 3 outs, whichever comes first.

Questions
Q: What was the goal of the game for the offense and for the defense?
A: Get to first ahead of the throw and get the runner out at first.

Q: Today we are focusing on the defensive team's performance. What did you do to get the runner out at first?
A: Moved feet to the ball, watched the ball into the glove, and threw quickly to first.

Q: Were you successful? If not, let's practice.

PRACTICE SITUATION

Setup
Two players in the field (minimum) at second and first base, pitcher (optional), and three players hitting (the battery). Extra players serve as catchers. From a ball rolled, pitched, or placed on a tee, hitter (kicker) hits (kicks) grounder to the right side of the infield and then runs hard and fast to first. Players each field three balls from each position. The task can also focus on footwork used to cover first base on a force play.

Goals
- Successfully field three balls in a row at second and at first.
- Throw batter out 5 of 6 times.

Cues
- Feet to the ball.
- Watch it in.
- Catch and cover.
- Recover to throw.

GAME 2

Repeat game 1.

Tactical Problem
Getting on base

Lesson Focus
Situation is 0 to 2 outs, no runners on base

Objectives
- Hit a grounder to the left side of the infield.
- Run to first as quickly as possible (running through or past the base).

GAME 1

Setup
0 runners on base, 0 to 2 outs

Goal
Get on first base safely.

Conditions
- Play 4v4 minimum, 5v5 optimum, 6v6 maximum.
- Defensive players play first base and as many other infield positions as possible.
- Hitter (kicker) must hit (kick) a ground ball to the infield and get to first before the throw.
- Player scores a run by safely reaching first base.
- Whether safe or out, the runner returns to the dugout area.
- Inning is over after 3 runs or 3 outs, whichever comes first.

Questions

Q: *To where did you have to hit or kick the ball to get on first base?*
A: Along the third baseline, on the left side of infield, close to third.

Q: *So, when there are 0 to 2 outs and no runners on base, where is the best place on the left side of the infield to hit or kick the ball?*
A: Along the third baseline.

Q: *How did you run to get to first before the throw?*
A: Ran fast without looking at the ball and ran through first base.

PRACTICE SITUATION

Setup
Three players in the field (minimum) at shortstop, third base, and first base and three players hitting (the battery). Extra players serve as pitchers and catchers. From a ball rolled or thrown from the pitcher's mound or placed on a batting tee, batter hits grounder to left side of the infield and then runs hard and fast over first base to a cone 20 feet (6 meters) past first on the first baseline. Batter hits and runs five times, attempting to knock down cones (one cone on third baseline 10 feet, or 3 meters, past the base and the other cone just beyond but between third base and the shortstop). After five hits, the batter replaces a defensive player. Defensive players make a play on every ball and attempt to throw runner out at first (all rules related to backups, calling the ball, and so on remain in effect).

Note
You may use 3 or 4 cones as targets, depending on abilities of players.

Goals

- Angle bat to hit (or approach to kick) toward third baseline or between third base and the shortstop.
- Run hard and fast through first base.

Cues

- Hit, step, and drive.
- Run hard and through first base.
- Adjust angle of the bat to hit the ball toward left field.
- Approach (if kicking) or bat (if batting) to send ball toward left field.

GAME 2

Repeat game 1 and match the final score with the score of the previous game.

Lesson 4 Level I

Tactical Problem

Defending space by outfield position

Lesson Focus

Situation is 0 to 2 outs, runner on first, ball hit to left side of outfield

Objectives

- Field grounders, line drives, and fly balls in outfield.
- Back up adjacent outfielder.
- Make an accurate throw to second base.

GAME 1

Setup

Runner on first, 0 to 2 outs

Goals

- Defensive team gets runner out at second.
- Offensive team safely moves runner to second.

Conditions

- Play 4v4 minimum, 6v6 maximum.
- Defensive players play left field, left center field, second base, and first base.
- Offensive team must have a runner on first at all times.
- Batter must hit ball to left side of outfield and run to first base.
- Balls hit to the right of second base are considered outs.
- Player scores a run by safely reaching second base.
- Whether safe or out, the runner returns to the dugout area.
- Inning is over after 3 runs or 3 outs, whichever comes first.

Questions

Q: What was the goal of the game for the offensive team and for the defensive team?
A: Safely move the runner to second and get the runner out at second.

Q: Today we're focusing on the defense. How were the defensive players, the left fielder and the left center fielder, able to get the ball to second base ahead of the runner?
A: By getting to the ball quickly and throwing to second as quickly as possible.

Q: Why is it important for the outfielders to get the ball to the infield as quickly as possible?

A: To keep runners from advancing or scoring.

Q: What should the nonfielding outfielder do and why?

A: Back up the player fielding the ball and be ready in case the fielder misses the ball to stop it and get it to the infield as quickly as possible.

PRACTICE SITUATION

Setup

Four players on defense (minimum) at left field, left center field, second base, and first base and four players on offense—the battery and a base runner. Batter hits a ball from the pitcher or batting tee to the left side of the outfield and then runs hard and fast to first base. The runner on first advances to second except on a fly ball. After players field three balls from each position (left and left center), they rotate to second base and then to first or into battery. Fielding player calls the ball and nonfielding player backs up.

Goals

- Successfully field the ball and throw the runner out at second base.
- Perform proper backup on every play.

Cues

- Feet to the ball.
- Watch it in.
- Catch and cover over throwing shoulder.
- Recover and throw quickly.
- Back up to get appropriate angle—pretend fielder isn't there or assume he will miss the ball.

GAME 2

Repeat game 1. Defense scores a bonus run by throwing out base runner at second base on a throw from an outfielder.

Lesson 5 Level I

Tactical Problem
Defending space by outfield position

Lesson Focus
Situation is 0 to 2 outs, runner on first, ball hit to right side of outfield

Objectives

- Field grounders, line drives, and fly balls in outfield.
- Back up adjacent outfielder.
- Make an accurate throw to second base.

GAME 1

Setup
Runner on first, 0 to 2 outs

Goals

- Defensive team gets runner out at second.
- Offensive team safely moves runner to second.

Conditions

- Play 4v4 minimum, 6v6 maximum.
- Defensive players play right center field, right field, second base, and first base.
- Offensive team must have a runner on first at all times.
- Batter must hit ball to right side of outfield and run to first base.
- Balls hit to the left of second base are considered outs.
- Player scores a run by safely reaching second base.
- Whether safe or out, the runner returns to the dugout area.
- Inning is over after 3 runs or 3 outs, whichever comes first.

Questions

Q: Today we're focusing on the defense. How were the defensive players, the right fielder and right center fielder, able to get the ball to second base ahead of the runner?
A: By fielding the ball quickly and throwing quickly to second base.

Q: How were you able to quickly catch and throw the ball?
A: By catching the ball over the throwing shoulder and running forward if possible.

Q: What should the nonfielding outfielder do?
A: Back up and field the ball or bases.

Q: What's the best angle to take when backing up the player fielding the ball?
A: Cut behind her so if she misses the ball you'll be in a position to catch it.

PRACTICE SITUATION

Setup

Four players on defense (minimum) at right field, right center field, second base, and first base and four players on offense—the battery and a base runner. The batter hits the ball from the pitcher or from a tee to the right side of the outfield and then runs hard and fast to first base. Runner on first advances to second except on a fly ball. After fielding three balls from each position (right and right center), players rotate to second base and then to first or into the battery. Fielding player calls the ball and nonfielding player offers backup.

Goal

Successfully field the ball and throw the runner out at second base.

Cues

- Feet to the ball.
- Watch it in.
- Catch and cover over throwing shoulder.
- Recover and throw quickly.
- Back up to get appropriate angle—pretend fielder isn't there or assume he will miss the ball.

GAME 2

Repeat game 1. Defense scores a bonus run by throwing out base runner at second base on a throw from an outfielder.

Tactical Problem

Defending bases on a throw from outfield positions

Lesson Focus

Situation is 0 to 2 outs, runner on first, ball hit to outfield

Objective

Demonstrate proper positioning and footwork when covering second base on a throw from the outfield.

GAME 1

Setup

Runner on first, 0 to 2 outs

Goals

· Defensive team gets runner out at second.
· Offensive team safely moves runner to second.

Conditions

· Play 5v5 minimum, 6v6 maximum.
· Defensive players play all four outfield positions, second base, and shortstop.
· Offensive team must have a runner on first at all times.
· Batter must hit ball to right side of outfield and run to first base.
· Balls hit to the left of second base are considered outs.
· Player scores a run by safely reaching second base.
· Whether safe or out, the runner returns to the dugout area.
· Inning is over after 3 runs or 3 outs, whichever comes first.

Questions

Q: When the ball is hit to the left side of the outfield, which infielder covers second?
A: Player at second base.

Q: When the ball is hit to the right side of the outfield, which infielder covers second?
A: Shortstop.

Q: What part of the base should you tag with your foot?
A: The outside edge closest to the person throwing the ball (this may require repositioning).

Q: Why?
A: To keep from interfering with the runner.

PRACTICE SITUATION

Setup

Six players are on defense (minimum) playing left field, left center field, right field, right center field, second base, and shortstop and six players are on offense—the battery and a base runner. Batter hits a ball from pitcher or a tee to the outfield and then runs hard and fast to first base. The runner on first advances to second except on a fly ball. Runner can tag up on a fly ball. After catching three balls from the outfielders while playing second base and the shortstop, players rotate to the battery. From the battery, players rotate through the outfield positions. Players use speed of incoming runner and position of incoming throw to adjust their foot position when covering second base.

Goals

- Keep runner from advancing to second.
- Appropriate player (shortstop or second base) covers second.
- Cover second using proper footwork and outside edge of base.

Cues

- Give them a target.
- Foot on edge is closest to the incoming throw.
- Use incoming runner and incoming throw to adjust position used to cover second base.
- Catching the ball is first priority.

GAME 2

Setup

Repeat game 1. Defense scores a bonus run by throwing the base runner out at second base.

Lesson 7

Tactical Problem

Advancing to second base

Lesson Focus

Situation is 0 to 2 outs, runner on first, ball hit to outfield

Objectives

- Take off from first base at appropriate time and run to second base and execute proper stop.
- Tag up and run to second base on a fly ball to outfield.

GAME 1

Setup

Runner on first, 0 to 2 outs

Goals

- Defensive team gets runner out at second.
- Offensive team safely moves runner to second.

Conditions

- Play 5v5 minimum, 6v6 maximum.
- Defensive players play all four outfield positions, second base, and shortstop.
- Offensive team must have a runner on first at all times.
- Batter must hit ball to right side of outfield and run to first base.
- Balls hit to the left of second base are considered outs.
- Player scores a run by safely reaching second base.
- Whether safe or out, the runner returns to the dugout area.
- Inning is over after 3 runs or 3 outs, whichever comes first.

Questions

Q: *As a runner, when should you leave first base?*
A: When the batter steps.

Q: How should you stop at second base?

A: Slide, lean back as you approach, and hang onto the base with your foot.

Q: Can the runner on first advance to second on a fly ball to the outfield?

A: Yes, but she must tag up.

Q: What should the runner do to tag up?

A: Wait until the fielder touches the ball and then run as fast as possible to the next base.

Q: Does she have to run if she is unable to make it to the next base?

A: No. The runner does not have to advance if her team has fewer than 2 outs.

PRACTICE SITUATION

Setup

Six players are on defense (minimum) at left field, left center field, right field, right center field, second base, and shortstop. Six players are on offense—battery and a base runner. Batter hits to the outfield and then runs hard and fast to first base. Runner on first advances to second except on a fly ball. Runner can tag up on a fly ball. Batter hits and runs to first three times. The base runner runs from first to second three times (batter should attempt to hit at least one fly ball so the runner can practice tagging up). After running, the player should rotate to an infield position and then rotate from an infield position to an outfield position.

Goals
- Runner takes off when batter steps.
- Runner tags up, taking off as soon as any defensive player touches the ball.

Cues
- Be in ready position.
- Take off (or step off) on batter's step.
- On a fly ball, go when ball contacts glove of any defensive player.
- Run hard and prepare to slide.

GAME 2

Setup
Repeat game 1. Defense scores a bonus run by throwing out base runner at second base.

Level II

Students who have completed level I or who have previous playing experience, such as on a recreational team, should be ready for level II. Most of the lessons in level II focus on the situation in which there are no outs or 1 out and a runner on first base. In this situation defenders focus on force plays at second base, including plays from outfield throws and double plays from second to first. Many of these plays require crossover play. In crossover play the shortstop covers second base when the ball is hit to the right side of the infield or outfield. The fielder at second base covers it when balls are hit to the left side of the infield or outfield. We also introduce relays during level II, focusing on when to use a relay, how to perform a relay, and how to line up a relay.

In level II, students also solve the problem of where to hit the ball in order to get on base or to advance the runners. The situation of no outs or 1 out with a runner on first provides opportunities for students to refine their base running, specifically, they continue to learn how to hit and run to first and advance from first to second quickly and safely.

Players must be able to accurately throw in from the outfield.

Lesson 8

Tactical Problem
Getting on base

Lesson Focus
Situation is 0 to 2 outs, no runners on base, grounder to left infield

Objectives
- Hit a ground ball to the left side of the infield.
- Hit and run hard to first base.

GAME 1

Setup
No runners on base, 0-2 outs

Goals
- Offensive batter places ball in an area of the field that allows her to get on first base.
- Defense throws ball to first, ahead of the runner.

Conditions
- Play 4v4 minimum, 5v5 optimum, 6v6 maximum.
- Defensive players play first, second, third, and shortstop.
- Batter must hit a ground ball to the infield and get to first before the throw.
- Player scores a run by safely reaching first base.
- Whether safe or out, the runner returns to the dugout area.
- Inning is over after 3 runs or 3 outs, whichever comes first.

Questions

Q: When there are 0 to 2 outs and no runners on base, where is the best place to hit the ball?

A: To the left side of the infield, down the third baseline.

Q: Why?

A: It requires a longer throw to first and you are more likely to get on base.

Q: How did you have to run to get to first before the throw?

A: Fast without looking at the ball.

PRACTICE SITUATION

Setup

Place cones on the left field line (3 or 4 abreast) between third base and shortstop and between shortstop and second base. Hitting from a tee or pitch, the batter attempts to hit cones. Batter gets five tries and runs to first base following the fifth attempt. Remaining players field at third, shortstop, and first and others can back up infielders from outfield positions. Remaining players can practice running to first base as the batter hits the first 4 of her 5 attempts.

Goals

- Angle bat to hit toward third baseline or between third and shortstop.
- Hit and run hard.

Cues

- Use normal to open stance.
- Make contact in the power zone.
- Angle bat toward target.
- Follow through target.

GAME 2

Setup

Repeat game 1. Defensive team scores a bonus run when fielder at third base or shortstop throws out the base runner.

Lesson 9 — Level II

Tactical Problems

Advancing to the next base (second); defending bases (second)

Lesson Focus

Situation is no outs or 1 out, runner on first, grounder to left infield

Objectives

- Base runner runs from first to second base.
- Fielder at second covers her base.

GAME 1

Setup

Runner on first, 0-1 out

Goals

- Offensive team safely gets runners to first and second.
- Defensive team turns a double play.

Conditions

- Play 3v3 minimum, 6v6 maximum.
- Batter must hit a ground ball to left side of the infield.
- Player scores a run by safely reaching first base.
- Whether safe or out, the runner returns to the dugout area.
- Inning is over after 3 runs or 3 outs, whichever comes first.

Questions

Q: *Who should cover second base when the shortstop or third-base player fields the ball?*

A: The player at second base.

Q: *How did the second-base player cover second base when the ball was fielded in front of the base path?*

A: Pivoted inside, moved to the inside edge of the base, and then stepped with the left foot (pivoted) to throw to first base.

Q: *How did second-base player cover second base when the ball was fielded behind the base path?*

A: Performed an outside crossover, moved to the outside edge of the base, and then crossed her feet on the throw to first.

Q: *What if there is a chance that the runner will interfere?*

A: Second-base player should use a rocker step, stepping on the base and then pushing away from the base to make the throw.

PRACTICE SITUATION

Setup

Ball hit to left side of infield, play at second base. Second-base player covers second base. Additional players serve as base runners. Offense should always have a runner on first base. Runners practice proper base running.

Goals

- Use proper footwork when covering second.
- Turn the double play.

Cues

- Adjust to position of ball, incoming throw, and incoming runner.
- Use crossover if ball is coming from behind base.
- Use inside pivot if covering inside base.
- Use rocker step if there is no need to cross the base.
- Catch ball first, get sure out.

GAME 2

Setup

Repeat game 1. Defensive team scores 3 bonus runs for every double play turned by second-base player.

Tactical Problems
Advancing to the next base (second); defending bases (second)

Lesson Focus
Situation is no outs or 1 out, runner on first, grounder to right infield

Objectives
- Run from first to second base.
- Cover second from shortstop position.

GAME 1

Setup
Runner on first, 0-1 out

Goals
- Offensive team safely gets runners to first and second.
- Defensive team turns a double play.

Conditions
- Play 3v3 minimum, 6v6 maximum.
- Batter must hit a ground ball to right side of the infield.
- Player scores a run by safely reaching first base.
- Whether safe or out, the runner returns to the dugout area.
- Inning is over after 3 runs or 3 outs, whichever comes first.

Questions
Q: *Who should cover second base when the first or second-base player fields the ball?*
A: Shortstop.

Q: *How did the shortstop cover second base when the ball was fielded in front of the base path (path from first to second)?*
A: Crossed over on the inside, came toward and touched the base while catching the throw, and then used the crossover step to throw to first.

Q: *How did the shortstop cover second base when the ball was behind the base path?*
A: Used outside crossover, crossed over and touched the base while catching the throw, and used the crossover step to throw to first.

PRACTICE SITUATION

Setup
Ball hit to right side of infield. Play at second base. Shortstop covers second base. Additional players serve as base runners. Offense should always have a runner on first base. Runners practice proper base running.

Goals
- Use proper footwork to cover second.
- Turn the double play.

Cues
- Adjust to position of ball, incoming throw, and incoming runner.
- Keep feet moving to first base after throw.

GAME 2

Setup
Repeat game 1. Defensive team scores 3 bonus runs for double play turned by the shortstop.

Lesson 11 Level II

Tactical Problems
Moving the runner; defending space by outfield positions

Lesson Focus
Situation is no outs or 1 out, runner on first, fly ball to outfield

Objectives
- Batter hits a fly ball to the outfield.
- Fielder fields a fly ball and throws to second quickly.
- Base runner tags up and runs from first to second.

GAME 1

Setup
Runner on first, 0-1 out

Goals
- Offensive players
  - Batter hits long fly ball to an outfield area to help the runner to advance to second.
  - Runner tags up on the catch and runs as quickly as possible to second base.
- Defensive players
  - Catch the ball on the fly and make throw to second ahead of the runner tagging up from first.

Conditions
- Play 6v6 minimum.
- Defensive players play all four outfield positions plus shortstop and second base.
- Offensive team starts with a runner on first.
- Batter must hit a ball out of the infield (ball cannot touch the ground in front of the base path).
- Runner scores when he reaches second safely.
- Whether safe or out, the runner returns to the dugout area.
- Inning is over after 3 runs or 3 outs, whichever comes first.

Questions
Q: *When is the best time to hit a fly ball?*
A: When there are 0 or 1 out and you want to move or score a runner.

Q: *How did you have to swing the bat to hit a fly ball?*
A: Hard and fast, hit through center of ball, and follow through.

Q: *What is the best way to field a fly ball so you can make a quick throw?*
A: Catch ball over throwing shoulder.

Q: On a fly ball, when can the runner advance to second?
A: When a fielder touches the ball.

Q: When should the runner leave the base?
A: As soon as a defensive player touches the ball.

PRACTICE SITUATION

Setup

Batter hits fly balls to outfield, with runner on first base. Each batter attempts to hit five fly balls and then rotates. Runner must tag up and run on a fly ball to provide a throwing situation for outfielders. Batters may have to move up in the infield so they can hit a fly ball to the outfield. Students may also choose to hit fly balls off a tee or to throw the ball.

Goal

Reach second base safely after tagging up on a fly ball hit to the outfield.

Cues

- Hitting a fly ball
  - Swing fast through center of ball.
  - Follow through toward outfield.
- Throwing from outfield
  - Catch over throwing shoulder.
  - Recover and throw immediately.
- Tagging up
  - Ready position.
  - Listen for coach to say "go."
  - Run hard.

GAME 2

Setup

Repeat game 1. Defensive team scores 1 bonus run for a putout at second base on a throw from an outfielder.

Lesson 12   Level II

Tactical Problem

Defending bases

Lesson Focus

Situation is no outs or 1 out, runner on first, grounder or line drive to outfield

Objective

Proper coverage of second base when ball hit to left side and right side of outfield.

GAME 1

Setup

Runner on first, 0-1 out

Goal

Appropriate defensive player covers second base on a ball hit to the outfield.

Conditions

- 6v6 minimum and defensive players play all four outfield positions plus shortstop and second base.
- Offensive team starts with a runner on first.
- Batter must hit the ball out of the infield (the ball cannot touch the ground in front of the base path).
- Runner scores when she reaches second safely.
- Whether safe or out, the runner returns to the dugout area.
- Inning is over after 3 runs or 3 outs, whichever comes first.

Questions

Q: *What was the goal of the game?*
A: To have the appropriate player cover second base on a hit to the outfield.

Q: *Which infield player should cover second base on a hit to the left side of the infield?*
A: The second-base player.

Q: *Which infield player should cover second base on a hit to the right side of the infield?*
A: The shortstop.

Q: *Which infield player should cover second base on a hit to center field? Why?*
A: The shortstop because she will be moving for a possible play on the ball.

PRACTICE SITUATION

Setup

3v3 to 8v8. Play with 2 to 4 outfielders, a shortstop, and a second-base player. The batter hits or throws three fly balls to each side of the outfield. Extra players run from first to second. Review proper footwork for base coverage on throws from outfield.

Goals

- Shortstop covers second on ball hit to right side of outfield.
- Second-base player covers second on ball hit to left side of outfield.

Cues

- Shortstop covers when ball is hit to the right.
- Second-base player covers when ball is hit to the left.

GAME 2

Setup

Repeat game 1. Defensive team scores 1 bonus run for a putout at second base on a throw from an outfielder if the appropriate player is covering second.

Lesson 13 Level II

Tactical Problem
Defending bases

Lesson Focus
Situation is no outs or 1 out, runner on first, a long ball to outfield

Objective
Use cutoff to get ball to the infield from the outfield.

GAME 1

Setup
Runner on first, 0-1 out

Goal
Use cutoff to get ball to the infield from the outfield.

Conditions
- Play 6v6 minimum.
- Defensive players play all four outfield positions plus shortstop and second base.
- Offensive team starts with a runner on first.
- Batter must hit a ball out of the infield (ball cannot touch the ground in front of the base path).
- Runner scores when he gets to second or third safely.
- Once runner reaches third, she returns to the dugout area.
- Inning is over after 3 runs or 3 outs, whichever comes first.

Questions
Q: *When should a shortstop or second-base player move toward the fielding outfielder to cut the ball off?*
A: When the runners have already advanced and you need to keep them from running to the next base.

Q: *Which player is responsible for cutoff when the ball is hit to left?*
A: The shortstop.

Q: *Which player is responsible for cutoff when the ball is hit to the right?*
A: The second-base player.

Q: *What should the other infielders do while the cutoff is being taken?*
A: Cover bases (except for the pitcher).

Let's practice using a cutoff player to keep runners from advancing.

PRACTICE SITUATION

Setup
Use 2 or 3 outfielders, shortstop, second-, third-, and first-base players. Extra players run from first base. Batter attempts six hits to outfield. Runners who safely advance to second stay and advance to third on the next hit. Runners must continue running until the cutoff player cuts the throw. Outfielders must throw to the cutoff, who is the only player who can throw a runner out.

Goals
- Do not let runners score.
- Throw to keep lead runner from advancing.

GAME 2

Setup
Repeat game 1. Defensive players score a bonus run every time they keep a runner from advancing to third base.

Tactical Problem
Defending bases

Lesson Focus
Situation is no outs or 1 out, runner on first, a long ball to the outfield

Objective
Use relay to get ball to infield from the outfield.

GAME 1

Setup
Runner on first, 0-1 out

Goal
Use relay from shortstop or second-base player to get runners out at bases.

Conditions
- Play 6v6 minimum.
- Defensive players play all four outfield positions plus shortstop and second base.
- Offensive team starts with a runner on first.
- Batter must hit a ball out of the infield (ball cannot touch the ground in front of the base path).
- Runner scores when she safely gets to second or third.
- Once runner reaches third, she returns to the dugout area.
- Inning is over after 3 runs or 3 outs, whichever comes first.

Questions

Q: What is the difference between a cutoff and a relay?
A: A cutoff is used to stop runners, while a relay is used to get the ball in quickly and to possibly make a play at a base.

Q: How does the shortstop or second-base player know where to stand to set up the relay?
A: Whichever of the two (shortstop or second-base player) covering the base should tell the relay player to move left or move right to help him adjust position.

Q: Should you throw the ball to the relay the same way you throw to a cutoff and why?
A: Yes, because if the throw is late she might need to just hold runners.

Q: How will she know whether to cut or to relay the ball?
A: The player covering the base (or the pitcher) should call, "Cut!"

PRACTICE SITUATION

Setup
Three players stand about 10 to 15 yards/meters apart. The middle player practices receiving a throw and pivoting to throw to the other player. The end players practice receiving the throw from over the throwing shoulder and throwing quickly and accurately to the pivot player.

Goal
Relay as quickly as possible from one player to another (compete with another group of three).

Cues
- Catch and cover over throwing shoulder.
- Pivot left on right foot (if right side is dominant).
- See target (glove).
- Transition quickly from catching to throwing position.

GAME 2

Setup

Repeat game 1. Defensive team scores a bonus run every time it keeps a runner from advancing to third base.

Level III

Lessons in level III advance tactical complexity by increasing the complexity of conditioned games, requiring players to use more refined skills and tactics. Students work on offensive situations that require a batter to place the ball (e.g., down the right-field line, between infielders, and down the left-field line) in order to get on base and to advance runners. Situations with a runner on second provide players opportunities to advance runners into scoring position, practice looking back the runner, and practice covering third base. We provide a few examples of these types of lessons in this section.

It takes knowledge and skill to determine where would be the best place to hit the ball or where to avoid hitting it, and to follow through by hitting it to that position.

Tactical Problem

Defending space by infield position

Lesson Focus

Situation is 0 to 2 outs, no runners, a grounder to the infield

Objectives

- Determine best place to hit ball in this situation.
- Hit and run hard to first.
- Understand when to run through or round first base.

GAME 1

Setup

0 runners on base, 0-2 outs

Goal

Given the situation of 0 to 2 outs and no runners on base, runner advances to as many bases as possible.

Conditions

- Use 4v4 at the minimum, 5v5 for the optimum, and 6v6 at the maximum.
- Batter must hit a ground ball.
- Runs are scored for each base safely reached after the initial hit.
- Inning is over after 3 runs or 3 outs, whichever comes first.

Questions

Q: *How did you run to first when there was absolutely no chance of advancing to second?*

A: Ran hard and fast, through or over first base.

Q: *How did you run to first when there was a possibility of advancing to second base?*

A: Rounded the base and observed the position of the ball (or listened to the coach).

Q: *What is the advantage of listening to a coach?*

A: You do not have to hesitate before advancing to second and you know when and where to run without having to watch the ball.

PRACTICE SITUATION

Setup

Three players in the field (minimum), to include first base, second base, third base, or shortstop, and three players batting. Have one player serve as a coach. The batter should hit a grounder to the left side of infield and then run hard and fast to first base. The coach should tell the runner whether to round or go to second.

Goal

Do what the coach says.

Cues

- Coach lets runner know what to do as soon as possible.
- Runners listen and don't watch the ball.

GAME 2

Setup

Repeat game 1. Coach gets a bonus run for her team for every base runner that advances safely (if the runner gets out at any base, no bonus runs are earned).

Lesson 16

Tactical Problem

Moving the runner

Lesson Focus

Situation is no outs or 1 out, runner on first, grounder behind runner

Objectives

- Determine best place to hit the ball.
- Run from first to third.

GAME 1

Setup

Runner on first, 0 to 1 out

Goals

- Offensive batter places ball to allow runner to get to third safely.
- Defense gets the lead runner out.

Conditions

- Play 4v4 minimum, 5v5 optimum, 6v6 maximum.
- Defensive players play first base, second base, shortstop, pitcher, and as many other infield positions as possible.
- Player scores a run by safely reaching third base.
- Inning is over after 3 runs or 3 outs, whichever comes first.

Questions

Q: *Into what area of the field should the batter place the ball in order to advance the runner?*
A: Behind the runner.

Q: *As a right-handed batter, how do you have to position yourself in the batter's box if you want to hit to right field?*
A: Angled toward the right side of the field.

Q: *At what point in the power zone should you contact the ball if you're attempting to hit down the right-field line?*
A: Outside toward the right-field side of the plate, between the plate and the area of the field you want to hit to.

Q: *How should you follow through?*
A: Follow through toward right field.

PRACTICE SITUATION

Setup

Batter hits three balls from a batting tee, attempting to hit down the right-field line. Then the batter hits three pitched balls, attempting to hit down the right-field line. Repeat the drill with the batter attempting to hit the ball between players covering first and second.

Goals

- Hit balls down right-field line.
- Hit balls between first- and second-base players.

Cues

- Pick a target (before the pitch).
- Angle body and bat toward target.
- Follow through toward target.
- Know where in the power zone you want to contact the ball before it is pitched.
- Contact ball in the power zone.

GAME 2

Setup

Repeat game 1. Batter scores 2 bonus runs for hitting a grounder behind the runner and through the right side of the infield.

Lesson 17 ☉   Level III

Tactical Problem

Defending bases

Lesson Focus

Situation is no outs or 1 out, runner on second, grounder down right-field line

Objective

Hold the lead runner.

GAME 1

Setup

Runner on second, 0-1 out

Goal

Get the lead runner out.

Conditions

- Play 4v4 at the minimum, 5v5 for the optimum, or 6v6 at the maximum.
- Defensive players play first base, second base, shortstop, pitcher, and as many other infield positions as possible.
- Offensive team must always have a runner at second base.
- Batter must hit a ground ball.
- Player scores a run by safely reaching third base.
- Once runner reaches third, he returns to dugout area.
- Inning is over after 3 runs or 3 outs, whichever comes first.
- Defensive team scores an additional run if it keeps the lead runner from advancing to third base.

Questions

Q: *After fielding the ball, what did you do to keep the runner from advancing?*
A: Looked the runner back.

Q: Once a throw is made to first, what should the first-base player do if the runner is advancing to third?

A: If the base player has a play, he should step off first and throw to third. If he doesn't have a play, he should get the sure out at first and then put the ball in his throwing hand and move toward third to hold the runner there.

Q: When the runner attempts to advance, what does the third-base player need to do?

A: Cover third base and provide a good target.

Q: How should the third-base player position herself to make a tag on the runner?

A: Straddle the bag.

Q: How should the third-base player tag the runner? Why?

A: Sweep low across the edge of the base closest to the runner because if the base player sweeps at the runner, the runner may move and avoid the tag.

PRACTICE SITUATION

Setup
Defensive team needs 4 or 5 infield players. Offensive team must have a runner on second base. Batter hits and runs. On the hit, the runner must run to third, hesitating if the fielder looks her back, but proceeding to third if the throw is made to first.

Goal
Get lead runner out at third using sweep tag.

Cues
- Look runner back.
- Players covering bases provide target.
- Sweep tag at base.

GAME 2

Setup
Repeat game 1. Offensive team scores a bonus run when the runner safely advances to third. Defensive team scores 2 bonus runs for a putout at third and 5 bonus runs for a double play (first to third).

Lesson 18   Level III

Tactical Problems
- Moving the runner
- Advancing to the next base

Lesson Focus
Situation is 2 outs, runner on second, line drive to outfield

Objective
Hit a line drive from left to middle of field.

GAME 1

Setup
Runner on second, 2 outs

Goal
Offense gets on base and moves runner to third.

Conditions

- 8v8 (you can have fewer players if you place restrictions on where batters can hit).
- Batter can hit ball anywhere on playing field.
- Player scores a run by reaching first safely and scores another run if the runner on second reaches third safely.
- Once runner reaches third, she returns to the dugout area.

Questions

Q: What did the batter do to advance the runner from second to third and to get on base?

A: Hit a line drive from the middle to the left side of the outfield.

Q: Why is this the best place to hit the ball?

A: If the ball makes it to the outfield, the infield still has to make a long throw to get the batter out at first and the runner still has a chance to advance to third.

Q: Where in the power zone is the best place for batters to contact the ball if they're trying to hit from left to left center?

A: Between the plate and left field or left center field.

Q: How should the batter contact the ball?

A: Swing level, hit through the middle of ball, and follow through to the target. The batter should know where to hit the ball before the pitch.

Q: What should the base runner do in this situation?

A: Watch to be sure that the ball gets through the infield and that the ball isn't caught on the fly in the outfield, then go to third (and home if possible).

PRACTICE SITUATION

Setup

From a batting tee or pitch, practice hitting (5 to 10 times in a row) line drives over or between infielders on the left side of the field. Base runners practice running from second to third as batters hit line drives.

Goal

Hit line drives between or over infielders and in front of or between outfielders.

Cues

- Know where you want to hit and where you want to make contact.
- Contact in the power zone and swing through toward target.

GAME 2

Setup

Repeat game 1. Line drives score 2 bonus runs.

Level IV

Lessons at level IV are for students with extensive experience in softball or baseball. Structure the lessons to provide many competitive experiences to motivate these players. For example, have students play the conditioned games against another team. They can then practice with another team or within their team. You can add some element of competition that allows players to compete against themselves or other members of their team.

Situations in level IV should provide opportunities for players to work individually and as a team. More advanced situations include batting and fielding with a runner on second, a runner on third, or even runners on second and third. These situations require more complex tactical play such as positioning for rundowns and backups and defending space as a team. Hitting during these situations requires placing the ball to allow the batter to get on base and score or to advance runners already on base. Students can refine their base running. Sliding and maneuvering to draw a throw are often considered part of advanced play.

Placing students in competitive situations helps them learn to think fast about what tactics should be used.

Lesson 19 — Level IV

Tactical Problem
Getting on base

Lesson Focus
Situation is 0 to 2 outs, no runners, grounders to left side of infield

Objective
Batter places ball between players on the left side of the infield.

GAME 1

Setup
No runners, 0 to 2 outs

Goal
Offense hits grounders between infielders.

Conditions
- Play 4v4 minimum, with defensive players at first, second, third, and shortstop.
- Batter must hit a ground ball.
- Player scores a run by safely reaching first base.
- Whether safe or out, the runner returns to the dugout area.
- Offensive team scores an additional run if the grounder goes through the infield.

Questions

Q: Where in the infield was the best place for the batter to hit the ball to get on base?

A: To the right side of the infield, down the third baseline or between third and shortstop.

Q: How should the batter position her body to place the ball?

A: In an open stance and slightly toward left field.

Q: Where in the power zone should the batter make contact if he is trying to hit through the left side of the infield?

A: Out in front, but the contact point and follow-through should be in the direction of the target.

Q: How many players were able to consistently hit where they were aiming?

A: Most players could not.

PRACTICE SITUATION

Setup

Put large cones or hoops between each infield position and put one on the foul line, behind the base. Batter attempts to hit a cone or hoop with the ball, scoring 5 bonus runs if she is successful. Each player should hit five balls from a tee, soft toss, or pitch and should run on the fifth trial.

Goal

Place ball between players on left side of the infield.

Cues

- Mentally see (visualize) where you want to hit the ball.
- Contact ball in power zone.
- Follow through toward target.
- Watch ball contact bat.

GAME 2

Setup

Repeat game 1. Offensive team scores 2 bonus runs by hitting the ball between or past the third-base player and shortstop.

Lesson 20   Level IV

Tactical Problem

Getting on base

Lesson Focus

Situation is 0 to 2 outs, runner on first, grounder to right side of the infield

Objective

Batter places ball between players on right side of the infield.

GAME 1

Setup
No runners, 0 to 2 outs

Goal
Offense hits grounders between infielders.

Conditions
- Play 4v4 minimum, with defensive players at first, second, third, and shortstop.
- Batter must hit a ground ball.
- Runner scores when she safely reaches second.
- Whether safe or out, the runner returns to the dugout area.
- Offensive team scores an additional run if the grounder goes through the infield.

Questions
Q: *Where in the infield was the best place for the batter to hit the ball to advance the runner to second base?*
A: To the right side of infield, down first baseline, or between first and second.

Q: *How should the batter position his body to place the ball?*
A: In a closed stance and slightly toward right field.

Q: *Where in the power zone should the batter make contact if she is trying to hit through the right side of the infield?*
A: Out in front, but the contact point and follow-through should be in the direction of the target.

Q: *How many players were able to consistently hit where they were aiming?*
A: Most players could not.

PRACTICE SITUATION

Setup
Put large cones or hoops between each infield position and put one on the foul line, behind the base. Batter attempts to hit a cone or hoop with the ball, scoring 5 bonus runs if successful. Each player hits five balls from a tee, soft toss, or pitch and runs on the fifth trial.

Goal
Place ball between players on right side of the infield.

Cues
- Mentally see (visualize) where you want to hit the ball.
- Contact ball in power zone.
- Follow through toward target.
- Watch ball contact bat.

GAME 2

Setup
Repeat game 1. Offensive team scores 2 bonus runs by hitting the ball between or past the first- and second-base players.

Tactical Problem
Defending bases

Lesson Focus
Situation is 0 to 2 outs, runner on first, grounder fielded by first-base player

Objective
Pitcher covers first base.

GAME 1

Setup
Runner on first, 0 to 2 outs

Goals
- Batter gets to first ahead of the pitcher.
- Defense gets ball to the pitcher (covering first) ahead of the runner.

Conditions
- Play 3v3 minimum, with defense playing first, second, and pitcher.
- Batter must hit a grounder to the right side of the infield.
- Only the pitcher can make the play at first base, unless she fields the ball.
- Player scores a run by safely reaching first base.
- Whether safe or out, the runner returns to the dugout area.
- Inning is over after 3 runs or 3 outs, whichever comes first.

Questions
Q: *What did the pitcher do to make the play at first base?*
A: Run to first ahead of the runner.

Q: *How did the pitcher need to run to avoid colliding with the runner?*
A: Parallel along the base path.

Q: *Where should fielders throw the ball so that the pitcher has the best opportunity to make the play?*
A: Directly over the base.

PRACTICE SITUATION

Setup
Batters hit grounders to the right and run to first base. Pitcher covers first and attempts to make the play ahead of the runner. Each player gets 3 to 5 attempts as pitcher. Each player should get at least three attempts to field and throw to first.

Goal
Pitcher gets runner out at first.

Cues
- Pitcher runs parallel with runner.
- Pitcher gets to first ahead of runner.
- Pitcher gives a good target.
- Fielders time throw to base.

GAME 2

Setup

Repeat game 1. Pitcher scores a bonus run for his team for every putout at first base.

Lesson 22

Tactical Problem

Defending bases

Lesson Focus

Situation is no outs or 1 out, runner on second, line drive through the middle

Objectives

- Double play from third to first.
- Perform sweep tag and throw.

GAME 1

Setup

Runner at second, 0-1 out

Goals

- Offense advances runner by hitting a line drive over or through middle of infield.
- Defense gets lead runner out, holds at second base, or turns three-to-one double play if runner tries to advance.

Conditions

- Play 4v4 minimum.
- Defensive players play first, second, third, shortstop, and pitcher.
- Batter must hit grounder or line drive between the shortstop and second base (place cones behind infield positions to mark area).
- Batter scores a run by reaching first while other runner reaches third safely.
- Once the runner reaches third, she returns to the dugout area.
- The defensive team gets 5 bonus runs for a three-to-one double play.
- The inning is over after 3 runs or 3 outs, whichever comes first.

Questions

Q: *When a three-to-one double play occurred, what type of tag was used by the third-base player?*
A: Sweep tag.

Q: *Why is the sweep tag best for a three-to-one double play?*
A: It keeps the fielder covering the base out of the way of the runner and it keeps the runner from knocking the ball out of the fielder's glove.

Q: *What's the advantage of a three-to-one double play?*
A: It cuts the lead runner and keeps a runner from getting into a scoring position.

PRACTICE SITUATION

Setup

Third-base player practices three-to-one double play, sweep tag, and throw. Set up a runner at second. Batter hits or throws ball toward or over second and runs to first.

Infielders attempt to field and throw to third. Provide at least five opportunities for each player to cover third base and to field and throw to third.

Goals
- Successfully complete the three-to-one double play.
- Use sweep to tag runner.

Cues
- Sweep with two hands.
- Sweep and step toward first (play).
- Sweep ball toward throwing shoulder (if possible).

GAME 2

Setup
Repeat game 1. Defensive team scores 5 bonus runs for three-to-one double play.

Lesson 23   Level IV

Tactical Problems
- Advancing to the next base
- Moving the runner

Lesson Focus
Situation is no outs or 1 out, runner on second, grounder or line drive to right side

Objectives
- Base runner serves as a decoy to delay throw.
- Player fielding ball looks runner back before throwing.

GAME 1

Setup
Runner on second, 0-1 out

Goals
- Offense gets on base and moves runner to third.
- Defense gets batter out and holds runner at second.

Conditions
- Play 8v8 (you can have fewer players if you place restrictions on where batters can hit).
- Offensive team must have a runner at second.
- Batter must hit to the right side of the field.
- Batter scores a run when she gets to first and the runner advances to third safely.
- Once the runner reaches third, he returns to the dugout area.
- The inning is over after 3 runs or 3 outs, whichever comes first.

Questions
Q: What should the runner on second do to delay the throw to first base?
A: Act like he is going to run.

Q: Where is the best place to hit to move the runner from second to third?

A: Hit toward the left side of the infield, between the third baseline and the shortstop.

Q: Why?

A: It requires a longer throw by the fielder and so the batter is more likely to move the runner and get to first safely.

Q: If the runner gets to third and a throw is made to first, what should the runner at third do?

A: Lead off toward home. Run home if the first-base player throws to third but return to third if she can't make it home.

Q: What should the runner on first do if the throw goes to third?

A: Run to second.

Q: As a defender, what would you do to hold runners?

A: Stand next to one of the runners with the ball in your throwing hand and look at the other runner; call for a time-out.

PRACTICE SITUATION

Setup

Use minimum of four infielders. Batter hits ball to right side of the infield and runs to first. The runner at second attempts to advance to third. After the batter gets to first, the runner on third attempts to lead off to draw a throw. Runners advance depending on throwing or until offense has ball under control and has called time-out.

Goals

- Base runners advance to as many bases possible.
- Fielders keep runners from advancing past second.

Cues

- Have ball ready to throw as you look runner back.
- Fake or take quick steps toward next base to delay or draw throw.
- Be ready to run.
- Keep moving or running until offense controls ball.

GAME 2

Setup

Repeat game 1. Offensive team scores 1 run for every runner reaching home safely. Defensive team scores 5 bonus runs for three-to-one double play.

Lesson 24   Level IV

Tactical Problem
Defend bases

Lesson Focus
Situation is no outs or 1 out, runner on first, grounder or line drive to right side

Objective
Execute a rundown.

GAME 1

Setup

Runner on first, 0 to 1 out

Goals

- Offense gets on base and moves runner to third.
- Defense gets batter out and holds runner at second.

Conditions

- Play 8v8 (you can have fewer players if you place restrictions on where batters can hit).
- Offensive team must have a runner at second.
- Batter must hit to the right side of the field.
- Batter scores a run when he gets to first and the runner advances to third safely.
- Once the runner reaches third, she returns to the dugout area.
- The inning is over after 3 runs or 3 outs, whichever comes first.

Questions

Q: What should you do when the runner is caught between bases?
A: Attempt to run her back to the base she came from.

Q: What should off-the-ball players do during a rundown?
A: Back up to the closest base.

Q: What if someone else is backing up a base?
A: Move in behind him.

Q: Why is support important in a rundown?
A: It keeps runners from advancing and scoring.

PRACTICE SITUATION

Setup

Practice in groups of three with two bases and one runner. Play running bases, and when the runner is caught between bases, attempt to tag her or run her back to the other base. Repeat on the base path with other players moving into backup positions.

Goals

- Get runner out.
- If you can't get runner out, keep him from advancing to the next base.

Cues

- Run the runner back to original base.
- Have ball ready to throw while running runner back.
- Know when to step out (and let backup continue rundown).
- Support, support, support.

GAME 2

Setup

Repeat game 1. Defensive team scores 5 bonus runs for tagging the runner out while in a rundown.

Summary

Chapter 11 has provided sample lessons for teaching softball tactically. You can extend or refine many of these lessons to create new ones focusing on a variety of off-the-ball movements and on-the-ball skills. The key to creating new lessons is to remember that for each situation (e.g., 1 out, runner on first) every offensive and defensive player has a role. As you examine a situation, ask yourself, "What off-the-ball movements or on-the-ball skills does the player need to adequately perform her role?" Having identified these movements and skills, you can create game and practice conditions to help your students understand what to do and how to do it.

If you find that a particular game is not working, try to identify where the game is breaking down. Then devise and implement a condition (or rule) that will force students to do what you want them to do. For example, if players are not throwing to second base to cut the lead runner, give the defensive team 2 additional runs each time it successfully gets the lead runner out. If a game is breaking down because students are unable to perform a particular skill, stop the game and ask students why they think the game is breaking down. Students know when things are not going well and are usually able to identify why. Having identified poorly executed skills as the reason for breakdown, students will be more motivated to practice these skills. Now students know *why* skill practice is necessary. Play ball!

CHAPTER 12

Cricket

Adrian Turner

Bowling Green State University

© Glyn Kirk

This chapter focuses on offensive and defensive tactical principles and skills for striking and fielding that can be developed in modified cricket games and practices. As in other striking and fielding games such as baseball, softball, and rounders, tactical problems in cricket include striking an object and running between safe areas to score and restricting scoring and getting batters out. In cricket, offensive (batting) principles include scoring runs, avoiding getting out or defending the wicket (staying in), and hitting into space in order to achieve these offensive goals. Defensive (bowling and fielding) principles include restricting runs scored, getting batters out, and preventing hitting into space in order to achieve these defensive goals. The simple offensive goals in cricket are to hit the ball into the field so that it eludes the fielders and to not get out. The defense attempts to restrict run scoring and to get batters out.

As with other games, cricket is best taught from a tactical approach by using small-sided games. Specific pedagogical principles are embedded in all of the games activities in this chapter in an attempt to maximize learning opportunities for participants. In small groups, students practice offensive (batting) and defensive (bowling and fielding) concepts in modified contexts replicating real game situations. Players equally practice each striking and fielding role. Though cricket is a team game, solo (or pair) activities are used to regularly rotate students through batting, bowling, and fielding roles. Batters of different abilities receive the same number of deliveries in many of the games and practices, so participants equally experience the offensive and defensive components of cricket. Most of the lessons in this chapter involve only 6, 7, or 8 players who compete either by themselves or as part of a pair. For a class of 24 up to 32 students to be active, you will need to set up three or four games simultaneously. At no time in any of these activities does a player sit out—players simply rotate into the next batting, bowling (pitching), or fielding role.

All lessons in this chapter begin with a game form, but some of the associated practices use smaller numbers than used in the initial game. For example, a lesson on bowling uses a triad practice but a batting game, Hit the Gap, involves five students. Other specific practices like Drive Cricket allow students to develop an offensive tactic and skill under similar conditions to those experienced in the real game. While the focus in Drive Cricket is offensive (a batting shot played to a specific ball), most of the game contexts in cricket are reciprocal and so defensive skills and tactics (catching, picking up, throwing, covering a teammate) are also practiced in these activities. The modified scoring used in the various levels of tactical complexity in this chapter rewards players for their defensive performances (bowling and fielding) in addition to their batting scores. Using small numbers and providing students with multiple opportunities to improve can instill motivation and confidence in players experiencing success in scaled-down situations representing similar pressures to those in the real game of 11 players per side.

Short lessons are a challenge to teaching cricket due to its time-consuming nature. Nevertheless, a conceptual, question-driven approach facilitates players' understanding. In addition, restricting the length (i.e., where the ball bounces) and line (i.e., direction) of the bowler's delivery encourages players to think tactically. In many of the games bowlers are given a numbered target zone (marked by lines, chalk, or spots) in which the ball should bounce. Different types of batting strokes played into specific sectors of the field are learned as responses to different lines and lengths of bowling in various games and practices. In this chapter, all of the concepts and terms used are for a right-handed batter or bowler. For a left-handed batter, whenever the chapter references to the off or leg side, the concepts and terms are reversed.

Diagrams have been provided for many of the lessons' activities. All figures relating to conditioned games are an oval, illustrating a cricket field. Some figures for the Practice Tasks show a rectangle as these practices take place in a specific context.

Some other issues to consider when teaching cricket include:

- **Facilities and equipment.** All of the game's activities can be adapted to specific environments (indoors or outdoors). The dimensions of the playing area (of both modified games and practices) can be varied to suit individual teaching contexts and specific student needs. Inexpensive, lightweight, and safe equipment such as tennis, Nerf, and Wiffle balls can be used in the games to slow the speed of the ball for smaller spaces and novice players. Large cones, chairs, or even trash cans can be used to simulate the wickets. Regulation trainer bats for softball (flat bats) are ideal as modified cricket bats for elementary children. Bats can also be shaped from wood (ideally willow), although these bats tend to be heavy for younger children. Three cutoff broom handles (28 inches, or 71 centimeters, high and together spanning 9 inches, or 23 centimeters, across) glued onto a piece of wood can be used as a makeshift wicket. Plastic wickets and bats made by Kwik Cricket are also available from physical education retailers around the world. All that is really required for playing cricket is a comparatively flat surface indoors or outdoors and space in which to hit a relatively soft ball.

• **Tactical framework.** Several features of cricket provide players with greater flexibility and many more opportunities for decision making than do other games in the fielding/run-scoring category. A tactical framework and three levels of tactical complexity for teaching cricket are presented in tables 12.1 and 12.2. Several key features of cricket are introduced in the first level of tactical complexity, and these features have major implications for the subsequent tactics and skills learned by the players.

Table 12.1   Tactical Problems, Movements, and Skills in Cricket

Tactical problems	Movements	Associated skills
SCORING AND STAYING IN		
Defending the wicket (staying in)	• Batting • Judging line and length of the ball	• Batting — Grip — Stance — Backlift — Taking guard
	• Moving forward or backward • Keeping the ball out • Defending a good length • Defending the short ball	• Defensive strokes — Front foot off-side and leg side (forward defense) — Back foot off-side and leg side (backward defense) — Leaving the ball
Scoring runs	• Moving forward or backward to attack • Looking for space • Attacking the half volley or low full toss	• Attacking strokes — Front foot off-side and leg side drive
	• Attacking the short ball	— Back foot — Across the line—leg side (pull shot) — Across the line—off-side (cut shot)
	• Working the short ball	— Down the line (fine, back foot leg glance) — (Back foot drive)
	• Working the full length ball	— Down the line (front foot leg glance) — Across the line (sweep/paddle)
	• Running between the wickets • Communication (calling) • Backing up	• Turning and changing hands • Grounding the bat

(continued)

Table 12.1 *(continued)*

Tactical problems	Movements	Associated skills
PREVENTING SCORING		
Getting the batter out	• Bowling – Making the batter play – Straight line and length – Attacking the off-stump – Moving the ball away – Looking for the edge – Moving the ball in – Slower or faster ball – Over or around the wicket – Moving wide on the crease • Bowling to a field – Leg side – Off-side	• Bowling – Basic action – Running up • Seam (I) – Leg cutter – Off-cutter – Yorker • Spin – Off-break – Leg break – Arm ball
	• Fielding – Field placements – Working the batter out – Attacking the batter • Ready position • Moving in	• Fielding • Catching – Close – Long
	• Running out the batter – Deciding where to throw	• Intercepting, picking up and throwing
Restricting run scoring	• Fielding • Defending space in front of the wicket • Field placements – Ready position – Moving in – Saving a single – Saving 4 runs • Backing up in the field	• Fielding • Ground fielding • Long barrier • Fielding on the move • Throwing the ball – Underarm – Overarm
	• Defending space behind the wicket • Communication in the field • Wicket keeper • Backing up in the field	Wicket keeper • Stance • Position • Takes and returns • Catching
Umpiring	• Umpire decisions – Out – No-ball – Bye – Wide – Six – Four	

Table 12.2 Levels of Tactical Complexity for Cricket

Tactical problems	Levels of tactical complexity		
	I	II	III
SCORING AND STAYING IN			
Defending the wicket (staying in)	• Judging line and length of the ball • Moving forward • Keeping the ball out (defending a good length)	• Judging line and length of the ball (moving forward or backward) • Moving backward • Keeping the ball out (Defending a short ball)	

Scoring runs	• Moving forward
	• Looking for space (Attacking the half volley or low full toss, down the line—off-side or leg side)
		• Moving backward
		• Looking for space
		  – Attacking the short ball, across the line—leg side
		  – Working the short ball, fine-leg side
		• Running between the wickets
		• Communication
			• Moving backward
			• Looking for space
			  – Working the short ball, down the line—off-side or leg side
			  – Attacking the short ball, across the line—off-side
			• Moving forward
			• Looking for space
			  – Working the full length ball, fine, down the line, leg side and across the line—leg side
			  – Running between the wickets
			  – Backing up
			  – Turning and changing hands

PREVENTING SCORING			

Getting the batter out	• Bowling
	  – Making the batter play
	  – Line and length
	  – Attacking the 'off stump'
	  – Moving the ball away/Looking for the edge
		• Bowling
		• Making the batter play
		  – Moving the ball into the batter
		  – "Yorking" the batter
		  – Achieving an L.B.W.
		  – Slower/faster ball
		  – Over/around the wicket
			• Bowling spin to tempt the batter (leg breaks, off breaks)
			• Bowling from wider on the crease

	• Fielding
	  – Slip catching
		• Attacking the batter
		• (Field placement
		  – close catching)	

		• Running out the batter – Deciding where to throw	

(continued)

Table 12.2 *(continued)*

Tactical problems	Levels of tactical complexity		
	I	II	III
PREVENTING SCORING			

Restricting run scoring	• Defending space in front of the wicket
	  – Ground fielding
	• Defending space behind the wicket
	  – Wicket keeping
	• Communication with the field
		• Field placement
		  – Saving a single
		  – Saving four runs
		• Backing up in the field
			• Bowling to a field
			  – Leg-side
			  – Off-side

Umpiring		• Umpire decisions
		  – Out
		  – No-ball
		  – Bye
		  – Wide
		  – Six
		  – Four	

Level I

In the first level of tactical complexity, teachers are encouraged to focus on both defensive (bowling and fielding) and offensive (batting) concepts as students are introduced to the game. Bowlers develop a basic understanding of a good line and length when attempting to restrict run scoring and to get batters out. Batters are taught the importance of defending a good line and length delivery and of attacking a ball that lands close by moving forward to play their shots. At this level students also develop an understanding of defending space behind and in front of the wicket.

Specifically:

- **The bowler delivers the ball with a straight arm to the batter.** It is illegal for the bowler to throw the ball (called a no ball—if the bowler throws the ball, the batting team receives another delivery and scores a run). All other defensive players are allowed to throw the ball when fielding.

- **The ball is allowed to bounce before it reaches the batter.** The bowler can use the bounce to make the ball deviate and thereby make batting more difficult. Doing so helps restrict run scoring and helps get the batter out.

- **Fielders can attempt to get one of two players out.** In games with two batters, this rule forces fielding players to decide where to throw the ball in order to execute an out (as in other striking and fielding games).

- **The batter is permitted to play the ball through 360 degrees.** This range allows for a greater variety of strokes and provides challenge for field placements. It also allows the defense to get a batter out behind the wicket.

While batting and bowling appear to be the more glamorous offensive and defensive activities, explain to your players that they will spend more time defending in the field than in any other activity in the game. In order to introduce this concept to students, fielding is the focus for the initial lesson at level I.

A bowler must deliver the ball with a straight arm.

Lesson 1 Level I

Tactical Problem
Defending space in front of the wicket

Lesson Focus
Getting the batter out with effective fielding

Objectives
- Successfully catch the ball.
- Field ground balls consistently.
- Return ball efficiently to the bowler.

GAME 1

Setup
Nonstop Cricket (6-8 players; see figure 12.1)

Goal
Defensive team gets ball back to the bowler safely.

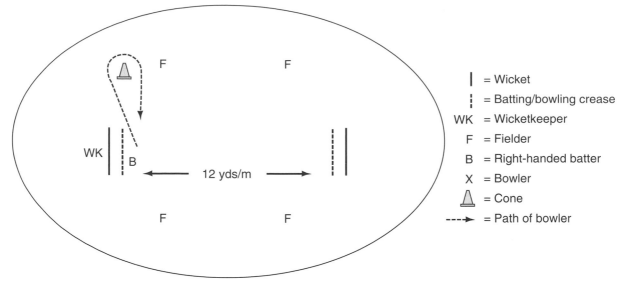

FIGURE 12.1

Conditions

- The bowler tosses the ball underhand to the batter, who stands in front of the wicket.
- The ball must be tossed to where the batter has a chance to hit it.
- If the batter misses the ball and it hits the wicket, he is out (bowled).
- The ball can bounce once before it gets to the batter.
- If the batter hits the ball into the air and it is caught by one of the fielders, the batter is out.
- There is no foul territory and the ball can be hit anywhere.

When the batter hits the ball, she runs around the cone and returns to her initial batting position in order to score a run. The batter bats until she is out or for a maximum of six pitches (one over). The fielders must return the ball to the bowler as quickly as possible once they field it. As soon as the bowler has the ball, he may toss it toward the wicket, regardless of whether or not the batter is there and ready to defend.

Each time a batter is out, a new bowler takes over and the fielders rotate one position clockwise. Each batter counts how many runs she scores, and the player with the most runs wins the game.

Questions

Q: What was the goal of your game when you were in the field?
A: To get the batter out.

Q: What did you do when you were fielding?
A: Tried to cover space along with other fielders by spreading out in a semicircle, or horseshoe, around the batter (similar shape to the infield in baseball or softball).

Q: When a batter consistently hits the ball past fielders in a certain area, what should the fielding players do?
A: Move one fielder deeper to cover a hard or high hit (to act as an outfielder does in baseball or softball).

Q: So moving a fielder deeper allows the batter to score a run in the area closer to the wickets?

A. Yes, but only 1 run rather than 2 or 3.

Q: How can fielders make the batter think that they are deeper (farther from the batter) than they really are?

A: As the bowler is about to deliver the ball, they should take three steps toward the batter. The exception is the wicketkeeper (a position similar to a catcher in softball or baseball), who remains crouched behind the wicket.

Q: Where are your hands positioned to be ready to field?

A: At your sides and a little in front (like a gunfighter in the Old West).

Q: When the ball is hit toward you, what are your options?

A: Catch the ball or field the ball (if it cannot be caught) and return it to the bowler.

Q: What position were your hands in to catch a ball coming from high in the air?

A: Either palms turned upwards until about at chest level or thumbs together (for higher balls).

Q: How did you field the ball if you were not able to catch it?

A: Moved feet and body in line with the ball and watched the ball safely roll into both hands.

Q: If the ball bounced awkwardly just in front of you, what did you do to keep from missing it?

A: Crouched low behind the ball.

Q: When you threw the ball back to the bowler, what type of throw did you use?

A: It depended on the distance to the bowler. For short distances an underhand toss worked well but for longer distances an overarm throw was better.

PRACTICE TASK 1

Setup
Partners use underarm throws to pass the ball high into the air. The receiver moves into position, catches the ball (with either thumbs or little fingers together), and brings it into his body. To extend the practice, have partners throw the ball overhand with a flatter trajectory.

Goal
Successfully catch seven consecutive throws.

Cues
- Catching
  - Watch the ball and move into position.
  - Form a cup with your hands.
  - Relax your arms, elbows away from body, and draw the ball into your body.

PRACTICE TASK 2

Setup
Practice with a partner. Partner 1 rolls the ball underhand to partner 2, who is already moving toward the ball. Partner 2 fields the ball and returns it with a throw. Partner 1 uses an overarm throw to bounce the ball just in front of partner 2. Partner 2 uses a long-barrier technique to safely field the bouncing ball.

Goal
Successfully field and return seven consecutive balls.

Cues

- Long barrier
  - Move in line with ball and field ball with little fingers touching and hands pointing down.
  - Position kneeling leg inside heel of other leg (to form a sideways barrier at a right angle to the oncoming ball).
  - Make kneeling leg the one opposite of your throwing arm (to allow a quick step forward and the throw return in one movement).

GAME 2

Setup
Nonstop Cricket

Conditions
- Every catch or fielding assist back to the bowler that results in a batter being out counts as 1 point.
- Player with the most points (not runs) wins.

Lesson 2 Level I

Tactical Problem
Restricting run scoring and getting the batter out

Lesson Focus
Bowling straight from stationary position

Objectives
- Make the ball pitch in line with the wicket or outside the off (outside) stump.
- Understand bowling line and length.
- Learn basic bowling action.

GAME 1

Setup
Nonstop Cricket (6-8 players)

Goal
Prevent batter scoring in target area through accurate bowling.

Conditions
- The batter scores 4 runs (like for a home run in baseball) and does not have to run around the cone to score if she hits the ball between the two cones on the leg side (see figure 12.2).
- Only one fielder may stand between the cones.
- If the batter hits the ball anywhere other than between the two cones she still has to run to score (as in the previous game of Nonstop Cricket).

Questions

Q: What type of pitch is easy for a batter to hit between the cones?
A: A pitch that arrives at a comfortable height (between thigh and abdomen), either on the fly or after bouncing in imaginary zones 4, 5, 6 (see figure 12.2).

Q: What type of shot will the batter play to this kind of ball?
A: He will pull the ball with a softball-style (horizontal) swing.

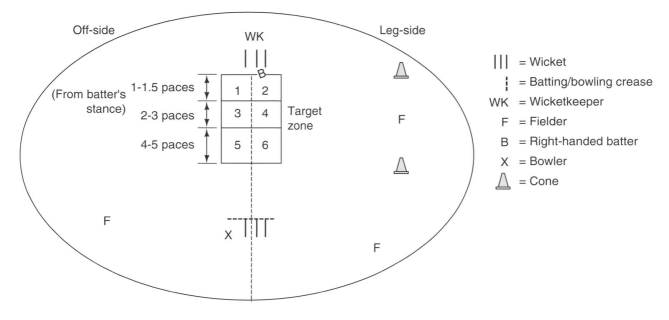

FIGURE 12.2
Bowling target zones.

Q: What type of pitch is harder for the batter to hit between the cones?
A: A pitch that bounces within 1 to 3 yards/meters of the batter and that comes at a low height (see zones 1 and 3 in figure 12.2).

Q: Where does this ball land in relation to the batter and the wicket?
A: The side opposite the batter's legs (the off-side—see figure 12.2).

Q: So in this game, what has the bowler learned?
A: To pitch the ball into zones 1 and 3 (close to the batter and in-line with or outside the batter's off (outside) stump (wicket) in order to prevent the ball from being hit (pulled) between the cones. This would be a good line and length.

Notes
- In cricket, three stumps constitute a wicket: the off (outside), middle, and leg (closest to the batter's legs) stumps (see figure 12.2).
- For a left-handed batter, all of the concepts and terms are reversed.
- The positions of the cones in the game also need to be reversed for a left-handed batter.

Now that the bowler knows where to make the ball land, she has to learn the technique of bowling because underarm tossing or throwing is not allowed in cricket.

PRACTICE TASK

Setup

Students are grouped in pairs, with partners standing about 12 to 15 yards/meters apart. Each bowler uses an overarm bowling action (keeping his arm straight) to bounce the ball 1 to 2 paces in front of his partner. The partner gathers the ball and then bowls the ball back. A set of wickets or a cone can be used to focus the bowler's aim.

FIGURE 12.3
Cricket triad.

Goal
Make the ball land in target zones 1 and 3.

Variation
A batter can be added to play shadow strokes only, deliberately missing the ball and allowing it to hit the wicket or reach the wicketkeeper. (The player who is not bowling can act as wicketkeeper). Ground targets (plastic strips or even bandanas) can also be placed in front of the batter's wicket to represent the target (zones 1 and 3) for the bowler. A triad practice can now include a batter, bowler, and wicketkeeper. Each batter receives six balls (an over) before rotating to the next position. See figure 12.3.

Cues
- Bowling
  - Grip the ball with your fingers (middle and index fingers form a "V" on top, thumb and third finger underneath).
  - Turn sideways with your arm holding the ball at your side.
  - Make a cross with your arms.
  - Raise front knee and nonbowling arm as high as possible and look at wicket (batter) behind the nonbowling arm.
  - Swing the nonbowling arm down past the hip while your bowling arm remains straight, traveling past your head and releasing the ball.
  - Let your bowling arm follow across your body as you step forward.
- Remember:
  - Lift your front leg, bending your knee.
  - Swing your nonbowling arm down behind your body and your bowling arm past your head (like a windmill).
  - Stay sideways as long as possible.
  - Action of bowling arm is analogous to drawing a number 6.

GAME 2

Setup
Repeat Nonstop Cricket with bowlers now focusing on the line (accuracy) and length (position of bounce) of each delivery. Use a cricket bowling action. Force the batter to hit across the line of the ball in order to score between the cones.

   · Each time a batter is out (caught or bowled), the bowler earns a wicket.
   · Bowler with the most wickets wins the game.

Lesson 3 Level I

Tactical Problem
Defending the wicket (moving forward, using front foot)

Lesson Focus
Defending a good length ball and pushing to space

Objectives
   · Block the ball by coming forward to meet the bounce.
   · Take guard, grip, stance, and backlift.
   · When to leave a good ball.

GAME 1

Setup

Tip and Run. Bowler bowls the ball, aiming at zone 3. After successfully contacting the ball, the batter runs from the batting crease to the bowling crease (see figure 12.4).

   The ball can be hit anywhere inside the modified boundary (15-yard/meter radius around the batting strip, which is the area between the two wickets). A run is scored when the batter touches his bat over the bowling crease. He then walks back to the batting crease and the bowler and fielders prepare for his (the same player's) next at bat. The batter can only be run out at the end to which he runs. A run-out is made when the ball is thrown to the bowler and the bowler hits the wicket where

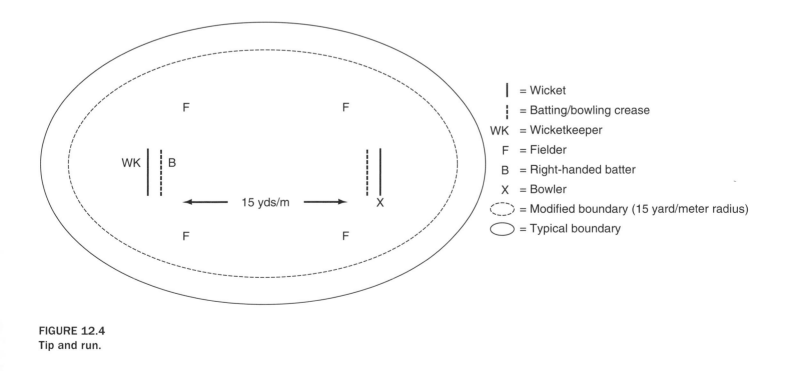

FIGURE 12.4
Tip and run.

she is standing with the ball before the batter gets past the bowling crease. A direct hit by a fielder throwing at the bowler's wicket also runs out the batter. Additionally, the batter can be out if he is bowled (he lets the bowler's pitch hit the wicket) or if a fielder catches the ball on the fly. Each batter faces a maximum of 4 to 6 deliveries (or depending on time, bats until he is out). Each time a batter is out (or his 4-6 ball innings are over), a different bowler bowls at the new batter. When all players have batted, the player with the most runs wins.

Condition
If the ball rolls outside the 15-yard/meter inner boundary, the run is discounted.

Questions

Q: When you were batting what were you trying to do?
A: Make contact with the ball and send it to a space inside the inner boundary.

Q: What actions help you to do this?
A. Looking to see where the fielders are positioned before each delivery and then pushing the ball into gaps in the field.

Q: Where do you stand in relation to the wicket?
A: Take guard by lining up with the middle wicket or stump and by marking the batting crease with the bat (or chalk if the ground is hard) so you know where to stand each time.

Q: How far from the wicket do you stand?
A: Straddle the batting crease so you can pick up the bat without hitting the wicket behind you during the backlift (which results in the batter being out).

Q: When the bowler made the ball pitch in zones 1 and 3 and it was likely to hit the wicket, what kind of swing did you use?
A. A vertical swing with a straight bat.

Q: Why did you use this type of swing?
A. Less chance of missing the ball.

Q: When swinging the bat vertically, where does your backlift begin?
A. The toe of the bat points almost at the wicketkeeper at the top of the backlift.

Q: When do you pick up the bat?
A. Just as the bowler lifts her front arm.

Q: If the ball lands about 2 paces in front of you and will hit the wicket if you miss it, what do you do to make sure you contact the ball?
A. Step toward the ball with your front foot.

Q: If the ball was likely to miss the outside (off) wicket, what could you do?
A. Allow it to pass without attempting a shot.

Q: Why would you want to do this?
A. To prevent a slight deflection or edge to the wicketkeeper that would result in an out (caught behind).

Q: By letting the ball pass, aren't you giving up a scoring opportunity?
A. Yes, but the ball is often harder to track when you begin to bat than when you have been batting for a while so you have a chance of hitting the edge, rather than the middle, of the bat.

PRACTICE TASK 1

Setup
Divide the class into pairs, with one bat per pair

Goal
Partners check each other's grip, batting stance, and backlift and help each other take guard in front of a wicket.

Cues
- Grip
  - Hands close together toward top of handle.
  - Form Vs with the thumb and index finger on each hand that are in line along the handle.
- Stance
  - Feet are shoulder-width apart and parallel with the crease.
  - Slightly flex knees.
  - Keep eyes level and watching bowler's hand at delivery.
- Backlift
  - Front shoulder and elbow point to bowler.
  - Swing bat straight back above off stump with face of bat open.
  - Keep elbows clear of body.

PRACTICE TASK 2

Setup
Practice for "push in the box" includes a batter, bowler, fielder, and wicketkeeper. Each batter receives one over before rotating to the next position. The bowler attempts to deliver the ball into zones 1 and 3. If the bowler has difficulty with accuracy, an underhand toss or dart throw can be used by the bowler at a closer distance (see figure 12.5).

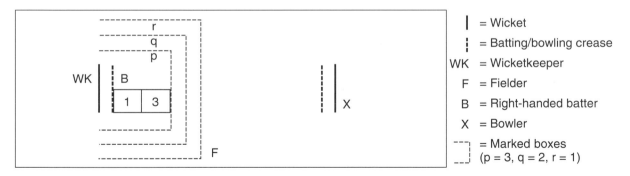

FIGURE 12.5
Push in the box.

Goal
Batter attempts to play the ball with a vertical, straight bat and soft hands.

Conditions
- Batter scores 3 runs if ball remains inside box p, 2 if it remains inside box q, and 1 if it remains inside box r.
- The batter also scores 1 run for leaving a ball that is wide of her off-stump.

- If the batter is out, caught, or bowled, 4 runs are deducted from her score.
- The batter with the most runs wins.

Cues
- Forward defense stroke.
  - Move your head into line with the ball.
  - Step with the foot nearest the bowler and bend the same knee.
  - Angle bat vertically down alongside knee.
  - Let ball hit bat and do not follow through.
  - Control bat with top hand, gripping bat with thumb and first two fingers of bottom hand.

GAME 2

Setup
Tip and Run

Goals
- Stay in and avoid getting out (for greater opportunity to win the game).
- Push the ball to a space inside the inner boundary.

Conditions
- If the ball rolls outside the 15-yard/meter inner boundary, the run is discounted.
- Score 1 run for leaving a ball that passes outside the off stump.
- Player with most runs wins.
- If the batter is out before the end of his allotted over (six balls), then he is out in this game—no second chances.

Lesson 4 Level I

Tactical Problem
When to attack the ball by moving forward

Lesson Focus
Attacking the half volley or low full toss on the front foot

Objective
Look for space and drive the ball along the ground.

GAME 1

Setup
Second-Chance Cricket

Goal
Hit the ball into space in the sector.

Conditions
- Bowler bowls the ball at target zones 1 and 2 (trying to make the ball land 1-1.5 steps from the batter's stance and in line with the wicket or outside the off stump).
- Batter attempts to hit the ball into the sector (see figure 12.6), the only area in which she can score (and so the fielders align to protect this area).
- Batter scores a run each time she hits the ball and runs from the batting crease to the bowling crease.

- Batter scores 4 points and does not have to run if she hits the ball through the field to the outer boundary of the sector.
- Batter can be out by being bowled, caught, or run out at the bowler's wicket.
- Each time a batter is out (or her allotted number of deliveries finishes), a different bowler has a turn to bowl at the new batter.
- Players rotate through the roles of batter, bowler, fielder, and wicketkeeper.
- The player with the most runs after all players have batted wins.

Variation

If the ball does not land in zones 1 and 2 or the batter misses the ball (as long as it does not hit the wicket), he can hit the ball off a low tee (3-4 inches or 7.6-10 centimeters)—he gets a second chance. See figure 12.6.

Questions

Q: *What type of ball did you hit successfully into the sector?*
A: A ball that bounced about a pace away from my batting stance or that could be hit on the fly.

Q: *In order to hit the ball, what did you do with your feet?*
A: Stepped the front foot toward where the ball pitched.

Q: *What batting techniques helped you hit the ball effectively?*
A. Swinging the bat vertically and following straight through.

Q: *If the ball pitched in line with or just outside your off-stump (wicket), where did your stroke finish?*
A. Pointing where the hit went on the off-side of the wicket.

Q: *If the ball pitched on your leg stump, where did your stroke finish?*
A. Pointing where the hit went on the leg side of the wicket.

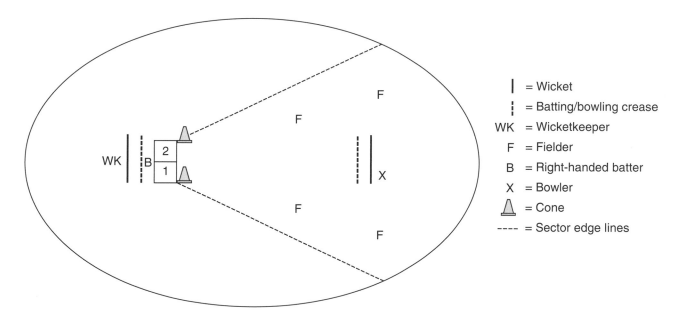

| = Wicket
┊ = Batting/bowling crease
WK = Wicketkeeper
F = Fielder
B = Right-handed batter
X = Bowler
⬣ = Cone
---- = Sector edge lines

FIGURE 12.6
Second-chance cricket.

Q: What might cause you to miss the ball?
A. Not watching the ball, swinging too hard, or lifting the head.

Q: When did you lob the ball into the air, giving a fielder an easy catch?
A. When the ball pitched farther away than one big step and bounced up a little higher on the bat.

Q: What stroke could you have played to that ball instead?
A. Forward defensive stroke because the ball was a good length ball.

Q: So the drive is just an extension of the forward defensive shot for a ball landing a little bit closer?
A. Yes, a half volley or low full toss.

Q: Is it always good to hit the ball along the ground?
A. Generally yes, but sometimes hitting the ball into the air gets the ball over the fielders and can reach the sector boundary so more runs are scored. The risk of hitting into the air is that the ball can get caught.

PRACTICE TASK

Setup
Drive Cricket
The bowler tosses the ball to the batter so that it bounces in zone 1 (see figure 12.7). The ball could also be hit off a low tee placed in that zone if the batter is having difficulty hitting. The batter attempts to drive the ball between the cones where the fielders are positioned. If the ball goes past the cones, a run is scored. The batter can double his score by running to the crease where the bowler stands, touching his bat over the bowling crease, and returning to the batter's wicket (this simulates the 2 runs that would be earned in the real game). Fielders attempt to run out the batter by throwing the ball to the wicketkeeper before the batter returns. The batter decides whether to risk the additional run, and he loses all runs on the shot if he is out. Each

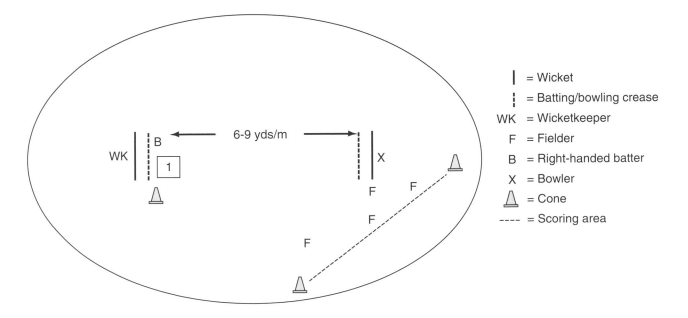

FIGURE 12.7
Drive cricket (off-drive).

batter receives six deliveries and attempts to score as many runs as possible. If a fielder catches a fly ball from the batter, no runs are scored on that shot.

Goals
- Batter uses off drive to hit a ball on the off-side.
- Batter elects to hit the ball into the air or attempts a second run in order to double her score.

Variation
Bowler tosses ball into target zone 2 (see figure 12.2, page 369) and cones are set up on the leg, or on, side for an on-drive.

Cues
- Watch the ball.
- Step front foot toward ball.
- Use straight backlift.
- Swing bat vertically.
- Follow through in the direction of the hit.

GAME 2

Setup
Second-Chance Cricket

Goal
Use off- and on-drives to score runs.

Conditions
- Batter elects to run or not run (he assesses the risk on each shot).
- May remove second-chance condition.

Lesson 5

Tactical Problem
Making the batter play

Lesson Focus
Bowling line and length and moving the ball away from the batter

Objectives
- Attack the off-stump.
- Add a run-up to the bowling action.
- Look for the outside edge of the bat.

GAME 1

Setup
Off-Side Cricket

Goal
Bowler aims at zone 3 around the batter's off-stump.

Conditions
- Batter attempts to hit the ball into the off-side (see figure 12.8).

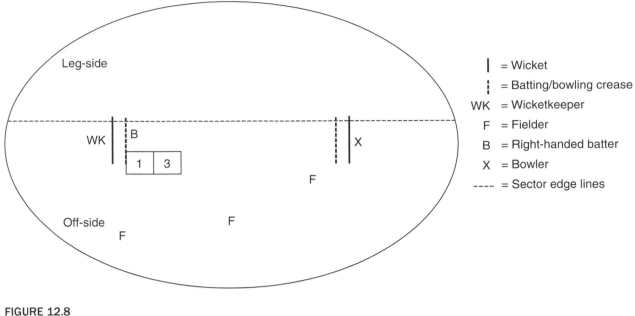

FIGURE 12.8
Off-side cricket.

- Batter can score only in the off-side and so fielders protect this area while also helping the bowler get the batter out.
- A ball hit on the leg side of the wicket (see figure 12.8) is dead and no runs can be scored.
- Other conditions are similar to Second-Chance Cricket but if the batter misses the ball there is no second chance in this game.

Questions

Q: *When you are bowling in this game, what are you trying to do?*
A: Bowl the batter out or have her shot get caught in the field.

Q: *What type of shot will the batter try to play to a ball that lands in zone 1?*
A: If the ball lands about a pace in front of her feet, the drive is likely, but if the ball lands farther away she may play a forward defensive stroke.

Q: *Why can't the batter let the ball pass by?*
A: It's too close to judge whether the ball will hit the wicket so she has to play a shot.

Q: *What else can happen here if the batter tries to hit at a ball that is close to but outside the line of the wickets?*
A: The ball can be deflected off the outside edge of the bat to the wicketkeeper.

Q: *So bowling into zone 3 (see figure 12.2) and in line with the off-stump is an effective place to bowl the ball?*
A: Yes, it is a good line and length.

Q: *How can you make it even harder for the batter to make good contact with the ball?*
A: By bowling a little faster and also by making the ball deviate away from the batter.

Q: *What else could you do to tempt the batter into driving the ball on the off-side?*
A: Show the batter a big gap in the field by moving a fielder out of the way.

Q: Where could you place the fielder when the ball deflects off the edge?

A: Close to the wicketkeeper in case the ball deflects wide of the wicketkeeper. (The fielder is called a slip, see figure 12.9.)

Q: Is there any other time when the batter has difficulty hitting the ball?

A: When the ball lands in line with his toes. (This bowling delivery is called a Yorker.)

PRACTICE TASK 1

Setup

- Have students line up on the edge of the instructional area and practice running up and bowling a ball that bounces once (in target zone 3).
- Review overarm bowling position (see cues for lesson 2).
- Have students lift the arm they bowl with and stamp the opposite foot (the one they will jump off of).
- Build the following sequence (critical features): Run, jump off the foot opposite the bowling arm, throw both arms in the air, and turn so that the landing foot is perpendicular to the direction of travel (finishing in the overarm bowling position, as practiced in lesson 2).
- Bowl an imaginary ball.

Goal

Four out of six pitches land in target zone 1.

- Work on increasing delivery speed.

Cues

- Bowling from run-up.
  - Run, jump, and land in overarm bowling position.
  - Look where you want the ball to pitch.
  - Bowl an imaginary ball by drawing a number 6 with your bowling arm.

PRACTICE TASK 2

Setup

Looking for the edge requires a bowler, batter, wicketkeeper, and slip (see figure 12.9). The bowler aims at target zone 3 around the batter's off-stump. The bowler's front foot must be on or behind the batting crease at the bowler's end as she releases the ball

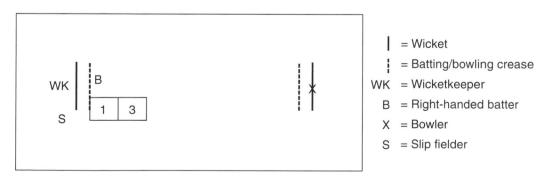

FIGURE 12.9
Looking for the edge.

in the bowling action. If the foot is not properly aligned, the bowl is a no ball and the batter can hit the ball but can only be run out (not caught or bowled). The batter also releases another bowl as a penalty for the bowler's mistake.

Conditions

- Batter attempts to hit the ball into the off-side but bats with a softball bat or cricket bat (playing with the edge of the bat facing the bowler).
- Playing with the edge of the bat facing the bowler should facilitate a lot of small deflections resulting in catches to the wicketkeeper and slip.
- Each batter receives six deliveries and then players rotate.

Goals

- Bowl batter out or have batter caught behind the wicket.
- Bowl leg cutter (move the ball away from the right-handed batter after it hits the ground).

Cues

- Seam of the ball is vertical or pointed in the direction of the slip.
- Middle finger runs along seam, with index finger placed 1/2 inch (1.3 centimeters) away.
- Ball rests between thumb and third finger.
- As the ball is released the index and middle fingers work down the inside of the ball (as right-handed bowler views it when starting with it above right shoulder) so that the thumb passes under ball, generating turn on the ball.

GAME 2

Setup

Off-Side Cricket
The batter can be out by being bowled, caught, or run out at the bowler's wicket. Each time a batter is out (or her allotted number of deliveries finishes), a different bowler has a turn to bowl at the new batter.

Goal

Bowler uses pace, good line and length, and leg cutter to tempt batter and make the batter play.

Conditions

- Bowler decides whether to attack batter with 1 or 2 slips or place fielders in defensive (run-saving positions) as in figure 12.8.
- Bowler can also place a fielder very deep to save 4 runs and therefore virtually give the batter 1 run for a good drive.
- Bowler can change the positions of her fielders anytime during a batter's innings.
- Batter receives another delivery and 1 run for a no ball or can score off the no ball but not be out unless it's by a run-out.

Tactical Problem
Defending space behind the wicket

Lesson Focus
Wicketkeeper's role

Objectives
  · Use basic wicketkeeper stance and position.
  · Learn takes and returns.
  · Communicate with the field.

GAME 1

Setup
Stoolball (Know the Game Indoor Cricket 1989)
The rules and organization are similar to the previous modified games but there are two differences. The ball can be hit anywhere in the field and there are always two batters (striker and nonstriker) at the respective wickets.

Conditions
  · The nonstriker is located at the wicket next to the bowler (see figure 12.10).
  · After the batter hits the ball, 1 run is scored when both batters cross and get to the creases or the opposite wickets (they switch places).
  · The ways a batter can be out remain the same, but now a run-out can occur at either crease (wicketkeeper's or bowler's end).
  · Only one batter can be out at a time—the one closest to the wicket hit by the fielding team.
  · Each batting pair faces 12 pitches (two overs).
  · After every six pitches (one over), a different bowler bowls from the wicket at the other end.
  · Bowlers aim for zone 3 (they now have a run-up), but the ball often strays in direction as the bowlers try to bowl faster, making it harder for the wicketkeeper to collect a ball missed by the batter.

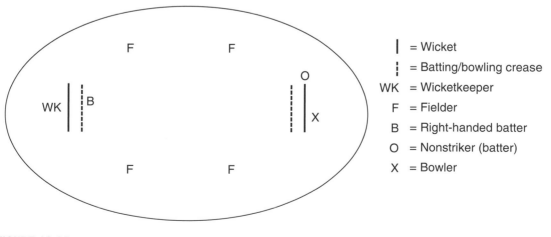

| = Wicket
⋮ = Batting/bowling crease
WK = Wicketkeeper
F = Fielder
B = Right-handed batter
O = Nonstriker (batter)
X = Bowler

FIGURE 12.10
Stoolball.

Questions

Q: When the batter hits the ball into the field, what does the wicketkeeper do?

A: If he is standing back for a faster bowler, he runs to the wicket and stands next to it on the opposite side from where the ball was hit. He lines up with the ball and waits for the fielder's throw to arrive just above the wicket.

Q: If there is the chance the batter will not reach the crease before the throw, what does the wicketkeeper do?

A: Catches the ball and, keeping it in the hands (gloves), touches the ball to (breaks) the wicket.

Q: Anything else?

A: Wicketkeeper appeals, "How's that?" to the umpire standing square of the wicket on the leg side (square leg), and the umpire signals if the batter is out.

Q: If the bowler is aiming for zone 3, where does the wicketkeeper stand?

A. In line with zone 3 so that if the batter misses the ball or lets it pass the wicketkeeper can field it.

Q: How far away from the wicket should the wicketkeeper stand?

A: It depends on the speed of the bowler. If the bowler is fast, the wicketkeeper may have trouble reacting to the ball if she stands close to the wicket.

Q: What else could happen that would cause the wicketkeeper a problem?

A: The bowler might bowl the ball into zones 2, 4, or 6 (leg side) (see figure 12.2, page 369). If the bowler was bowling fast the wicketkeeper would have to get from in line with zone 1 to in line with zone 2 and her view would be obstructed by the batter.

Q: Why is this problematic?

A: If the ball gets past the wicketkeeper, even though the batter didn't hit it she can run (and score a bye), or worse, the ball can go all the way to the boundary and the batters could score 4 runs (4 byes).

Q: So for a faster bowler the wicketkeeper stands farther from the wicket but for a slower bowler the wicketkeeper stands closer?

A: Yes.

Q: How close does the wicketkeeper want to stand?

A: Close enough that when the ball comes through to the wicketkeeper it has bounced only once. That way, if the batter touches the ball, the wicketkeeper can catch the batter out (the batter is caught behind).

Q: What height is comfortable for catching the ball?

A: Between the knee and waist as the ball begins to drop after having bounced once before reaching the batter.

PRACTICE TASK

Setup

Looking for the Edge

Requires a bowler, batter, wicketkeeper, and slip (see figure 12.9). The bowler bowls to the batter, varying the line and length between imaginary zones (1 to 3 off-side and 2 to 4 leg side).

Conditions

- Batter uses a softball bat or cricket bat (with the edge of the bat facing the bowler) to generate lots of small deflections and near misses that result in catches to the wicketkeeper.

- Each batter receives six deliveries before players rotate through the other defensive positions.

Goal
Wicketkeeper to take 5 of 6 bowling deliveries cleanly (assuming batter does not make good contact).

Cues
- Wicketkeeping
  - Stand with feet shoulder-width apart, weight on balls of feet, knees bent, hands (gloves) touching ground, little fingers together, palms open.
  - Raise hands with the ball after it bounces—depending on the height and direction of the bounce the hands will point to the ground, sky, or side.
  - For fast bowlers, slide sideways to take the ball while it is level with your inside hip.
  - For slow bowlers, keep your eyes over your hands and slide your feet across the crease in a straight line, with your weight on the foot nearest the wicket, in order to allow the ball to be brought to wicket for a potential stumping (similar to a run-out in which the batter leaves her batting crease when attempting to hit the ball but misses the ball).
  - Watch the ball, not the bat.
  - Let the ball come from the bowler—avoid snatching it.

GAME 2

Setup
Stoolball
The player who takes the most catches and is involved in the most run-outs when playing wicketkeeper wins the game.

Q: Why do fielders usually throw to the wicketkeeper in the real game?
A: The wicketkeeper is an expert fielder and has not just bowled a ball like the bowler (who then has to recover to wicket). In the real game the wicketkeeper is the only fielder permitted to wear protective gloves because of the frequency with which she handles the ball.

Q: When the ball is hit into the field, what else does the wicketkeeper do once she is in position to receive the throw?
A. Tells the fielders if they have time to field the ball or if they should return the ball very quickly to execute a run-out. Usually the wicketkeeper will say, "Time," or "Hit them," referring to her gloves.

Condition
Fielders use wicketkeeper only as the point of return for the throw.

Level II

At level II players learn the importance of using effective defense (ground fielding, catching, field placements) to restrict scoring and get batters out. Bowlers gain a greater understanding of using variations in their deliveries (variations in movement off the pitch, speed, bounce, and angle of delivery) to impair a batter's decisions and to limit the batter's scoring opportunities. Batters learn to judge the line and length of a delivery and to decide whether to move forward or backward to play shots. At this level, lessons emphasize offensive and defensive strokes on the back foot in response to specific variations in bowling deliveries. Batters also learn to communicate when running between the wickets, another feature of cricket introduced at level II.

In cricket, the batter does not have to run upon contact with the ball (see level II, lesson 8). This condition enables the batter to play shots to defend the stumps rather than to score runs. It also necessitates communication between both batters to ensure that they both know whether or not to run.

Batters must learn to judge the line and length of a delivery so they will know how to respond in order to hit the ball.

Lesson 7 Level II

Tactical Problem
Running out the batter

Lesson Focus
Ground fielding, deciding where to throw

Objectives
- Move in.
- Pick up and throw.
- Back up the fielder or throw.

GAME 1

Setup
Stoolball

Goal
Create scenarios for run-outs that fielders must solve to get the batter out.

Conditions
- Batters must run upon making contact with the ball.
- Fielders all save 1 run (they're not deep enough in the field to allow a single run).

Questions

Q: When the batter hits the ball into the field and it is not a catch, what do you do?
A: Run the batter out or prevent or restrict scoring.

Q: How do you anticipate where the ball will go?
A: Watch the batter's footwork, backlift, and bat angle to see what type of shot is likely.

Q: What do you do to be quick off the mark?
A: Walk toward the batter as the bowler runs up to bowl, taking short steps and preparing to move in any direction.

Q: Where do you want to return the ball?
A: Usually to the wicketkeeper but it depends on the position and speed of the batters, the time available to pick up and throw, and the distance to the respective wickets.

Q: What type of throw do you use?
A: It depends on the distance to the wickets. For short distances an underhand throw, for longer distances an overarm throw.

PRACTICE TASK 1

Setup
Run-Out Cricket (see figure 12.11)

Goal
Fielders run out the batters.

Conditions
- Batters do not hit the ball but avoid being run out.
- Wicketkeeper rolls the ball into the field and calls the name of one of the fielders in that half of the field.
- Once the ball is released both batters run.
- The fielder (F3 at cover point in figure 12.11) attempts a quick pickup and throw to either the wicketkeeper or the bowler in an attempt to run out one of the batters.
- The other fielder (F4 at extra cover) covers her teammate in case of a misfield.
- The other two fielders (F1 at square leg and F2 at midwicket) back up the wicketkeeper and bowler, respectively, in case the ball is overthrown.
- If the ball rolls over the boundary because of a fielder's throw, it results in the 1 run the batters score plus an additional 4 runs.
- Each pair of batters begins with 6 runs and receives six rolls.
- If one of the batters is run out, the batters lose 1 run from their total.
- If both batters make their ground, they score 1 run.
- The pair with the most runs wins the game.

Variation
The batter can hit the ball from a tee and call a fielder's name rather than have the wicketkeeper roll the ball.

Cues
- Interception
  - Move quickly into line and attack the ball.
  - Bend knees slightly and turn sideways as ball approaches.
  - Extend hands to meet ball.
  - Keep head down and watch the ball roll into your hands.
  - Field ball in line, with foot on throwing side, and step with other foot (two-handed pickup).

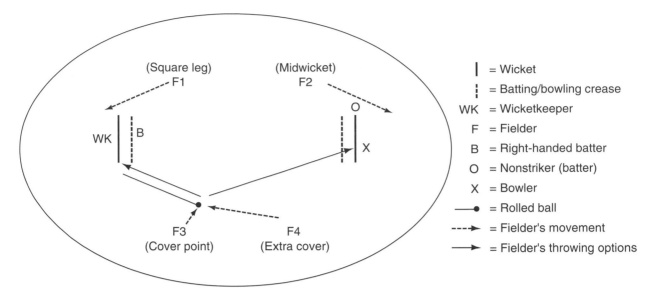

FIGURE 12.11
Run-out cricket.

- Underarm throw (one-handed pickup)
  - As you approach, point both feet in direction of target.
  - Pick up ball along your foot on throwing side, step on other foot, and release.
  - Arm follows through to target.
- Overarm throw
  - Throwing arm extends behind body with wrist cocked and arm slightly bent.
  - Step to target with lead foot and turn hips, transferring your body weight.
  - Elbow of throwing arm comes through first and arm finishes on other side of your body.

PRACTICE TASK 2

Goal
Fielders run out the batters.

Conditions
- Same as Run-Out Cricket except fielders are positioned on the boundary (see figure 12.12).
- Batters must attempt to score 2 runs (finishing back at their initial positions as striker and nonstriker).
- Fielders back up and cover throws as in previous practice.

GAME 2

Setup
Stoolball

Goal
Create run-out scenarios that fielders must solve to get the batter out.

Conditions
- Batters must run on making contact with the ball.
- Bowler decides which fielders will save a single run and which fielders will be positioned deep on the boundary to prevent 4 runs (see figure 12.13).

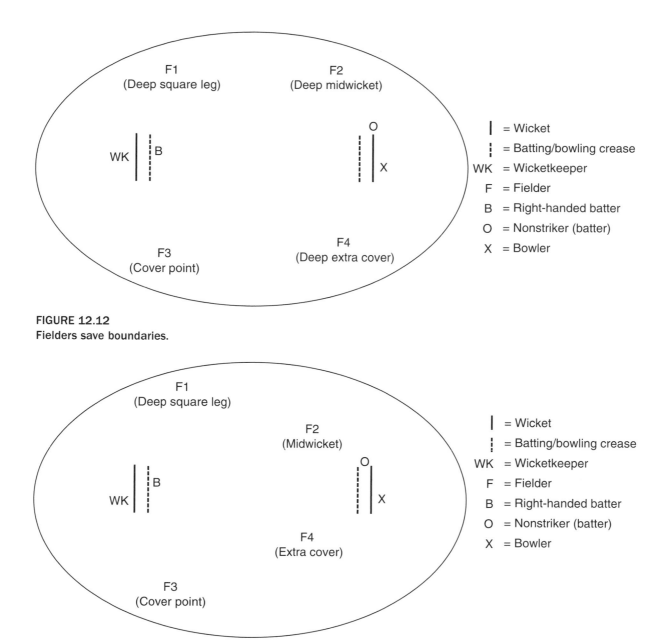

FIGURE 12.12
Fielders save boundaries.

FIGURE 12.13
Bowler sets field.

Lesson 8

Tactical Problem
Making the batter play

Lesson Focus
Bowling line and length and moving the ball into the batter

Objectives
- Attack the off-stump.
- Bowl an off-cutter.
- Vary the angle of delivery (over and around the wicket).
- Achieve and understand leg before wicket (LBW).

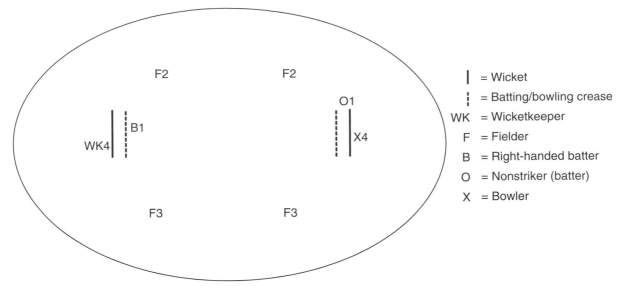

FIGURE 12.14
Pairs cricket.

GAME 1

Setup

Assuming that there are four pairs of players (see figure 12.14):

- Pair 1 bats first.
- Pair 2 fields on the leg side.
- Pair 3 fields on the off-side.
- Pair 4 includes the bowler and wicketkeeper (who change roles after one over or 6 bowls).

Each new over starts from the opposite end wicket from the previous over. The bowler counts the number of balls she has bowled and rotates at the end of her over. If the ball is not delivered to where the batter can play it from a normal batting stance (in his crease), a run is added to the batting pair's total (called a wide) and another ball has to be bowled in that over. The batting players announce the number of runs they scored in their two overs: 10 runs scored plus 2 outs (–6) equals 4 runs total. When all pairs have batted, the pair with the most runs wins.

Conditions

- Each batting pair faces 12 pitches (two overs).
- Batters score runs as in stoolball.
- Batters decide whether to run based on the chance of being run out.
- When the ball crosses the boundary, four runs are scored and the batters do not have to run.
- When a batter is out (caught, bowled, or run out), 3 runs are deducted from the batting pair's score.
- Every time there is an out the batters change ends.
- At the end of two overs each pair rotates to its next activity.

Questions

Q: *What type of shot does the batter try to play to a ball that lands in zone 1?*
A: If the ball lands about one pace in front of her feet the drive is likely, but if it lands a little farther away she may play a forward defensive stroke.

Q: So bowling to zone 3 in line with or just outside the batter's off-stump is an effective place to bowl the ball?

A: Yes, it is a good line and length. But the batter can now predict what the ball will do when it hits the ground.

Q: What could make it harder for the batter to make good contact with the ball?

A: Bowling the ball a little faster or slower and making the ball deviate back toward the right-handed batter make it dangerous for the batter to drive the ball.

Q: Why is doing this problematic for the batter?

A: The ball could hit his wicket by traveling between the batter's front leg and the bat or the ball could hit the batter on the leg and he could be out because of leg before wicket (LBW).

Q: What does LBW mean?

A: If the batter misses the ball with the bat and the ball hits his body when it would have (in the opinion of the umpire at the bowler's end) hit the batter's wicket, the batter is out (LBW). The bowler also has to appeal ("How's that?") to the umpire.

Q: What else can cause the batter a problem?

A: If the ball bounces higher than expected or quickly comes back into the batter after pitching and hits her bat and body, it can gently lob into the air for a catch on the leg side.

PRACTICE TASK 1

Setup

Bowler, batter, wicketkeeper, short leg, slip (see figure 12.15).

Goals

- Bowl for an edge or LBW.

Conditions

- Bowler aims at zone 1 in line with the batter's off-stump. The bowler can bowl "around" or "over" the wicket.
- Batter attempts to play the ball on the front foot but bats with a softball bat or cricket bat (with the edge of the bat facing the bowler) to facilitate a lot of wickets for the bowler or catches at short leg or slip (see figure 12.15).
- Each batter receives six deliveries before players rotate positions.

Cues

Off-cutter (moving the ball into the right-handed batter after it hits the ground)
- Seam of the ball is vertical or pointed in the direction of the short leg.
- Index finger runs along seam with middle finger half an inch away.
- Thumb is underneath the ball on the seam and the ball rests on the third finger.
- As ball is released, the index and middle finger work down the outside of the ball (as right-handed bowler views it when it is held above right shoulder) so that the thumb passes over the top of the ball, generating turn on ball.

PRACTICE TASK 2

Setup

Repeat task 1 with bowler bowling from where nonstriker normally stands (on the right of the wicket, or around the wicket).

Goal

Bowl ball that straightens after it bounces.

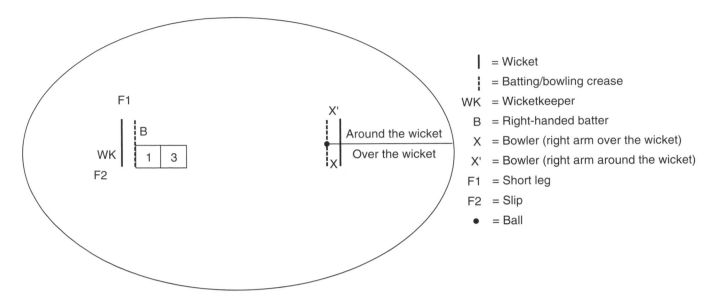

FIGURE 12.15
Off-cutter attack.

Cue

Right-handed bowler (see X' in figure 12.15) angles the ball across the right-handed batter and tries to make the ball straighten so that the batter has problems defending the wicket.

Conditions

- If ball does not straighten it can also find the outside edge of the bat.
- The batter cannot be out LBW to a ball that pitches outside the line of his leg stump.

Note

It is virtually impossible to get an LBW decision by bowling around the wicket because the angle is so difficult for an umpire to judge whether the ball would have really hit the wicket.

GAME 2

Setup

Pairs Cricket

Goal

Make the batter play by using change of pace, good line and length, and off-cutter to tempt the batter.

Conditions

- Bowler decides whether to attack batter with a leg slip or slip and whether to place fielders in defensive positions (to save runs).
- Bowler can also decide to attack batter around the wicket.

Tactical Problem
Attacking the short-pitched ball (delivery)

Lesson Focus
Moving onto the back foot, looking for space, and playing the ball square of the wicket

Objective
Play the pull shot.

GAME 1

Setup
Pairs Cricket

Goal
Move onto the back foot.

Conditions
- Bowlers aim at zones 5 and 6 or farther away from the batter (see figure 12.16).
- Bowlers attempt to bowl fast.

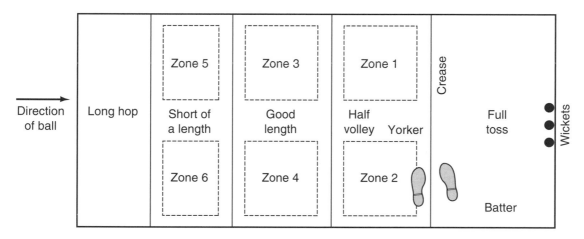

FIGURE 12.16
Target zones and types of delivery.

Questions

Q: *When the ball pitches in zones 5 and 6 or farther away (a long hop), what height does the ball arrive at as you attempt to hit it?*
A: Around waist height or higher.

Q: *If you step toward this ball, what is likely to happen?*
A: It may hit my body rather than the bat.

Q: *Where should you first move for this type of delivery?*
A: Move backward in order to hit the ball, which is bouncing high.

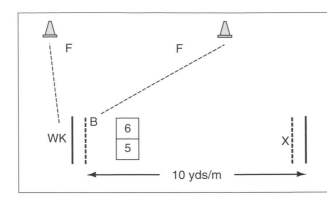

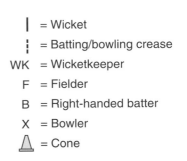

| = Wicket
⋮ = Batting/bowling crease
WK = Wicketkeeper
F = Fielder
B = Right-handed batter
X = Bowler
△ = Cone

FIGURE 12.17
Hit the gap.

PRACTICE TASK

Setup
Hit the gap

Goal
Batter hits ball in front of square on the leg side so that it goes between the target cones to score (see figure 12.17).

Conditions
- Bowler makes the ball pitch in zones 5 or 6 or shorter by using a modified overarm throw with minimal arm extension on the backswing.
- Batter receives six balls (one over) and scores 4 runs every time the ball beats the fielders and passes between the cones (simulating a boundary).
- Batter can be out by being bowled, caught, or LBW.
- If the ball remains inside the scoring arc but does not go past the cones the batter can score two runs by running to the bowler's crease and returning to the batting crease before the throw is returned to the wicketkeeper.
- Batter elects whether to run and can be run out.
- Player with most runs wins.

Cues
Pull shot
- High backlift.
- Head is steady and left behind.
- Back foot moves back and across toward batter's off-stump.
- Throw front foot out to leg side.
- Swing the bat horizontally at full arm's length (chest opens to ball).
- Roll wrists over ball on contact.

Variations
- Hit ball from high tee.
- Ball is tossed on the full by the bowler so that it arrives at waist height.

GAME 2

Setup
Pairs Cricket

Goals
- Pairs score as many runs as possible.
- Bowlers make ball pitch in zones 5 or 6 or shorter.

Conditions

- Leg side only, ball cannot be hit on the off-side of the wicket (opposite of game in figure 12.8).
- If ball clears the leg-side boundary on a pull shot without bouncing, the batter scores 6 runs (4 runs if the ball bounces before crossing the boundary).
- The pair with the most runs wins.

Lesson 10 — Level II

Tactical Problem
Working the short-pitched delivery

Lesson Focus
Running between the wickets and moving onto the back foot

Objectives
- Backward defense.
- Back-foot leg glance.

GAME 1

Setup
Pairs Cricket

Goal
Bowler sets field and makes ball pitch in front part (closest to the batter) of zones 5 and 6 or beginning of zones 3 and 4.

Conditions
- Ball can be hit anywhere inside the modified boundary.
- If the ball rolls outside the 16-yard/meter inner boundary, the run is discounted and the batters must return to their original positions (see figure 12.18).
- Batters should communicate whether to run a single.
- Bowlers attempt to bowl fast.

Questions

Q: *When you were batting, what were you trying to do?*
A: Make contact with the ball and send it to a space inside the inner boundary.

Q: *What helps you to do this?*
A: Looking to see where the fielders are positioned before each delivery and then pushing the ball into gaps in the field.

Q: *Who decides when to run?*
A: If the ball is hit anywhere in front of the batter's wicket the batter calls for the run.

Q: *What happens when the ball goes behind the wicket?*
A: The nonstriker calls for the run because she sees the ball before the batter sees it.

Q: *What do you call to indicate your intention to run?*
A: "Yes," "No," or "Wait" followed by "Yes" or "No." Nothing else is required.

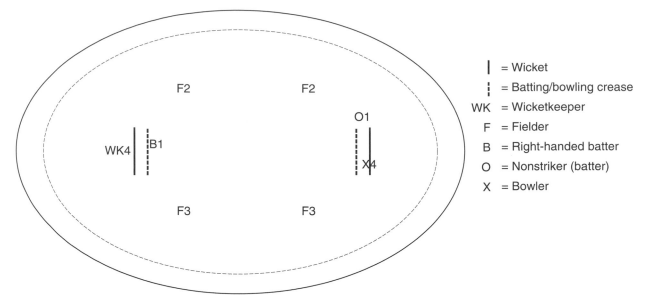

FIGURE 12.18
Pairs cricket with modified boundary.

Q: When you previously played the short-pitched ball using the pull shot, where did the ball bounce?
A: Usually around zones 5 and 6 (short of a length) or even farther away (long hop), and the ball came around waist height or above.

Q: If the ball pitches around the front half of zones 5 and 6 (see figure 12. 16) or the beginning of zones 3 and 4, what might be a problem with pulling the ball?
A: The ball comes through quickly and may be a little low and if you miss the ball it could hit the wicket.

Q: Would you still play the ball with a cross bat?
A: No, a straight bat would provide a better chance of defending the wicket and making good contact with the ball.

Q: If the ball bounced outside your off-stump and is in no danger of hitting the wicket, what else can you do?
A: Allow the ball to pass without playing a stroke.

PRACTICE TASK 1

Setup
Backward Defense

Goals
• Batter defends ball on the back foot.
• Wicketkeeper and four fielders catch the batter out (see figure 12.19).

Conditions
• Each batter receives one over before rotating.
• Bowler attempts to pitch the ball into zones 3 and 4 (part farthest from the batter) from 10 yards/meters away using an overarm throw, making the ball reach the batter off the bounce around thigh height or above.

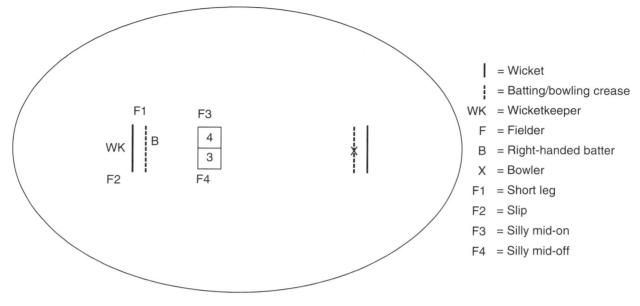

FIGURE 12.19
Backward defense.

- Wicketkeeper and the four fielders attempt to catch the batter out.
- No attacking shots can be played by the batter when fielders are close to the bat in front of the wicket (for safety).
- Batter who is out the least wins the practice.

Cues
Backward defense
- As ball is thrown, step back toward wicket with back foot.
- Front foot follows back (with down swing of bat) and finishes next to back foot (parallel with batting crease).
- Front elbow kept high.
- For right-handed batter, arms and bat form a P.
- Bat is held vertically at slight angle, facing down.
- Ball hits bat and drops down.
- Top hand is firm and bottom hand is relaxed on bat.

PRACTICE TASK 2

Setup
Back-foot leg glance

Goal
Play shot to a ball that pitches around leg stump in zones 4 or 6 by deflecting ball off hip toward fine leg (see figure 12.20) using the speed of the bowled ball to generate the power.

Condition
Use same field set for backward defense but with short leg now saving a boundary at fine leg.

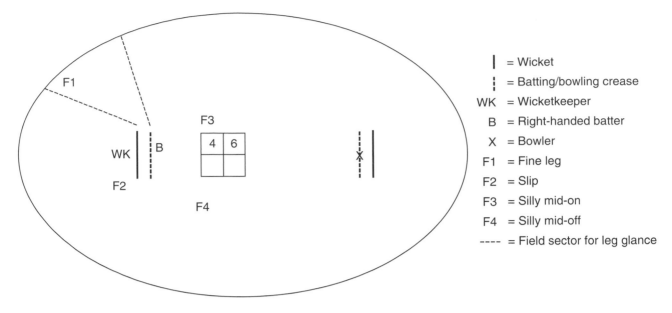

FIGURE 12.20
Back-foot leg glance.

Cues
Back-foot leg glance
- Similar to setup for backward defense.
- Ball flicked off hip area.
- Bat angled very slightly toward fine leg.
- Rotate wrists after contact to send ball toward fine leg.

GAME 2

Setup
Pairs Cricket

Goals
Bowler sets field and makes ball pitch in closest part (to the batter) of zones 5 and 6 or farthest part (from the batter) of zones 3 and 4.

Conditions
- Batters must call for every run.
- Ball can be hit only inside the modified boundary as in game 1 (batters use backward defense) except when the batter uses a back-foot leg glance, in which case the ball can travel in the arc indicated in figure 12.20 and over the outer boundary for 4 runs.
- Nonstriker should call for any runs in this area.
- Bowler sets field.

Tactical Problem
Judging length when batting

Lesson Focus
Moving forward or backward

Objective
Select appropriate defensive stroke.

GAME 1

Setup
Pairs Cricket

Goal
Bowler sets field and pitches the ball in any target zone.

Condition
Ball can be hit anywhere.

Questions

> Q: *When you are batting, what is a major decision regarding your movement at the crease?*
> A: Deciding whether to move forward to play the ball or to move backward.
>
> Q: *If the ball is a half volley (landing in zones 1 and 2), where will you go?*
> A: Forward to play the ball.
>
> Q: *If the ball is short of a length (landing in zones 5 and 6), where will you go?*
> A: Backward to play the ball.
>
> Q: *What about a ball that is a good length (landing in zones 3 and 4)?*
> A: That's what makes it a good length—you are unsure whether to move forward or backward.

PRACTICE TASK

Setup
Each batter receives two overs before rotating. The bowler delivers the ball to the batter using an overarm throw, varying deliveries to land before or after the bowling decision line (see figure 12.21). Batter scores 1 point for each correct decision, playing a vertical (defensive) shot on either the back foot or front foot.

Goal
Decide whether to move forward or backward.

Conditions
- Use bowler, batter, wicketkeeper, and two fielders (midwicket, extra cover).
- Mark bowling decision line at appropriate length (see dashed line in figure 12.21).
- Mark batting lines one step behind and one step in front of the batter's crease.
- For any ball that pitches before (shorter than) the dotted line (from the batter's view), the batter steps back past the back-foot line to play the ball.
- For any ball that pitches after the dotted line, the batter steps over the front-foot line to play the ball.

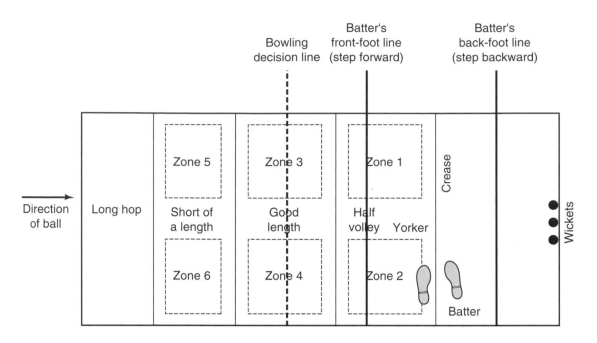

FIGURE 12.21
Footwork decisions.

GAME 2

Setup
Pairs Cricket

Goal
Bowler sets field and elects to pitch the ball in any target zone.

Condition
Ball can be hit anywhere.

Questions

Q: *Unfortunately, the bowling decision line (for the batter) varies from one bowler to the next. Why?*

A: The speed and subsequent bounce of the ball means that for quicker bowlers the decision line is slightly closer to the batter. The ball bounces higher so the batter should move onto the back foot. For a slower bowler the decision line moves slightly away from the batter. The ball tends not to bounce as high so the batter wants to be on the front foot.

Q: *So a ball pitching in the same spot (around zones 3 and 4) could be played on the front foot to a slow bowler and on the back foot to a fast bowler?*

A: Yes, because the two bowlers are getting a different amount of bounce from the ball hitting the ground.

Q: *What else can bowlers do to cause problems for the batter?*

A: They can change the speed of individual deliveries, bowling faster or slower than usual. To make it harder for the batter to time the stroke, the ball may not bounce as high as the batter anticipates. The batter could easily play an inappropriate shot to this kind of ball.

Tactical Problem
Attacking the batter

Lesson Focus
Working the batter out (making defense offense)

Objectives
- Field placement close to the wicket.
- Close catching.
- Umpiring.

GAME 1

Setup
Kwik Cricket

Play with two teams of six players per team (batting and fielding). The batting team starts with 0 runs. Each batter bats for a maximum of two overs (12 pitches per player) unless he is out. The batter does not have to run every time the ball is hit. When a batter is out (caught, bowled, LBW, or run out), no runs are deducted from the batting team's score and the next batter on the team then replaces him. Bowling must be overarm and take place from the same end throughout the game. Each bowler must bowl six legitimate balls in an over (no balls and wides count as a run and an additional ball for the batting team). At the end of every over, the fielding team rotates clockwise through one position and the batters change ends. If a fielding team has less than six players, the batting team must provide the fielding team with a wicketkeeper who subsequently also rotates to other positions in the field but does not bowl. The batting team must provide two impartial umpires (at the bowler's end and square leg) to count the bowler's pitches (indicate if the batter is caught, LBW, bowled, or run out) and to signal wides, byes, and no balls and to signal boundaries, awarding 4 or 6 runs (see figure 12.22). The batting team also records the score on

Four runs (boundary)

Six runs

Bye

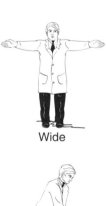
Wide

No ball

Out

Batter ran a short run

Leg bye

FIGURE 12.22
The umpire's signals.

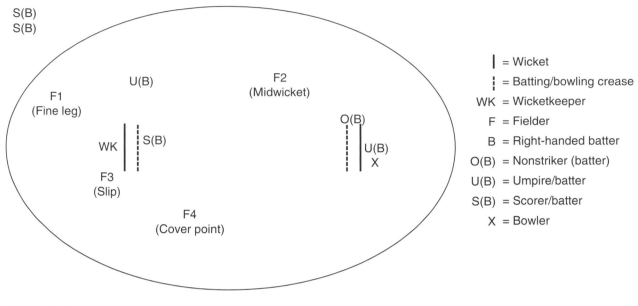

FIGURE 12.23
Bowler sets field.

the scoreboard (two scorers). Having faced 12 deliveries (assuming batter was not out), the batter retires and is replaced by another until the whole team has batted.

Players rotate through batting, umpiring, and scoring duties (see figure 12.23 for a potential setup for Kwik Cricket). If a team's last two batters are batting and one of the batters is out, the batter who is out may act as a nonstriking partner (runner) until the final batter is either out or has faced two overs. After 12 overs (assuming a team of six batters) or when all the batters are out, the batting team's total is recorded. The fielding team becomes the batting team and attempts to beat the target set by the team that batted first.

Goal
Work the batter out.

Condition
Bowler places the fielders in positions of her choice but must have at least one player in addition to the wicketkeeper in a close catching position (see figure 12.19 for examples of close catching positions).

Questions

Q: When you are bowling, where is your close fielder positioned and why?
A: At slip because the leg cutter is the delivery of choice.

Q: Any other reason?
A: For bowling a full length and because the batter likes to try to drive the ball.

Q: If you are bowling off-cutters, where is the fielder positioned?
A: At leg slip and possibly at regular slip if the ball keeps going straight and doesn't cut back.

Q: When you field at first slip (off-side) or you are the wicketkeeper, what should you watch?
A: The ball from the time it leaves the bowler's hand.

Q: In all other close catching positions (including leg slip), what does the fielder watch?
A: The batter's bat.

PRACTICE TASK 1

Setup
Catch It

Goal
Two catchers (6-8 feet, or 1.8-2.4 meters, apart) attempt to make the ball land in the opponent's target square (8 by 8 feet or 2.4 by 2.4 meters) using an underhand throw from below knee height (see figure 12.24)

Conditions
- Score 1 point when the ball hits the ground in the opponent's square.
- Prevent opponent from scoring by catching the ball before it lands in your square.
- If the ball hits the ground outside the square, the receiving player scores a point.

Cues
Close catching
- Feet shoulder-width apart.
- Knees and hips bent.
- Weight primarily on balls of feet.
- Elbows slightly bent and not resting on knees.
- Hands together just below knee height, fingers pointing down.

Variations
- Vary height and speed of underarm throw.
- Reduce or increase size of target square.

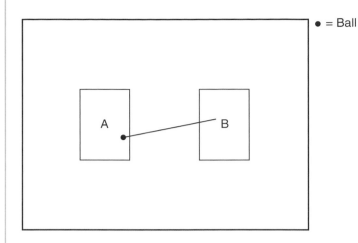

FIGURE 12.24
Catch it.

PRACTICE TASK 2

Setup
Repeat practice task 1 of lesson 10 in level II (see figure 12.19).

GAME 2

Setup
Kwik Cricket

Condition
For first four overs, defense must have two fielders in addition to the wicketkeeper in close catching positions (for safety reasons fielders should be 8 to 10 yards/meters from the bat if they are in front of the batter).

Level III

Levels I and II emphasize developing batting techniques to help batters stay in (defend the wicket) and use all of the allotted deliveries during their overs. You may advise students that in the real game of cricket, once a batter is out he does not bat again during his team's innings (usually does not bat for the remainder of the day). Remind batters that avoiding getting out is always a tactical objective, so defending a good length (a delivery from the bowler likely to strike the wicket or find the edge of the bat) is sensible. As defensive (bowling and fielding) tactics and skills develop in the first two levels, batters need greater tactical understanding and associated skills to help them attack the different types of delivery from the bowler. Level III focuses on a variety of sophisticated offensive batting strokes. Batters increase their offensive stroke armory as more advanced bowling techniques (spin) and associated field placements are introduced. Defensive players recognize the need to bowl to a field and force the batter to hit the ball in a specific area in order to restrict scoring and to get batters out. Batters no longer surrender their wickets as cheaply as they once did because of the tactical understanding and skills developed in the first two levels.

Batters have an array of batting strokes that they can employ to make the best offensive play.

Lesson 13

Tactical Problem
Scoring runs

Lesson Focus
Back-foot drive and running between the wickets

Objectives
- Communicate.
- Ground the bat.
- Change hands when turning.

GAME 1

Setup
Circle Cricket (6-8 players) played in pairs

Goal
Batters score runs by pushing the ball out of the circle and running between the wickets.

Conditions
- All fielders (including the wicketkeeper) must be positioned outside the 13-yard/ meter circle (see figure 12.25).
- Bowler aims for good length (target zone 3, see figure 12.21 on page 398).
- Each batting pair receives two overs.
- When the ball is hit outside the circle the batters can run if they wish.
- Fielders field the ball and throw only at the batter's wicket (not at the bowler's wicket).
- No fielder can enter the circle or run with the ball.

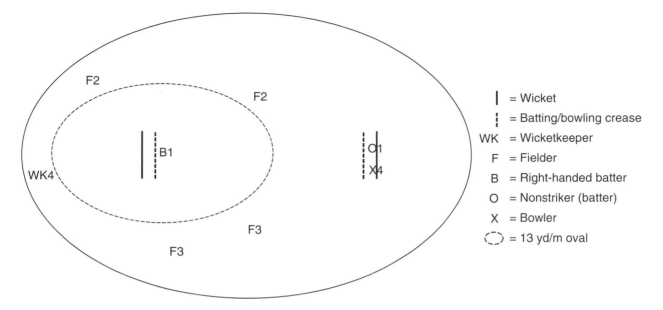

FIGURE 12.25
Circle cricket.

- Batters keep running until the wicket is hit or until a maximum of 4 runs have been scored.
- Batters bat until two overs are completed and then the next pair bats.
- The pair with the most runs wins.

Questions

Q: *When batting, who decides when to run?*
A: If the ball is hit anywhere in front of the batter's wicket the batter calls for the run.

Q: *What happens when the ball goes behind the wicket?*
A: The nonstriker calls for the run because she sees the ball before the batter sees it.

Q: *What do you call to indicate your intention to run?*
A: "Yes," "No," or "Wait" followed by "Yes" or "No." Nothing else is required.

Q: *As the bowler releases the ball what is the nonstriker doing?*
A: Moving toward the other wicket (backing up) and continuing to do so as the ball is hit.

Q: *If the batter calls "Yes," what is the advantage of backing up?*
A: The nonstriker has already gained 2 to 3 yards/meters for the run, reducing the distance to the striking batter's crease.

Q: *If the batter calls "No," what does the nonstriker do?*
A: Returns to her crease by extending the bat and touching the ground inside the nonstriker's batting (bowling) crease. This is the act of grounding the bat.

Q: *Grounding the bat is important whether or not a batter attempts a run?*
A: Yes, because it reduces the distance to safety (inside the batter's crease) by almost 2 yards or meters at either end (crease). It makes the run shorter and is the reason why batters carry their bats.

Q: Does it matter which hand a batter uses to carry the bat?

A: Yes, the batter always wants to see the ball when turning to attempt a second or third run.

Q: So if a right-handed batter hits the ball into the off-side through extra cover and is looking for a second run, when he turns to call for the second run the bat should be in which hand?

A: In his left hand. The nonstriker should be turning with the bat in her right hand.

Q: If the ball were hit into the leg side by the same right-handed batter, what would be the hand positions?

A: The players' hands would be reversed so the players could track the ball when turning.

PRACTICE TASK

Setup
Back-foot drive and run in pairs

Goal
Practice back-foot push and running between wickets.

Conditions
- Each batting pair receives two overs.
- Bowler aims at target zones 3 and 4 (around or just short of a good length).
- Batter attempts to drive the ball off the back foot into the sector (see figure 12.26).
- After successfully contacting the ball the batters can run as many times as they wish.
- Batters can be caught, bowled, or run out.
- Pairs rotate through batting, fielding, bowling, and wicketkeeping.
- When all pairs have batted, the pair with the most runs wins.

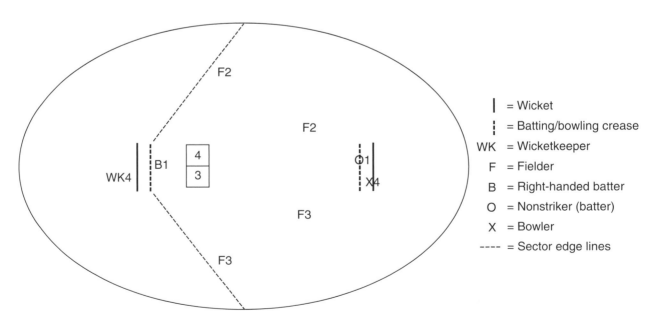

| = Wicket
⋮ = Batting/bowling crease
WK = Wicketkeeper
F = Fielder
B = Right-handed batter
O = Nonstriker (batter)
X = Bowler
---- = Sector edge lines

FIGURE 12.26
Back-foot drive and run.

Cues
- Running and turning
  - Nonstriker backs up.
  - Call for each run.
  - Carry the bat in the correct hand.
  - Slide the bat over the crease (ground the bat).
  - Turn low, using the bat as an extension of the hand.
  - Accelerate out of the turn.
- Back-foot drive (extension of backward defense)
  - Step back toward wicket with back foot.
  - Front foot follows back (with downswing of bat) and finishes next to back foot (parallel with batting crease).
  - Body is sideways to delivery.
  - Front elbow is high at contact.
  - Bottom hand punches through ball.
  - Blade of bat points in the direction the ball was hit.

GAME 2

Setup
Circle Cricket (6-8 players)

Goal
Batters score runs by using the back-foot drive and running between the wickets (communicating, grounding the bat, and turning).

Condition
May allow wicketkeeper to move to the stumps after the batter contacts the ball.

Note
Game is excellent review for fielding and intercepting skills.

Lesson 14 Level III

Tactical Problem
Restrict run scoring by bowling to leg side and get the batter out

Lesson Focus
Forcing the batter to play in a designated area and bowling to a leg-side field

Objective
Slow bowling (off break).

GAME 1

Setup
Modified Kanga 8s cricket. Four pairs of players rotate through batting, fielding, bowling, and wicketkeeping as done in Pairs Cricket. Batters can be bowled, caught, or run out or be out if they hit their own wicket (usually in the backswing with the bat). A pair of batters bats for two overs regardless of the number of times each pair is out. Pairs add run increments to their totals for the following bowling and fielding performances: 4 runs for a batter who is bowled, 2 runs for a catch to each fielder and to the bowler who was bowling when the catch was taken, and 4 runs for a run-out.

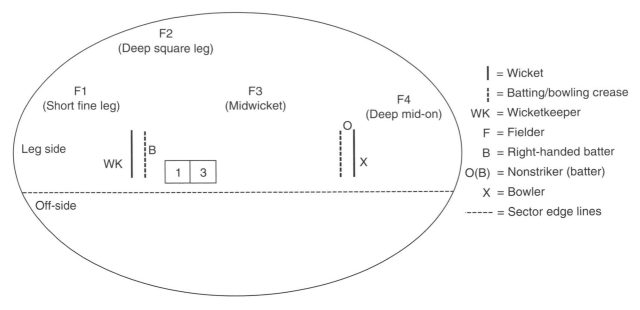

FIGURE 12.27
Off-break field.

Goal
Make batter play ball into the leg side to restrict run scoring and to get the batter out.

Conditions
- Batters can only score runs on the leg side (see figure 12.27).
- Bowlers may use no more than a three-step run-up.

Questions

Q: When you bowl, where would most batters like to hit a ball?
A: On the leg side.

Q: Suppose that when you bowl you encourage a batter to hit only on the leg side. How does doing that help the defense?
A: You can allocate most of your fielders to this side because you can predict the batter will hit in that direction.

Q: If you want a batter to hit on the leg side should you bowl to the leg side?
A: Not exactly, because you still want to get the batter out by bowling at the wicket (otherwise you lose the opportunity to bowl the batter or get an LBW decision).

Q: So what is your target when you bowl?
A: The off-stump.

Q: Which target zones will you aim at?
A: Zones 1 and 3 (and not 4, 5, or 6 because a ball that is short of a length will easily be pulled by a batter).

Q: If the batter wants to hit on the leg side, what does it mean for the batter's stroke?
A: The batter is hitting across the line of the ball, which means he has a greater chance of mishitting or missing the ball completely, particularly when the ball pitches in zones 1 and 3 on a full length.

Q: What else can you do to tempt the batter into hitting on the leg side when the ball pitches in line with the off-stump?
A: Make the ball deviate sharply in the direction of the leg side.

Q: What else can you do to tempt the batter?

A: Bowl the ball fairly slowly, and by spinning the ball you can cause it to fly into the air unless the batter makes solid contact with the middle of the bat.

PRACTICE TASK 1

Setup
Off break with partner

Goal
Spin the ball using off spin.

Conditions
- Partners stand 11 yards/meters apart and throw the ball from in front of their face (like throwing a dart).
- Ball should land 1 to 2 yards/meters in front of partner, who collects the ball and returns it with a similar action.
- For a right-handed bowler, the ball should hit the ground and spin from left to right.

Cues
- Off spin
  - Middle joints of the index and second fingers spread across the seam.
  - Ball rests against the third finger and the thumb (children with small hands may need a modified grip allowing the third finger to help hold the ball).
  - Turn the wrist and index finger to generate a clockwise spin on the ball.
  - Wrist is cocked initially, and then the first finger drags sharply down the side of the ball while the thumb flips up.

PRACTICE TASK 2

Setup
Bowler, batter, wicketkeeper, and two leg-side fielders positioned at bowler's discretion inside the sector (see figure 12.28)

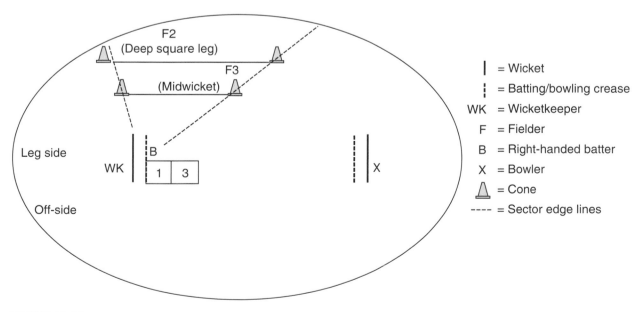

FIGURE 12.28
Defending square on the leg side.

Goal

Turn ball using off spin, forcing batter to play the ball on the leg side across the line.

Conditions

- Bowler aims at target zones 1 and 3 around the batter's off-stump, causing the batter to hit across the line of the ball but with the spin.
- Batter attempts to hit the ball into the sector.
- If the ball goes past the first set of cones the batter scores 1 run, if it goes past the next set of cones she scores 2 runs, and if it goes past the boundary she scores 4 runs.
- Each batter receives six deliveries before players rotate.
- Run increments are awarded for defense as in modified Kanga cricket.
- The player with most runs wins.

Cues

- Vary speed of delivery.
- Vary position on bowling crease (tight to nonstriker's wicket or wider on batting crease).
- Bowl a straight ball occasionally with no spin (arm ball).
- Try bowling around the wicket (as with off-cutter, see figure 12.15).

GAME 2

Setup

Modified Kanga 8s Cricket

Goal

Make batter play ball into the leg side to restrict run scoring and to get the batter out.

Conditions

- Batters can only score runs on the leg side (see figure 12.27).
- Bowlers may use no more than a three-step run-up.

Questions

Q: Why is the fielder at short fine leg (in figure 12.27) saving a single run and not on the boundary?

A: The batter may attempt to glance the ball in that direction, but there is little pace on the ball. The fielder could also be positioned at leg slip to attack the batter in this game.

Q: Why is the fielder at deep square leg on the boundary?

A: To prevent a boundary from a pull shot and to cover the fielders at midwicket and short fine leg who are saving the single. A batter may also hit the ball hard and give a catch in the deep near the boundary.

Q: Why is the fielder at midwicket fairly close to the batter?

A: To prevent the batter from pushing the ball into space and scoring a quick single.

Q: Why is the fielder at deep mid-on near the boundary?

A: To prevent a straight, hard hit. A good batter will try to drive an off spinner hard in this direction to minimize the effect of the spin imparted by the bowler.

Tactical Problem
Scoring on the leg side

Lesson Focus
Attacking an off-break bowler, working the ball off the legs, and hitting with the spin square on the leg side

Objective
Play sweep, paddle, or front-foot leg glance

GAME 1

Setup
Modified Kanga 8s

Goals
- Play ball into the leg side to score runs.
- Take what the defense offers.

Conditions
- Batters can only score runs on the leg side.
- Batters' score is doubled if they hit ball for runs into the target sector on the leg side (see figure 12.29).
- Bowlers may use no more than a three-step run-up and must bowl off breaks pitching in line with the wicket.

Questions
Q: *When attacking an off-break bowler, what are your options?*
A: Driving the ball with a vertical bat through the leg- or off-side (on-side only in this game).

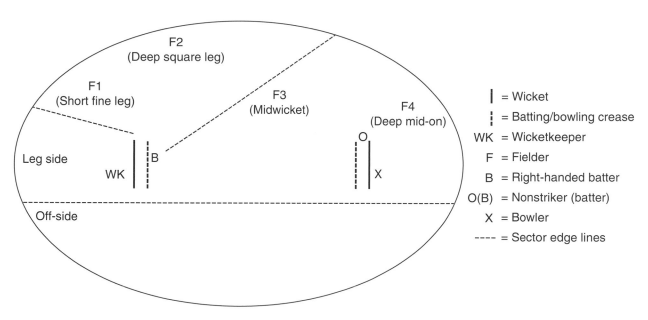

FIGURE 12.29
Kanga cricket (double your score in the zone).

Q: What about hitting the ball square, into the space on the leg side, for a single?
A: Pulling a ball that is short of a length (pitching in zones 5 and 6).

Q: What kind of ball from an off-break bowler is hard to hit with a cross stroke on the leg side?
A: A ball that is on a good or full length around the front border of zone 2 (half volley) or is just about a good length (zone 4) and is in line with the leg stump of the wicket. Either ball arrives too low to pull effectively.

Q: So what are your options for hitting the ball into the bonus sector in the game?
A: Sweeping or glancing the ball to the leg side.

PRACTICE TASK 1

Setup
Bowler, batter, wicketkeeper, and two leg-side fielders positioned at bowler's discretion inside the sector (see figure 12.30)

Goal
Batter hits ball into the sector by using a sweep.

Conditions
- Bowler (from position X') throws ball like a dart from about 11 yards/meters (using off-spin technique) to land on a full length in line with or just outside of batter's leg stump.
- Line of bowler's throw can vary.
- Batter hits across the line of the ball but hits with the spin.
- Batter attempts to hit the ball into the sector and if it goes past the first set of cones she scores 1 run, if it goes past the next set of cones she scores 2 runs, and if it goes past the boundary she scores 4 runs.
- Each batter receives six deliveries before players rotate.
- The player with most runs wins.

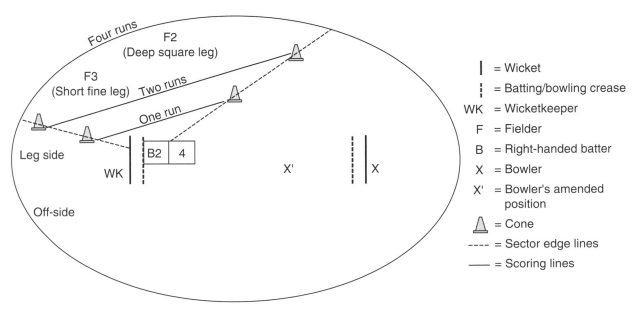

FIGURE 12.30
Practicing the sweep or leg glance.

Variation

Have batter hit from low (4-inch or 10-centimeter) tee.

Cues

- Sweep shot
  - High backlift.
  - Ball is hit on half volley.
  - Step forward with front leg (bending knee) to pitch of ball.
  - Back leg bends (knee can be in contact with ground).
  - Legs now cover the line of the ball.
  - Weight is forward, head leaning over ball, watching closely.
  - Bat is horizontal at impact.
  - Roll wrists to keep ball down.
  - Sweep goes roughly square of wicket.
- Paddle (variation of sweep)
  - Late sweep.
  - Ball goes toward fine leg.
  - Played with wrists, just a gentle tap.

PRACTICE TASK 2

Setup

Repeat task 1 (sector can be increased to encompass midwicket area).

Cues

Front-foot leg glance

- Set up as in forward defensive stroke to ball on leg stump.
- Head over ball.
- Front foot to pitch of ball.
- Weight on front foot.
- Bat is in front of front leg—not alongside it as in forward defense.
- At impact bat is turned, allowing ball to run to fine leg.

Variation

- Flick wrists at moment of contact to angle bat face toward midwicket.
- Shot is about timing, not power.

GAME 2

Setup

Modified Kanga 8s

Goals

- Play ball into the leg side to score runs.
- Take what the defense offers, using sweep, paddle, and leg glance.

Conditions

- Batters can only score runs on the leg side (see figure 12.29).
- Batter's score is doubled if he hits the ball for runs into the target sector on the leg side.
- Bowlers may use no more than a three-step run-up and must bowl off breaks pitching in line with the wicket.
- The pair with the most runs wins.

Tactical Problem
Restrict run scoring by bowling to an off-side field and get the batter out

Lesson Focus
Forcing the batter to play in a designated area and bowling to an off-side field

Objective
Slow bowling (leg break).

GAME 1

Setup
Modified Kanga 8s. Four pairs of players rotate through batting, fielding, bowling, and wicketkeeping as in pairs cricket. Batters can be out by being bowled, caught, run out, or hit wicket. A pair of batters bats for two overs regardless of the number of times each pair is out. Pairs add run increments to their totals for the following bowling and fielding performances: 4 runs for a batter who is bowled, 2 runs per catch to each fielder and to the bowler who was bowling when the catch was taken, and 4 runs for a run-out.

Goal
Make batter play ball into the off-side to restrict run scoring and to get the batter out.

Conditions
· Batters can only score runs on the off-side (see figure 12.31).
· Bowlers may use no more than a three-step run-up.

Questions

Q: *When you bowl, where would most batters like to hit a ball?*
A: On the leg side.

Q: *How can you encourage the batter to play the ball on the off-side?*
A: Make the ball deviate sharply in the direction of the off-side after it pitches.

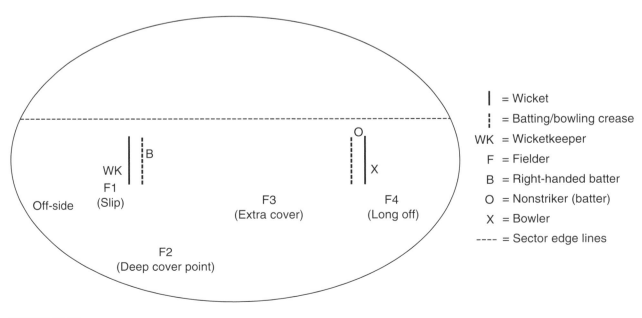

FIGURE 12.31
Leg-break field.

Q: How does that deviation help the defense?

A: You can allocate most of your fielders to the off-side because you can predict that the batter will hit in that direction.

Q: If you want a batter to hit on the off-side, should you bowl to the off-side?

A: To some extent, yes, but you still want to get the batter out by bowling at the wicket.

Q: So what is your target when you bowl?

A: Around the middle and off-stump in target zone 3 so that the ball can turn away from the batter toward the off-side after it pitches. (If the ball is really turning, a leg-break bowler may aim at the middle and leg stump and may also take advantage of the bowler's footmarks, from the other end—this happens only in a real game—and sometimes may even try to bowl the batter around her legs.)

Q: What are the two possibilities of getting the batter out in this tactical scenario?

A: The ball finds the edge of the bat for a catch to the wicketkeeper or slip or the ball does not turn but travels straight after it hits the ground and possibly hits the wicket (an arm ball).

Q: If the batter wants to hit on the leg side, what does doing so mean for his stroke?

A: The batter is hitting across the line of the ball and against the direction of the spin, which means he has a greater chance of mis-hitting or missing the ball completely.

Q: What else can you do to tempt the batter?

A: Bowl the ball fairly slowly, and by spinning the ball you can cause it to fly into the air for a catch to a fielder on the off-side unless the batter makes excellent contact.

PRACTICE TASK 1

Setup
Leg break with partner

Goal
Spinning the ball using leg spin

Conditions
- Partners stand 11 yards/meters apart and throw the ball underhand.
- Ball should land 1.1 to 2.2 yards/meters in front of partner, who collects and returns with a similar action.
- For a right-handed bowler, the ball should hit the ground and spin from right to left.

Cues
- Leg break.
  - Middle joints of the index and second fingers are across the seam (not spread).
  - Ball rests against a bent third finger and the thumb.
  - As ball is released, straighten the fingers (most work is done by the third finger), turning the ball counterclockwise with a flick of the wrist.
  - Wrist turns from facing in to facing batter as fingers flick outward.
  - Palm of the hand finishes facing down.

PRACTICE TASK 2

Setup
Bowler, batter, wicketkeeper, slip, and two defensive off-side fielders positioned at bowler's discretion inside the sector (see figure 12.32)

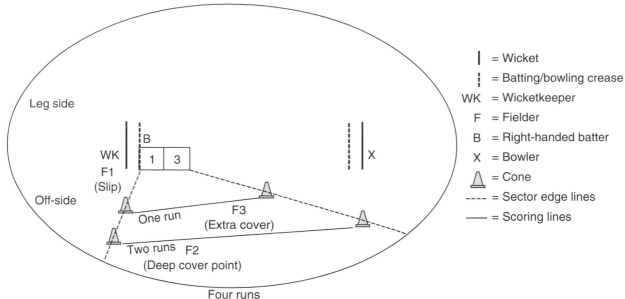

FIGURE 12.32
Defending the off-side.

Goal

Turn ball using leg spin, forcing batter to play ball on the off-side.

Conditions

- Bowler aims at target zone 3 around the batter's off- or middle stump, causing the batter to hit with the spin.
- The batter attempts to hit the ball into the sector.
- If the ball goes past the first set of cones the batter scores 1 run, if it runs past the next set of cones she scores 2, and if it runs past the boundary she scores 4.
- Each batter receives six deliveries before players rotate through the other positions.
- Run increments are awarded for defense as they are awarded in modified Kanga cricket.
- Player with most runs wins.

Cues

Tactical bowling

- Vary speed of delivery.
- Vary position on bowling crease (tight to nonstriker's wicket or wider on batting crease).
- Bowl a straight ball occasionally with no spin (arm ball).

GAME 2

Setup

Modified Kanga 8s

Goal

Make batter play ball into the off-side to restrict run scoring and get the batter out.

Conditions

- Batters can only score runs on the off-side (see figure 12.31).
- Bowlers may use no more than a three-step run-up.

Q: Why is the fielder at slip (see figure 12.31)?
A: The batter may attempt to drive the ball and the leg spin will cause an edge to go to this area.

Q: Why is the fielder at deep cover point on the boundary?
A: To prevent a boundary from a horizontal bat shot or a square drive from a wide ball bowled on the off-side. This fielder could also cover the player at extra cover, who is saving a single.

Q: Why is the fielder at extra cover fairly close?
A: To prevent the batter from pushing the ball into space with the spin and scoring a quick single.

Q: Why is the fielder at deep long-off?
A: To prevent a hard, straight hit. Good batters will try to hit a leg spinner hard in this direction to minimize the effects of the spin.

Lesson 17   Level III

Tactical Problem
Scoring on the off-side

Lesson Focus
Attacking a leg-break bowler and hitting with the spin square on the off-side

Objective
Play cut shot.

GAME 1

Setup
Modified Kanga 8s

Goal
Take what the defense offers and play the ball into the off-side to score runs.

Conditions
- Batters can only score runs on the off-side (see figure 12.33).
- Batter's score is doubled if she hits a ball for runs into the target sector on the off-side.
- Bowlers may use no more than a three-step run-up and must bowl leg-break pitching on- or outside the off-stump.

Questions

Q: When attacking a leg-break bowler, what are your options?
A: Driving the ball with a vertical bat through the leg- or off-side (in this conditioned game, only the off-side).

Q: What about hitting across the line in a real game where the leg side is available?
A: This hit is very risky—not only are you hitting across the line but you are also hitting against the spin.

Q: Could you hit the ball square of the wicket on the off-side into the space for a single?
A: Yes, in two ways: A square drive to a ball that pitches in zone 1 (very wide outside the off-stump) or cutting a ball that is short of a length (pitching in zone 5) and well outside the off-stump (see figure 12.21).

Q: What does a batter need for hitting the ball square of the wicket on the off-side?
A: Good footwork to make room for him to play the shot.

PRACTICE TASK

Setup
Bowler, batter, wicketkeeper, two off-side fielders positioned at bowler's discretion inside the sector (see figure 12.34)

Goal
Batter attempts to hit ball into sector by using the cut shot.

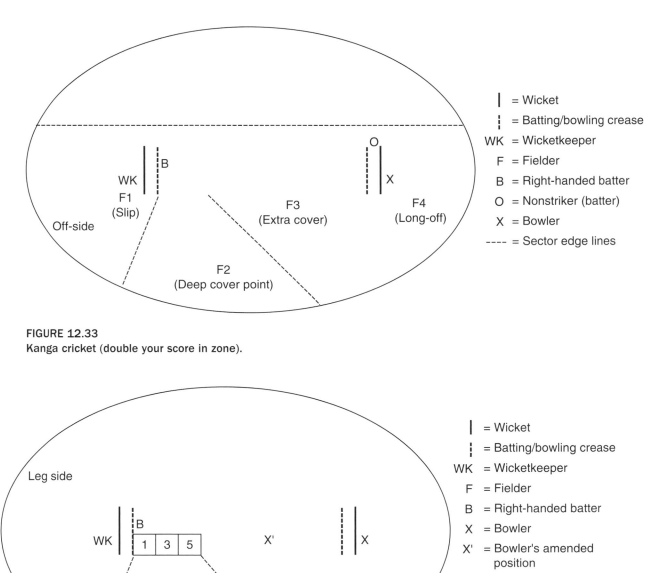

FIGURE 12.33
Kanga cricket (double your score in zone).

FIGURE 12.34
Practicing the cut shot.

Conditions

- Bowler (X') throws ball underhand or overhand (using leg spin) from about 11 yards/meters to land short of a length in target zone 5 outside the batter's off-stump.
- Batter hits with the spin.
- Line of bowler's throw can vary to middle or leg stump depending on amount of spin generated.
- The batter attempts to hit the ball into the sector. If the ball goes past the first set of cones she scores 1 run, if it runs past the next set of cones she scores 2, and if it passes a boundary she scores 4. Each batter receives six deliveries before players rotate through the other positions. Player with most runs wins.

Variation

- Have batter hit from a high tee.

Cues

Square cut

- High backlift.
- Step back and across with back foot toward off-stump.
- Get head in line with ball.
- Turn front shoulder toward direction of point.
- Fling bat horizontally (keep hold of it), fully extending arms and hands at the ball.
- Lean over ball, not back.

GAME 2

Setup

Modified Kanga 8s

Goals

- Play ball into the off-side to score runs.
- Take what the defense offers using the cut shot.

Conditions

- Batters can only score runs on the off-side (see figure 12.33).
- Batter's score is doubled if he hits the ball for runs into the target sector on the leg side (see figure 12.33).
- Bowlers may use no more than a three-step run-up and must bowl leg-break pitching outside the off-stump.
- The pair with the most runs wins.

Questions

Q: *When the batter hits the cut shot, what can happen to the ball when less than perfect contact is made?*

A: The ball can slice into the air behind square on the off-side.

Q: *What can the defense do to restrict run scoring and potentially get the batter out when this happens?*

A: Place a fielder in a catching position wide of slip and almost square with the wicket (a gully fielder) or a little farther away (a backward-point fielder).

Q: *So how does this fielder affect the batter?*

A: The batter must keep her body weight over the ball and hit down or run the risk of being caught in the gully or at the backward point when playing the cut shot and slicing the ball upward. The cut shot is also commonly used against faster bowlers who bowl short and wide of the wicket on the off-side (ball pitches in target zone 5). See figure 12.21 on page 398.

Summary

We hope the ideas in this chapter provide physical educators with the basic tools for teaching cricket from a tactical approach. Students are generally very responsive to learning the concepts of cricket. They understand their responsibilities in offensive and defensive situations and align this understanding with the ability to solve tactical problems using offensive (batting) and defensive (bowling and fielding) skills. The motivation to learn to play cricket seems to be high.

CHAPTER 13

Golf

Golf is a target game with many unique tactical problems. Approximately one-third of all shots taken during a game of golf require a full swing, a complex skill. The complexity of a full swing increases when the golfer uses drivers and fairway woods. We recommend starting with the putter and working up through irons for short, middle, and long distances and using the driver and fairway woods only with advanced players. In fact, a full swing with a middle iron is all that players need off the tee and, in the long run, adds to the novice's success and enjoyment of the game. Encourage novice players to play short, par-3 courses to help them gain confidence, skill, and tactical understanding of the game.

Safety

Safety is a major consideration when teaching golf to a whole class. Arranging students so they are far enough apart yet close enough to monitor is not an easy feat. For easy management and observation of students when indoors, try arranging runners or strips of carpet like the spokes of a wheel (see figure 13.1), with putting cups at the center. You can use the same arrangement for chipping practice, this time positioning small pieces of artificial turf or carpet squares about 10 feet (3 meters) beyond the end of the runner. This setup allows students to chip onto the green.

Partners are a must. They are useful for providing feedback to their peers and can serve as the primary observers for safety infractions. Select a safety cue such as "freeze," "fore," or "no!" When a safety cue is given, everyone should stop and wait for your command to restart activity. Practice this safety cue with your students and periodically yell it out to ensure that students are alert and safety conscious.

Check clubheads after every class, as the constant pounding caused by multiple swings into the floor or ground can cause them to loosen. Also, check the club grips periodically.

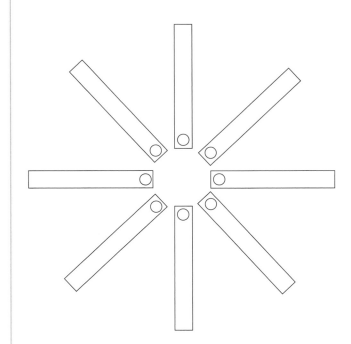

FIGURE 13.1

Arranging putting cups in a circle with runners radiating outward provides an efficient layout for observing students.

Grips can become slippery after many uses. Replacing grips is an easy task, and replacement kits are inexpensive. Get to know the owner or manager of a local golf course, who can often provide tips for club repair and may even volunteer her services. Local courses are also a good source of scorecards, pencils, tees, and other golf gadgets that you can use in class or as prizes for tournaments like the 9-Hole Putt-Putt Golf Classic (just an example).

Instruction Tips

We do not advocate teaching the proper grip, the parts of a club, or the history of the game in the beginning. Let students acquire their own grips and only intervene when you observe a dysfunctional grip. Use proper terminology as you demonstrate each swing, referring to the *sweet spot* on the *clubface*, for example. As for the history of the game, assign students the task of finding out how golf got its start. They can ask parents and grandparents about it or look it up in the library or on the Internet. While in class, get the clubs in their hands and let them play. Once students are engaged and having fun, they will want to learn about the game and how to be successful playing it.

Tactical Reality Golf

To grasp the tactical concepts of golf (learn golf tactically), students will need to understand the conditions under which they make each shot. How far the ball is from the hole, obstacles between the ball and the hole, and the lie of the ball are all important aspects of a golf shot. The decisions made before the shot, the preshot decisions, are as important as the shot itself. We recommend using visual aids to help students understand how to use each type of shot within the game of golf (see figure 13.2). You can use posters, colored chalk drawings, overheads, and so forth to illustrate a situation on the golf course. Be sure to include bunkers, hazards, trees, and so on to keep illustrations real. We have often copied diagrams of golf holes from magazines, scorecards, and promotional materials for golf resorts. If the diagram is too small, enlarge it. Then laminate these diagrams and use them as instructional aids or let the students pretend to play a few holes in class in the game of tactical reality golf which can be played outdoors or indoors on mats (see reproducible on page 424).

When starting out, it is important to use proper terminology as you teach each lesson.

We present the tactical framework and levels of tactical complexity for golf in tables 13.1 and 13.2. Throughout the chapter, we also describe each level before providing its lesson outlines.

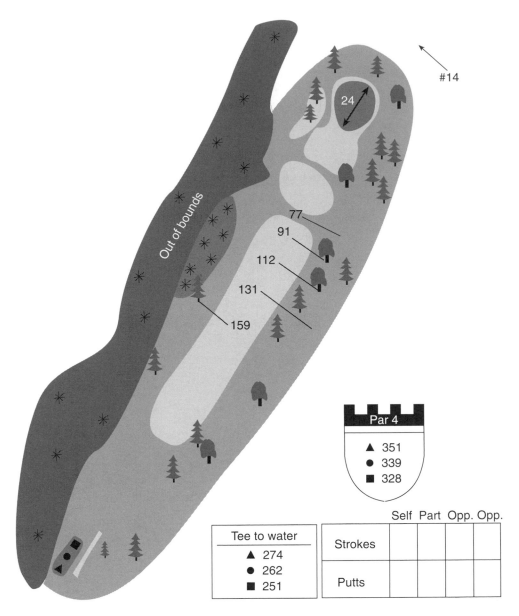

Par 4
▲ 351
● 339
■ 328

Tee to water
▲ 274
● 262
■ 251

	Self	Part	Opp.	Opp.
Strokes				
Putts				

FIGURE 13.2

From *Teaching Sport Concepts and Skills: A Tactical Games Approach,* Second Edition, by Stephen A. Mitchell, Judith L. Oslin, and Linda L. Griffin, Champaign, IL: Human Kinetics.

Table 13.1 Tactical Problems, Decisions, and Skills in Golf

Tactical problems	Preshot decision	Shot execution
REDUCE NUMBER OF STROKES		
Hitting ball the proper distance	· Club selection · Ball placement · Judge distance · Tee the ball · Determine swing length	· Setup routine · Stance · Swing plane · Drive · Putt 1-1, 2-2 · Swing 6-8, 3-9, 2-10, full

Tactical problems	Preshot decision	Shot execution
REDUCE NUMBER OF STROKES		
Hitting the ball in the intended direction	· Select target · Intermediate target · Read green	· Setup · Stance · Swing plane · Putt
Hitting out of hazards	· Club selection · Ball placement · Reading the lie	· Stance · Swing plane · Sand shot
Uphill, downhill, sidehill, and uneven lies	· Club selection · Ball placement · Reading angle of the lie	· Stance · Swing plane

Hitting the ball with spin	· Determine
	  – Backspin
	  – Left to right
	  – Right to left
	  – Hook
	  – Slice
		· Setup
		· Stance
		· Swing plane

Table 13.2 Levels of Tactical Complexity for Golf		
Tactical problems	**I**	**II**
REDUCE NUMBER OF STROKES		

Hitting ball the proper distance	· Club selection
	· Ball placement
	· Setup routine
	· Determine swing length
	· Putt 1-1, 2-2
	· Swing 6-8, 3-9, 2-10, full with midiron
		· Full swing
		  – Long irons
		  – Woods
		· Fairway woods

Hitting the ball in the intended direction	· Select intermediate target · Read green · Setup · Swing plane	
Hitting out of hazards	· Ball placement · Reading the lie · Deep, dense grass	· Sand shot
Uphill and downhill lies Side-hill lies and uneven lies		· Club selection · Stance · Ball placement · Swing plane
Hitting the ball with spin		· Backspin · Left to right · Right to left

Tactical Reality Golf

Player 1 _____   Player 2 _____

Instructions

1. Select a partner and have at least one bag of clubs between you.

2. Choose a hole to play (consult the diagrams of golf holes).

3. Begin with a tee shot from a rubber tee using a Wiffle ball and hit remaining shots from turf mats.

4. Let your partner decide how far and in which direction your ball has gone and then tell you where to play your next shot.

5. For each shot, select an appropriate club. The club you select will depend on your distance from the hole and any obstacles in your path (i.e., you might have to hit over a bunker, in which case you will need to get plenty of height).

6. When you reach the green, use your regulation ball and putter and putt the hole out on the artificial green.

7. Record the number of strokes made from tee to green and the number of putts made on the green and add these two numbers to get your score on the hole.

Maximum Distances Allowed with Each Club

Driver—230 yards/meters

3-wood—210 yards/meters

3-iron—190 yards/meters

4-iron—180 yards/meters

5-iron—170 yards/meters

6-iron—160 yards/meters

7-iron—150 yards/meters

8-iron—140 yards/meters

9-iron—130 yards/meters

Wedge—120 yards/meters

Name	1	2	3	4	5	6	7	8	9	Score

From *Teaching Sport Concepts and Skills: A Tactical Games Approach,* Second Edition, by Stephen A. Mitchell, Judith L. Oslin, and Linda L. Griffin, Champaign, IL: Human Kinetics.

Level I

Level I begins with the putt and ends with a full swing using a middle iron. Lessons focus on club selection, setup, preshot routine, selection of intermediate target, stance, and swing. Through numerous games and practices, students encounter many problem-solving experiences to help them understand the relationship between the loft of the club and the placement of the ball within the stance.

Many drills require players to observe their partner's swing or the flight characteristics of their partner's ball. This observation requires keen skills that must be taught. Take time to instruct how to observe (i.e., stand in this location, watch one critical element at a time, and view multiple trials). Use a marker to stripe the golf balls, because the direction of spin can provide feedback about the swing. By becoming competent observers and evaluators, students can improve their own skills and game performance.

Students should work on their putting skills to help them get the golf ball to the hole in fewer strokes.

Lesson 1

Tactical Problem
Hitting for proper distance

Lesson Focus
Putt, club selection

Objective
Putt ball into hole in fewest number of strokes.

GAME 1

Setup
Putt 10 balls at 3 feet (1 meter) and 10 balls at 10 feet (3 meters), keeping score

Goal
Put ball in hole in fewest number of strokes.

Conditions

- See figure 13.1 on page 420 for equip-ment setup.
- Ask students to select the club that will best allow them to complete the task.
- Impose a safety rule that students should not raise the clubhead higher than their feet.
- Place balls 3 feet (1 meter) and 10 feet (3 meters) from a hole on a green (a smooth, flat surface). Use diagrams, posters, overheads, and so on to give students a mental picture of the green and ball position relative to the hole (see figure 13.3 for an example).

Questions

Q: What stance, grip, and body position helped you get the ball in the hole with one stroke?

A: Square and balanced stance, comfortable grip, ready position with head and nose over ball.

Q: How did you swing your club to achieve the goal?

A: Smoothly, keeping blade straight.

Q: How was your swing for the 3-foot (1-meter) putt different from your swing for the 10-foot (3-meter) putt?

A: The 3-foot putt swing was shorter than the 10-foot putt swing.

Q: Why is it important to know how long your swing should be when you're attempting a 3-foot (1-meter) putt?

A: So that every time you putt from 3 feet your swing is the same.

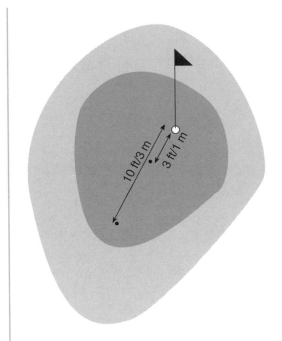

FIGURE 13.3

PRACTICE TASK

Setup

Putt between rulers, yardsticks, or measured boards. Putt 10 1-1 strokes (1-1 means a 1/2- to 1-foot, or 0.15- to 0.3-meter, backswing and forward swing) and have partner measure the distances the ball travels on the last five strokes (using a measuring tape). Switch roles and then repeat the task for 2-2 strokes (2- to 3-foot, or 0.6- to 0.9-meter, swings) and for 3-3 strokes (3- to 4-foot, or 0.9- to 1.2-meter, swings). Partner also serves as coach, repeating cues and giving feedback. Have students calculate the average distance the ball traveled at each stroke length.

Goal

Develop a consistent swing for the 1, 2, and 3 putts.

Cues

Stance and swing

- Balanced.
- Square blade.
- Comfortable grip.
- Quiet body.
- Nose over ball.
- Smooth, even stroke.

GAME 2

Repeat game 1.

Conditions

- Putt balls at 3 feet (1 meter), 10 feet (3 meters), and 15 feet (5 meters), keeping score.
- Compare scores at 3 feet (1 meter) and 10 feet (3 meters) with scores of first game.

Lesson 2

Tactical Problem
Hitting ball in proper direction

Lesson Focus
Intermediate target

Objective
Use an intermediate target to putt ball into hole in fewest number of strokes.

GAME 1

Setup

Putt five balls each at 10, 15, and 20 feet (3, 4.6, and 6 meters), keeping score.

Goal
One putt.

Conditions

- See figure 13.1 for equipment setup.
- Ask students to select the club that will best allow them to complete the task.
- Impose a safety rule that students not raise the clubhead higher than their feet.
- Place balls 8 and 15 feet (2.4 and 5 meters) from a hole on a green, using an uneven surface (place rope under the green to change the surface).

Questions

Q: *Where did you aim to get the ball in the hole?*
A: Right at the hole and at the area or spot between the hole and the ball.

Q: *Why use a spot between the hole and the ball?*
A: A closer target allows you to be more accurate.

Q: *When you use a target between the ball and the hole, we refer to it as an intermediate target. Where is the best place for this intermediate target: closer to the ball or closer to the hole?*
A: Don't know.

Let's experiment to find out the best place for your intermediate target.

PRACTICE TASK

Setup
Playing under the conditions from game 1, students use stickers, stars, or small markers to find the best place for an intermediate target when attempting 8-foot (2.4-meter) and 15-foot (5-meter) putts. Have them place their markers between the ball and the hole and then gradually move the marker closer to the hole. When they think

they have selected a good place for an intermediate target at 8 feet (2.4 meters) and at 15 feet (5 meters), let them move to another green to try their target placement.

Goal
Determine the best location for an intermediate target when putting.

Cues
- Pick intermediate target before setup.
- Once lined up, focus on swing length.

Questions
Q: *What was the goal of the practice task?*
A: To find the best place for an intermediate target.

Q: *Where did you determine to be the best place for an intermediate target?*
A: Fairly close to the ball.

Q: *Why is this better than an intermediate target at a farther distance?*
A: The closer target is easier to hit, with less chance for error.

GAME 2

Setup
Repeat game 1. Keep score and compare with score of first game.

Lesson 3  Level I

Tactical Problem
Hitting the ball the proper distance and in the intended direction

Lesson Focus
Club selection, selection of intermediate target, and chipping

Objective
Select and execute a chip shot from 20 feet (6 meters), landing the ball within one short putt of the hole.

GAME 1

Setup
Ball 3 feet (1 meter) off green on first cut, ball 10 feet (3 meter) off green in rough

Goal
Hit ball within 3 feet (1 meter) of hole.

Conditions
- Ask students to select the club that will best allow them to complete the task.
- Impose a safety rule that students should not raise the clubhead higher than their knees.
- Place two balls 20 feet (6 meters) from hole, one 3 feet (1 meter) off the green and the other 10 feet (3 meters) off the green. (Use diagrams, posters, overheads, and so on to give students a mental picture of the green, the surrounding area, and the ball position relative to the hole.)
- Students hit the ball onto the green, then putt out.
- Students record scores.

Questions

Q: What club did you use for each shot?
A: You can use the 3- to 7-irons for 3 ft (1 meter) and the 9-iron or wedge for 10 feet (3 meters) because of deep grass.

Q: What stance, grip, and body position worked best for reaching the goal?
A: Open stance, comfortable and choked down, and a ready position with head over the ball.

Q: What swing was best for reaching the goal from 3 feet (1 meter)?
A: Square and smooth, with a follow-through toward the hole.

Q: How were you able to control the direction your ball traveled?
A: By selecting an intermediate target.

PRACTICE TASK

Setup
Chip the ball from between two yardsticks or metersticks into a target about one-third the distance between the ball and the hole (use a small rope or cord to mark a target). Chip 10 balls each from 3 feet (0.9 meter) and 10 feet (3 meters). Then select a longer distance (between 12 and 20 feet, or 3.6 and 6 meters) and adjust your swing and target.

Goal
Use appropriate form to chip ball into a target.

Cues
Chipping
- Open stance, hands ahead of blade.
- Weight on front foot, hands to target.
- Lag clubface, quiet body.

GAME 2

Setup
Repeat game 1 and compare score with score of first game.

Lesson 4   Level I

Tactical Problem
Hitting ball with proper distance, direction, and trajectory

Lesson Focus
Club selection, pitch shot

Objective
Use one-quarter (6:00 to 9:00) and one-half (6:00 to 12:00) swing with a short iron to pitch ball over a hazard and land it close to the hole 10 feet (3 meters) from that hazard.

GAME 1

Setup
Place balls 30 feet (9 meters) and 60 feet (18 meters) from hole, with a sand trap between the ball and the hole, and the hole within 10 feet (3 meters) of the hazard. Hit 5 to 10 balls from each distance.

Goals

- Put ball in hole in fewest number of strokes.
- Land ball within 5 feet (1.5 meters) of hole.

Conditions

- Ask students to select the club that will best allow them to complete the task.
- Impose a safety rule that students not raise the clubhead higher than their shoulders.
- Place balls at 30 feet (9 meters) and 60 feet (18 meters) from the hole, with a sand trap between the ball and the hole.
- Hole is 10 feet (3 meters) on the other side of the trap. (Use diagrams, posters, overheads, and so on to give students a mental picture of the green, the sand trap, and the ball position relative to the hole.)
- Students record scores.

Questions

Q: What club was best for reaching the goal? Why?
A: The wedge or 9-iron because it gave more loft and more control.

Q: What stance, grip, and body position worked best for reaching the goal?
A: A square stance; a comfortable, overlapping, and interlocking grip; and a natural, ready position.

Q: The farther you are putting from the hole, the longer should be your swing. How does that concept apply to pitching?
A: The farther you are from the hole, the longer should be the backswing.

Q: Some people use the face of a clock to refer to the distance of a backswing. How could we use the face of the clock to measure the length of our backswings?
A: A one-quarter swing is 6:00 to 9:00 and a one-half swing is 6:00 to 12:00.

PRACTICE TASK 1

Setup

Use the situation from game 1 to practice one-quarter and one-half swings for pitching the ball onto the green. Use a partner checklist to evaluate swing form and length. Each partner takes 10 practice swings, and then takes 10 more swings for his partner to evaluate his form. Rotate after 20 swings and then move to other distances (30 or 60 feet, or 9 or 18 meters).

Goals

- Use good form on one-quarter and one-half swings to perform a pitch shot.
- Evaluate partner's pitch shot.

Questions

Q: Were your setup routine, selection of intermediate target, and ball placement similar or different from that for the chip and putt?
A: Setup and selection of intermediate target were the same but ball placement was different.

Q: Relative to the stance, where was the best place for the ball to be?
A: Don't know.

Let's find out.

PRACTICE TASK 2

Setup

Use the situation from game 1 to practice ball placement from 30 feet (9 meters) or 60 feet (18 meters). Each student hits two balls placed off the front, middle, and rear of the foot. Partners chart the trajectory of each shot and then players switch roles and repeat the task.

Questions

Q: How does the placement of the ball in the stance influence its flight?
A: The farther back the ball is, the lower its trajectory.

Q: What other factor influences the trajectory of the ball?
A: The loft of the club.

Q: If you want the ball to have a high trajectory, what should you do?
A: Place the ball toward the middle of your stance and select a club with more loft (a 9-iron or wedge).

GAME 2

Setup

Repeat game 1 and compare results with first game.

Lesson 5

Tactical Problem

Hitting ball the proper distance, direction, and trajectory

Lesson Focus

Hitting over a lake and landing on the green

Objective

Use three-quarter and full swings with a short iron to pitch the ball within 15 to 20 feet (5 to 6 meters) of the hole.

GAME 1

Setup

Place balls 90 feet (27 meters) and 120 feet (37 meters) from hole, with a lake between the ball and the hole, and the hole within 20 feet (6 meters) of the hazard.

Goal

Land ball within 10 to 15 feet (3 to 4.6 meters) of the hole.

Conditions

- Ask students to select the club that will best allow them to complete the task.
- Impose a safety rule that students should not raise the clubhead unless their partners give the all clear.
- Place balls 90 feet (27 meters) and 120 feet (37 meters) from the hole, with a lake between the ball and the hole.
- Place the hole 20 feet (6 meters) on the other side of lake.
- Students hit 5 to 10 balls from each distance.
- Record the number of balls landing within 15 feet (5 meters) of the hole (see figure 13.4).

Questions

Q: What club was best for these shots?
A: The wedge or 9-iron.

Q: How did your swing differ from 90 feet (27 meters) to 120 feet (37 meters)?
A: A bigger swing was needed for 120 feet (37 meters).

Q: How was this swing similar to the one-quarter or one-half swings?
A: It was the same but longer, with a greater range of motion.

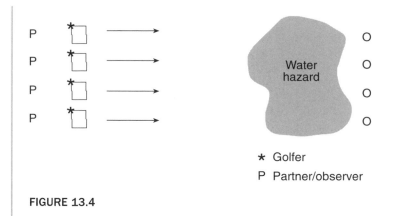

FIGURE 13.4

PRACTICE TASK

Setup

Use the situation from game 1 to practice the three-quarter to full swings for pitching the ball onto the green. Use partner checklist to evaluate swing form and length. Each partner takes 10 practice swings and then takes 10 more swings for her partner to evaluate. Rotate after 20 swings, and then go to 90 feet (27 meters) or 120 feet (37 meters).

Goals

- Use good form to perform the three-quarter to full-swing pitch shot.
- Evaluate partner's swing.

GAME 2

Repeat game 1 and compare score with score of first game.

Lesson 6   Level I

Tactical Problem

Hitting ball the proper distance and direction

Lesson Focus

Hitting ball with low trajectory

Objective

Use a three-quarter to full swing with a middle-distance iron to approach the green.

GAME 1

Setup

Ball under a tree and 150 feet (46 meters) from hole

Goal

Get ball onto the green.

Conditions

- Ask students to select the club that will best allow them to complete the task.
- Impose a safety rule that students should not raise the clubhead unless their partners give the all clear.
- Students hit 10 balls and then hit 3 to 5 balls, playing each all the way out. (Use

diagrams, posters, overheads, and so on to give students a mental picture of the green, the surrounding area, and the ball position relative to the hole.)

· Students record scores of last 3 to 5 balls.

Questions

Q: Where was the best place to land the ball and why?
A: Short of the green, letting it roll to avoid a penalty for losing a ball in the woods.

Q: Which club was best for achieving the goal?
A: The middle-distance or long-distance iron, but choke up to keep the ball low.

Q: What swing length was best for achieving the goal?
A: Three-quarter to full swing.

Q: Where was the best ball placement?
A: Forward in stance to keep trajectory low.

PRACTICE TASK 1

Setup

Each partner takes 10 practice swings, adjusting placement to achieve proper trajectory, and then takes 10 more swings so his partner can evaluate his form. Players rotate after 20 swings. Repeat the task if partner needs more time to evaluate.

Goals

· Adjust ball placement to get low trajectory.
· Evaluate partner's performance of full swing.

PRACTICE TASK 2

Setup

Use the situation from game 1 and practice using a full swing to get out from under a tree and to land the ball in front of the green. Use a partner checklist to evaluate swing errors and causes of errors based on the flight of the ball.

Goal

Land ball in front of green for good approach shot.

Cues

· Ball placement and club selection necessary for achieving low trajectory.
· Even, smooth swing.

GAME 2

Repeat game 1 and compare score from first game.

Lesson 7

Level I

Tactical Problem

Hitting ball the proper distance and trajectory

Lesson Focus

Full swing with middle iron

Objectives

· Drive ball from tee.
· Play five holes of golf on a tactical reality golf course (par-3 holes).

GAME 1

Setup

From a tee box, hit the ball down the fairway so you can reach the green on your second (approach) shot

Goal

Land drive within 100 feet (31 meters) of green.

Conditions

- Ask students to select the club that will best allow them to complete the task.
- Impose a safety rule that students should not raise the clubhead unless their partners give the all clear.
- Place tee box 250 feet (76 meters) from the hole, with a lake between the ball and the hole, and place the hole 20 feet (6 meters) on the other side of lake. (Use diagrams, posters, overheads, and so on to give students a mental picture of the green, the surrounding area, and the ball position relative to the hole.)
- Students record scores.

Questions

Q: Why do you want to land the drive within 100 feet (31 meters) and in front of the green?
A: To set up an easy second shot.

Q: Did you change any part of your setup or swing to help you achieve the goal?
A: Used a tee.

Q: How did using the tee help?
A: It made it easier to hit the ball by setting up the ball clear of the grass.

Q: Did any of you try placing the ball in different places within your stance? If so, what happened?
A: No.

Let's practice to determine which ball placement will give you the best distance and trajectory.

PRACTICE TASK 1

Setup

From a tee, all students should hit two balls placed off the front, the middle, and the rear of the foot. Partners should chart the trajectory and approximate distance and trajectory of each shot. Players switch roles and repeat the task.

Goal

Determine best placement for ball during a drive.

Questions

Q: Where was the best ball placement for obtaining the proper distance, direction, and trajectory?
A: In front of the foot.

Q: How high should you tee the ball?
A: There should be approximately the width of an index finger from the ball to the ground.

Q: What is the effect of ball height on the trajectory of the ball?
A: If the ball is too high, the trajectory will be high. If the ball is too low, the trajectory will be low.

Let's practice to determine how high the ball should be teed up.

PRACTICE TASK 2

Setup
From the tee, students hit balls placed high, medium, and low on the tee (two balls at each height). Partners should chart the trajectory and approximate distance of each shot. Players switch roles and repeat the task.

Goal
Determine the proper height for teeing the ball.

Questions

Q: How did the height of the ball influence the trajectory?
A: If you tee up the ball too high, you get a high trajectory.

Q: What was the best height?
A: Low to medium for an iron, medium for a driver.

Cues
- Work on setup and ball placement.
- Swing easy, hit hard.
- Fix eyes on spot (on the ball).

GAME 2

Setup
Play 3 to 5 holes of tactical reality golf (see figure 13.2) and compare score with score of first game.

Lesson 8

Tactical Problem
Reducing number of strokes

Lesson Focus
Rules and etiquette of golf

Objectives
- Drive ball from tee.
- Play five holes of golf on a tactical reality golf course (par-3 holes).

GAME 1

Setup
Play 5 to 9 holes of tactical reality golf

Goals
- Score par (or better) on every hole.
- Demonstrate knowledge of proper club selection, shot selection, setup, and swing length.

Conditions
- Play on tactical reality golf holes (see figure 13.2).
- All players must follow the rules or assume the appropriate penalties.
- Players must follow course etiquette.

Questions (after 3 or 4 holes)

Q: *What did you do when your ball went into the woods or other hazard, causing you to lift or pick up your ball?*
A: Added a penalty stroke to my score.

Q: *Can you describe other instances where penalty strokes are assessed?*
A: Playing the wrong ball, moving the ball while setting up a shot, and so forth.

Q: *How did you know whose turn it was?*
A: The player with the lowest score on the previous hole went first.

Q: *What did you do with your bag on the tees and the green?*
A: Left the bag off the tees and green. (You can include other questions about rules and etiquette.)

Let's continue play using official rules and proper etiquette.

Level II

Lessons at level II focus on the full swing with a driver and the fairway woods. Once students have developed consistent swing patterns, they should work on altering their swing planes and club positions to hit a ball left to right or right to left. Once the swing pattern becomes consistent, the player can work on uneven lies, uphill and downhill lies, and sidehill lies. Two of the following lessons focus on these irregular lies.

Students must practice their full swing to produce accuracy.

Tactical Problem
Hitting the ball the proper distance and direction

Lesson Focus
Full swing with a fairway wood, club selection

Objective
Use a fairway wood to hit ball to intended target.

GAME 1

Setup
Play 3 to 5 holes of tactical reality golf, par-5 holes.

Goal
Land all shots to allow easiest approach to the green.

Conditions
  · Ask students to select the clubs that will best allow them to complete the task.
  · Impose a safety rule that students should not raise the clubhead unless their partners give the all clear.
  · Place tee box 450 yards/meters from hole, with a lake between the ball and the green, and the green 30 feet (9 meters) on the other side of the lake. (Use diagrams, posters, overheads, and so on to give students a mental picture of the green, the surrounding area, and the ball position relative to the hole.)
  · Students record scores.

Questions

  Q: *When you had 200 yards/meters or more to the green after your drive, what club did you select? Why?*
  A: The long iron or wood because the longer club and larger clubhead give a longer distance.

  Q: *What other factors influence club selection?*
  A: The distance the person can hit, the lie of the ball, and the distance to the green.

  Q: *How is hitting with a fairway wood different from hitting a drive from the tee?*
  A: The ball lies lower and is not teed up.

  Q: *What do you think were some of the causes for mis-hitting the ball?*
  A: Setup and stance were not right.

PRACTICE TASK 1

Setup
With a partner, practice using a fairway wood (2/3 or 4/5). One partner hits five balls from the forward, middle, and back positions as the other partner charts the direction and trajectory of each ball. Partners then switch roles.

Goal
Determine proper ball placement when hitting with a long iron or fairway wood.

Questions

  Q: *What was the best ball placement for hitting with a fairway wood?*
  A: Forward. The exact spot may vary from player to player.

Q: How far from your body was the ball?
A: Close, medium, or far away.

Q: What distance did you find was best?
A: Not sure.

Let's look at ball placement and the distance the ball is placed from your feet.

PRACTICE TASK 2

Setup
With a partner, use a fairway wood (2/3 or 4/5). One partner hits 15 to 20 balls, placing the ball at various distances from his body. His partner should provide feedback on his form and the flight of the ball. Once he thinks that he's found the proper distance, partners switch roles. (Prompt students to use findings from the problem posed in practice task 1 to place the ball in relation to their stances.)

Goal
Determine proper placement of ball during shot with a fairway wood.

GAME 2

Setup
Repeat game 1, playing 3 to 5 holes of tactical reality golf, and compare score with score of first game.

Lesson 10 — Level II

Tactical Problem
Hitting ball the proper distance and direction

Lesson Focus
Full swing with a driver from the tee box

Objective
Use a driver to hit the ball down the center of the fairway.

GAME 1

Setup
Play 3 to 5 holes of tactical reality golf, par-4 holes.

Goal
Land the drive in a place that will allow the easiest approach to the green.

Conditions
- Ask students to select the club that will best allow them to complete the task.
- Impose a safety rule that students should not raise the clubhead unless their partners give the all clear.
- Place tee box 300 yards/meters from hole, with a lake between the ball and the hole, and place the green 20 feet (6 meters) on other side of lake. (Use diagrams, posters, overheads, and so on to give students a mental picture of the green, the surrounding area, and the ball position relative to the hole.)
- Students record scores.

Questions

Q: For most holes, where was the best place to land the ball?
A: In the middle of the fairway, with an open shot to the green.

Q: Were you able to hit the ball straight most of the time?
A: Not many students consistently hit straight.

Q: How can the flight of the ball help you determine swing errors?
A: If the flight is too low or too high, then perhaps there was not a good placement during setup; if the ball spins left or right, then perhaps the swing plane was incorrect or the blade was not square at impact.

Q: Let's practice swinging and reading the flight and spin of the ball. If ball is too high or too low, hooking, or slicing, what should you do?
A: Adjust your swing.

PRACTICE TASK 1

Setup

Students hit Wiffle balls into a curtain or wall or hit real or restricted balls in a cage or outside. As one partner practices her drive, the other partner evaluates her, using a checklist and providing feedback. Partners should rotate after 10 to 20 swings.

Goals

- Improve full swing.
- Evaluate partner's full swing.

PRACTICE TASK 2

Setup

Students hit Wiffle balls into a curtain or wall or hit in cage or outside. As one partner hits 5 to 10 balls, the other partner evaluates the direction and trajectory of the ball and gives feedback.

Goal

Read the trajectory and spin of the ball and use them to provide feedback about swing performance.

GAME 2

Setup

Repeat game 1, playing 3 to 5 holes of tactical reality golf, and compare score with score of first game.

Lesson 11 Level II

Tactical Problem
Hitting out of hazards

Lesson Focus
Sand shots

Objective
Hit the ball out of a sand trap, landing the ball in the target zone.

GAME 1

Setup

Place the ball in sand, with a hole 30 feet (9 meters) from the trap and the ball 10 feet (3 meters) from the lip of the trap, or 40 feet (12 meters) from the hole.

Goal

Get the ball out of the sand and onto the green in one stroke.

Conditions

- Ask students to select the clubs that will best allow them to complete the task.
- Impose a safety rule that students should not raise the clubhead unless their partners give the all clear.
- You can use a sandbox or pit to create the sand trap.
- Set up identical lies and have students play against a partner to see who can get the ball out of the trap and into the hole in the fewest number of strokes. (Use diagrams, posters, overheads, and so on to give students a mental picture of the green, the surrounding area, and the ball position relative to the hole.)
- Students record scores.

Questions

Q: *How were you able to get the ball out of the sand and onto the green?*
A: Use a firm, open stance and swing through the ball.

Q: *How did you know how big of a swing you needed to get the ball out of the sand?*
A: The swing depended on how deep the ball was lying in the sand.

PRACTICE TASK 1

Setup

Students work with partners to evaluate form and provide feedback. Each student takes 10 practice swings and then switches roles with the partner.

Goals

- Consistently get the ball out of the sand and onto the green in one stroke.
- Evaluate partner's sand shot.

PRACTICE TASK 2

Setup

Students work with partners and place the ball at different depths in the sand. The other partner observes and provides feedback relative to the point of contact in sand and the swing length required to remove the ball from the sand.

Goal

Identify point of contact for removing ball during sand shots.

GAME 2

Setup

Repeat game 1 and compare scores with those of first challenge.

Tactical Problem
Hitting out of hazards

Lesson Focus
Hitting a ball lying deep in dense grass

Objectives
- Select the proper club, setup, and intermediate target.
- Adjust swing plane to hit down and through the ball.

GAME 1

Setup
Hit balls out of deep, dense grass about 30 yards/meters from the green

Goal
Hit ball out of the grass and to the intended target with one swing.

Conditions
- Ask students to select the clubs that will best allow them to complete the task.
- Impose a safety rule that students should not raise the clubhead unless their partners give the all clear.
- If dense grass is not available, use sand or loose dirt to simulate this shot.
- If possible, place balls 60 to 70 yards/meters from the green.
- Have students alternate hits with a partner.
- Students record scores and subtract 5 strokes from their scores every time a ball lands and stays on the green or area designated as the green. (Use diagrams, posters, overheads, and so on to give students a mental picture of the green, the surrounding area, and the ball position relative to the hole.)

Questions
Q: *What did you do to get the ball out of the grass and to your intended target?*
A: Hit the ball high and landed it short.

Q: *How did you adjust your swing to get the ball out of the high grass?*
A: Swung down and through the ball and used a firm grip and a good follow-through.

Q: *How many of you were able to consistently land the ball on the green?*
A: Not many.

Let's practice.

PRACTICE TASK

Setup
Use the situation from game 1 and add a hula hoop to provide a target in which to land the ball. With a partner, students take five shots each and then switch. Partner should serve as a coach, providing feedback following each shot.

Goal
Adjust swing to get the ball out of dense grass.

Cues
- Select an intermediate target.
- Select a place to land the ball.
- Swing down and through.

GAME 2

Setup
Repeat game 1 and compare scores at the end of class.

Lesson 13

Tactical Problem
Hitting downhill and uphill lies

Lesson Focus
Setup for downhill and uphill lies

Objective
Determine club, setup, stance, and ball placement for uphill and downhill lies.

GAME 1

Setup
Compete with a partner. Hit five uphill lies and five downhill lies into a target area about 30 feet (9 meters) away.

Goal
Land ball within 10 feet (3 meters) of intended target with one swing.

Conditions
- Ask students to select the clubs that will best allow them to complete the task.
- Impose a safety rule that students should not raise the clubhead unless their partners give the all clear.
- If possible, place the ball 10 to 20 yards/meters from a target if hitting a Wiffle ball.
- Students record their partners' scores, adding 1 stroke for every shot that misses the target area and subtracting 2 strokes for every shot that lands in the target area. (Use diagrams, posters, overheads, and so on to give students a mental picture of the uphill and downhill lies, the surrounding area, and the ball position relative to the hole.)

Questions
Q: *How did you adjust your preshot setup to successfully hit uphill and downhill lies?*
A: Took a practice swing to determine where to place ball in the stance and positioned the ball high toward the foot.

Q: *How did you adjust your swing to successfully hit uphill and downhill lies?*
A: Adjusted swing length to the degree of the slope and used a choke-up grip (about 3 inches, or 8 centimeters, from the top) with shoulders parallel to the slope. Shots for uphill lies tended to hook. We moved closer to the ball on downhill lies.

Q: *How successful were you at consistently making contact with the ball?*
A: Not many students respond positively.

Perhaps we should practice.

PRACTICE TASK

Setup
Use partner evaluation, such as a checklist. Partners alternate after 10 to 20 shots. Include evaluation of preshot routine.

Goals

- Set up properly to allow for good contact.
- Improve swing used for uphill and downhill lies.

Cues

- Bear weight on uphill foot.
- Use practice swing to help with ball placement.
- Swing parallel with the slant of the hill.

GAME 2

Setup

Repeat game 1 or allow students to play 2 or 3 holes of tactical reality golf, with each fairway shot played as either an uphill or a downhill lie.

Lesson 14 Level II

Tactical Problem
Hitting sidehill lies

Lesson Focus
Setup for hitting sidehill lies

Objectives
- Determine club, setup, stance, and ball placement for sidehill lies.
- Refine preshot routine.

GAME 1

Setup

Compete with a partner. Hit 10 sidehill lies (5 sloping away from target, 5 sloping toward target) into a target area.

Goal

Land ball within 10 feet (3 meters) of intended target with one swing.

Conditions

- Students hit ball from about 30 feet (9 meters) away and score 1 stroke for every shot that misses the target area and −2 strokes for every shot that lands in the target area.
- Ask students to select the clubs that will best allow them to complete the task.
- Impose a safety rule that students should not raise the clubhead unless their partners give the all clear.
- If possible, place ball 10 to 20 yards/meters away from a target if hitting a Wiffle ball. (Use diagrams, posters, overheads, and so on to give students a mental picture of the uphill and downhill lies, the surrounding area, and the ball position relative to the hole.)
- Students record their partners' scores.

Questions

Q: *How did you adjust your preshot setup to successfully hit a sidehill lie?*
A: Took a practice swing to determine where to place ball in stance; selected an intermediate target.

Q: How did you adjust your swing to successfully hit sidehill lies?
A: Adjusted swing length to the degree of the slope and used a choke-up grip (about 3 inches, or 8 centimeters, from the top). Stood closer when the ball was below the feet and shifted weight toward heels and insteps.

PRACTICE TASK

Setup
Use partner evaluation, such as a checklist. Partners alternate after 10 to 20 shots. Evaluation should include preshot routine.

Goals
- Set up properly to allow good contact.
- Improve swing used for sidehill lies.

Cues
- Use practice swing to check for proper ball placement.
- Always use preshot routine.
- Use a closed blade on a downward slope (slopes away from golfer).
- Use an open blade on an upward slope (slopes toward golfer).

GAME 2

Setup
Repeat game 1 or allow students to play 2 or 3 holes of tactical reality golf, with each fairway shot played as a sidehill lie.

Lesson 15 — Level II

Tactical Problem
Hitting a ball with spin

Lesson Focus
Hitting a ball with backspin

Objective
Land a pitch shot on a green from 40 to 80 yards/meters.

GAME 1

Setup
Three holes of stroke play with a foursome

Goal
Play three partial holes in as few strokes as possible.

Conditions
- Pin is close to the front edge of the green and the ball is on the fairway, about 60 yards/meters from the hole.
- Students play three holes, beginning with a short fairway shot.

Questions
Q: What was the best club for the first shot?
A: A 9-iron, pitching wedge, or sand wedge.

Q: Where was the best spot on the green to place the ball?
A: Close to the hole so you could putt once.

Q: How were you able to get the ball to land close to the hole?
A: Used a high trajectory so the ball would stay where it landed.

Q: How successful were you at landing the ball close to the hole and getting it to stay there?
A: Not very.

Let's practice!

PRACTICE TASK

Setup
Work on varying the loft of the ball. With a partner, one student uses a 9-iron to hit three balls: one off the target heel, one off the rear heel, and one from the center. Partner observes ball spin and flight and records observations. Partners switch and repeat task. They repeat the task again with a pitching wedge and with a sand wedge.

Goal
Observe differences in loft and flight caused by different clubs and ball placements.

Cues
- Narrower stance.
- Forward swing length, 2:00 or 3:00.
- Hands to target.

Questions

Q: How did the position of the ball influence its trajectory and spin?
A: The farther back in stance the ball is placed, the lower the trajectory.

Q: How did the type of club influence the trajectory and spin of the ball?
A: The greater the loft, the higher the trajectory and the greater the spin.

GAME 2

Setup
Play 2 to 4 par-3 holes of tactical reality golf.

Goal
Make as few strokes as possible.

Conditions
- Use visual aids to illustrate conditions of each par-3 hole.
- Do not use a tee when hitting from tee box.

Lesson 16   Level II

Tactical Problem
Hitting a ball with spin

Lesson Focus
Modifying the flight pattern of the ball

Objective
Determine the elements of the swing that influence the direction the ball travels.

GAME 1

Setup
Follow the Leader

Goal
Imitate flight path of ball hit by partner.

Conditions
- In a field or down the length of a gym, partners alternate shots.
- First partner attempts to hit the ball right to left or left to right, and then the other partner attempts to imitate that shot.
- After 10 shots, partners switch.

Questions
Q: What elements of the swing influenced the direction of the ball?
A: The angle of the clubface at contact, the angle of the swing during the forward swing, and a setup that was not square.

Q: What was the position of the clubface when the ball rotated right (clockwise)? When it rotated left (counterclockwise)?
A: Open. Closed.

Q: What swing plane caused the ball to move left? To move right?
A: Outside-in. Inside-out.

Q: How many of you were successful at imitating your partner's swing?
A: Not many.

Let's practice!

PRACTICE TASK

Setup
One partner swings as the other observes and records flight patterns. First partner attempts five full swings with an open face and five full swings with a closed face. Partners then switch roles. First partner attempts five full swings moving the club outside-in (with clubface staying square) and five full swings moving the clubface inside-out (again, with clubface remaining square). Partners switch roles. First partner combines outside-in swing with an open clubface for five shots and then with a closed clubface for five shots. Partners switch again. First partner combines inside-out swing with an open clubface for five shots and then with a closed clubface for five shots. Partners switch roles and repeat task.

Goal
Intentionally hit hook, slice, and fade shots.

Cues
- Swing normal when clubface is open or closed.
- Adjust swing plane only slightly from normal swing.
- Read flight of ball for feedback.
- Set up right and then let the club do the work.

GAME 2

Setup
Play 2 or 3 holes of tactical reality golf

Goal

Fewest strokes possible.

Conditions

- During drive and long fairway shots, partners predetermine flight patterns.
- Use a one-stroke penalty for flight patterns not matching the predetermined ones, or, if possible, select holes that require certain types of shots to approach the green (e.g., narrow fairways, doglegs, strong breezes).

Lesson 17 Level II

Lesson Focus

Rules and etiquette

Objective

Play 4 or 5 holes of golf, scoring par or better.

GAME 1

Setup

Play golf on an actual course or play tactical reality golf, in twosomes, threesomes, or foursomes

Goal

Play 4 or 5 holes in as few strokes as possible.

PRACTICE TASK

Setup

Students analyze the 4 or 5 holes just completed and assess (in writing) their game performances (skills such as drives, approach shots, and putting and game play such as shot selection, performance of preshot routine, and selection of intermediate target).

Goal

Assess your golf game to improve your play and lower your score.

GAME 2

Setup

Play golf on an actual course or play tactical reality golf, in twosomes, threesomes, or foursomes

Goal

Play same 4 or 5 holes in fewer strokes.

Summary

There are several videotapes, books, magazines, and Internet sites on tactical and skill development. You can modify many drills and practice situations found in these resources for your students. Experienced players enjoy working on various aspects of their games, as they realize the value of consistent and accurate shots. Assign students the task of searching for new drills and tips to improve their games so you can help them identify available resources for future reference. Then you will not only provide players with golf experience, but you will also offer them experience with identifying sources for developing personal skill and improving game performance.

Encourage students to play golf on a regulation course. Give them credit for a family golf outing or for playing a round of golf with friends. Let students know that it's OK to play even if they are not very skilled. After all, most golfers are far from skilled. Teach students that etiquette and courtesy count most on the golf course. As long as they allow faster groups to play through, repair divots, rake traps, and treat the golf course gently, they will be welcome. You may also want to identify three or four local courses that would be best for beginners. Visit these courses yourself to see if you can get some coupons or other deals (e.g., two games for the price of one, or 18 holes for the price of 9).

CHAPTER 14

Bowling

Bowling, with its tactical simplicity and potential as a lifelong activity, is an essential component of secondary physical education. Most of the tactics fundamental to bowling apply to almost every other target game, and these tactics embrace a primary concept of movement: accuracy requiring control of both speed and direction. Like golf, bowling requires numerous decisions before rolling the ball, such as determining a starting spot and an intermediate target. These decisions, referred to as preshot decisions, can help even the novice bowler solve tactical problems related to rolling the ball in the intended direction and achieving the desired pin action (see table 14.1).

Organization of Lanes and Equipment

Set up as many lanes as possible to maintain high levels of student engagement. Keep the lane distance shorter rather than longer, as the longer is the distance the more the ball moves (follows the slight undulation in the gym floor) and the harder it is for students to control the ball. Lanes should end within 3 to 5 feet (1-1.5 meters) of a wall to keep balls from roll-

Table 14.1 Tactical Problems, Decisions, and Skills in Bowling

Tactical problems	Preshot decisions	Skill execution
Knocking down all pins on first ball (strike)	• Ball selection • Select starting point • Select an intermediate target	
Rolling the ball in the intended direction	• Select starting point • Select an intermediate target	• Setup routine (stance) • Approach • Release and follow-through • Release point and angle

Attaining proper pin action	• Ball selection
	• Determine:
	  – Speed of the approach
	  – Length of arm swing
	  – Angle of entry or contact point
	  – Spin (amount and direction)
		• Adjust:
		  – Setup position
		  – Approach speed
		  – Release point and follow-through

Adjusting for lane conditions	• Ball selection
	• Read lane conditions (shadow bowling)
	• Consider and adjust target and approach to accommodate lane conditions
		• Adjust:
		  – Setup position
		  – Approach angle
		  – Approach speed
		  – Release point and follow-through

Knocking down remaining pins with one ball (spare) Adjusting starting position and intermediate target	• Determine:
	  – Starting position
	  – Intermediate target
		• Adjust:
		  – Setup position
		  – Approach angle or direction
		  – Release point and follow-through

Picking up splits	• Determine:
	  – Best place to contact the pin
	  – Starting position
	  – Intermediate target
		• Adjust:
		  – Setup position
		  – Angle and speed of approach
		  – Release point and follow-through

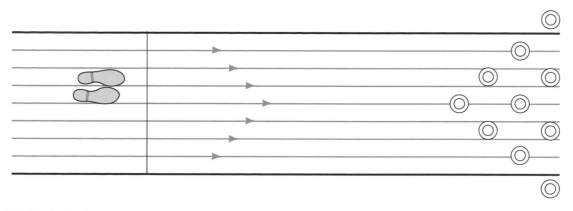

FIGURE 14.1 Arranging bowling lanes at the appropriate length and adjusting the number of pins to align with tactics and skills provide for an efficient environment and a high success rate.

ing into high-traffic areas. Mark the approach with spots, just as with real bowling lanes, and place arrows just ahead of the foul line (see figure 14.1). Most gymnasiums will accommodate 10 to 12 lanes. Use 3 or 6 pins rather than 10, as many of the basic tactics can be learned with fewer pins, which require far less time for setup. If you do not have plastic bowling pins, use wooden pins or soda bottles. If you do not have bowling balls especially designed for gymnasium instruction, consider using 8- to 10-inch (20- to 25-centimeter) playground balls. Since playground balls bounce, students are less likely to loft the ball, instead rolling the ball to avoid the bounce.

To maximize participation, keep groups small. Groups of four are recommended: two players to set up pins and return the ball and two players to bowl and record the score. Each pair can provide feedback on performance and etiquette and watch for safety infractions. Two safety rules for the pair resetting the pins are a must: (1) When returning the ball, you must roll it, and (2) when stopping a ball, use the foot (as if trapping a soccer ball), because pins often fly about when struck.

Get to know the owner or manager of a local bowling establishment. He can often provide coupons for free or discounted games and information on equipment and bowling leagues and may even volunteer his services. Local bowling proprietors are also a good source of score sheets, pencils, and other bowling paraphernalia. Some proprietors and local bowling associations may also have portable lanes, pins, balls, and instructional materials, which they lend to schools and nonprofit organizations as a means of promoting the sport.

Instruction Tips

We do not advocate initially teaching the parts of the ball, pins, or lanes or the history of the game. If using balls with holes, show students where to place their fingers and thumb and let them bowl. Intervene only when you observe a dysfunctional grip or an unsafe approach. Use proper terminology as you present each tactic or skill, referring to the *spots and arrows* on the *lane* or hitting the *pocket* between the *1-3 pins*. As for the history of the game, assign students the task of finding out how bowling got started. They can ask parents or grandparents about it or look it up on the Internet or in the library. Get the pins set up and the balls in their hands and let them play. Once students are engaged and having fun, they will want to learn about the game and how to be successful in playing it.

Establishing an Authentic Context

To grasp the tactical concepts of bowling, students will need to understand the situation each time they roll the ball. Where is the best place to stand given the pin setup and pins remaining, lane conditions, and score to win a game or match? The decisions made before the ball is rolled, or the preshot decisions, are as important as the shot itself. We recommend using visual aids to help students understand how to determine the best angle of approach, where to strike the pins, and what the effects of various spins and approaches are. You can use posters, colored chalk drawings, overheads, and so forth to illustrate a situation in an actual bowling alley. Be sure to include gutters, balls of different weights, and lane conditions to illustrate the reality of a bowling alley. We have often copied diagrams of lanes, grips, and approaches from magazines, Web sites, scorecards, and materials from bowling association tournaments and promotions. If the diagrams are too small, enlarge them. Then laminate these diagrams and use them as instructional aids or let the students pretend to play a few frames in class. Increasing authenticity may increase transfer to the real context.

We present the tactical framework and levels of tactical complexity for bowling in tables 14.1 and 14.2. Throughout the chapter, we describe the focus of each level before presenting lesson outlines. In figures 14.2 and 14.3 we provide an example of a bowling score sheet and a sample chart highlighting key points and targets for bowlers. These may be reproduced for student use.

Table 14.2   Levels of Tactical Complexity for Bowling

Tactical problems	I	II	III	IV
KNOCKING DOWN ALL PINS ON FIRST BALL (STRIKE)				
Rolling the ball in the intended direction	• Select starting point			• Release point • Release angle
Attaining proper pin action	• Select an intermediate target	• Adjust ball speed		
Adjusting for lane Conditions	• Setup routine (stance)	• Determine: – Starting point – Intermediate target	• Determine: – Starting point – Intermediate target	• Shadow bowling
Knocking down remaining pins with one ball (spare)	• Approach			
Adjusting starting position and intermediate target		• Adjust: – Setup routine (stance) – Approach – Release and follow-through – (1, 2, 3, 4, 5, 6, 1-2, 1-3, 2-4, 3-5, 3-6 pin spares)	• Adjust: – Setup routine (stance) – Approach – Release and follow-through – (4-7, 4-8, 7, 5-8, 5-9, 5, 6-9, 6-10, 10 pin spares)	
Picking up splits	• Release and follow-through		• 5-7 and 5-10 splits	

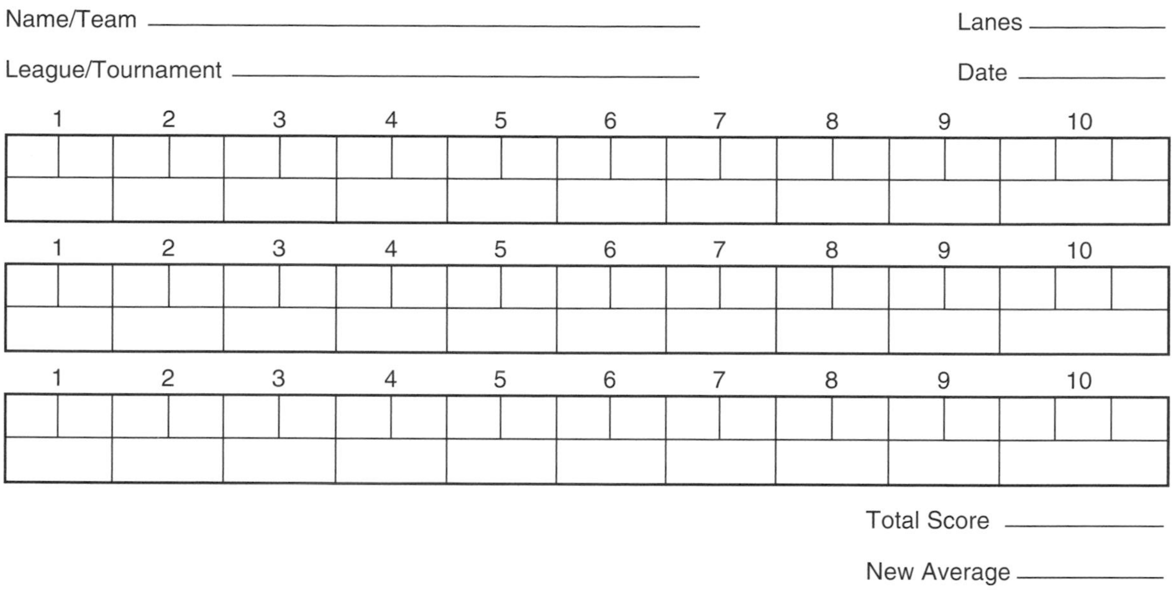

Name/Team _____   Lanes _____

League/Tournament _____   Date _____

	1	2	3	4	5	6	7	8	9	10

	1	2	3	4	5	6	7	8	9	10

	1	2	3	4	5	6	7	8	9	10

Total Score _____

New Average _____

FIGURE 14.2 Bowling score sheet.

From *Teaching Sport Concepts and Skills: A Tactical Games Approach,* Second Edition, by Stephen A. Mitchell, Judith L. Oslin, and Linda L. Griffin. Champaign, IL: Human Kinetics.

Score	**Foot Placement** (Starting spot)	**Lane Markings** (Intermediate target)	**Pins** (Use arrow to show point of contact)

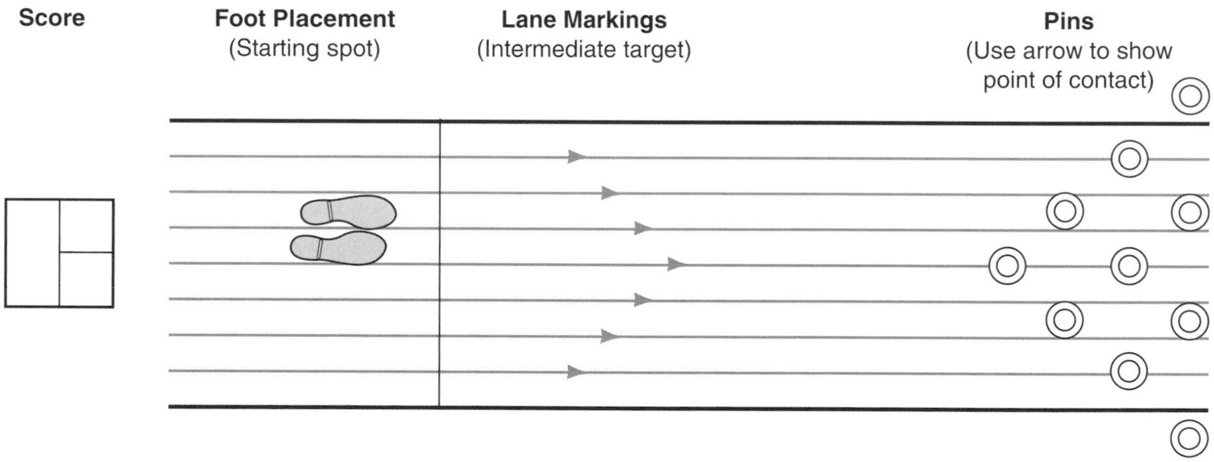

FIGURE 14.3 Sample chart. Charting the start point, intermediate target, and point at which the ball contacts the pins is useful for clarifying tactical concepts, reinforcing preshot decisions, and highlighting the need for consistency.

From *Teaching Sport Concepts and Skills: A Tactical Games Approach,* Second Edition, by Stephen A. Mitchell, Judith L. Oslin, and Linda L. Griffin. Champaign, IL: Human Kinetics.

Level I

Lessons in level I focus on rolling the ball in the intended direction and should build on rolling lessons taught in the primary grades. Lesson 1 begins with locating the pocket, so students come to understand where to hit the pins. Lessons 2 and 3 focus on preshot decisions (specifically, determining the starting spot and intermediate target), and they will help students hit the pocket more consistently. Lesson 4 emphasizes using a consistent setup, approach, and delivery, and it should build on rolling lessons taught during primary and intermediate grades. Lesson 5 allows students to put it all together, promoting authentic, gamelike conditions that will prepare them for bowling in a public setting. Depending on the level of your students, you may combine two or more level I lessons or extend some lessons to allow students more time to refine their bowling skills and preshot decisions.

A consistent setup, approach, and delivery will help students hit the pocket consistently.

Lesson 1

Tactical Problem
Rolling the ball in the intended direction

Lesson Focus
Locating the pocket

Objective
Identify the pocket as the best place to strike the pins so that they can all be knocked down with one roll of the ball.

GAME 1

Setup
Three pins in the 1, 2, 3 position

Goal
Determine the best place to strike the three pins to knock them down with one roll.

Conditions

- Groups of two or four play on lanes 30 feet (9 meters) long that are marked with spots on the approach and with arrows on the lane.
- One or two players set pins while the others bowl.
- Each player takes two consecutive trials to knock down all three pins.
- Player or partner records number of pins knocked down on each trial and adds cumulative score (see figure 14.2 on page 453).
- Each player bowls at least four frames. (Remind students of cues from previous rolling lessons, such as bend and send.)

Questions

Q: *Where was the best place to strike the three pins to knock them down with one roll?*
A: Between the 1 and 3 (if right-handed) or between the 1 and 2 (if left-handed).

Q: *Why is the 1-3 (or 1-2 for left-handed bowlers) better than right down the middle?*
A: Ball is more likely to knock down all three pins when it approaches from an angle.

Q: *What is the area between the 1-3 pins called?*
A: The pocket.

PRACTICE TASK

Setup

Students return to lanes and repeat game 1, using the pocket as the target. Record score for each ball bowled and compare with scores of game 1.

Goal

Hit the pocket.

Cues

- Bend and send.
- Aim for the 1-3 pocket (right-handed player).
- Aim for the 1-2 pocket (left-handed player).

Lesson 2

Level I

Tactical Problem

Rolling the ball the intended direction

Lesson Focus

Determining a starting spot

Objective

Select a starting spot for improving accuracy and consistency in knocking down all pins with the first ball.

GAME 1

Setup

Three pins in the 1, 2, 3 position

Goal

Hit the pocket four times in a row.

Conditions

- Groups of two or four play on lanes 30 feet (9 meters) long that are marked with spots on the approach and with arrows on the lane.
- One or two players set pins while the others bowl.
- Each player takes two consecutive trials to knock down all three pins.
- Player or partner records number of pins knocked down on each trial and adds cumulative score (see figure 14.2 on page 453).
- Each player bowls at least four frames.

Questions

Q: *What did you do to consistently hit the pocket?*
A: Started and stood in the same place, rolled the ball the same way, and aimed.

Q: *What can you do to be sure that you start in the same place every time?*
A: Use the spots on the approach lane.

PRACTICE TASK

Setup

Students try different starting spots to determine which spot allows them to more consistently hit the pocket. Provide students with stickers or dry-erase markers to mark their spots. Each student should select a spot and roll three balls and then adjust the spot and roll three more balls. If more adjustment is needed, the student should wait until all other group members have had two attempts at finding their spots. The student should then continue until she has found a spot that increases consistency. (Encourage students to select a spot that is to the right of the center, as this location leads to a better angle from which to enter the pocket and it will result in better pin action once more pins are added.)

Goal

Find your starting spot.

Cues

- Mark your spot and roll three balls.
- Use the same foot on the starting spot each time you roll.

GAME 2

Setup

Repeat game 1.

Goal

Hit the pocket every time.

Conditions

- Students start from their spot on every trial.
- Record scores and compare with those of first game.

Lesson 3 Level I

Tactical Problem

Rolling the ball the intended direction

Lesson Focus

Determining an intermediate target

Objective

Select an arrow as an intermediate target to improve accuracy and consistency in knocking down all the pins with the first ball.

GAME 1

Setup

Three pins in the 1, 2, 3 position

Goal

Determine the best place to aim to knock down all pins with the first ball.

Conditions

- Groups of two or four play on lanes 30 feet (9 meters) long that are marked with spots on the approach and with arrows on the lane.
- One or two players set pins while the others bowl.
- Each player takes two consecutive trials to knock down all three pins.
- Player or partner records number of pins knocked down on each trial and adds cumulative score (see figure 14.2 on page 453).
- Each player bowls at least four frames.

Questions

Q: *Everyone look at this lane and show me (by pointing) where you aim.*
A: At the pocket, at the arrows just beyond the foul line, and at the arrows farther down the alley.

Q: *Why do you aim at an arrow that is close rather than at the pocket that is far away?*
A: A closer target is easier to hit.

Q: *What do you call a target between you and the pins?*
A: An intermediate target.

PRACTICE TASK

Setup

Students try different arrows as intermediate targets to determine which arrow allows them to more consistently hit the pocket. Provide students with stickers or dry-erase markers for marking their intermediate targets. Each student should select an intermediate target and roll three balls, adjust the intermediate target, and roll three more balls. If more adjustment is needed, the student should wait until all other group members have had two attempts at finding their intermediate targets. Then the student should continue until she has found an intermediate target that increases her consistency.

Goal

Find your intermediate target.

Cues

- Mark your arrow (intermediate target) and roll three balls.
- Aim and roll the ball over the intermediate target.

GAME 2

Setup

Repeat game 1.

Conditions
- Each student starts from his spot and uses his intermediate target on every trial.
- Record scores and compare with those of the first game.

Lesson 4 Level I

Tactical Problem
Rolling the ball the intended direction

Lesson Focus
Consistent setup, grip, and approach

Objective
Determine and use a consistent setup, grip, and approach.

GAME 1

Setup
Three pins in the 1, 2, 3 position

Goal
Knock down all three pins four times in a row.

Conditions
- Groups of two or four play on lanes 30 feet (9 meters) long that are marked with spots on the approach and with arrows on the lane.
- One or two players set pins while the others bowl.
- Each player takes two consecutive trials to knock down all three pins.
- Player or partner records number of pins knocked down on each trial and adds cumulative score (see figure 14.2 on page 453).
- Each player bowls at least four frames.

Questions
Q: *Besides starting at the same spot and using the same arrow as an intermediate target, what can you do to knock down all three pins four times in a row?*
A: Use the same stance, same grip, and same approach.

Q: *Let's watch three volunteers as they perform their stance, grip, and approach. What parts of their stance, grip, and approach are the same? What parts are different?*
A: Their stance and approach are different. Their grips are all the same.

Q: *Notice that they all take a different number of steps, but they end on the foot opposite the one they began on. Why?*
A: So they can slide on the last step, which allows them to bend and send the ball low.

PRACTICE TASK

Setup
Students try different stances and approaches to determine which ones allow them to more consistently hit the pocket. Each student should pick a stance and approach and roll three balls, try a different stance and approach, and then a third stance and approach. Students should select the stance and approach that feels the best and allows them to consistently knock down all three pins.

Goal

Find the stance and approach that is comfortable and results in consistency.

Cues

- Stance
  - Still and focused
- Approach
  - Smooth and controlled
  - Bend and send

GAME 2

Setup

Repeat game 1.

Conditions

- Each student starts from her spot, uses her intermediate target, and uses a consistent stance and approach on every trial.
- Record scores and compare with scores of first game.

Lesson 5

Tactical Problem

Rolling the ball the intended direction

Lesson Focus

Putting it all together, including scoring and etiquette (consistency) and adjusting for lane conditions

Objectives

Consistently use the same starting point, intermediate target, setup routine, approach, and delivery to knock down all three pins. Follow proper bowling etiquette and scoring procedures during partner or team competition.

GAME 1

Setup

Three pins in the 1, 2, 3 position

Goal

Knock down all three pins at least 5 out of 10 times.

Conditions

- Groups of two or four play on lanes 30 feet (9 meters) long that are marked with spots on the approach and with arrows on the lane.
- One or two players set pins while the others bowl.
- Players take turns with the opponent on the lanes as in league or tournament play.
- Players also take turns setting up pins and scoring.
- Scorer records number of pins knocked down on each trial and adds cumulative score on a regulation bowling sheet (see figure 14.2 on page 453).
- The players on each team total their scores to determine the winner.

Questions (Ask questions after most students have bowled five frames.)

Q: *How many of you knocked down all three pins in the first five frames?*
A: None. One.

Q: *Where does the ball go when you miss?*
A: Left or right.

Q: *If your setup, intermediate target, and form are consistent and you are consistently missing to the right, in which direction should you shift your starting spot (left or right)?*
A: To the right, in the direction of the error.

Q: *If you are missing the pins sometimes to the left and sometimes to the right, what should you do?*
A: Work on using a consistent setup, intermediate target, approach, release, and follow-through.

Level II

Lessons in level II focus on shooting spares, using six pins to teach tactical concepts related to adjusting the starting spot and the intermediate target, as well as the ball speed. As level II progresses, students are required to be increasingly accurate. As with lesson 5 of level I, lesson 10 at level II emphasizes putting it all together.

It is important to know how to adjust the starting spot and intermediate target to shoot spares consistently.

Tactical Problem
Attaining proper pin action

Lesson Focus
Adjusting ball speed

Objectives
- Adjust speed of the approach and length of arm swing to vary the speed of the ball.
- Determine the amount of speed necessary to create sufficient pin action to knock down all six pins on one ball.

GAME 1

Setup
Six pins in the 1 through 6 positions

Goal
Knock down all six pins with one ball four times in a row.

Conditions
- Groups of two or four play on lanes 30 to 40 feet (9-12 meters) long that are marked with spots on the approach and with arrows on the lane.
- One or two players set pins while the others bowl.
- Each player takes two consecutive trials to knock down all three pins.
- Player or partner records number of pins knocked down on each trial and adds cumulative score (see figure 14.2 on page 453).
- Each player bowls at least four frames.

Questions

Q: *How was bowling at three pins the same as bowling at six pins?*
A: Same setup, intermediate target, approach, and release.

Q: *How was bowling at three pins different from bowling at six pins?*
A: Need more force and more speed to create more pin action.

Q: *What kinds of things did you do to increase the speed of the ball?*
A: Increased the speed of the approach and the length of the arm swing.

PRACTICE TASK

Setup
Students try adjusting the speed of their approaches and note the difference in pin action that occurs when the ball is rolled slower and faster. After each student has had 3 or 4 trials, she should try adjusting the length of her backswing. (If cameras are available, have students record pin action when backswing is short versus when backswing is long.) Once each student has tried varying approach speeds and lengths of backswing, he should establish a consistent approach with sufficient speed to consistently knock down all six pins.

Note
Students may need to adjust their starting points to accommodate the change in ball speed.

Goal

Adjust your approach or length of backswing to attain sufficient pin action.

Cues

- Step a bit quicker.
- Match backswing with intended speed.

GAME 2

Setup

Repeat game 1.

Condition

Record scores and compare with scores of first game.

Lesson 7 Level II

Tactical Problem

Adjusting starting spot and intermediate target

Lesson Focus

Shooting spares

Objective

Determine which spares can be made without adjusting first ball's starting spot or intermediate target.

GAME 1

Setup

Six pins in the 1 through 6 positions

Goal

Knock down remaining pins with a second ball.

Conditions

- Groups of two or four play on lanes 30 to 40 feet (9-12 meters) long that are marked with spots on the approach and with arrows on the lane.
- One or two players set pins while the others bowl.
- Each player is allowed two balls to knock down all six pins.
- Player or partner records number of pins knocked down on each trial, using a slash (/) in the appropriate place on the score sheet to indicate a spare, adding 10 points to the number of pins knocked down on the next ball, and adding the cumulative score (see figure 14.2 on page 453).
- Strikes are recorded with an X, with 10 points plus the number of pins knocked down on the next two balls added to the cumulative score.
- Each player bowls at least four frames before gathering for questions.

Note

Students who know how to score should help those who do not. Assign worksheets and Web sites for homework and recruit assistance from classroom teachers and parents.

Questions

Q: What is it called when you knock all the pins down with one ball? With two balls?
A: Strike. Spare.

Q: How is shooting for a spare different from shooting for a strike?
A: The pins are in a different location, which means you have to use a different starting spot and intermediate target.

Q: Are there any spares in which you do not have to change starting spots or intermediate targets?
A: 1, 2, 3, and 5, plus some combinations such as 1-2 and 1-3.

PRACTICE TASK

Setup
Groups of two or four play on lanes 30 to 40 feet (9-12 meters) long that are marked with spots on the approach and with arrows on the lane. One or two players set up six pins while the others bowl. One player bowls and the other charts (see figure 14.3 on page 453) pins contacted by the strike, or first ball. Switch after each player has had three attempts. Players then review everyone's charts to determine which spares could be made using the strike ball.

Goal
Determine which pins are most likely to be contacted by the strike, or first ball.

Cues
- Use strike ball on center spares.
- On the chart, put an X through the pins that came in direct contact with the ball.

GAME 2

Setup
One pin, two pin, three pin

Goal
Every team member knocks down each pin in order on three consecutive attempts.

Conditions
- If the 1 pin is knocked down, set up the 2 pin, and if the 2 pin is knocked down, set up the 3 pin.
- Repeat for the next bowler.
- If a pin is missed, rotate to the next bowler. That bowler can then resume from where he left off. For example, if a bowler gets the 1 pin and misses the 2 pin, he should start with the 2 pin on his next turn.

Lesson 8 Level II

Tactical Problem
Adjusting starting spot and intermediate target

Lesson Focus
Shooting spares

Objective
Adjust starting spot or setup position and intermediate target to successfully make spares.

GAME 1

Setup

Six pins in the 1 through 6 positions

Goal

Knock down remaining pins with a second ball.

Conditions

- Groups of two or four play on lanes 30 to 40 feet (9-12 meters) long that are marked with spots on the approach and with arrows on the lane.
- One or two players set pins while the others bowl.
- Each player is allowed two balls to knock down all six pins.
- Player or partner records number of pins knocked down on each trial, using a slash (/) in the appropriate place on the score sheet to indicate a spare, adding 10 points to the number of pins knocked down on the next ball, and adding the cumulative score (see figure 14.2 on page 453).
- Strikes are recorded with an X, with 10 points plus the number of pins knocked down on the next two balls added to the cumulative score.
- Each player bowls at least four frames before gathering for questions.

Questions

Q: *For which spares was it necessary to adjust your starting spot and intermediate target?*
A: 2, 3, 4, 6, 2-4, 3-5, 3-6, and so on.

Q: *When shooting at the four pin, where is the best starting spot?*
A: The right side of the lane (as you are facing the pins).

PRACTICE TASK 1

Setup

Groups of two or four play on lanes 30 to 40 feet (9-12 meters) long that are marked with spots on the approach and with arrows on the lane. One or two players set up four pin (six pin for left-handed bowlers) while the others bowl. One player bowls three consecutive times at the four pin, adjusting starting point or intermediate target, and scores (see figure 14.2) a pin for every successful attempt. Switch after each player has had three attempts.

Goal

Make the spare three consecutive times.

Cue

Shoot across on corner spares.

PRACTICE TASK 2

Setup

Repeat with six pin (four pin for left-handed bowlers).

GAME 2

Setup

Repeat game 1.

Condition

Record scores and compare with scores of first game.

Tactical Problem
Adjusting starting spot and intermediate target

Lesson Focus
Shooting spares

Objective
Adjust starting spot or setup position and intermediate target to successfully make spares.

GAME 1

Setup
Six pins in the 1 through 6 positions

Goal
Knock down all 6 pins in six consecutive frames.

Conditions
- Groups of two or four play on lanes 30 to 40 feet (9-12 meters) long that are marked with spots on the approach and with arrows on the lane.
- One or two players set pins while the others bowl.
- In the first frame all players get one turn to knock down the 1 pin, in the second frame all players get one turn to knock down the 2 pin, and so on through the sixth frame.

Questions

Q: *What did you need to do to be successful?*
A: Adjust starting spots and intermediate targets.

Q: *Which pins did you hit? Which did you miss?*
A: Various answers.

Q: *Is there a rule of thumb that could help you adjust?*
A: If you want the ball to go right, move left—assuming you use the same intermediate target.

PRACTICE TASK

Setup
Each player bowls five times at all six pins, beginning with the strike ball. On the next ball, move one spot to the right and roll again, using the same intermediate target. On the third ball, move one more spot to the right and roll again, using the same intermediate target. On the fourth ball, move one spot left of the strike-ball starting spot and roll again, using the same intermediate target. On the fifth ball, move one more spot left and roll again, using the same intermediate target. Another player or partner should chart the point at which the ball contacted the pins, using a small circle and recording the numbers of balls thrown in the sequence (see figure 14.3 on page 453). For example, place a 1 in the circle of the first ball thrown and a 2 in the circle of the second ball thrown.

Goal
Recognize that when you move to the right, the ball goes left, and when you move to the left, the ball goes right.

Cue
Change starting spot, keep same intermediate target.

GAME 2

Setup

Repeat game 1.

Lesson 10

Tactical Problem

Adjusting starting spot and intermediate target

Lesson Focus

Shooting spares

Objectives

- Adjust the starting spot or intermediate target to successfully shoot spares.
- Demonstrate appropriate etiquette and rotation, consistent with league or tournament play.

GAME 1

Setup

Six pins in the 1 through 6 position

Goal

Knock down remaining pins with the second ball.

Conditions

- Groups of two or four play on lanes 30 to 40 feet (9-12 meters) long that are marked with spots on the approach and with arrows on the lane.
- One or two players set pins while the others bowl.
- Each player is allowed two balls to knock down all six pins.
- Player or partner records number of pins knocked down on each trial, using a slash (/) in the appropriate place on the score sheet to indicate a spare, adding 10 points to the number of pins knocked down on the next ball, and adding the cumulative score (see figure 14.2 on page 453).
- Strikes are recorded with an X, with 10 points plus the number of pins knocked down on the next two balls added to the cumulative score.
- Players take turns on lanes with the opponent, as is done in league or tournament play.
- Bowl and score 10 frames.

Questions

Q: *What happens when you get a strike in the 10th frame?*
A: You get to bowl two more balls and add the number of pins knocked down to the total score.

Q: *What happens when you get a spare in the 10th frame?*
A: You get to bowl one more ball and add the number of pins knocked down to the total score.

Q: *Besides the score, how can you analyze your game play?*
A: Chart the pins missed on the first and second balls of each frame (see figure 14.3).

Lessons in level III utilize 10 pins to emphasize common spares and the tactics needed to consistently pick up these spares. In lessons 11 through 14, game 1 highlights tactical problems related to adjusting the starting spot and intermediate target. The spares are in groups of three, positioned on the left, center, and right, which should require little to no adjustment when two of the three pins are remaining and slight adjustment when one of the three pins is remaining. Lesson 14 highlights the 5-7 and 5-10 splits, two splits that are very doable. Of course, other splits can be included here or covered in additional lessons. The final game is a regulation game that can be set up as a competition with other teams to mimic league play.

Lessons at level III and IV can be extended to create a sport education season. Consistent with the sport education model, we suggest awarding points for fair play to teams demonstrating proper etiquette before, during, and after league play. These points can be added to team standings during league play and can level the playing field and contain celebrations that often ensue after strikes. We do not suggest eliminating the celebration, but suggest stressing proper forms of it.

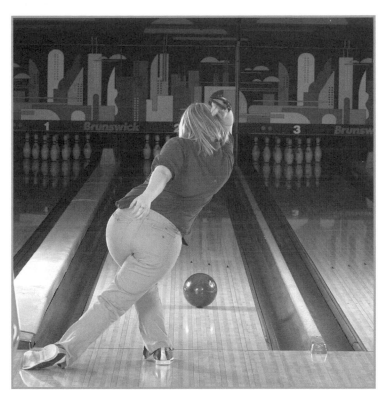

In order to keep those points racking up, students must use the dots and arrows on the lane to adjust their shot and pick up spares.

Lesson 11

Tactical Problem
Adjusting starting spot and intermediate target

Lesson Focus
Shooting spares

Objectives
Adjust the starting spot or intermediate target to successfully shoot the 4-7, 4-8, and 7 pin spares.

GAME 1

Setup
4-7-8 pins

Goal
Knock down the 4-7-8 with one ball.

Conditions

- Three or four students play on lanes 30 to 40 feet (9-12 meters) long that are marked with spots on the approach and with arrows on the lane.
- Set up 4, 7, and 8 pins only.
- Score as though seven pins are knocked down with first ball.
- One or two players set up pins while the others bowl.
- Allow time for students to score 3 or 4 frames.

Questions

Q: *Point to the spot on which you started.*
A: Students point to spots, most of which are to the right of the center when facing the pins.

Q: *Why is right of center better than left of center?*
A: It's a better angle of approach with less chance of the ball going into the gutter.

Q: *If only the 4-7 pins were remaining, where would your starting spot and intermediate target be? Where for the 4-8 pins? The 7 pin?*
A: Same place.

PRACTICE TASK

Setup

Students take turns shooting at the 4-7 pin spare, four times each, and then at the 4-8 spare, and then at the 7 pin spare. Repeat the task, but alternate lanes as in league play so students can adjust to various lane conditions. Each bowler charts her starting spot and intermediate target, along with pins remaining (see figure 14.3 on page 453).

Goal

Score a spare.

Cues

- Focus on your intermediate target.
- Use feedback to adjust next shot.

GAME 2

Setup

Regulation bowling game

Goal

No missed frames—spare or strike.

Conditions

- League play.
- Play 3v3, alternate lanes, display proper etiquette, and score on an official score sheet.
- Team with the highest total score wins.

Note

Points for fair play can be awarded to teams who demonstrate proper etiquette at all times.

Tactical Problem
Adjusting starting spot and intermediate target

Lesson Focus
Shooting spares

Objective
Adjust the starting spot or intermediate target to successfully shoot the 5-8, 5-9, and 5 pin spares.

GAME 1

Setup
5-8-9 pins

Goal
Knock down the 5-8-9 with one ball.

Conditions
- Three or four students play on lanes 30 to 40 feet (9-12 meters) long that are marked with spots on the approach and with arrows on the lane.
- Set up 5, 8, and 9 pins only.
- Score as though seven pins were knocked down with the first ball.
- One or two players set up pins while the others bowl.
- Allow time for students to score 3 or 4 frames.

Questions

Q: *Point to the spot on which you started.*
A: Students point to their individual starting spots.

Q: *How similar is this starting spot to the starting spot on your first ball?*
A: Similar. The same.

Q: *If only the 5-8 pins were remaining, where would your starting spot and intermediate target be? Where for the 5-9 pins? The 5 pin?*
A: Same place. Similar place. Not sure.

PRACTICE TASK

Setup
Students take turns shooting at the 5-8 pin spare, four times each, then at the 5-9 spare, and then at the 5 pin spare. Repeat the task, but alternate lanes as in league play so students can adjust to various lane conditions. Each bowler charts his starting spot and intermediate target, along with pins remaining (see figure 14.3 on page 453).

Goal
Score a spare.

Cues
- Focus on your intermediate target.
- Use feedback to adjust next shot.

GAME 2

Setup
Regulation bowling game

Goal
No missed frames.

Conditions
- League play.
- Play 3v3, alternate lanes, display proper etiquette, and score on an official score sheet.
- Team with the highest total score wins.

Note
Points for fair play can be awarded to teams who demonstrate proper etiquette at all times.

Lesson 13 Level III

Tactical Problem
Adjusting starting spot and intermediate target

Lesson Focus
Shooting spares

Objective
Adjust the starting spot or intermediate target to successfully shoot 6-9, 6-10, and 10 pin spares.

GAME 1

Setup
6-9-10 pins

Goal
Knock down the 6-9-10 with one ball.

Conditions
- Three or four students play on lanes 30 to 40 feet (9-12 meters) long that are marked with spots on the approach and with arrows on the lane.
- Set up 6, 9, and 10 pins only.
- Score as though seven pins were knocked down with the first ball.
- One or two players set up pins while the other players bowl.
- Allow time for students to score 3 or 4 frames.

Questions
Q: Point to the spot on which you started.
A: Students point to spots, most of which are to the left of the center when facing the pins.

Q: Why is left of center better than right of center?
A: It is a better angle of approach with less chance of the ball going into the gutter.

Q: If only the 6-9 pins were remaining, where would your starting spot and intermediate target be? Where for the 6-10 pins? The 10 pin?
A: Same place.

PRACTICE TASK

Setup
Students take turns shooting at the 6-9 pin spare, four times each, then the 6-10 spare, and then the 10 pin spare. Repeat the task, but alternate lanes as in league play so students can adjust to various lane conditions. Each bowler charts her starting spot and intermediate target, along with pins remaining (see figure 14.3 on page 453).

Goal
Score a spare.

Cues
- Focus on your intermediate target.
- Use feedback to adjust next shot.

GAME 2

Setup
Regulation bowling game

Goal
No missed frames.

Conditions
- League play.
- Play 3v3, alternate lanes, display proper etiquette, and score on an official score sheet.
- Team with the highest total score wins.

Note
Points for fair play can be awarded to teams who demonstrate proper etiquette at all times.

Lesson 14   Level III

Tactical Problem
Adjusting starting spot and intermediate target

Lesson Focus
Shooting spares

Objectives
Adjust the starting spot or intermediate target to successfully shoot the 5-7 and 5-10 splits.

GAME 1

Setup
5-7 or 5-10 splits

Goal
Knock down the split with one ball.

Conditions

- Three or four students play on lanes 30 to 40 feet (9-12 meters) long that are marked with spots on the approach and with arrows on the lane.
- Set up 5-7 pins on one lane and 5-10 pins on adjacent lane.
- Bowlers alternate lanes.
- Score as though eight pins were knocked down with the first ball.
- One or two players set up pins while the others bowl.
- Allow time for students to score at least four frames.

Questions

Q: *Point to the spot on which you started when shooting for the 5-7 split.*
A: Students point to their individual starting spots.

Q: *How does this spot differ from your starting spot for the 5-10 split?*
A: Students may have different answers as to which starting point works best.

Q: *Why is it important to have a specific starting spot for each split or spare?*
A: It increases your chance of knocking down the split or spare.

PRACTICE TASK

Setup

Students take turns shooting at a 5-7 pin split, four times each, and then at a 5-10 pin split. Repeat the task, but alternate lanes as in league play so students can adjust to various lane conditions. Each bowler charts his starting spot and intermediate target, along with pins remaining (see figure 14.3 on page 453).

Goal

Knock down the 5-7 and 5-10 splits.

Cues

- Focus on your intermediate target.
- Use feedback to adjust spot on next shot.

GAME 2

Setup

Regulation bowling game

Goal

No missed frames.

Conditions

- League play.
- Play 3v3, alternate lanes, display proper etiquette, and score on an official score sheet.
- Team with the highest total score wins.

Note

Points for fair play can be awarded to teams who demonstrate proper etiquette at all times.

Tactical Problem
Adjusting to lane conditions

Lesson Focus
Using spin and speed to adjust to lane conditions

Objective
Adjust ball spin and speed to align with lane conditions.

GAME 1

Setup
Regulation bowling game

Goal
Knock down all 10 pins on each roll.

Conditions
- Groups of three play on lanes 30 to 40 feet (9-12 meters) long that are marked with spots on the approach and with arrows on the lane.
- One or two players set pins while the others bowl.
- Each player is allowed one ball to knock down all 10 pins.
- Alternate lanes, with one lane designated as the slow lane where bowlers must roll the ball slowly.
- The other lane is designated as the fast lane where bowlers must roll the ball quickly (but with control).
- Player or partner records the number of pins knocked down on each trial.
- Each player charts the points where the ball contacted the pins (see figure 14.3 on page 453).
- Each player bowls at least four frames before gathering for questions.

Questions

Q: *Where did the ball contact the pins most often when you rolled it slowly?*
A: To the left of the center (as you are facing the pins).

Q: *Why would the ball be more likely to roll to the left of the center?*
A: The slower the ball is rolling, the more likely it is to break or move with the lane conditions.

Q: *Where did the ball contact the pins most often when you rolled it quickly?*
A: To the right of the center (as you are facing the pins).

Q: *Why would the ball be more likely to roll to the right of the center?*
A: It is not as affected by lane conditions.

Q: *Besides speed, what else can affect how the ball rolls?*
A: Spin.

PRACTICE TASK

Setup
Students take turns shooting at all 10 pins, two times in a row on one lane and then two times in a row on the other. Students try different speeds and spins and use the feedback from their charts (see figure 14.3) to determine the most appropriate amounts of spin and speed.

Goals

- Determine the amount of ball speed and spin needed to consistently knock down all 10 pins.
- Determine how to adjust ball speed and spin to achieve the desired results (get strikes, spares, and adjust to lane conditions).

Cues

- Control speed.
- Use feedback to adjust next shot.

GAME 2

Setup

Regulation bowling game

Goal

No missed frames

Conditions

- League play.
- Play 3v3, alternate lanes, display proper etiquette, and score on an official score sheet.
- Team with the highest total score wins.
- League standings from the past five lessons can be used to set up tournament play (level IV).
- Individual standings can be used to calculate handicaps.

Note

Points for fair play can be awarded to teams who demonstrate proper etiquette at all times.

Level IV

Lessons at level IV focus on integrating the sport education model (Siedentop, 1994) and emphasize customary roles, rituals, and sporting behaviors common to bowling. Levels III and IV can be combined, but ought to be extended to last 18 to 20 days. At first, most teachers think that students will get bored. But with careful integration of roles and responsibilities, bowling rituals, scoring, calculating averages and handicaps, league play, and tournament competition, students will find multiple ways to engage and may even be motivated to participate in leagues outside of school.

We integrate the tactical approach and sport education models into all of our classes so that our physical education majors have firsthand experience with these approaches. For example, lesson 16 focuses on shadow bowling to ensure good preparation before actually bowling. Lesson 17 emphasizes appropriate sporting behavior and allows the students to set up their own rules, which they are more likely to uphold than any you may choose or post. Some lessons may be less active, such as lesson 18, but integrate math skills. You may choose to do this in class, assign it as homework, or work with classroom teachers to integrate it into their lessons.

Lesson 19 provides an example of how you can teach content within a tactical and sport education lesson. Similar to lessons in level III, the problem is posed in the first game, which is followed by questions to guide students to the solution and then followed by practice. Practice is followed by league or tournament play. The final lesson integrates bowling festivities, which are often left out of the traditional unit but are very much a part of the bowling league experience. We offer numerous suggestions for increasing participation by local bowling proprietors, parents, and administrators. Besides providing an authentic sport experience for the students, sport education allows you to promote your program beyond the gymnasium and throughout the community.

Proper bowling etiquette should be followed so that everyone in every lane can have a good time.

Lesson 16 {Level IV}

Tactical Problems
- Rolling the ball in the intended direction
- Adjusting for lane conditions

Lesson Focus
Shadow bowling

Objective
Use shadow bowling to determine starting spot and intermediate target on alternate lanes.

GAME 1

Setup
Shadow bowling—no pins

Goal
Locate and adjust starting spots and intermediate targets for first ball.

Condition
Play 3v3, alternate lanes, and bowl without pins.

Questions

Q: What is the purpose of shadow bowling?

A: To warm up, locate and adjust starting spots and intermediate targets, and get used to lane conditions.

Q: How did you decide whose turn it was to shadow bowl?

A: We stood in line behind the approach, waited for an open lane, and bowled a couple of balls.

Q: If you need to throw more shadow balls than most players, what should you do?

A: Take more turns, but wait until the end when fewer players are shadow bowling.

Extensions

- League Meeting: Elect a secretary (or two) to assist with scheduling and with calculating averages, handicaps, and final standings.
- Team Meeting: Elect a team captain. Using individual averages from league play, determine a team lineup and enter it on the score sheet. Besides team captain, roles can include a statistician (to calculate individual averages and handicaps) and a technical support person (to troubleshoot automated scoring machines or to set up a team Web site).
- Tournament Play: For first round, play 3v3, alternate lanes, and use an official score sheet or technological device (see appendix for software and Web site resources).

Goal

Bowl on alternate lanes and take turns scoring.

Lesson 17   Level IV

Tactical Problem

Adjusting for lane conditions

Lesson Focus

Appropriate sporting behavior

Objective

Demonstrate proper etiquette, decorum, and fair play before, during, and after league play.

GAME 1

Setup

Shadow bowling—no pins

Goal

Locate and adjust starting spots and intermediate targets for first ball.

Condition

Play 3v3, alternate lanes, and bowl without pins.

Extensions

- League Meeting: Determine the rules of etiquette necessary to allow all bowlers to participate in a fair and respectful environment. Each team should contribute one or two possible rules of etiquette. Limit the number of rules to no more than five and post them for all to see.

- Tournament Play: In second round, play 3v3, alternate lanes, and use official scoring. Teams following all rules of etiquette before, during, and after league play score 1 point for fair play.

Goal
Always follow rules of etiquette.

Lesson 18

Lesson Focus
Calculating averages and handicaps

Objective
Demonstrate how to calculate individual averages and handicaps and use handicaps to establish fair competition between teams.

GAME 1

Setup
Regulation bowling game

Goal
Bowl head-to-head against another bowler.

Condition
Students select an opponent and bowl five frames of regulation play.

Questions

Q: *How many of you were within 10 pins of your opponent's score? How many were more than 10 pins from your opponent's score?*
A: A few. Many.

Q: *When bowling against an opponent that has more (or less) experience, what can you do to set up a fair competition?*
A: Spot the less-experienced bowler some pins. Use a handicap.

Q: *What do you need to know to calculate a handicap?*
A: Individual averages.

PRACTICE TASK

Setup
Students work with team captains and a league secretary to calculate their averages and handicaps. Teams work together to calculate the team handicap and the handicap for the next tournament game. An average is the total score divided by the number of games bowled. Individual handicap is calculated based on 80% to 100% of a 200-point scale, but 100% is used most often and is easiest to calculate (200 minus individual average = individual handicap). Individual or team handicaps can be used in league or tournament play. The number of games needed to establish an average can be determined during a league meeting, with recommendations from you and the league secretary.

Goal

Calculate individual averages and handicaps and team handicaps for league and tournament play.

Cue

200 – your average = your handicap

GAME 2

Setup

In third round of tournament, play 3v3, alternate lanes, and use official score sheet

Goal

Calculate new average and handicap after tournament.

Lesson 19 Level IV

Tactical Problem
Rolling the ball the intended direction

Lesson Focus
Release point and angle

Objective
Demonstrate a proper release point at the very bottom of the downswing (not beyond the toe) and a release angle that is low and extended out (rather than up).

GAME 1

Setup

Regulation bowling game

Goal

Smooth, consistent release

Conditions

- Teams of three or four bowl five frames on their home lanes.
- Bowlers use stickers to mark where their balls land on the lane and score and chart the results.
- At the end of five frames, each player notes her pattern to check for consistency or lack of consistency.

Questions

Q: *Were you able to demonstrate a consistent release–that is, were you able to release the ball at just about the same place (or along the same line) on the lane every single time?*
A: Sometimes, but not consistently.

Q: *Why is it important to have a consistent release?*
A: To control speed, keep the ball from bouncing, and increase overall control.

PRACTICE TASK

Setup

Shadow bowl to allow students to focus on the release and not the pins. Emphasize the acceleration of the hand at the bottom of the downswing that should begin about

12 inches (31 centimeters) before the release. This acceleration requires precise timing, so encourage students to focus on the rhythm of their swings. The hand motion is similar to that for accelerating a golf club through the ball. The release angle (or loft) should be outward, as a natural extension of the release point. After about 10 to 15 rolls per player on the home lane, have players alternate lanes and roll 10 to 15 more times. Set up pins on the last 3 or 4 rolls.

Goal
Accelerate through the bottom of the release and consistently land the ball on the same spot.

Cues
- Bend and send as low as possible.
- Keep shoulders square.
- Do not tilt shoulder beyond knee (on the release).

GAME 2

Setup
In the fourth round of the tournament, play 3v3, alternate lanes, and use an official score sheet

Goals
- Consistent release point and angle.
- More strikes and fewer open frames.

Lesson 20 — Level IV

Lesson Focus
Bowling festivities—end-of-the-year league banquet

Objective
Organize and participate in a league banquet following league and tournament play.

GAME 1

Setup
10 pins

Goal
Determine league and tournament standings.

Conditions
Regulation game play with 3v3, alternating lanes, and official scoring.

Note
This lesson could be a field trip to a local bowling establishment.

Extension: Bowling Banquet
Have students and parents arrange for refreshments (e.g., juice and cookies). Consider asking the principal or a member of the school board to hand out awards. Allow students to organize as much of this banquet as possible. Involve the proprietor of a local bowling establishment, members of local bowling associations, and parents or grandparents with league experience. Consider various alternatives for awards, such as

having winning teams sign a bowling pin that is displayed in the school trophy case or adding the winning team's name to a (donated) bowling trophy. Post team pictures on the school Web site or on the Web site of the physical education department.

Summary

We have provided four levels of lessons in this chapter. At the first level, we recommend using only three pins so students can establish consistent form and essential preshot decisions. The recommended number of pins increases to six in level II. Using six pins keeps the context efficient while allowing students to focus on adjusting their starting spots and intermediate targets so they can gain sufficient control to consistently knock down spares. The emphasis on adjusting starting spots and intermediate targets to knock down spares continues in level III, with students shooting at all 10 pins. Level IV illustrates the integration of the sport education model with the tactical approach. For more ideas and examples of the sport education model, we recommend starting with the following Web sites: www.bowlingindex.com and www.Ten-PinBowling.com.

Lessons at all levels also include a progression for score keeping that begins with adding cumulative scores at level I and moves to adding spares and strikes at level II. Encourage students to share scoring responsibilities so everyone can learn how to score. Although bowling scores are automated, there are often errors and miscalculations that an educated bowler can catch. Calculating bowling scores, averages, and team and individual handicaps can be used to integrate physical education content into the classroom as well as mathematics content into physical education.

We encourage establishing and maintaining an authentic context throughout all four levels. This context includes etiquette, safety, and fair play before, during, and after bowling. Both the tactical approach and sport education models provide a framework through which appropriate sporting behavior can and should be taught. Etiquette, safety, and fair play must be addressed directly and include measures of accountability, such as points for fair play. Providing an authentic context is also important for fostering transfer of bowling tactics, skills, and positive sporting behavior to public venues, where bowling can be played for a lifetime.

PART III

Tactical Games Curriculum

CHAPTER 15

Tactical Games Curriculum Model

Kirk (2005) has argued that tactical approaches to games teaching can become "mainstream practice" within physical education and youth sports programs. For this possibility to become reality Kirk suggested that, in addition to revising the research agenda, proponents of tactical approaches focus on conceptualizing a model for tactical games teaching and base instructional resources on this formalized approach.

In *Instructional Models for Physical Education,* Metzler (2000) calls for "model-based instruction" as a means of focusing on long-term, holistic learning outcomes. He describes a teaching model as a set of teaching patterns that "ties together theory, planning, classroom management, teaching-learning processes, and assessment" (p. xxiv). In this book we have attempted to tie together these facets of curriculum and instruction. As in *Sport Foundations for Elementary Physical Education: A Tactical Games Approach,* we support Metzler's call for model-based instruction using a tactical games approach by proposing a conceptual framework for a tactical games model and linking the elementary and secondary levels to suggest how a tactical games model can span the physical education curriculum for K through 12. In this chapter, we revisit the concepts underpinning the original model, simplify this model for the teacher, and reemphasize the ties among planning, management, teaching–learning processes, and assessment that have been described in the preceding chapters.

Assumptions Underpinning a Tactical Games Curriculum

A curriculum model is not value-free, and there are several assumptions underpinning the tactical games model. To make our values clear, we should identify these assumptions.

First, proponents of the model believe that games are important to the physical education curriculum because they are enjoyable lifetime physical activities and they are based on sport, which is a prominent social institution in our society. Educators who implement games instruction in physical education at all levels value games playing as an activity in its own right. Proponents value games for their educational benefits, including emphases on decision making, problem

Tip Box

Proponents of the tactical games model argue differently, suggesting that younger students of perhaps lower abilities can play a game if that game is modified to enable meaningful play.

solving, communication, teamwork, and skillfulness.

Second, all students can understand and play games at their particular ability levels. Unfortunately it is not uncommon to hear that some students cannot play games because they lack skill—we have even been told this by high school teachers. This is exactly the reason for the small-sided game play and the distinct modifications to games made throughout chapters 4 through 14.

Third, and related to the previous assumption, games can be modified to represent their mature forms and they can be conditioned (i.e., exaggerated by rule changes) to emphasize tactical problems encountered within the game. Each lesson in chapters 4 through 14 contains examples of modifications designed to place students in problem-solving situations.

These tactical problems form the basis of the games classification system presented in table 3.1. Both preservice teachers and experienced teachers sometimes express the concern that they don't know games well enough or, more frequently, do not know a particular game sufficiently enough, to modify and teach with any expertise. Clearly it is advantageous for teachers to be games players or at least to know games if they are to successfully use a tactical games model in their teaching.

Our response to the "knowledge" concern is that most teachers probably know a lot more about most games than they realize, particularly if they apply what they know about one game to another. For example, a college basketball player once told

Tip Box

Games have common tactical elements, or problems, and understanding these elements can help students transfer learning from one game to another.

us that she was not sufficiently comfortable with the game of soccer to develop its scope and sequence and then teach it successfully. We suggested that she might begin by taking what she knew about basketball, which was extensive and specific, and applying it to soccer. Using this approach she was able to develop lesson content based around deciding when to shoot, pass, or dribble and around defensive aspects of the game such as marking or guarding. Although knowing a game will obviously help you teach it, you do not need to know all games well! As we suggest in chapter 3, if you are not familiar with games content, try to learn one game from each category and then apply that knowledge to other games within the same category. Knowing one game gives you a good understanding of the main rules of game play,

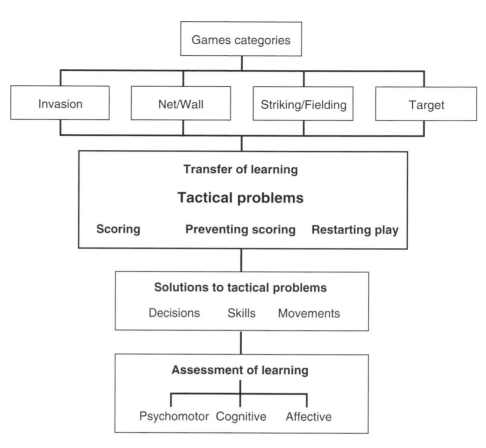

FIGURE 15.1 A conceptual framework for the tactical games curriculum model.

an appreciation for basic tactical considerations, knowledge of starting and restarting play, and an appreciation for the spirit in which games can and should be played. For teachers with little or no games experience, printed resources (including this book) are a good place to begin seeking lesson ideas.

Conceptual Framework

A curriculum model is sometimes best understood by referring to a diagram, or conceptual framework, outlining its major components. A conceptual framework for the tactical games model is presented in figure 15.1. Central to the model are the tactical problems the various games present. Tactical problems are those that must be overcome in order to score, to prevent scoring, and to restart play. Having identified the relevant tactical problems of a game, students solve them by making appropriate decisions and applying appropriate movements and skills. Again, many

games within each category have similar tactical problems, and understanding these similarities can assist in transferring performance from one game to another.

We believe that it is possible and desirable to develop a progressive and sequential tactical games curriculum across the compulsory education spectrum, beginning at second grade (about age 7). In *Sport Foundations for Elementary Physical Education: A Tactical Games Approach* (2003) we suggested a thematic approach, while in this book we use a more sport-specific approach to allow for greater specificity and greater development of performance competence. Choosing an approach is clearly an issue of content development, with the conceptual framework (figure 15.1) forming the foundation for developing tactical frameworks to identify relevant content for learning. These frameworks are then used to develop levels of game complexity to ensure that content is planned in developmentally appropriate progressions based on the development of game understanding and performance skill.

Model-Based Instruction

Here we address the tactical games curriculum in light of Metzler's (2000) characteristics of model-based instruction. Our point in doing this is to emphasize the development of tactical games teaching from a teaching model (Bunker and Thorpe 1982) to a curriculum model.

Planning

Chapters 4 through 14 include numerous lesson outlines using the planning format presented in chapter 2. This format represents a simplification of the original six-stage Teaching Games for Understanding (TGFU) model (Bunker and Thorpe 1982). This original model is presented in figure 15.2, with the simplified format again shown for comparison purposes in figure 15.3.

The original TGFU model presented by Bunker and Thorpe (figure 15.2) described a more complex six-stage model for developing decision making and improved performance in game situations. The simplified three-stage model presented in figure 15.3 focuses on the essential lesson components of the model, namely modified game play, development of tactical awareness and decision making through questioning, and development of skill.

Management

Often in physical education there are time constraints that make it necessary to put in place sound and efficient management procedures. Too often in both elementary and secondary gymnasiums we see students enter a gym and immediately sit in squad lines for attendance and wait for the teacher to begin the lesson warm-up (often stretches and calisthenics). Teachers who adopt this and other time-inefficient procedures are usually the first to raise concerns as to their ability to implement a tactical games lesson within the allocated time.

This alleviates the need for transitions between lesson segments and immediately focuses students on the content (i.e., tactical problem) that is the focus of

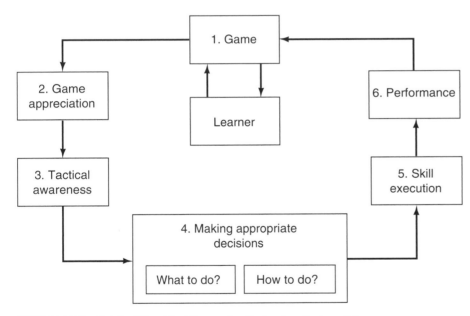

FIGURE 15.2   Original Teaching Games for Understanding model

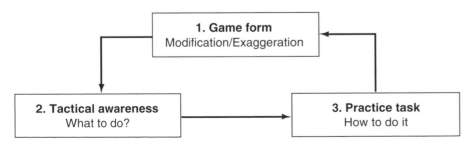

FIGURE 15.3   Simplified tactical games model.

Adapted, by permission, from R.D. Thorpe and D.J. Bunker, 1986, A model for the teaching of games in secondary schools. In *Rethinking games teaching*, (Loughborough University), 8.

instruction for the lesson. With students assigned to permanent "home" courts or fields, the need for attendance squads is alleviated. If attendance taking is required it can simply be accomplished by observation once students are actively engaged in game play. The management structures that are an integral facet of sport education provide an effective framework through which a tactical games model can be implemented.

The organization of teams, assignment of simple roles and responsibilities, and identification and designation of field spaces and home fields or courts can facilitate effective management and place your tactical games teaching within an appropriate sport context. In this section we advocate the use of Sport Education (Siedentop, Hastie, and van der Mars 2004) to provide mechanisms for team, equipment, and game organization as a means of developing student game play and sport behaviors. The Sport Education curriculum model has several features designed to help students develop into competent, literate, and enthusiastic participants. It is not our intention to describe these features in depth. Rather we will briefly describe the way we have used the model to facilitate use of a tactical approach to games instruction at both the elementary and secondary levels.

The sidebar (page 488) provides a sample contract that might be used at the secondary level. In fact we have used this type of contract with groups ranging from fourth grade to undergraduate students and across a range of games. Each student accepts responsibility for one of the roles on the contract and signs her name next to that role to confirm a willingness to carry out the necessary responsibilities. Once responsibilities are defined, students enter the gymnasium and begin play immediately under the direction of the team coach. Each team is assigned a home court to which they go upon entering the gym. The equipment manager distributes vests of the appropriate color and sets up goals (if needed for the game being played). Coaches report to you, the teacher, to find out the introductory activity (game), or they might go to a "coaches' corner" to read the starting activity from the chalkboard. Alternatively the coach might have some latitude to work with her team on things previously learned. The administrator takes attendance, and warm up and stretching can begin under the direction of the athletic trainer. Teams remain the same throughout the sport "season," which includes both a regular season and a postseason. Introductory game play is often done within teams, as are skill practices, which are organized at the home court by the coach, eliminating the need for time-consuming transitions to alternative playing areas and saving confusion on the part of the students as to where they should conduct practices.

Team Contract

Class _____

Semester _____

Sport _____

Team name _____

The team members and especially the coaches should demonstrate the following:

   I. Good sporting behavior.

   II. Fair play—Know and play by class and game rules.

   III. Hard work—Practice and work your hardest to be a good team player.

   IV. Cooperation—Whenever possible team decisions should be made by all team members together.

   V. Respect—For classmates, teachers, and equipment.

   VI. Positive attitude—Work hard to encourage team members to be positive.

   VII. Responsibility—Help with lesson organization by carrying out your role.

We will do our best to carry out our roles and to cooperate and work as a team under the leadership of our coach.

Team members' signatures:

(Coach—Organize practices) _____

(Assistant coach—Help coach as requested) _____

(Athletic trainer—Organize warm-up and stretching) _____

(Equipment manager—Give out and collect equipment) _____

(Reporter—Sports reporting) _____

(Statistician—Collect and organize team statistics) _____

From *Teaching Sport Concepts and Skills: A Tactical Games Approach,* Second Edition, by Stephen A. Mitchell, Judith L. Oslin, and Linda L. Griffin Champaign, IL: Human Kinetics.

With all students aware of their responsibilities to the team, lessons can begin and run to conclusion smoothly and in a time-efficient manner. Small changes are communicated by the teacher to the coaches, thereby eliminating the need to communicate information by gathering in the whole class. Students, primarily each team's statistician, keep track of win–loss records and fair play or performance points (awarded by the teacher) to decide on a regular season champion prior to commencing "playoffs." In addition to effective management, this system is also designed to teach appropriate sport behaviors. In using the Sport Education model we have seen and heard quality discussions within and among teams concerning individual members' responsibilities and the importance of ensuring that these responsibilities are fulfilled. Sport behavior has also been discussed and the importance of fair play and effective leadership by coaches becomes apparent. Disputes are resolved by a replay, and the value of shaking hands and congratulating your opponents on a well-played game is also stressed.

Teaching and Learning

Using a tactical games model means using mixed teaching strategies, including direct and indirect teaching styles, and problem-solving strategies. Teachers trained in movement education should feel a high degree of comfort with this approach. In fact, some teachers have first come to understanding tactical games teaching as a movement education approach to games instruction. Problems or goals are set and students are given opportunities to seek solutions to these problems. Solutions to the problems are identified through the questioning process and these solutions then become the focus of a practice task. Direct instruction might be the preferred teaching style at this point, though this may depend on the specificity of the required solution. Take care to modify practice tasks to simplify or challenge students, as their abilities require. Lesson outlines in chapters 4 through 14 provide examples of task extensions, but be creative with this aspect of your teaching. As stressed in chapter 2, the quality of questions asked will be critical and these should be an integral part of the planning process. While we have provided many questions in chapters 4 through 14, we encourage you to develop your own questions that are meaningful to your students.

Assessment

The issue of learner assessment in education is of such importance that assessment ideas are an integral component of K-12 National Content Standards for Physical Education (NASPE 2004). Our concerns for learner assessment are threefold:

- **Assessment should be an ongoing part of instruction.** Assessment of learning takes time. For that reason, assessment cannot be left until the end of an instructional unit. Ongoing assessment is a fairer and more accurate means of assessing student learning.

- **Assessment should be authentic and therefore related to instructional objectives.** Where improvement of game performance is the goal of instruction, assessment should be conducted within the context of the game.

- **Assessment of learning should be completed in all domains, but particularly the psychomotor domain.** The original Teaching Games for Understanding model (Bunker and Thorpe 1982) focused on outcomes in all domains. Understanding of games was a key goal, as was the motivation to practice and become effective games players. While we also attach value to learning in all domains, we encourage you to remember that what makes physical education unique is its opportunity to achieve learning outcomes in the psychomotor domain. To this end, game performance assessment tools such as the Game Performance Assessment Instrument (GPAI) and the Team Sport Assessment Procedure (TSAP) (Grehaigne,

> **Tip Box**
>
> Making learner assessment an ongoing and habitual process, perhaps assessing one team every lesson, allows you to ensure that the learning of all students is determined on more than one occurrence to account for uncharacteristically good or poor performances.

Godbout, and Bouthier 1997) described in chapter 16 have been developed to measure psychomotor outcomes during game play.

Summary

As we did in *Sport Foundations for Elementary Physical Education: A Tactical Games Approach,* we hope we have encouraged you not only to rethink the way you teach games, but also to view tactical games teaching as a curriculum model rather than simply a teaching method. Increasingly the tactical games literature seeks to take the approach beyond planning for a single lesson by attempting to formulate ideas for constructing curriculum scope and sequence based on the tactical similarities among games. Many secondary school physical educators now group games for instruction in such a way as to maximize the principle of transfer. For example, following one invasion game with another in consecutive units of instruction enables students to see the common principles of play across invasion games, a key component of tactical games teaching. For reasons such as these, we believe that a tactical games model is a viable and increasingly mainstream way of organizing games curriculum and games instruction within the context of physical education.

CHAPTER 16

Assessing Outcomes

This chapter was modified from chapter 8, by permission, from S. Mitchell, J.L. Oslin, and L.L. Griffin, *Sport foundations for elementary physical education: A tactical games approach* (Champaign, IL: Human Kinetics), 147-168.

This chapter addresses the role of assessment in teaching and learning games. How can we accurately and fairly assess what students have learned? When understanding is the purpose of instruction, assessment is more than evaluation; it is a substantive contribution to learning (Blythe 1998). Assessment that fosters understanding (i.e., that goes beyond evaluation) has to be more than a test at the end of the unit. It must inform students and teachers of what students currently understand and of how to proceed with subsequent teaching and learning. Integrated performance and feedback is exactly what students need as they develop their understanding of a particular concept. Ongoing assessment is the process of providing students with clear responses to their demonstrations of understanding in a way that improves subsequent performances.

Integrating assessment can help learning by providing feedback that teachers and their students can use to assess themselves and one another and to modify their activities. According to Black and colleagues (2004) there are two main problems with assessment: (a) the methods that teachers use do not promote good learning and (b) feedback often has a negative impact, particularly on low-achieving students, who then believe that they lack ability and so are not able to learn. As Oslin (2005) points out, the role of assessment in tactical games teaching is that it ensures that students develop the skillfulness, competence and confidence needed to play games. In this chapter we examine what to assess and what your students should know and be able to do (i.e., learning outcomes), aligning assessment with the National Association for Physical Education and Sport (NASPE) standards (National Association of Sport and Physical Education 2004). We share our beliefs about assessment and then outline practical considerations for assessing students.

Assessment Beliefs

We have four major beliefs about assessment: (a) it should be ongoing and regular, (b) it should be authentic, (c) planning what to teach is the same as planning what to assess, and (d) assessment should serve as a system of checks and balances for teaching and learning.

We believe that assessment should be an ongoing and regular part of teaching sport-related games: ongoing in that it is an expected part of a unit and regular in that it is routine to every lesson. Assessment can be for summative purposes (assigning grades) and for formative purposes (checking on student progress, providing feedback for diagnosing strengths and weaknesses). Summative assessment, usually evaluation, involves systematically determining the extent to which objectives have been met (Veal 1993). Summative assessment can be based on several formative assessments taken over the course of a unit. Formative assessment provides feedback for the teacher and the individual students about strengths and weaknesses of performance as well as checks on student progress. Every tactical games lesson includes a segment of questions and answers that is a measure of formative assessment. Using a variety of summative and formative assessments throughout a unit not only gives a picture of student learning but also provides students with in-depth knowledge about what they should learn in the unit (Zessoules and Gardner 1991).

Another valuable aspect of ongoing assessment is that it provides teachers with many opportunities to find out what their students already know about games. The role of prior knowledge in games teaching is important for two reasons. First, students generally know about games because they have played them in their neighborhoods or in community leagues or have watched them as a spectator. Because of all of these possible experiences, the students' knowledge may differ from the desired knowledge (Clement 1993; Griffin and Placek 2001; Wandersee, Mintzes, and Novak 1994). Second, students may have alternative conceptions about various aspects of game play. For example, they may have ideas about their roles in particular games positions or about how to get open in an invasion game in order to support teammates. Alternative conceptions are reasonably different ideas about an aspect of game play that are based on a learner's experience and are brought into formal instruction (Dodds, Griffin, and Placek 2001; Wandersee, Mintzes, and Novak 1994). A teacher should acknowledge that her students usually know something about games playing and that she thus needs to have a sense of this

> **Tip Box**
>
> To assess improvement in student performance, assessment should 1) measure all aspects of performance and 2) measure game playing in context.

prior knowledge so she can better build developmentally appropriate instruction.

Assessment should be authentic. When implementing a tactical games approach, the teacher's goal is for students to focus on successful game play and so assessment should also focus on game play (Veal 1993).

Typically physical educators rely on skill testing to assess game performance, and there are many examples of common skill tests in any measurement textbook. Using skill tests to assess game performance is problematic for four reasons: skill tests do not predict playing performance, they do not take into account the social dimensions of games, they measure skills out of context, and they do not reflect a broader view of game performance (Mitchell, Oslin, and Griffin 2003; Oslin, Mitchell, Griffin 1998).

Planning what to teach is the same as planning what to assess. This notion of integrating instructional goals with instructional processes and assessment is known as instructional alignment (Cohen 1987). Instructional alignment helps the teacher establish a relationship of assessment to the goals and learning activities of a lesson or unit, thus informing students of expected learning outcomes. Each tactical lesson in the earlier chapters begins with the tactical problem to be solved, a lesson focus, and specific lesson objectives. Considering these aspects of instructional alignment in your planning will help you limit your scope of content (to do a few things well), allowing time for assessment and enhancing your ability to sequence the games' content appropriately. The relationship of the assessment criteria to what has been taught is critical for performance in game situations (Mitchell and Oslin 1999a). Ongoing assessment should have established criteria. Criteria for each performance of understanding need to be

- clear—articulated explicitly at the beginning of each performance,
- relevant—closely related to the goals for the unit, and
- public—all students in the class know and understand the criteria (Blythe 1998).

For example, in a tactical games lesson the teacher is asking the students to confront a situation or problem to solve, engage in an action situation (i.e., practice or game) to solve the problem, and reflect on their actions (i.e., critical thinking). This instructional process will help you and your students stay focused during each learning activity as you ask yourself, "What aspects of the lesson do I want my students to reflect upon?" Answering this question will help you decide what type of assessment measures (e.g., assessing game play, asking questions) to use.

Assessment can serve as a system of checks and balances for teaching and learning in that it holds teachers accountable for teaching and students responsible for learning (James, Griffin, and France 2000). It helps teachers improve their instruction and students understand expected learning outcomes. As noted by Oslin, Collier, and Mitchell (2001), assessment is necessary not only to evaluate the extent to which students have learned lesson content, but also to ensure that they stay focused. Ongoing assessment should provide feedback. Feedback needs to

- occur frequently from the beginning to the end of the unit,
- be both formal and planned and more casual and informal,
- provide students with information not only about how well they have carried out performances but also how they might improve them,
- inform planning of subsequent classes and activities, and
- come from a variety of perspectives, including from student's reflections, from peers, and from the teacher (Blythe 1998).

The goal of student assessment is not simply to measure student performance, but to improve it. The primary focus of a tactical games approach is to encourage students to become better games players (i.e., competent). Assessment helps teachers and students establish ongoing feedback about solving a particular tactical problem and demonstrate whether students have achieved particular goals or standards relative to game performance. These considerations are important to successfully using assessment in the everyday life of a physical education teacher's classroom.

While we have shared why we believe assessment is vital to the teaching and learning process, we also recognize that there are practical considerations for making assessment work in your classroom. Many teachers believe that there is too much paperwork and there is not enough time to make assessment part of classroom life, but these factors should not keep teachers from providing students with a complete learning experience, which includes assessment and accountability. In the next section, we identify the decisions the teacher needs to make about assessment and the various assessment strategies the teacher can use.

Assessment Strategies

As the teacher you know that you have many decisions to make in your classroom. One of these decisions deals with keeping track of student learning. The first assessment decision has to do with matching the assessment to the focus of the lesson (i.e., lesson objective). Next teachers need to decide whether assessment will be formative or summative, and then they need to consider the assessment strategy they will use. The assessment strategy will take into account who will do the assessment and the type of assessment tool to be used.

Who will do the assessment is one of the keys to addressing the issues of paperwork and time. Two types of individuals can assess in a classroom: teachers and students. Teachers can and should assess, but they should not do all the assessment, all the time. They can assess for both formative and summative purposes. Students can also assess and should do so in various formative situations. Students can assess themselves (i.e., self-assessment or reporting), assess each other (i.e., peer assessment), and assess as a group (i.e., group problem solving). Students can attain a specific learning goal only if they understand that goal and can assess what they need to do to reach it (Black

Tip Box

Involving students in assessment is cost-effective for you, and in our work with students they have shared how much they enjoy being involved in assessment and benefit from the opportunity.

et al. 2004), making self-assessment an important part of the learning process. Peer assessment adds value because students may accept feedback from one another that they might not take seriously from their teacher. When involving students in assessment, you should consider the following guidelines.

1. Teach students how to assess, what assessment means, and how to use the information gathered from the assessment process. These three important considerations will set you up for success when involving students with assessment. Take the time to teach all three of these considerations. For example, after the first two lessons of a badminton unit with a combined fifth- and sixth-grade class, a teacher introduced partner assessment to her students. The students were to keep track of overhead clears. The teacher set up a demonstration game for the students to practice. She organized the students to observe in pairs so that they could check for understanding, and then she had students share their results as a class. The activity was repeated a second time to make sure students understood their roles and expectations. The time spent was short but the teacher was clear about her expectations through practice. She used this example to teach the students what the information meant as well as set up students to give feedback to each other in a meaningful way.

2. Establish an assessment routine. For assessment to be a regular part of your class it is necessary to create a solid routine. You will need a system for organizing students, equipment, and space. First, students need to know whom they are assessing. There are endless ways to organize; the following are just two examples:

- Partner assessment in which student A assesses student B, then switches roles, and then continues alternating these roles throughout the unit.

- Team assessment in which teams take turns observing game play and assessing a member of another team.

A second consideration involves organizing the equipment for assessment. On what and with what will the students write? How will the assessment forms be collected? There are several options, such as pencils attached to clipboards or student or team portfolios or envelopes taped to a wall (some for blank assessment sheets and some for completed sheets). Finally, you need to consider space in the assessment process. How will observers use the space? Where will they sit to assess each other? Where will the equipment be prior to assessment and at the end of class? We trust that you know yourself as a teacher, your students, and your facilities to develop a smooth routine.

3. Hold students accountable. Simply put, you need to follow up on all aspects of assessment. If you do not value assessment and take care when integrating it into the teaching and learning process, neither will your students. Take time to briefly discuss results and their meaning because this indicates the importance you place on the process of assessment.

4. Consider doability in assessment. Doability involves considering how much to do and who will do the assessment. You should limit how much to observe and measure in a particular lesson or across a whole unit regardless of whether the teacher or student is involved in the assessment. This will ensure that you set assessment tasks that can be accomplished within constraints of available time, equipment, facilities, and people.

Next we consider the type of assessment to be used. Assessment might range from the use of an observation instrument to the use of student self-reporting. Table 16.1 shows the various types of assessment and who is a better fit when using them—teacher or student.

When considering the logistics of assessment you need to consider yourself as the teacher, your students, and your equipment and facilities, but work with them and around them as needed. It is important to balance type of assessment with who does the assessing because this balance provides you and your students with a broader picture of progress toward becoming better games players.

Assessing Learning Outcomes

The concept of four domains of learning outcomes—psychomotor, cognitive, personal and social, and affective—is a way to identify the range of learning outcomes that reflects a broad view of game performance. Figure 16.1 presents our proposed learning outcomes and indicates the relationships among these outcomes. We have argued that improvement in game performance, the primary goal of a tactical games approach, will lead to increased enjoyment, interest, and perceived competence. These motivational outcomes increase the likelihood that students will play games later in life, hence increasing the likelihood that they will maintain a physically active lifestyle after school and into adulthood, as specified by NASPE content standard 3 and 4 (NASPE 2004). Figure 16.1 matches tactical games outcomes with the NASPE standards.

Improved game performance stems from increased tactical awareness. Tactical awareness is the ability to identify problems and their solutions in game situations and thus become better decision makers. The link between tactical awareness and game performance occurs through the integration and interaction of the psychomotor, cognitive, social, and affective domains.

Table 16.1 Possible Types of Assessment for Teachers and Students

Assessment type	Teacher	Students
Written test	Yes	No
Question–answer session	Yes	No
Game Performance Assessment Instrument (GPAI)	Yes	Yes
Monitoring and observation	Yes	No
Rubric	Yes	Yes
Checklist	Yes	Yes
Self-report or journal	No	Yes

Adapted, by permission, from S. Mitchell, J.L. Oslin, and L.L. Griffin, *Sport foundations for elementary physical education: A tactical games approach* (Champaign, IL: Human Kinetics), 150.

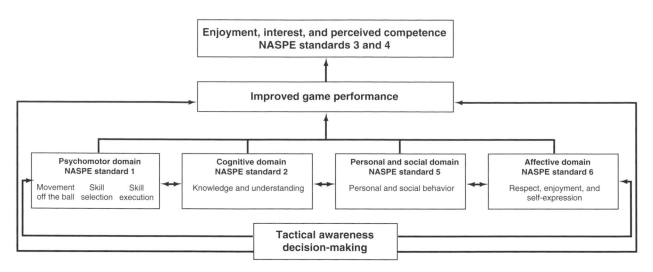

FIGURE 16.1 Anticipated learning outcomes.

The psychomotor domain encompasses game performance; the cognitive domain reflects the understanding of game-related knowledge; and the social and affective domains consider behavioral and social dimensions of sport and games, such as good sporting behaviors, teamwork, and cooperation. In the end, one domain influences the other and this combination reflects the dimensionality and complexity of game play. The following sections discuss assessment as they relate to each domain.

Psychomotor Domain

In teaching and learning tactical games, the psychomotor domain encompasses off-the-ball movement, such as support, and on-the-ball skills, which include skill selection and skill execution (see figure 16.1). This domain parallels the NASPE content standard 1 (NASPE 2004), which states, "A physically educated person demonstrates competency in motor skills and movement patterns needed to perform a variety of physical activities" (p. 11). A tactical games approach primarily focuses on improved game performance (i.e., competent players). Assessment of game-playing ability should include decisions players make about what to do with the ball and movements players make when they do not have the ball because both on- and off-the-ball skills are vital to becoming competent or proficient games players (NASPE 2004). For example, in a small-sided (3v3) basketball game, we can assess what players are doing with the

ball. But it is also just as important to assess how a player moves in positive ways to get the ball.

Recent efforts to measure performance more completely in game play have included assessing aspects of decision-making, skill execution, and individual performance (French, Werner, Rink, Taylor, and Hussey 1996; Grehaigne, Godbout, and Bouthier 1997; Grehaigne, Richard, and Griffin 2005; Mitchell, Oslin, and Griffin 1995; Nevett, Rovegno, and Babiarz 2001; Oslin, Mitchell, and Griffin 1998; Oslin 2005; Turner and Martinek 1992). These types of measurements are valuable for three reasons.

- They assess students in game play.
- They can provide information about a player's thinking process. For example, in an invasion game a player may receive credit for attempting to pass to an open player even if the pass is not well executed.
- They can be a valuable source of information for planning the next lesson.

As we have maintained, game play should be measured authentically, that is, within the context of actual game-playing situations (Oslin 2005). The authentic assessment of game performance requires observing participants when they are not in possession of the ball. Therefore, carefully planned observation is essential. In this section we will introduce two formal methods for assessing both individual and team performance: the Game Performance Assessment Instrument (GPAI) and the Team Sport Assessment Procedure (TSAP) (Grehaigne, Godbout, and Bouthier 1997; Grehaigne, Richard, and Griffin 2005). We will also share an invasion games rubric that we have used with students for peer assessment.

Game Performance Assessment Instrument (GPAI) The GPAI was developed as a comprehensive assessment tool for teachers to use and adapt for a variety of games. This flexibility means that teachers can use the GPAI for different games across the classification system (e.g., invasion, net and wall) or within a particular classification (e.g., basketball, soccer). We designed the GPAI to provide teachers and researchers a means of observing and coding performance behaviors. The GPAI includes behaviors that demonstrate the ability to solve tactical problems by making decisions, moving appropriately, and executing skills. We initially developed performance components for the GPAI through consultation with five teacher-coaches who had expertise in each classification category discussed in chapter 2 (see table 2.1). Our aim was to identify observable components of game performance that applied across game categories. After identifying seven components, we formulated descriptions of each component and reformulated them until all experts reached consensus.

Seven components of game performance are defined in the GPAI (see table 16.2). Not all components apply to all games. For example, in tennis the base component is critical to court coverage, but players do not have to guard or mark opponents. The seven components in table 16.2 constitute a broad definition of game performance that entails much more than skill execution (Mitchell and Oslin 1999a).

Following are brief descriptions and examples of each component of game performance.

- **Base** is a position to which players should return between skill attempts. For example, in net games, players should return to a specific place on the court that provides them with optimal opportunity for court coverage. Table 16.3 provides some examples of how base applies to various games.

- **Decision making** is choosing which movement or skill to execute in response to a tactical problem. Table 16.4 provides some examples of decision making across the games classification system.

- After players decide what they are going to perform, **skill selection and execution** must be efficient to achieve the desired outcome. Table 16.5 lists some examples of skill execution in various games.

- **Support** is important primarily to invasion games, where keeping possession is vital to scoring. To keep possession as a team, players with the ball must be able to pass to teammates who are ready and available to receive a pass. Hence, being available to support teammates (an off-the-ball movement) is critical to keeping possession of the ball and scoring and thus to solid overall game performance.

- Off-the-ball movements are critical aspects of defensive game play. All invasion games require players to **guard or mark** their oppo-

Table 16.2 Components of Game Performance*

Base	Appropriately returning to a recovery (base) position between skill attempts
Decision making	Appropriately deciding about what to do with the ball (or projectile) during a game
Skill execution	Efficiently executing selected skills
Support	Appropriately supporting teammate with ball (or projectile) by being in position to receive a pass
Guard or mark	Appropriately guarding or marking an opponent who may or may not have the ball (or projectile)
Cover	Appropriately providing defensive cover, help, or backup for a player making a challenge for the ball (or projectile)
Adjust	Moving either offensively or defensively as necessitated by the flow of the game

*Note: All text is compiled from Griffin, et al. 1997; Mitchell and Oslin 1999a; Oslin et al. 1998)

Table 16.3 Examples of Base Applied in Various Games

Game	Example
Badminton	**Net/Wall Games** Player returns to about the "T" at center court in between shots
Tennis	**Net/Wall Games** Player returns to the center of the baseline in between shots
Volleyball	**Net/Wall Games** Player returns to a designated playing area when ball is returned over the net during a rally
Softball	**Striking/Fielding Games** Player starts in base (fielding position) before each pitch
Golf	**Target Games** Player starts in a setup or stance position
Basketball	**Invasion Games** Player sets up in position in a zone defense

Table 16.4 Examples of Decision Making in the Four Games Categories

Game category	Skill selection
Invasion games	Decide whether to shoot, pass, or dribble
Net/wall games	Decide shot selection and placement
Striking/fielding games	Batters—decide pitch and placement of shot Fielders—decide where to throw the ball Pitchers—decide how to deliver the ball
Target games	Golf—decide what club to use

Adapted, by permission, from S.A. Mitchell, J.L. Oslin, and L.L. Griffin, 2003, *Sport foundations for elementary physical education: A tactical games approach* (Champaign, IL: Human Kinetics), 153.

Table 16.5 Examples of Skill Execution

Invasion games	Player shoots on target Player passes accurately to open player Player controls the ball from a pass
Net/wall games	Player executes clear to deep court Player executes drop shot close to net in front of service line Player passes ball to set up move (more than one hit on a side)
Striking/fielding games	Player fields cleanly Player throws accurately to target Player hits effectively (maximizes scoring, minimizes outs)
Target games	Player executes a chip to within 6 ft (1.8 m) Player shoots an arrow and hits the target Player delivers the ball Player throws a horseshoe

Adapted, by permission, from S.A. Mitchell, J.L. Oslin, and L.L. Griffin, 2003, *Sport foundations for elementary physical education: A tactical games approach* (Champaign, IL: Human Kinetics), 154.

nents in order to deny them the ball and prevent them from scoring.

- **Covering**, another defensive aspect, usually involves providing backup to teammates who make challenges for the ball. In invasion games defenders make a challenge for the ball and teammates cover the space behind them. In basketball this is called "help" defense, and in soccer it is simply known as cover. In striking/fielding games such as softball, the fielder making a play on a ball should have a teammate covering the fielder in case of a fielding error. In net/wall games such as volleyball, players provide cover for teammates who are attempting to spike.

- **Adjust** refers to the ability to adjust positioning as needed in the game. In other words, don't stand rooted during a game. Table 16.6 provides examples of adjustments players may make in invasion, striking/fielding, and net/wall games.

The appeal of the GPAI is that you can adapt and use the instrument according to the type and aspect of the game being played, your students, and your gymnasium or playing area. There are two basic scoring methods for using the GPAI: the 1 to 5 system (see reproducible 16.1 at the end of this chapter) and a tally system (see reproducibles 16.2, 16.3, and 16.4 at the end of this chapter).

Mitchell and Oslin (1999a) pointed out that the 1 to 5 scoring system is efficient for two reasons. First, observers (primarily the teacher) do not have to record each time a player is involved in the game. In invasion games and some net/wall games, this is impossible to do effectively because of the tempo, flow, and unpredictability of those games when players have a wide range of skill levels. Second, the 1 to 5 scoring system provides for a wide range of scoring but not so broad as to make consistency of scoring difficult to achieve. You need to create criteria for the five indicators, that is, from very effective performance to very weak performance—or you could modify this by using a scale from always to never. These indicators should be based on your objectives, student abilities, and time available for physical education.

The tally system can be used with striking/fielding and some net/wall games because they are played at a slower pace, which gives the observer an opportunity to score or tally every event. The tally system also provides a more precise performance measure. As you can see in the net/wall and striking/fielding game GPAI forms (see reproducibles 16.3 and 16.4), components are scored as either "appropriate" or "inappropriate," or "efficient" or "inefficient." You can then develop percentage scores for assessed GPAI components (Mitchell and Oslin 1999a). For example, an appropriate decision-making percentage would be calculated by dividing the number of appropriate decisions made by the total decisions made. Likewise you could calculate a skill-execution percentage by dividing efficient execution attempts by total execution attempts.

You can also give your students the bigger picture of their game play by calculating game involvement and overall game performance scores.

Table 16.6   Examples of Adjustment Across Game Categories

Game category	Adjustment
Invasion games	Ball at the opposite end of the field—defender adjusts position by moving at least to the halfway line in a position to support the attack if needed and to deny space should opponents counterattack
Net/wall games	Badminton doubles players adjust offensive front-back formation to a defensive side-side formation when necessary Volleyball players in the front row adjust (open up) when the ball goes to the back row (face the ball)
Striking/fielding games	Softball or cricket fielders adjust their positions according to strengths and weaknesses of batters and to whether the batter is left- or right-handed

Adapted, by permission, from S.A. Mitchell, J.L. Oslin, and L.L. Griffin, 2003, *Sport foundations for elementary physical education: A tactical games approach* (Champaign, IL: Human Kinetics), 155.

Game involvement can be measured by adding together all responses that indicate involvement in the game, including inappropriate decisions made and inefficient skill execution. Do not include inappropriate guarding and marking, supporting, adjusting, and covering because an inappropriate response in these components indicates that the player was not involved in the game. Game performance is a more precise measure and is calculated by adding scores from all components assessed and dividing by the number of components assessed:

(% decisions made + % skill execution) / 2.

Following are examples of possible performance measures.

- Game involvement = number of appropriate decisions + number of inappropriate decisions + number of efficient skill executions + number of inefficient skill executions + number of appropriate supporting movements
- Decision-making index (DMI) = number of appropriate decisions made / (number of appropriate decisions made + number of inappropriate decisions made)
- Skill execution index (SEI) = number of efficient skill executions / (number of efficient skill executions + number of inefficient skill executions)
- Support index (SI) = number of appropriate supporting movements / (number of appropriate supporting movements + number of inappropriate supporting movements)
- Game performance = (DMI + SEI + SI) / 3

Let's now examine some GPAI data from a soccer unit in which the components measured were decision making, skill execution, and support (see table 16.7).

The data in table 16.8 has been collected from observations of Matthew's team playing soccer and we have assessed players' decision making, skill execution, and support (see table 16.8). Each tally on the recording sheet represents one observation.

After adding up his scores for each component of game performance, we applied the formulas suggested previously to come up with the following measures of Matthew's game play:

Game involvement = 7 + 7 + 6 = 20

Decision making = 6 / 7 = 0.86

Skill execution = 6 / 7 = 0.86

Support = 6 / 10 = 0.60

Game performance = (0.86 + 0.85 + 0.60) / 3 = 0.77

Game performance is the arithmetical average of the decision making, skill execution, and support indexes. This calculation ensures that players whose scores indicate strong game performance do have contact with the ball, make good decisions, and execute skills well within the game. If percentages are easier to report (and for students to understand) for the DMI, SEI, and SI, simply multiply the figure you get by 100 in each case.

Matthew has been highly involved in the game and his decision-making and skill-execution scores indicate a high degree of success, though there were some occasions in which he failed to give support to teammates. Nicholas, on the other hand, was not particularly involved in the game either with or without the ball. Using the formulas, his respective measures of game performance are 3,

Table 16.7 GPAI Criteria for a Soccer Unit

GPAI Component	Criteria
Decision making	Player attempts to pass to an open teammate Player attempts to shoot when appropriate
Skill execution	Reception—control of pass and setup of the ball Passing—ball reaches target Shooting—ball stays below head and is on target
Support	Player appears to support the ball carrier by being in or moving to an appropriate position to receive a pass

Table 16.8 Observation of Soccer Performance

Name	Decision made		Skill execution		Support	
	A	IA	E	IE	A	IA
Matthew	xxxxx	x	xxxxx	x	xxxxxx	xxxx
Nicholas					xxx	xxx
Katie	xxxxx	x	xxxxx	x	xxxx	x
Jamal	xx	x	xxx	x	xxxxx	xx
Jenn	xxx	xx	xx	xxx	xx	x
Sasha	x	xx	x	xx	xxxxxxx	x

A = appropriate
E = efficient
IA = inappropriate
IE = inefficient

Table 16.9 Tactical Complexity Level II in Soccer

	Tactical problem	Level II
Scoring	**Maintaining possession of the ball** Attacking the goal	Supporting Shooting, turning
Preventing scoring	**Defending space** Defending the goal	Marking, pressuring the ball Goalkeeper, positioning, receiving, throwing

0, 0, 0.5, and 0.17. Katie's performance was strong overall. Sasha's scores are interesting—though not particularly successful in either decision making or skill execution, Sasha was involved in the game. Her scores for support provide evidence of this, suggesting that she worked hard to be in a position to receive the ball. As you can see, the GPAI provides useful information about the strengths and weaknesses of your students' game play.

GPAI scores can be used for both formative and summative purposes. You could set targets for students relative to GPAI scores, for example, "See if you can score 75% on decision making today." If you choose to use GPAI scores for grade assignment, we recommend reporting both game-performance and game-involvement scores to give students credit both for quality of performance and for attempts to be fully involved in game play. You can easily build criteria for assessment into a game-specific record sheet. For example, in table 16.8

we coded Matthew's supporting runs to space as appropriate, but we coded his lack of support for teammates as inappropriate. We can code appropriateness each time Matthew makes a decision about what to do with the ball. For example, when he passes to a teammate who is closely marked (guarded) we tally the decision as inappropriate. If such a pass is technically well struck, we code it as efficiently executed.

Each sport chapter has been designed to assist you in creating GPAIs that align with each lesson and across the unit. Let's take a closer look at the chapters and possible GPAI modifications for those chapters. For example, each sport-specific chapter has levels of game complexity. In chapter 4, on soccer, there are five levels of tactical (game) complexity, which provide a scope and sequence to your instructional unit. Table 16.9 shows only tactical complexity level II; as you can see, it limits instructional focus to two offensive tactical problems (maintaining possession of the ball and attacking the goal) and two defensive components (defending space and defending the goal). The level also limits the size of the games to be played (level II uses 3- and 6-sided maximum) as well as the skills and movements that you will teach.

You can limit the focus of your GPAI instrument to the objectives of the overall unit. Reproducible 16.3 is a possible GPAI for an invasion game unit. This GPAI focuses on the offensive components of level II skill execution, decision making, and support. Spaces are provided for six players since level II calls for 3- or 6-sided games. Now you have an idea of how the levels of tactical complexity can help you link assessment with instruction.

Next, we'll examine how the lessons are designed by looking at a specific lesson (level II, lesson 9, in chapter 4). All lessons begin with the same format by stating the tactical problem to be solved, the general lesson focus, and the specific objective for the lesson. The following is from lesson 9:

- Tactical problem–Maintaining possession of the ball
- Lesson focus–Supporting the ball carrier
- Objective–Constant support for the ball carrier

In this lesson the focus is on constant support for player with ball, which means you should limit your GPAI use to support only. Games are complex, so we recommend that you limit the observation focus for yourself as well as your students (Mitchell and Oslin 1999a). In this lesson you might use the GPAI in reproducible 16.2 that focuses only on support and limit the number of students by observing just one team or use this form as a peer-assessment tool. The goal is always to align your instruction by linking objectives, instructional activities, and assessment.

At this point, you are probably asking yourself, "Can I really do this and be accurate?" The answer is yes! Assessments by both teachers and students who used a version of the GPAI in live settings have been considered reliable. That is, in their assessment of performance, observers have been consistent with a fellow observer approximately 80% of the time (Oslin, Mitchell, and Griffin 1998; Griffin, Dodds, and James 1999). You can make your

GPAI measures more objective and less subjective by having two observers independently collect GPAI data and then compare scores to establish interobserver agreement. The key to establishing reliability is in the quality of the criteria stated for observation: the criteria should be specific and observable (Mitchell and Oslin 1999a).

Team Sport Assessment Grehaigne, Godbout, and Bouthier (1997) developed the Team Sport Assessment Procedure (TSAP) as another authentic assessment instrument designed to reflect student learning in relation to real-life applications. The TSAP was developed for use in formative and summative assessment scenarios where tactical learning is the primary focus. It is a peer-assessment procedure based on two basic questions: (1) how did the player gain possession of the ball (i.e. "conquering" the ball, receiving a pass from a teammate in the course of play) and (2) how did the player dispose of the ball (i.e., passing the ball off, playing an offensive pass or shot, or losing the ball)? According to these questions a player's specific behaviors are observed and coded during the game play in six different components to reflect a student's offensive performance in invasion games. Table 16.10 identifies and defines the observed components, while reproducible 16.5 (page 513) provides a recording sheet. The information provided by the individual variables, performance indexes, and performance score are all indicators of both technical and tactical performance, which are related to successful game play.

The TSAP combines "volume of play" and "efficiency" to compute team performance or what Grehaigne and colleagues (1997) referred to as "rapport of strength." Table 16.11 provides formulas that you may want to use to help your students make meaning of their data.

Let's take a closer look at a student's data after playing in a 3v3 game of basketball (see table 16.12).

Kevin's game-play data tell us the following:

- Volume of play (game involvement) = 5 + 7 = 12
- Efficiency index (effective play) = 5 + 4 + 3 + 10 = 22
- Performance score (overall performance) = (12/2) + (22 × 10) = 6 + 220 = 226

Table 16.10 TSAP Components of Game Play

Components	Definitions
GAINING POSSESSION OF THE BALL	
Conquering the ball (CB)	Interception, stealing the ball from the opponent, or recapturing the ball after an unsuccessful shot on goal or near-loss to the other team
Receiving the ball (RB)	Receiving the ball from a teammate and not immediately losing control of it
DISPOSING OF THE BALL	
Playing a neutral ball (NB)	Passing the ball to a teammate, or any pass that does not put the other team in jeopardy
Losing the ball (LB)	Losing the ball to the other team without having scored a goal
Playing an offensive ball (OB)	Passing the ball to a partner, thus pressuring the other team, which most often leads to a shot on goal
Executing a successful shot (SS)	Scoring or maintaining possession of the ball following the execution of a shot

Adapted from Grehaigne, Richard, and Griffin 2005.

Table 16.11 Formulas for Calculating TSAP Outcome Variables

Outcome variables	Calculation
Volume of play (VP)	CB + RB
Efficiency index (EI)	CB + P + (SS / LB) + 10
Performance score (PS)	(Volume of play / 2) + (Efficiency index × 10)

SS = executing a successful shot
CB = conquering the ball
RB = receiving the ball
LB = losing the ball
VP = volume of play

Table 16.12 Game Play Data from a 3v3 Basketball Game

Name	CB	RB	LB	NB	P	SS
Kevin	5	7	2	5	4	6
Shelly	2	6	4	4	2	2
Karen	1	4	1	6	6	4

CB = Conquering the ball
RB = Receiving the ball
LB = Losing the ball
NB = Playing a neutral ball
P = Pass
SS = Executing a successful shot

Sample Game Rubric for Peer Assessment

Another possibility when seeking to assess students in game play is to create game-play rubrics. Reproducible 16.6 (page 514) provides a sample invasion-game rubric we developed to use for peer assessment in an ultimate Frisbee unit. This rubric focuses on solving the tactical problem of maintaining possession of the ball (i.e., object), particularly passing and supporting in game play. The rubric combines on-the-ball skills (pass and catch) and off-the-ball movements (support) to help guide students in their decision making. Students have the opportunity to learn a hierarchy for decision making. In using this type of rubric, students are encouraged to examine all possible solutions, thus guiding their own work and becoming independent learners through peer assessment.

Measuring a variety of performance components beyond skill execution provides an objective measure of participation, rewarding students who engage in game play on and off the ball. Students who have not had the opportunities to develop skill can be rewarded for moving into position to receive a pass (support play), making good decisions (when to pass, when to shoot), or appropriately marking players to keep them from scoring or gaining possession of the ball for their team (Oslin 2005).

The GPAI and TSAP are primarily *product* measures. Product measures make it easy for the observer to identify the effectiveness of the performance. For example, if a student scored low on supporting teammates and passing, both teacher and student will see that there is a need to work on those particular skills.

Process measures that focus on the execution of movements or skills are also important. Movement and skill forms can be assessed during practice situations using rubrics and checklists focused on critical elements of specific movements or skills. You probably use a number of these forms in your teaching on a regular basis. Both product and process measures can be used to develop a summative evaluation.

This section has familiarized you with two means for assessing game performance in the psychomotor domain that both teachers and students can use successfully. Because it provides all players with credit for simple game involvement and for decisions and performance with and without the ball, all students—regardless of skill level—will value game improvement.

Cognitive Domain

In teaching and learning tactical games, the cognitive domain encompasses the students' ability to know and articulate solutions to tactical problems (i.e., what to do) and explain how, when, and where they are going to execute particular skills and movements (i.e., how to do it, when it is best to do it, where you should do it).

The cognitive domain parallels NASPE (2004) content standard 2, which states, "A physically educated person demonstrates understanding of movement concepts, principles, strategies, and tactics as they apply to the learning and performance of physical activities" (p. 11). This standard refers to students' ability to articulate aspects of game understanding.

As a teacher, you know that there are many ways to assess students' knowledge and understanding about sport-related games. You will be familiar with many types of assessment tools such as written tests, reflective journals, checklists, portfolios, role playing, student logs, and demonstrations, to name a few. We encourage you to use other resources such as *Moving into the Future: National Standards for Physical Education* (NASPE 2004), *Teaching Middle School Physical Education* (Mohnsen 1997) and *Teaching for Outcomes in Elementary Physical Education* (Hopple 1995) for additional assessment tools. Following are some ways to get started assessing cognitive aspects of game performance, which foreground a tactical approach.

- Question–and–answer sessions such as those found in our books provide two opportunities for formative question-and-answer assessment. The first opportunity is right after the initial game, when the teacher can ask questions regarding what to do (i.e., tactical awareness) and how to do it (i.e., skill execution). A question-and-answer session that targets the specific objectives of the lesson serves three functions. First, it shifts the students to the center of the learning environment and you to the role of facilitator. Second, students share what they already know (prior knowledge) and begin to think critically about the tactical problem that you have presented in the small-sided conditioned game. Third, as students develop game understanding, they will begin to connect the tactical similarities between games, and this tactical understanding can transfer to other games (Mitchell and Oslin 1999b). The second opportunity in our lesson formats for a question-and-answer session is at the end of the lesson during closure. This is an opportunity to debrief your students by asking three questions: (1) what happened, (2) what does it mean, and (3) now what?

- A one-minute quiz is a written or verbal test used at the end of a lesson to a check for understanding (Griffin and Oslin 1990). Quiz questions are simple and hold students accountable for lesson content. Think tactically when you design questions. For example, have your students solve a tactical problem, make connections among games from the same category, and describe different skills and movements practiced in class. The following are examples of questions with a tactical focus:

  - *Q: What are the ways we tried to maintain possession of the ball?* The focus of this question is on the different skills or movements used to solve the tactical problem of maintaining possession of the ball in an invasion game (e.g., basketball, soccer, hockey).

    A: Pass, dribble, or support depending on the lesson focus.

  - *Q: How are volleyball, tennis, badminton, and handball similar?* The focus of this question is on understanding the similarities between these games because they are in the same classification (net/wall games).

    A: They are all net/wall games in which the primary goal is to propel an object over the net or against the wall that cannot be returned by an opponent.

  - *Q: What are the learning cues for support that we used today?*

    A: Quick straight movement, call for a pass.

- In scenario activities students are asked to solve tactical problems that you design as an activity. The figures on reproducibles 16.7 through 16.9 are examples of invasion-game scenarios, while the figures on reproducibles 16.10 through 16.12 are net/wall game examples. Scenarios could be completed by students as a worksheet on which they draw and write or they could be discussed orally as a class. Sometimes students know what to do in a game but cannot always execute it, so scenarios provide students with an opportunity to show their knowledge of game play.

- Self-report journals allow the teacher and students a simple way to keep track of written assignments. Students could self-report or use their journals for the one-minute quizzes or to reflect on their game-performance assessments (GPAI), such as how they might improve their performance. Self-report journals are a medium for students to give you feedback about their own performance. In addition they provide you with a permanent product that could be used either formally or informally and does not have to be evaluated immediately.

The following is one way for you to use the self-report journal so that students reflect on their game understanding. Either at the end of class or at home have students reflect on the results of a daily game-play assessment. Ask students to reflect on the following questions:

- What does the information tell you about your game play?
- How can you improve your play?
- What would you do differently?
- How could you help your team's performance?

Personal and Social Domain

In teaching and learning tactical games, the personal and social domain addresses socialization into sport. Students need to be aware that there is not only in-game knowledge (e.g., what to do, how to do it) but also knowledge about games in general. For example, for competition to be good and appropriate, players need to cooperate with each other as well as with their fellow teammates. The personal and social domain parallels NASPE (2004) content standard 5, which states, "A physically educated person exhibits responsible personal and social behavior that respects self and others in physical activity settings" (p. 11). Thus, assessing the personal and social domain involves assessing rule and procedure adherence, cooperation, etiquette, good sporting behaviors, fair play, and teamwork (including performing assigned or selected roles within teams such as equipment manager or statistician). These aspects of game performance are important. They simply do not just happen–they must be planned for and taught, and students must be held accountable for them.

The purpose of this section is twofold. First, we offer two ways to frame your game units to foster desirable sport behaviors and responsibility (i.e., sport citizenship). Second, we offer a few ways to assess your students for appropriate sport citizenship (i.e., behavioral and social domain) in a tactical games approach.

Promoting Sport Citizenship Suggestions for fostering sport citizenship include:

1. Integrate tactical games with sport education. Sport education (Siedentop 1994) has the personal and social dimensions of games built right in. Students form teams and take on roles such as coach, equipment manager, statistician, and so on. Teams can be assigned as special duty teams during tournaments, to be officials, and to keep score and game statistics. In sport education students are placed in teams for the duration of a season, which allows them to get to know each other better (see Collier 2005, for example). This makes it more likely that they can work on such things as teamwork and players' roles and responsibilities. Also, question–answer sessions that focus on positive sporting behaviors, fair play, and etiquette might be more meaningful when students are affiliated with a team.

2. Introduce Teaching Personal and Social Responsibility (TPSR) levels. As Hellison (1996) states, responsibility includes "learning to become more responsible and learning to take responsibility" as a games player. There are five TPSR levels, which can be considered a progression (adapted from Hellison 1996):

Level One: Respect

- Self control

Level Two: Participation and Effort

- Exploring effort
- Trying new things
- Developing a personal definition of success

Level Three: Self-Direction

- Demonstrating on-task independence
- Developing a sound knowledge base
- Developing, carrying out, and evaluating a personal plan
- Balancing current and future needs
- Striving against external forces

Level Four: Sensitivity and Responsiveness to the Well-Being of Others

- Developing prerequisite interpersonal skills
- Becoming sensitive and compassionate
- Contributing to the community and beyond
- Helping others without rewards

Level Five: Outside the Gym

- Trying out the levels in the classroom, on the playground, and at home
- Making decisions about the usefulness of the levels outside the gym

We suggest two ways to implement the TPSR levels. First, students report at the end of class by raising the number of fingers that corresponds to their perception of the level of their own behavior for the day or week. Second, you could have students complete a journal entry regarding their level, including a bit of reflection.

3. Integrating Cooperative Learning (CL). There is significant evidence to support the idea that students working in small cooperative groups can master material presented by the teacher better than students working on their own (Cohen 1994; Johnson and Johnson 1989; Slavin 1996). Dyson (2005) points to five main components of CL that can be integrated into TGM.

- Positive interdependence. Each group member learns to depend on the rest of the group while working together to complete the task.
- Individual accountability. Teachers establish and maintain student responsibility for appropriate behavior, task involvement, and outcomes (Siedentop and Tannehill 2000).
- Face-to-face interaction. Group members have head-to-head discussions in close proximity to one another (e.g., think-pair-share).
- Interpersonal and small-group skills. These include skills such as listening, sharing decision making, taking responsibility, learning to give and receive feedback, and learning to encourage each other (e.g., peer tutoring or coaching).

- Group processing. Time is allocated for the group to share how well it achieved its goals and maintained effective working relationships. Group processing is similar to the processing or debriefing (e.g., what happened and now what) that takes place in adventure education (see Dyson 2005, for example).

Assessing Sport Citizenship Many of the same tools and resources suggested for the cognitive domain can be designed to assess the behavioral and social domain. The following are ideas to get you started with assessment in this domain.

- **Use a class circle discussion.** The class circle discussion is similar to the question–answer sessions that are built into every lesson, and it could be used to discuss the social and behavioral dimensions of games. For example, one of your objectives for the lesson might be for students to demonstrate respect to their peers by making at least two supportive skill- or outcome-related statements to their classmates during a practice task or game. At the end of class you could then gather students into a circle to discuss some core values that make for appropriate sporting behavior, namely caring, respect, integrity, and responsibility.
- **Use self-report journals** for students to reflect on or rate their sport citizenship (using TPSR levels) for a particular day, event such as a tournament, or overall unit. Students could describe both positive and negative sporting behaviors.
- **Create a good-citizenship rubric** (table 16.13).

Affective Domain

In teaching and learning tactical games, the affective domain addresses the feelings and emotions students have developed about sport-related games. For example, teachers might ask students how they feel when they win or lose or how they feel about themselves after learning a particular game. A tactical games approach foregrounds students with the underlying goal of appealing to their interest in playing games so that they value or appreciate the need to work toward improved game performance. Improving performance should lead to greater enjoyment, interest, and perceived competence to become lifelong games players.

The affective domain parallels NASPE (2004) content standard 6, which states that "A physically educated person values physical activity for health, enjoyment, challenge, self-expression, and/or social interaction" (p. 11). Again, many of the ideas and resources in the cognitive and personal and social domain sections can be used to assess the affective domain in a tactical games approach. Following are some examples for assessing this tricky domain.

- **Self-report journals.** Students may record
  - how they felt about their particular games units,
  - how they felt when they scored or made a basket,
  - how they felt playing against an opponent,
  - how they felt when they tried a new game,
  - successes or challenges in learning a new skill or movement, and
  - successes or challenges when playing a particular game.

Table 16.13 Good Sport Citizenship Rubric	
Level	**Indicators**
	Makes no observational errors in interpreting or applying the rules of the game
	Refrains from actions or behaviors that endanger or injure another student
	Recognizes and acknowledges good play by a teammate or opponent

Level 3—Uses indicators in an extremely consistent manner
Level 2—Uses indicators with consistency most of the time
Level 1—Uses indicators with occasional consistency

- **Role play.** Ask students to create a play dealing with conflict resolution during a small-sided game that they usually play in class.
- **Affective domain rubric.** Reproducible 16.13 (page 525) provides a sample rubric for assessing the affective domain.

Summary

We have provided you with ways to assess students' learning through a tactical games approach. We have outlined the potential learning outcomes and aligned a tactical approach to four domains of learning (psychomotor, cognitive, personal and social, and affective) as well as to the NASPE (2004) standards. Formal and informal measures allow for ongoing assessment and can help the teacher provide a clear message that the intent of teaching sport-related games is to improve performance. Teachers should view themselves as the architects of games learning and create conditioned games and assessments that drive the skills, movements, and competencies that students should learn to be successful games players (Oslin 2005). The take-home message is simply that assessment matters. The teaching and learning process is not complete without assessment. By building assessment into your daily teaching you are making an investment in your students, yourself as a teacher, and physical education as a viable subject. Ongoing assessment ensures that students develop the competence and confidence to play games long after they leave your physical education programs.

Game Performance Assessment Instrument for Invasion Games

Class _____ Evaluator _____ Team _____ Game _____

Observation Dates (a) _____ (b) _____ (c) _____ (d) _____

Scoring Key

5 = Very effective performance (Always)

4 = Effective performance (Usually)

3 = Moderately effective performance (Sometimes)

2 = Weak performance (Rarely)

1 = Very weak performance (Never)

Components and Criteria

- **Skill execution**—Students pass the ball accurately, reaching the intended receiver.
- **Decision making**—Students make appropriate choices when passing (i.e., passing to unguarded teammates to set up a scoring opportunity).
- **Support**—Students attempt to move into position to receive a pass from teammates (i.e., forward toward the goal).

Name	Skill Execution	Decision Making	Support

Game Performance Assessment Instrument: Support in Invasion Games

Scorer _____ Player _____ Game _____

What to Look for

Support—Students should attempt to move into position to receive a pass form a teammate.

Appropriate Support

- Moving forward to space after pass is made
- Positioning self in a passing lane
- Moving quick and calling for the ball

Recording Directions

- Read the three previous points about good support.
- Use a tally to mark each player's attempt to support during the game.

Date	Appropriate (good supporting)	Inappropriate (not supporting)

Adapted, by permission, from S.A. Mitchell, J.L. Oslin, and L.L. Griffin, 2003, *Sport foundations for elementary physical education: A tactical games approach* (Champaign, IL: Human Kinetics), 157.

From *Teaching Sport Concepts and Skills: A Tactical Games Approach,* Second Edition, by Stephen A. Mitchell, Judith L. Oslin, and Linda L. Griffin, Champaign, IL: Human Kinetics.

Game Performance Assessment Instrument: Net/Wall Games

Class _____ Evaluator _____ Team _____ Game _____

Observation Dates (a) _____ (b) _____ (c) _____ (d) _____

Components and Criteria

- **Skill execution**—Students perform underhand ground strokes into opponent's court.
- **Decision making**—Students make appropriate choices of when to place a long or short shot.
- **Base**—Students return to recovery position between skill attempts.

Recording Procedures

- Use a tally to mark the observed category.
- Mark each player's responses during the game. If the student you are evaluating strikes the ball long or short, be sure to mark whether the player made an appropriate (A) or inappropriate (IA) decision and whether the underhand ground strokes were executed efficiently (E) or inefficiently (IE).

Name	SKILL EXECUTION		DECISION MAKING		BASE	
	E	IE	A	IA	A	IA

Game Performance Assessment Instrument: Striking/Fielding Games

Class _____ Evaluator _____ Team _____ Game _____

Observation Dates (a) _____ (b) _____ (c) _____ (d) _____

Components and Criteria

- **Skill execution**—Students field ball cleanly.
- **Decision making**—Students make the appropriate play for the situation.
- **Base**—Students are in an appropriate starting position.

Recording Procedures

- Use a tally to mark the observed category.
- Mark each player's responses during the game. If the student you are evaluating is fielding the ball, be sure to mark whether the player made an appropriate (A) or inappropriate (IA) decision and whether the fielding was executed efficiently (E) or inefficiently (IE).

Name	SKILL EXECUTION		DECISION MAKING		BASE	
	E	IE	A	IA	A	IA

From *Teaching Sport Concepts and Skills: A Tactical Games Approach,* Second Edition, by Stephen A. Mitchell, Judith L. Oslin, and Linda L. Griffin, Champaign, IL: Human Kinetics.

Team Sport Assessment Procedure for Invasion Games

Name _____ Class _____

Observer _____ Date _____

Directions

Observe student's game play and place a tally mark in the appropriate box.

Gaining Possession of the Ball		Disposing of the Ball			
Conquered Ball (CB)	Received Ball (RB)	Lost Ball (LB)	Neutral Ball (NB)	Pass (P)	Successful Shot (SS)

From *Teaching Sport Concepts and Skills: A Tactical Games Approach*, Second Edition, by Stephen A. Mitchell, Judith L. Oslin, and Linda L. Griffin, Champaign, IL: Human Kinetics.

Invasion Game: Peer Assessment Rubric Criteria

4 = Catchable pass; receiver open

3 = Catchable pass; receiver not open

2 = Uncatchable pass; receiver open

1 = Uncatchable pass; receiver not open

Directions

Circle the score for each pass according to the passing and catching rubric.

Player _____

Observer _____

Attempt	Rubric Score			
1.	1	2	3	4
2.	1	2	3	4
3.	1	2	3	4
4.	1	2	3	4
5.	1	2	3	4
6.	1	2	3	4
7.	1	2	3	4
8.	1	2	3	4
9.	1	2	3	4
10.	1	2	3	4

What would you tell the player to help the player improve?

Player _____

Observer _____

Attempt	Rubric Score			
1.	1	2	3	4
2.	1	2	3	4
3.	1	2	3	4
4.	1	2	3	4
5.	1	2	3	4
6.	1	2	3	4
7.	1	2	3	4
8.	1	2	3	4
9.	1	2	3	4
10.	1	2	3	4

From *Teaching Sport Concepts and Skills: A Tactical Games Approach,* Second Edition, by Stephen A. Mitchell, Judith L. Oslin, and Linda L. Griffin, Champaign, IL: Human Kinetics.

(continued)

Player _____

Observer _____

Attempt	Rubric Score			
1.	1	2	3	4
2.	1	2	3	4
3.	1	2	3	4
4.	1	2	3	4
5.	1	2	3	4
6.	1	2	3	4
7.	1	2	3	4
8.	1	2	3	4
9.	1	2	3	4
10.	1	2	3	4

What would you tell the player to help the player improve?

Player _____

Observer _____

Attempt	Rubric Score			
1.	1	2	3	4
2.	1	2	3	4
3.	1	2	3	4
4.	1	2	3	4
5.	1	2	3	4
6.	1	2	3	4
7.	1	2	3	4
8.	1	2	3	4
9.	1	2	3	4
10.	1	2	3	4

From *Teaching Sport Concepts and Skills: A Tactical Games Approach,* Second Edition, by Stephen A. Mitchell, Judith L. Oslin, and Linda L. Griffin, Champaign, IL: Human Kinetics.

Invasion Game Scenario 1

Solving the Tactical Problem

Attacking the goal (or basket)

Name _____ Date _____

Directions

Observe student's game play and place a tally mark in the appropriate box.

Situation

This is a 2v2 situation in an invasion game such as soccer, team handball, or basketball. Team O is on offense and Team X is on defense. You are player O1 with the ball. How can you and your teammate (O2) work together to beat the defenders on Team X and attack the goal? Try to think of two different ways. Explain what you would do and draw lines on the figure to show what you would do.

1. I could . . .

2. I could . . .

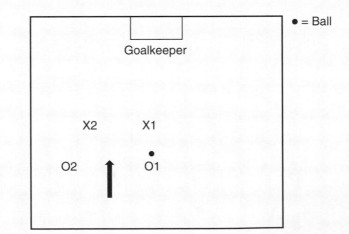

Adapted, by permission, from S.A. Mitchell, J.L. Oslin, and L.L Griffin, 2003, *Sport foundations for elementary physical education: A tactical games approach* (Champaign, IL: Human Kinetics), 162.

From *Teaching Sport Concepts and Skills: A Tactical Games Approach,* Second Edition, by Stephen A. Mitchell, Judith L. Oslin, and Linda L. Griffin, Champaign, IL: Human Kinetics.

Answers to Invasion Game Scenario 1

Answers

1. Player O1 can dribble at and attempt to beat defender X1. After getting around X1, player O1 can attack the goal to shoot.

2. Player O2 can run forward and behind defender X2. While this is happening, player O1 can send a pass between the two defenders so that O2 can move onto the ball, receive the pass, and attack the goal without slowing down (i.e., a lead pass).

Adapted, by permission, from S.A. Mitchell, J.L. Oslin, and L.L. Griffin, 2003, *Sport foundations for elementary physical education: A tactical games approach* (Champaign, IL: Human Kinetics), 162.

From *Teaching Sport Concepts and Skills: A Tactical Games Approach,* Second Edition, by Stephen A. Mitchell, Judith L. Oslin, and Linda L. Griffin, Champaign, IL: Human Kinetics.

Invasion Game Scenario 2

Solving the Tactical Problem

Maintaining possession of the ball

Name _____ Date _____

Situation

This is a 5v5 game. You are on Team O and your team has possession of the ball. You are player O2 with the ball. Your teammates (O1, O3, and O4) are not in very good positions—you cannot pass to them because they are close to or behind players on Team X. Draw arrows on the field to show where your teammates can move to so that you could pass to them and help your team keep the ball so you can attack the goal.

```
            ┌──────┐
            │  GK  │
        ┌───┴──────┴───┐
        │      X       │
        │      O1      │
        │          O3  │
        │         X    │
        │  O4  X       │
    ↑   │              │
        │         X    │
        │         •    │
        │         O2   │
        │              │
        │              │
        │  ┌──────┐    │
        └──┤  GK  ├────┘
           └──────┘
```

• = Ball   GK = Goalkeeper

From *Teaching Sport Concepts and Skills: A Tactical Games Approach,* Second Edition, by Stephen A. Mitchell, Judith L. Oslin, and Linda L. Griffin, Champaign, IL: Human Kinetics.

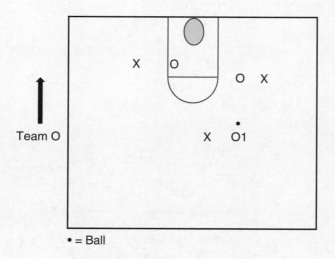

Invasion Game Scenario 3

Solving the Tactical Problem

Defending space

Name _____ Date _____

Situation

This is a 3v3 basketball game situation with Team O on offense. You are on Team X and player O1 on Team O has the ball. Team X is not defending very well! Draw arrows on the court to show where you and your teammates can position yourselves to make it harder for Team O to attack your basket.

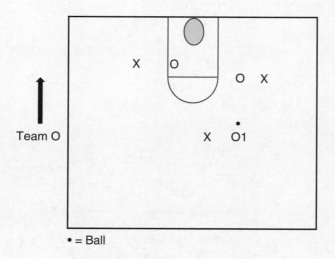

• = Ball

From *Teaching Sport Concepts and Skills: A Tactical Games Approach,* Second Edition, by Stephen A. Mitchell, Judith L. Oslin, and Linda L. Griffin, Champaign, IL: Human Kinetics.

Net/Wall Game Scenario 1

Solving the Tactical Problem

Creating space in your opponent's court

Name _____ Date _____

Situation

This is a diagram of a court for a net game. The lines represent the boundaries of the court and the thick line is the net. In this situation players A and B are playing a net game. You are player B. Player A hits the ball (or shuttle) to you.

1. Place an X where you want to make your next shot land.

2. Explain why you have placed the X in this position.

3. What type of shot would you need to use?

Adapted, by permission, from S.A. Mitchell, J.L. Oslin, and L.L. Griffin, 2003, *Sport foundations for elementary physical education: A tactical games approach* (Champaign, IL: Human Kinetics), 164.

From *Teaching Sport Concepts and Skills: A Tactical Games Approach,* Second Edition, by Stephen A. Mitchell, Judith L. Oslin, and Linda L. Griffin, Champaign, IL: Human Kinetics.

Net/Wall Game Scenario 2

Situation

In the figure displayed, player A is playing a singles game of tennis against player B. During the rally player B hits a ground stroke short to player A. If you are player A, where should you hit the ball to win the point?

Directions

Place an X on the court where you would hit the ball and be prepared to tell why (have students give a verbal or written response).

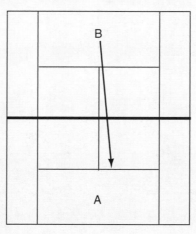

From *Teaching Sport Concepts and Skills: A Tactical Games Approach*, Second Edition, by Stephen A. Mitchell, Judith L. Oslin, and Linda L. Griffin, Champaign, IL: Human Kinetics.

Net/Wall Game Scenario 2 Answer

Answer

By hitting the ball short or crosscourt you give your opponent very little chance to return a volley.

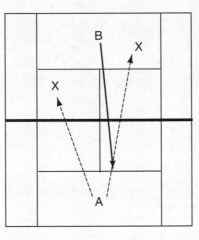

From *Teaching Sport Concepts and Skills: A Tactical Games Approach,* Second Edition, by Stephen A. Mitchell, Judith L. Oslin, and Linda L. Griffin, Champaign, IL: Human Kinetics.

Net/Wall Game Scenario 3

Situation

In the figure displayed, Team ABC is playing Team DEF in a 3v3 volleyball game. During a rally player E sends a free ball over the net to player C. What should player C do with the ball?

Directions

Draw a line to where player C should put the ball and be ready to explain how player C will do this.

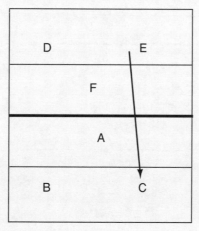

Adapted, by permission, from S.A. Mitchell, J.L. Oslin, and L.L. Griffin, 2003, *Sport foundations for elementary physical education: A tactical games approach* (Champaign, IL: Human Kinetics), 165.

From Teaching Sport Concepts and Skills: A Tactical Games Approach, Second Edition, by Stephen A. Mitchell, Judith L. Oslin, and Linda L. Griffin, Champaign, IL: Human Kinetics.

Net/Wall Game Scenario 3 Answer

Answer

Player C should pass the ball either using a forearm pass or overhead pass (set) to player A so that Team ABC could set up to attack.

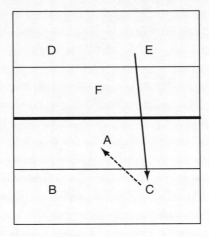

Adapted, by permission, from S.A. Mitchell, J.L. Oslin, and L.L. Griffin, 2003, *Sport foundations for elementary physical education: A tactical games approach* (Champaign, IL: Human Kinetics), 165.

From *Teaching Sport Concepts and Skills: A Tactical Games Approach,* Second Edition, by Stephen A. Mitchell, Judith L. Oslin, and Linda L. Griffin, Champaign, IL: Human Kinetics.

Affective Domain Assessment

Name _____ Date _____

The purpose of this assessment is to keep track of behaviors displayed by students during learning tasks and game play. Whether or not you assign a point value to the categories is your decision. Keep in mind that the games are self-officiated, so there will be opportunities to observe students taking responsibility for their behavior.

Directions

For the following behaviors keep track of a student during the class (you may track different students for a set interval of time). Look for a ratio of acceptable to unacceptable behaviors that you judge as appropriate (e.g., 4:1).

- You may substitute behaviors as you see fit for your class and your expectations.
- You could adapt this assessment sheet into a scale form. Instead of tallying each of the behaviors the extremes listed previously could be part of a 5-point scale. Then total points for students from the scale:

positive behavior identified   5   4   3   2   1   negative behavior identified

Acceptable behaviors		Unacceptable behaviors	
Supports and encourages teammates		Lacks any show of support or encouragement for teammates	
Makes an effort to pass to all members of the team		Looks for only a select few in which to pass the Frisbee	
Follows all calls without argument		Argues or breaks rules repeatedly	
Returns Frisbee to opposing team in respectful manner		Makes getting the Frisbee difficult for the opponents when unnecessary	
Does not taunt or demean anyone on either team		Taunts or demeans teammates or opponents	
Other		Other	
Total		Total	
Ratio: Acceptable Unacceptable			

Adapted, by permission, from V. Melograno, 1996, *Designing the physical education curriculum,* third ed. (Champaign, IL: Human Kinetics), 157.

From *Teaching Sport Concepts and Skills: A Tactical Games Approach,* Second Edition, by Stephen A. Mitchell, Judith L. Oslin, and Linda L. Griffin, Champaign, IL: Human Kinetics.

CHAPTER 17

Getting Started With Tactical Games Teaching

The tactical games approach is grounded in a constructivist learning perspective that recognizes the centrality of the learner to the construction of meaning across the psychomotor, cognitive, and social/personal domains. This approach places students in dynamic game play that requires them to make decisions and reflect upon these decisions through assessment and teacher facilitation. All parts of the process are important and teachers must take care in planning them.

Conceptual Framework for Planning Tactical Teaching

In this section we share a conceptual framework to guide your tactical thinking and planning (Griffin and Sheehy 2004) (see figure 17.1). The primary features of this planning framework include (a) the games classification system, (b) the game or game form focus, (c) the tactical problems and levels of tactical complexity, (d) the game or game form modifications, (e) the questions for teaching, and (f) the problem-solving skills as outcomes. Not only do you need to consider the goals and learning activities for the unit, you also need to think about the length of the unit. If the duration of your unit is short (8-10 lessons), limit the number of tactical problems you address in your unit. Using the tactical problems as the organizing feature for the unit provides you with a clear match between unit length and goals. Limiting the number of tactical problems gives you the opportunity to add depth to your unit, that is, to do a few things well. We advocate establishing a block plan that outlines a progression of learning tasks for each day of your unit. A block plan provides you with a view of the big picture and can help you focus. Table 17.1 provides a sample block plan for volleyball.

Games Classification System

The first feature to consider in your tactical games planning is the games classification system, which is a categorization scheme based on similarities among the primary rules that define games (Bunker and Thorpe 1982). The primary rules of a game identify how the game is to be played (tactics) and how winning can be achieved. Classifying games provides students with a more expansive view of games and helps students identify similarities of

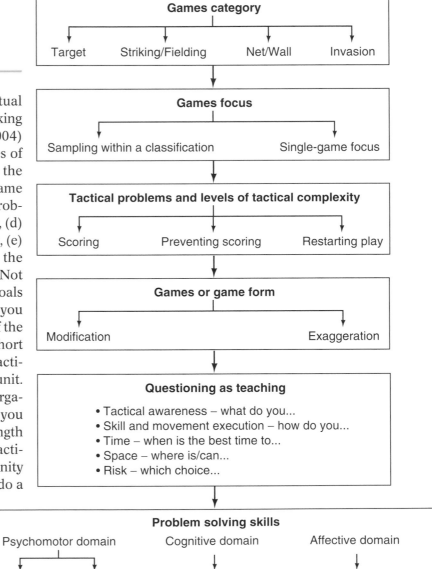

FIGURE 17.1 Conceptual framework for planning your teaching.

Table 17.1 Sample Volleyball Block Plan				
Day 1	**Day 2**	**Day 3**	**Day 4**	**Day 5**

· Introduction to unit
· 3v3 game
  – base position
  – Free ball (toss)
· Closure
	· 3v3 game
	· Setting up to attack
	  – forearm pass (FAP)
	· Practice = FAP
	· 3v3 game
	· Closure
		· 3v3 game
		· Setting up to attack
		  – setter open up
		· Practice = FAP and
		  open up
		· 3v3 game
		· Closure
			· 3v3 game
			· Setting up to attack
			  – setter pass to hitter
			· Practice = open up
			  and pass to hitter
			· 3v3 game
			· Closure
				· 3v3 game
				· Setting up to attack
				  and winning the point
				  – transition by hitter
				· Practice = pass, open
				  up, and transition
				· 3v3 game
				· Closure

Day 6	**Day 7**	**Day 8**	**Day 9**	**Day 10**

· 3v3 game
· Winning the point by
  attacking the ball
· Practice = hitting and
  spiking
· 3v3 game
· Closure
	· 3v3 game
	· Attacking the ball
	  – transition to hit or
	    spike
	· Extend practice
	· 3v3 game
	· Closure
		· 3v3 game
		· Review = setting up
		  to attack and winning
		  the point by attack
		· 3v3 game
		· Closure
			· 3v3 game
			· Review = setting up
			  to attack and winning
			  the point by attack
			· 3v3 game
			· Closure
				3v3 tournament
				· Closure

games that are usually considered quite different in terms of the specialized skills they employ. In using this approach, teachers may explicitly teach students to transfer knowledge they have about one game to another simply because the games are in the same classification. For example, the teacher needs to point out that volleyball is a net/wall game sharing tactical similarities with tennis and badminton.

Game Focus

In the game focus you consider the intent of the unit (e.g., exploring tactical problems across games) and the various games and game forms that you need to design to meet the goals of the lesson or unit. When creating games experiences, the teacher may organize the unit in one of two ways: game sampling or single game.

• **Game sampling.** The purpose of game sampling is to provide students with a variety of experiences that show similarities and differences among games (Holt, Strean, and Bengoechea 2002). The games classification system can facilitate the sampling process by providing a selection of various games with similar tactical problems rather than the traditional selection of teaching one specific sport as a unit topic. For example, a teacher might want students to experience solving the tactical

problems of setting up to attack and winning the point across various net/wall games such as pickleball, badminton, and volleyball. To assist students' ability to transfer their learning from one game to another, the students can encounter and the teacher point out the common tactical elements or problems in each of the three games.

• **Single game.** The purpose of a single-game focus within a unit is to provide students with an in-depth experience of the tactical problems and decision-making options associated with one particular game (e.g., volleyball). Selecting a single game for a unit in which the teacher holds a high level of content knowledge is strongly advocated for first-time users of the tactical games model. Either choice—game sampling or single game—provides a context for teachers to facilitate students' development and effective use of problem-solving skills.

Tactical Problems and Levels of Tactical Complexity

The next feature to think about is the tactical problems and the complexity of the problems you want your students to solve. As you know, central to the tactical games model are the tactical problems presented by various games. Tactical problems are those problems that must be overcome in order to score, prevent scoring, and restart play. Having identified the relevant tactical problems that a game presents, students need to solve these problems by making appropriate decisions and applying appropriate movements and skills. Levels of tactical complexity help teachers match tactical complexity with students' problem-solving development. As students develop an understanding of tactical problems and appropriate solutions, the complexity of the game can be increased; that is, working with levels of tactical complexity affords a way of teaching games in a developmentally appropriate manner.

Game and Game Form

This feature helps you with the design of your games and game forms. Games refer to small-sided competitive challenges where there are the same number of players on each team (e.g., 3v3) while game forms refer to highlighted tactical situations, often encountered during a full version of the game, where there might be an uneven number of players on a team (e.g., 3v2). Tactical problems are emphasized within game forms, thereby allowing students multiple opportunities to problem solve and practice the appropriate tactical response (French and McPherson 2003). Proponents of the tactical games model argue that all students can play a game if that game is modified to enable meaningful play to occur (Ellis 1986; Mitchell, Oslin, and Griffin 2003). This may mean beginning with few skills, few rules, and as few players as possible. Modified games or game forms, however, should be representative of the mature form, and conditioned (i.e., exaggerated by rule changes) to emphasize tactical problems encountered within the game (i.e., changing the secondary rules) (Mitchell, Oslin, and Griffin 2003). The following are five aspects of the game or game form that can help the teacher exaggerate a particular tactical problem.

- *Rules*. Rules define what players can and cannot do in a game. Rules can be changed (i.e., game conditions) to create a specific learning emphasis. For example, in 3v3 volleyball there might be a rule to alternate the serve using a free ball toss. Alternating the serve using a free ball toss makes initiation of the game simple and highly successful and allows both teams an equal chance to receive the serve.

- *Number of players*. Small-sided games or game forms (3v3 or 2v1) slow down the tempo and flow of a game, thus limiting the tactical complexity, which in turn simplifies the decision-making process. They also maximize the potential for every student to be a decision maker within a game or game form.

- *Playing area*. Altering the size of the playing area or changing the size of the goal may help students focus on learning a particular aspect of the game. For example, in a 3v3 volleyball game the court conditions might be a narrow court (e.g., one-half of a regular court) and lower net. Narrowing the court and lowering the net allow the students to focus on a small playing area.

- *Equipment*. Modifying the playing equipment makes the students feel safer, which allows for more successful execution of skills and movements. For example, students are more likely to attempt the forearm pass or dig in a volleyball unit when trainer volleyballs are used.

- *Scoring or modifying the goal*. Scoring allows the game to be shaped to reinforce practice. For example, in a volleyball lesson the final game goal might be to have teams earn points for containing the first pass on their side of the court.

Questioning As Teaching

Questioning is a critical teaching skill used in the tactical games model. Questions help the teacher guide students in identifying solutions to the tactical problem presented in the game. As facilitators, teachers need to know when to use questions and when to provide answers. Literature on tactical games teaching has been consistent in emphasizing the importance of quality questions (Bunker and Thorpe 1982; Den Duyn 1997). The quality of questions is critical to problem solving in a tactical games model and should be an integral part of the planning process. These questions fall into five categories:

- Tactical awareness   "What do you . . ."
- Skill and movement execution   "How do you . . ."
- Time   "When is the best time to . . ."
- Space   "Where is . . ."
- Risk   "Which choice . . ."

Each type of question is not necessarily asked during a single questioning session. The number and types of questions are determined by the teacher and are based on the readiness of the students.

Problem-Solving Skills

The tactical games model is a student-centered model in that the teacher facilitates the learning process. As the facilitator, the teacher sets problems or goals by organizing the game or game form, and students are given an opportunity to solve these problems. One of the basic premises of the tactical games model is that to become good games players students need to become good problem solvers. Students need to be able to define the problem, gather information about the problem, identify the decision-making options, make the decision, and put the decision into action. To do this, students need games experiences to help them develop their problem-solving skills. Through questions, the teacher helps the students explore possible solutions to the problem. These solutions then become the focus of a situated practice. The teacher also facilitates practice by either simplifying the game or introducing more challenging game conditions to meet student abilities. In this way the teacher works with the student's prior knowledge to develop new knowledge.

Putting the Planning Framework Into Action

Having explained the thinking behind the conceptual framework, in this section we will provide an example of the decisions the teacher makes that put the tactical games planning framework into action. Using the conceptual framework (see figure 17.1), let's say a physical education teacher at a middle school decides to further student understanding of net/wall games and chooses a single-game focus on volleyball since the students had completed a net/wall game sampling unit last year. The sampling unit focused on setting up to attack and winning the point in pickleball, table tennis, and volleyball. The teacher knows that the students are novice players and selects scoring as

the main tactical problem and determines the level of tactical complexity to be level I.

Now that the teacher has made decisions on the games category, game focus, tactical problems, levels of tactical complexity, and modifications, the teacher will use questioning as opportunities occur during the first lesson within this volleyball unit. The tactical problem for the first lesson is setting up to attack, with a lesson focus on base position and containing the ball on your side of the net. The 50-minute lesson begins with students involved in 3v3 games, each game played on half a court (a total of 12 students per court), with the goal of attempting to contain the first pass on their team's side of the court. The conditions of the game include a narrow court with a lower net. The game initiated from a playable, two-handed, overhead toss (free ball); an alternate free ball toss rotation after each rally; and up to three hits on a side. As the students play, the teacher observes.

After a short game of approximately 7 minutes, the games break down (meaning that students cannot direct consistent passes to the middle, the ball doesn't go over the net, and so on). At that point, the teacher begins to ask students questions with the purpose of encouraging self-directed, reflective analysis of their game play. The following is a representation of a typical exchange, designed to foreground problem-solving skills within the cognitive domain:

- Teacher: What did you do to contain the ball on your side of the net? (tactical awareness)

  Students: Hit the ball high.

- Teacher: Where would be the best place to pass the ball? (space)

  Students: The middle of the court.

- Teacher: How did you hit the ball to keep control? (skill selection and execution)

  Students: I used my hands (overhead pass) or bumped it using my forearms (forearm pass).

As illustrated, through the questioning process the students verbally identify issues related to solving the tactical problem of containing the first pass. Now that the students have identified these solutions there is a need to situate students in practice that rewards and reinforces good decision making, not just good skill execution (French and McPherson 2003). Further, when the skill is placed within the game context, the importance of being able to execute it consistently is highlighted, thereby increasing the focus of the students during practice.

At this point students return to their playing courts and practice in a triad formation with one tosser, one passer, and one setter. From the location on the court that simulates actual game play, the tosser sends a rainbow toss to the passer, who uses a forearm pass to direct the ball to the setter. The setter then catches the ball and bounce passes it back to the tosser. After three trials, the students switch roles, allowing each student to practice each of the roles during the majority of the class time. During practice the teacher circulates and asks students what they are thinking. Just asking questions can focus attention toward thinking about tactics (French and McPherson 2003). The lesson then ends with a 3v3 game using the same conditions as the initial game; however, the goal is now that a team earns a point (i.e., change in secondary rule) when they attempt a forearm pass as a way to contain the ball on their side of the court.

Skills and Attitudes for Teacher Change

In this section we present four skills and attitudes Joyce and Showers (1995) have identified that facilitate your learning potential as teacher. These are: putting your learning into action, persistence, meeting the cognitive demands of instruction, and flexibility.

Putting Learning into Action

You have probably attended many classes, conferences, and workshops and read books that have motivated you to consider change. But how do you turn your motivation into action? In other words, how do you make the transfer? Transfer is the ability to convey something you have learned from one situation to another. In this section we look at the phases of transfer every teacher goes through to make a new learning structure truly her own. Making changes is never easy and seeing the phases of transfer shows you that the difficulties are a normal part of the change process. As teachers, we vary in our ability to transfer a new teaching approach to our setting. You may want to consider these phases of transfer on a continuum. The notion of a continuum provides you with a way of thinking about struggles or discomfort you may have with new knowledge (Joyce and Showers 1995). For example, you may be uncomfortable beginning your lessons with a game (e.g., 3v3 in volleyball) because you have always begun your lessons with an exercise or skill warm-up. We invite you to consider where on the continuum in figure 17.2 you might be after reading this chapter, and we suggest that you return to it occasionally to see how you are progressing.

- *Imitative transfer* is an exact replication of skills, knowledge, or ideas. For example, you may use exact questions, games, or practice tasks from the lessons in the earlier part of the textbook. You may also attend a teacher-development workshop and use the exact drills or games as they were presented at the workshop.

- *Mechanical transfer* is horizontal transfer in the basic structure of lessons. For example, you start to change the format of your lesson by beginning the lesson with a game, such as playing 3v3 in a volleyball unit.

- *Routine transfer* is using skills and strategies at this stage with ease and comfort but not carrying them over throughout the curriculum. For example, you may choose to implement a tactical approach for teaching invasion games (e.g., soccer, team handball, and basketball) but not net games (e.g., tennis and badminton).

- *Integrative transfer* is taking the approach across subject areas. This means that you begin

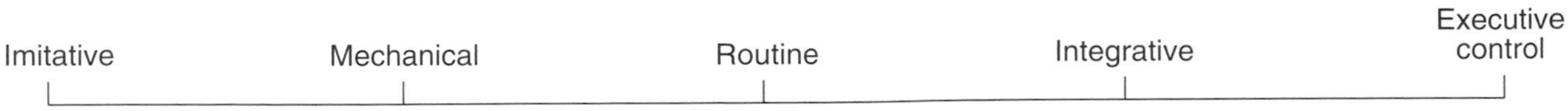

Imitative	Mechanical	Routine	Integrative	Executive control

FIGURE 17.2   Where on the continuum do you fall in your ability to transfer a new teaching approach to your classroom setting?

to view other teaching environments through this approach. Perhaps you teach health or coach a varsity sport and implement principles of the approach in that situation.

• *Executive control* happens when you are grounded in the theory and can select and implement materials appropriately and comfortably throughout the curriculum. You are able to make decisions and problem solve because you understand the principles. In other words you are in charge of the material and have completely made it yours.

We are not suggesting that transfer is a clean, clear, linear process. You may find yourself jumping along the entire continuum throughout one unit or even one lesson! Remember, change is a process, not an event. We encourage you to work toward executive control.

Persistence

Persistence is what Joyce and Showers (1995) call "driving through" the initial trials in which performance is awkward. For example, as a player you know how hard it is to change your golf swing or your tennis backhand. Think about how hard it is as a teacher to give up using calisthenics as warm-ups or to use a game *before* skill practice. The key to success often is pure determination (not necessarily talent); this will go a long way in overcoming the difficulty of changing behavior.

During a project that focused on learning to teach using a tactical approach, Danielle, a middle school physical education teacher, provided an example of persistence when we asked her how she felt about using a new approach with sixth graders. Danielle answered, "When you have taught one way and you are in the pressure of the moment, you have to work hard not to go back to your old way."

Meeting the Cognitive Demands of Instruction

Teachers have complained that their preservice program has overemphasized theory and neglected the practical aspects of teaching (Joyce and Showers 1995). Nonetheless, teachers who acknowledge the importance of understanding theory can better meet the cognitive demands

of instruction. When you know what to do and how to do it, you can be flexible and use the new knowledge appropriately in many situations.

Flexibility

Flexibility is the openness to consider that alternatives have something to offer. Being flexible is important in all aspects of teaching, and it can also serve you well when you participate in the teacher-as-learner process. For example, a teacher who has always used a technical approach to games teaching starts his volleyball unit by teaching the forearm pass and setting students up to practice this skill. Generally his role is that of *information giver* (direct instruction). Now this teacher shifts to implementing a tactical approach in the volleyball unit. He places students in small-sided games and, after game play, gathers them for discussion, using his questions to address the value of setting up to attack using the forearm pass. The teacher's role now shifts from information giver to *information processor* (indirect instruction). This role shift will require the teacher to be flexible.

Implementing Practices

We have developed implementing practices from our teacher-development efforts. These practices will help create a safe learning-by-doing climate (Stallings 1989):

• Examine your core beliefs.

• Change for you also means change for your students.

• Pick your favorite sport.

• Think *gamelike.*

• Lessons should reflect a game-questions-practice-game progression.

• Plan a unit.

• Find company.

Let's discuss each of these practices in detail.

• **Examine your core beliefs.** Beliefs are highly resistant to change and serve as a filter through which our experiences must pass (Lortie 1975; Pajares 1992). Beliefs help individuals understand their world and persevere even when contradictory evidence is presented (Nisbett and Ross 1980; Peterman 1991). Core beliefs form the center of a belief system. They are the most powerful beliefs and exert a strong influence over other beliefs. Core beliefs are also the most resistant to change because they become part of us at an early stage (Nisbett and Ross 1980; Rokeach 1968). Any significant innovation, if it is to result in change, requires individual implementers to work out their personal meanings (Fullan 1991).

We offer a games teaching continuum as a way of thinking about your core beliefs on games teaching (see figure 17.3).

On the left is the technical approach, on the right is a tactical games approach, and in the middle is a progression we refer to as a gamelike approach. A gamelike approach shifts practice from isolated technical drills (e.g., shuttle or circle drills in volleyball focused on one skill) to drills arranged within the tempo and flow of the game (e.g., triad drill in volleyball).

The games teaching continuum acts as a gauge to give you a reading of where you are and offer possible progressions for moving your games teaching toward a tactical approach. One teacher from our workshops and research shares her change in her core beliefs (Berkowitz 1996):

> I have always been concerned about the development of my students' skills. When first beginning to teach physical education, and up until a few years ago, I taught technical skills in isolation; detached from the game or activity, such as, forearm passing to oneself or set to the wall . . . Realizing that I made very little impact on the level of skill improvement in my students has caused me to reconsider my philosophical perspective. I no longer expect my students to demonstrate a specified level of skill proficiency. Rather, the expectation is utilization of various skills to accomplish the tactics within the game (page 44).

- **Change for you also means change for your students.** Part of the difficulty in introducing a new teaching process into the classroom is students' discomfort with change (Joyce and Showers 1995). Trying a new teaching approach for you is trying a new learning approach for your students, so it is change for all of you. We advocate starting with *one* class of your choice, giving a high priority to groups that can work together (Griffin 1996). Because the primary structure of a tactical approach is the small-sided game or game form, you need to feel comfortable teaching many small groups or pairs (Berkowitz 1996). By choosing one class, you have begun to build a safe environment to explore an alternative approach to games teaching and learning.

- **Pick your favorite sport.** Select the game you feel most comfortable with, which for us translates into a strong content knowledge. This strategy provides a way of linking prior knowledge to new information (Stallings 1989). We have had firsthand experience with this, and we have also observed and collaborated with preservice and inservice teachers as they grapple with a tactical games approach. For us and those teachers, strong content knowledge made transfer easier. For example, one teacher chose volleyball because she had played competitively at the college level and coached at the high school level. She felt this was her strongest sport, so it was a fit because she was able to break the game down into smaller tactical parts such as setting up for a pass-set-hit, receiving a serve, or defending against a free ball.

- **Think gamelike.** Thinking gamelike means considering how you can arrange the skills and tactics for practice within the flow and tempo of the game (Griffin 1996). For example, gamelike practice for volleyball is a triad formation. Figure 17.4 illustrates the triad with a focus on forearm passing. The triad formation involves a minimum of three players fulfilling three roles described as initiator, performer, and target player within each drill (Griffin 1994). If you have more than three players in the drill you can add roles such as collector, feeder, or an additional performer. Triad drills, such as toss and pass to target, serve and serve receive to target,

Technical	Gamelike	Tactical

FIGURE 17.3 Games teaching continuum.

toss-set-hit, pass-set-hit, or any other skill or tactical combinations of the game, simulate the tempo and flow of volleyball. Gamelike drills enhance the quality of practice.

Thinking gamelike increases the likelihood of carryover into the game. Consider drills such as practicing a volleyball skill against the wall, partners passing back and forth without the net, using a circle or semicircle to practice skills, and using a shuttle formation to practice skills. These drills provide many opportunities to practice but clearly have nothing to do with the flow and tempo of a volleyball game. Gamelike practice allows students to develop skills within the context of the game. It also promotes a cooperative learning environment.

- **Make your lessons reflect a game-questions-practice-game cycle.** Let us take a closer look at the lesson-plan format used in this book.

  - *Tactical problem (what you say to your students).* The tactical problem is the big picture feature that guides each specific lesson plan. The tactical problem is what you say to the student when you start your lesson. For example, "Today we will be working on solving the problem of setting up to attack in volleyball."

  - *Lesson focus (what you ask your students).* The lesson focus relates to the on-the-ball skills and off-the-ball movements you want your students to become aware of to solve a tactical problem. The lesson focus guides your questions. For example, if you want your students to understand the value of calling for the ball in volleyball, then your questions should reflect that lesson focus, such as, "What should you do if two teammates are close to the ball?" or "When is the best time to call for the ball?" The questions should align with the focus of the lesson.

  - *Objective (what your students practice).* The objective should help you design your practice. For example, if the objective is for the students to call for the ball ("mine"), then you should arrange a practice in which two players who are near each other work out who calls and when to call for the ball.

  - *Initial game.* First, game conditions refer to the essential components, such as number of students, size of the court or playing area, equipment type (i.e., regulation or modified ball) and modifications (i.e., net height), and specific conditions (i.e., two hits on a side, three passes before a shot).

Second, the goal of the game will directly reflect the focus of the lesson. We continue with the volleyball example in which students are engaged in a small-sided volleyball game. Game conditions are lower net, narrow and short court, modified volleyball, game initiated from a free ball, alternating toss, and rotation after each point. The goal of the game is for teams to score a point each time the pass goes to the setter.

- *Questions.* We have learned that constructing questions presents some difficulty at first. Three key aspects to questioning are (1) limiting the number of questions to two or three, (2) working with (incorporating) students' answers, and (3) aligning questions with the lesson focus. We offer these question stems to help guide you:

  What do you . . . ? (Tactical awareness)

  How do you . . .? (Skill selection and execution)

  When is the best time to . . .? (Timing)

  Where is or can . . . ? (Space)

  Which choice . . .? (Risk)

- *Practice task.* Essential elements for quality practice involve (a) running drills on the field or court because this is where games are played, (b) organizing gamelike practices to match the game-playing goal, (c) using specific feedback

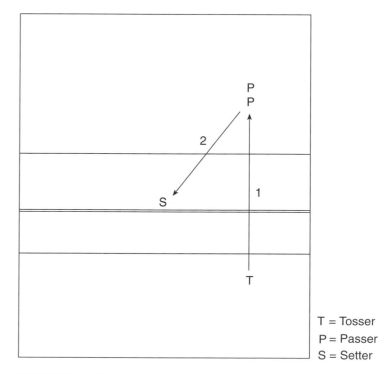

T = Tosser
P = Passer
S = Setter

FIGURE 17.4 Focus on forearm passing in a triad.

related to key words, (d) providing goals for practice, and (e) keeping activity compatible with skill levels of players. Going back to the volleyball lesson, students would practice the forearm pass in triads (see chapter 8, level I, lesson 1 for details).

- *Closing game.* The purpose of the closing game is to reinforce the focus or goal of your lesson and to allow application of practiced skills. The conditions of the game reflect all the essential game components. This game may or may not be different from the initial game you have read about in the specific sport chapters. You can consider it a way of reinforcing the goal of the lesson, perhaps by having students keep track of the number of shots taken in basketball games or number of passes completed in soccer. To finish the volleyball example, students return to the original game and the original conditions to reinforce the lesson goal. Students could compare the scores of the initial game to the closing game or count the number of successful forearm passes to target.

- **Plan a unit.** Consider how you might plan a whole unit. First, consider your goals or objectives. Ask yourself what tactical problems you want your students to solve. Here you have two choices: consult our levels of tactical complexity or use the tactical problems to organize your unit and develop your own levels. For example, if you are getting ready to teach a volleyball unit, you might focus only on the tactical problems of setting up to attack and winning the point. After you have decided on tactical problems, you can consult the levels of tactical complexity to establish the on-the-ball skills and off-the-ball movements appropriate for your students' level.

- **Find company.** We encourage you to learn in a supportive environment, that is, make productive use of peers. Research on teacher development (Joyce and Showers 1995) has documented the benefits of peers helping peers, meaning teachers helping teachers, implement innovations. You can then share problems and successes. A collaborative community can give you an opportunity for reflection and problem solving (Stallings 1989).

A specific strategy for making productive use of peers is the notion of the *coaching of teaching.* Follow up with help from each other as you imple-

ment a new teaching process, such as a tactical approach. Peer coaching uses a support community (cohort groups) with feedback procedures to improve or change classroom practice and is not tied to evaluation (Joyce and Showers 1995). Specific outcomes or educational benefits of peer coaching have indicated that coached teachers practice more, develop more skills, use new strategies more appropriately, have greater long-term retention of skills, are more likely to teach students new skills, and recognize purposes and uses of new skills (Showers 1982, 1984, 1985).

The possible benefits of teachers helping each other are endless. Knowing whom to approach, what to ask them for help with, and being sensitive to individual teachers' needs will go a long way in building a strong professional culture. Teachers need to have others to share successes with and to support each other in taking risks.

Reflections and Conclusions

A tactical games approach with an emphasis on authentic performance promotes an active, in-depth learning setting for students. An underlying goal of the tactical games approach is to appeal to students' interest in games playing so that they value the need to work toward improved game performance.

We believe that a tactical games approach enables students to understand games more deeply than a technical approach, to play more effectively, and to appreciate the similarities among games. Again, a teacher reflects on her feelings about implementing a tactical approach (Berkowitz 1996):

> There have been a number of positive outcomes using this approach. If my goal was to have students play the game more effectively, then letting them play the game was critical. Because my students have had increasingly more opportunities to play games and solve tactical problems, they seem to have a better understanding of games in general. Technical skill work still occurs but never in isolation, always as it would in the game and mostly as a means to accomplish the tactical problems. Students come in excited, positive, and ready to go because they know they are going to get to play a game of some form. I no longer hear, "Are we going to play a game today?" (45)

A tactical approach can provide students of all developmental levels with a greater understanding of games and improved game performance. Tactical awareness is a developmentally appropriate focus for teaching games (Mitchell, Griffin, and Oslin 1994). This approach also focuses on developmentally appropriate skill acquisition and ensures that students learn skills when they appreciate their value to the game. Students then practice these skills under conditions that enable them to relate the skills to game context. The process of teaching for tactical awareness is based on *playing the game*, an enjoyable activity for most students. Physical education programs promote lifetime participation in physical activity as a primary goal. Nevertheless, this goal will only be achieved if individuals experience enjoyment in physical activity. The identification and assessment of outcomes based on tactical awareness can contribute to progressive gains in game performance, critical thinking, and enjoyment at successive stages of development. We leave you with the challenge of matching content such as soccer, volleyball, and softball with a context that helps students make meaning—through playing games!

CHAPTER 18

Final Thoughts

In this final chapter we share our collective thoughts about tactical games teaching and its curriculum potential. These thoughts accumulated during the writing of this and our previous books and during the 20 years in which we individually and collaboratively applied our learning.

- **Collaboration makes life much easier.** In chapter 17, we suggest finding company when getting started with tactical games teaching. Collaboration is critical so that ideas, goals, materials, and frustrations can be shared. We learned the value of collaboration through sharing our work since 1992, and the ability to bounce ideas around has no doubt helped us develop our own understanding of tactical games. The international community of scholars interested in tactical games teaching has also recognized the importance of collaboration with its biannual conference on Teaching Games for Understanding. Conferences have been held in the United States (2001), in Melbourne, Australia (2003), and in Hong Kong (2005).

- **The name does not matter.** The original conception of tactical games teaching was developed by David Bunker and Rod Thorpe at Loughborough University in England. They called it Teaching Games for Understanding (TGFU) and presented it as a model for teaching decision making in secondary physical education. Since the early 1980s, the model has been viewed in different ways and various names have emerged. We initially saw it as a tactical approach to games teaching, and hence our use of "tactical games approach." We later saw, and hopefully developed the potential for, the use of tactical games in K-12 physical education. We also saw the tactical approach as a way of organizing games content within the curriculum—we saw it as a curriculum model, and hence our use of "tactical games model." Other names include "game sense" and "game-centered games." Regardless of nomenclature, scholars and practitioners interested in authentic approaches to games teaching within physical education have collaborated to develop a model that places the learner in problem-solving situations where decision making is of critical importance and where skill development occurs within its context. Therefore, the name does not matter.

- **It isn't rocket science.** Some teachers and many preservice teachers like to overcomplicate things! We have often witnessed our own preservice teachers develop complex game conditions and modifications, use numerous and sometimes unnecessary questions, and then wonder why their students switched off or did not get it. As a middle school student once said, "So we play a game, figure out what we need to do, practice it, then play again to see if we can do it. Right?" Right!

- **It doesn't take a games expert.** One school of thought is that you have to be a games expert to experience success with tactical games teaching. This view is one reason why tactical games approaches have been slow to take hold in physical education in grades K through 12. When told that expertise is needed, the nonexpert tends to avoid the challenge of tactical teaching and to stick with traditional skill-based teaching as a safer option. Remember the principle of transfer, which we have argued applies to you as teachers just as much as it applies to students. Having expertise in a broad range of games would no doubt comfort you in taking a new approach to games teaching, but not having expertise should not discourage you. In saying this, we also recognize that there are good physical educators who come from a specific background such as aquatics, gymnastics, dance, or track and field. If your range of expertise is narrow and you do not have extensive games knowledge, be prepared to learn one game from each tactical category and apply the principles of instruction for that game across others within the category. Reread chapter 3 to reassure yourself of your ability to transfer understanding. In fact, one might argue that being an expert hurts you because you develop strong beliefs about how a game should be taught. The key to tactical games teaching is to understand the model. Further, perhaps your comfort level is as much a result of what you value as it is what you know. If you value the game (and the problem-solving challenges it brings) as the essence of teaching, then tactical games teaching is more likely to make sense. However, if your focus remains on discrete skills you will have more difficulty getting it.

- **All students can play games.** We modify games so that students will believe that they can indeed play a game with some success. Beginning with the game counters the old argument that students must learn the skills before they can play the game. When we hear this argument, the proponent is inevitably referring to the full game. If we were to stick faithfully to the opinion that students must learn the skills before they can play the game, then some of the students would never play. Consider tennis and volleyball, perhaps the two most difficult games to learn in terms of their skill requirements. Unless the ball can be kept in play and sent in the necessary direction, a game cannot be played. It is no wonder that when novices play volleyball and tennis, points rarely last more that one or two hits. However, by appropriately modifying equipment, playing areas, and team sizes (in the case of volleyball), these games, and indeed all games, can be made playable by students of all abilities. Making the game playable is critical from a motivational standpoint since repeated failure only discourages students. Once the game is playable, skill development and refinement can continue.

• **It's not just about playing the game.** One of the greatest misconceptions about the tactical games model is that students "just play a game." It is not just "play," which would be spontaneous; rather, it is the game (and its required tactics and skills) that sets the learning activities for each lesson or unit. The learning activities range from the type of games to the type of questions to the type of practice tasks. All of these learning activities lead to solving the various tactical problems of games and thus they improve decision making. In sum, the initial modified game sets the problem, the skill focus provides solutions to the problem, and the closing game applies the solutions to their game context.

• **Competition is not a bad word.** When we teach games, competition becomes a natural part of the instructional context. Rather than avoid competition, we believe it is better to address issues that arise from heated competitions and student perceptions about sporting behavior acquired from popular media. Rather than waiting until tempers flair or trash talking begins, integrate con-

tent related to teamwork and appropriate social behavior before, during, and following competitive events. Address other social issues such as equity, inclusion of all players, and the values of lifelong participation. Sport can build character, but only by deliberately emphasizing appropriate sporting behavior can we increase sport's potential to build positive character.

• **Students respond when they are empowered.** Tactical games teaching places students at its center by making them responsible for running games and asking them to find solutions to problems posed by game situations. These responsibilities empower students to guide their learning, and in our experience students respond well when we require input from them. Empowering students also involves the teacher relinquishing some control, which may feel uncomfortable for some of you, but again, we have found that our students are able to assume responsibilities that are presented to them in a structured fashion.

• **Teaching and coaching have much in common.** Many of you are skilled tactical games teachers but do not know it. This is particularly true of those of you who coach. The game play emphasized in tactical games teaching lends itself to commonly used coaching strategies in which game play is frozen and situational responses are critiqued, reconstructed, and rehearsed in order to improve problem solving within the game. These behaviors make teaching and coaching interchangeable in games teaching. As a teacher in one of our early workshops said, "I do this all the time when I coach. I just never thought about doing it in a physical education class."

That you may unknowingly already be a skilled tactical games teacher is an encouraging note on which to close. Take what you already know, apply it as broadly as you can, and supplement it with available resources (including this book), and you will experience success in a motivational and engaging approach to the games curriculum. Good luck!

References

Almond, L. 1986. Reflecting on themes: A games classification. In *Rethinking games teaching,* ed. R. Thorpe, D. Bunker, and L. Almond, 71-72. Loughborough, England: University of Technology.

Australian Cricket Board. 2002. *Coaching youth cricket.* Champaign, IL: Human Kinetics.

Beard, C.H. 1993. Transfer of computer skills from introductory computer courses. *Journal of Research in Computing in Education* 25:413-430.

Benson, N.J. 1970. Training and transfer-of-learning effects in disabled and normal readers: Evidence of specific deficits. *Journal of Experimental Child Psychology* 64:343-366.

Berkowitz, R.J. 1996. A practitioner's journey from skill to tactics. *Journal of Physical Education, Recreation and Dance* 67 (4): 44-45.

Berman, R. 1994. Learners' transfer of writing skills between languages. *TESL Canada Journal* 12:29-46.

Black, P., C. Harrison, C. Lee, B. Marshall, B, and D. Wiliam. 2004. Working inside the black box: Assessment for learning in the classroom. *Phi Delta Kappan, 86*(1): 9-21.

Blythe, T., and Associates. 1998. *The teaching for understanding guide.* San Fransisco, CA: Jossey-Bass.

Booth, K. 1983. An introduction to netball. *Bulletin of Physical Education* 19 (1): 27-31.

Bowling Index. 1995. *Instruction: Tips from Bob Strickland.* Retrieved January 19, 2005, from http://www.bowlingindex.com/instruction/instruction.htm.

Bunker, D., and R. Thorpe. 1982. A model for the teaching of games in secondary schools. *Bulletin of Physical Education* 18 (1): 5-8.

Bunker, D., and R. Thorpe. 1986. Is there a need to reflect on our games teaching? In *Rethinking games teaching,* ed. R. Thorpe, D. Bunker, and L. Almond: 25-34. Loughborough, England: University of Technology.

Burrows, L. 1986. A teacher's reactions. In *Rethinking games teaching,* ed. R. Thorpe, D. Bunker, and L. Almond: 45-52. Loughborough, England: University of Technology.

Clement, J. 1993. Using bridging analogies and anchoring intuitions to deal with students' perceptions in physics. *Journal of Research in Science Teaching* 30:1241-1257.

Cohen, E.G. 1994. Restructuring in the classroom: Conditions for productive small groups. *Review of Educational Research, 64,* 1-35.

Cohen, S.A. 1987. Instructional alignment: Searching for the magic bullet. *Educational Researcher* 16 (8): 16-20.

Collier, C. 2005. Integrating tactical games and sport education models. In L. Griffin and J. Butler (Eds). *Teaching Games for Understanding: Theory, research and practice.* Champaign, IL: Human Kinetics.

Dan Ota, K., and J.N. Vickers. 1998. The effects of variable practice on the retention and transfer of two volleyball skills in male club-level athletes. *Journal of Sport and Exercise Psychology, NASPSA Abstracts* Suppl. no. 20: S121.

Den Duyn, N. 1997. *Game sense: Developing thinking players.* Belconnen, ASC: Australian Sports Commission.

Dodds, P., L.L. Griffin, and J.H. Placek. 2001. A selected review of the literature on development of learners' domain-specific knowledge. *Journal of Teaching in Physical Education* 20:301-313.

Doolittle, S., and K. Girard. 1991. A dynamic approach to teaching games in elementary PE. *Journal of Physical Education, Recreation and Dance* 62 (4): 57-62.

Dyson, B. 2005. Integrating Cooperative Learning and Tactical Games Models: Focusing on social interactions and decision-making. In Griffin, L. L., and Butler, J. I. (Eds.), *Teaching Games for Understanding: Theory, research and practice.* Champaign, IL: Human Kinetics.

Ellis, M. 1986. Making and shaping games. In *Rethinking games teaching,* ed. R. Thorpe, D. Bunker, and L. Almond, 61-65. Loughborough, England: University of Technology.

French, K.E., and J.R. Thomas. 1987. The relation of knowledge development to children's basketball performance. *Journal of Sport Psychology* 9:15-32.

French, K.E., and S.L. McPherson. 2003. Development of expertise. In *Developmental sport and exercise psychology: A lifespan perspective,* ed. M. Weiss and L. Bunker: 403-424. Champaign, IL: Human Kinetics.

French, K., P. Werner, J. Rink, K. Taylor, and K. Hussey. 1996. The effects of a 3-week unit of tactical, skill, or combined tactical and skill instruction on badminton performance of ninth-grade students. *Journal of Teaching in Physical Education* 15:418-438.

Fullan, M.G. 1991. *The new meaning of educational change.* 2nd ed. New York: Teachers College Press.

Grehaigne, J-F, J-F Richard, and L. L. Griffin. 2005. *Teaching and learning team sports and games.* NY: Routlege Falmer.

Grehaigne, J-F, P. Godbout, and D. Bouthier. 1997. Performance in team sports. *Journal of Teaching in Physical Education* 16: 500-516.

Griffin, L. 1994. Designing drills to make practice more perfect. *Strategies* 8 (3): 19-22.

Griffin, L. 1996. Improving games playing: Teaching net/wall games for understanding. *Journal of Physical Education, Recreation and Dance* 67 (3): 34-37.

Griffin, L., and J.H. Placek. 2001. The understanding and development of learners' domain-specific knowledge [Monograph]. *Journal of Teaching in Physical Education* 20: 299-419.

Griffin, L., J. Oslin, and S. Mitchell. 1995. Two instructional approaches to teaching net games. *Research Quarterly for Exercise and Sport* Suppl. no. 66 (1): 65- 66.

Griffin, L.L and D. Sheehy. 2004. Using a tactical games model to teach problem solving in physical education. In J. Wright, D. MacDonald, and L. Burrows (Eds). *Critical inquiry and problem solving in physical education: Working with students in schools*. London: Routledge.

Griffin, L.L. and J.L. Oslin, 1990. Got a minute: A quick and easy strategy for knowledge testing in physical education. *Strategies: A Journal for Physical and Sport Educators,* 4(2): 6-7, 23.

Griffin, L.L., P. Dodds, and A. James. 1999. *Game performance assessment in 5th/6th grade tactical badminton curriculum unit.* Paper presented at the annual meeting of the Association Internationale des Escles Superieures d'Education Physique World Sport Science Congress, Besancon, France.

Griffin, L.L., S.A. Mitchell, and J.L. Oslin. 1997. *Teaching sport concepts and skills: A tactical games approach.* Champaign, IL: Human Kinetics.

Harvey, L., and J. Anderson. 1996. Transfer of declarative knowledge in complex information-processing domains. *Human-Computer Interaction* 11:69-96.

Hellison, D. 1996. Teaching personal and social responsibility in physical education. In *Student learning in physical education: Applying research to enhance,* ed. S.J. Silverman and C.D. Ennis, 269-286. Champaign, IL: Human Kinetics.

Holt, N.L., W.B Strean, and E.G. Bengoechea. 2002. Expanding the teaching games for understanding model: New avenues for future research and practice. *Journal of Teaching in Physical Education* 21:162-176.

Hopple, C. 1995. *Teaching for outcomes in elementary physical education: A Guide for curriculum and assessment.* Champaign, IL: Human Kinetics.

James, A., L.L. Griffin, and T. France. 2000. Students', teachers', parents', and a principal's perceptions of assessment in elementary physical education. *Research Quarterly for Exercise and Sport* Suppl. no. 71: 73.

Johnson, D. W., and R. T Johnson. 1989. *Cooperation and competition: Theory and research.* Edina, MN: Interaction Book.

Jones, D. 1982. Teaching for understanding in tennis. *Bulletin of Physical Education* 18 (1): 29-31.

Joyce, B., and B. Showers. 1995. *Student achievement through staff development.* White Plains, NY: Longman.

Kirk, D. (2005). Future prospects for Teaching Games for Understanding. In L. Griffin and J. Butler (Eds). *Teaching Games for Understanding: Theory, research and practice.* Champaign, IL: Human Kinetics.

Know the Game Indoor Cricket 1989. London, England: A and C Black.

Lortie, D.C. 1975. *Schoolteacher: A sociological study.* Chicago: University of Chicago Press.

Magill, R.A. 1993. *Motor learning: Concepts and applications.* Madison, WI: Brown and Benchmark.

Martin, R.J. 2004. *An investigation of tactical transfer in invasion games.* Poster presented at the annual convention of the American Alliance for Health, Physical Education, Recreation and Dance, New Orleans, LA.

McAloon, N.M. 1994. Connections (from the teacher's desk). *Journal of Reading* 37: 698-699.

McPherson, S.L. 1994. The development of sport expertise: Mapping the tactical domain. *Quest* 46: 223-240.

McPherson, S.L. 1995. *Expertise in women's collegiate tennis: Development of knowledge and skill.* Paper presented at the annual conference of the North American Society for the Psychology of Sport and Physical Activity, Monterey, CA.

Melograno, V. 1996. *Designing the physical education curriculum.* 3rd ed. Champaign, IL: Human Kinetics.

Metzler, M.W. 2000. *Instructional models for physical education.* Boston: Allyn and Bacon.

Mitchell, S.A., and J.L. Oslin. 1999a. *Assessment series K-12 physical education series: Assessment in games teaching.* Reston, VA: National Association of Sport and Physical Education.

Mitchell, S.A., and J.L. Oslin. 1999b. An investigation of tactical understanding in net games. *European Journal of Physical Education* 4:162-172.

Mitchell, S.A., J.L. Oslin, and L.L. Griffin. 2003. *Sport foundations for elementary physical education: A tactical games approach.* Champaign, IL: Human Kinetics.

Mitchell, S.A., J.L. Oslin, and L. Griffin. 1995. The effects of two instructional approaches on game performance. *Pedagogy in Practice: Teaching and Coaching in Physical Education and Sport* 1:36-48.

Mitchell, S.A., L.L. Oslin, and J.L. Oslin. 1994. Tactical awareness as a developmentally appropriate focus for the teaching of games in elementary and secondary physical education. *The Physical Educator* 51 (1): 21-28.

Mohnsen, B. 1997. *Teaching middle school physical education: A blueprint for developing an exemplary program.* Champaign, IL: Human Kinetics.

National Association of Sport and Physical Education. 2004. *Moving into the future: National standards for physical education.* Reston, VA: National Association of Sport and Physical Education.

Nevitt, M., I. Rovegno, and M. Babiarz. 2001. Fourth-grade children's knowledge of cutting, passing and tactics in invasion games after a 12-lesson unit of instruction. *Journal of Teaching in Physical Education* 20: 389-401.

Nisbett, R.E., and L. Ross. 1980. *Human inference: Strategies and shortcomings in social judgment.* Englewood Cliffs, NJ: Prentice Hall.

Oslin, J. 2005. The role of assessment in teaching games for understanding. In *Teaching games for understanding: Theory, research and practice,* ed. L. Griffin and J. Butler, 125-135. Champaign, IL: Human Kinetics.

Oslin, J.L. 2004. Developing motor and tactical skills in K-2 physical education: Let the games begin. *Teaching Elementary Physical Education,* 15(3), 12-15.

Oslin, J., C. Collier, and S. Mitchell. 2001. Living the curriculum. *Journal of Physical Education, Recreation, and Dance* 72 (5): 47-51.

Oslin, J.L., S.A. Mitchell, and L.L. Griffin. 1998. The Game Performance Assessment Instrument (GPAI): Development and preliminary validation. *Journal of Teaching in Physical Education* 17:231-243.

Pajares, M.F. 1992. Teachers' beliefs and educational research: Cleaning up a messy construct. *Research of Educational Review* 62:307-332.

Peterman, F.P. 1991. An experienced teacher's emerging constructivist beliefs about teaching and learning. Paper presented at the annual meeting of the American Educational Research Association, Chicago, IL.

Pigott, B. 1982. A psychological basis for new trends in games teaching. *Bulletin of Physical Education* 18 (1): 17-22.

Rokeach, M. 1968. *Beliefs, attitudes, and values: A theory of organizational change.* San Francisco: Jossey-Bass.

Showers, B. 1982. *Transfer of training: The contribution of coaching.* Eugene, OR: Center for Educational Policy and Management.

Showers, B. 1984. *Peer coaching: A strategy for facilitating transfer of training.* Eugene, OR: Center for Educational Policy and Management.

Showers, B. 1985. Teachers coaching teachers. *Educational Leadership* 42 (7): 43-49.

Siedentop, D. 1994. *Sport education: Quality PE through positive sport experiences.* Champaign, IL: Human Kinetics.

Siedentop, D., and D. Tannehill. (2000). *Developing teaching skills in physical education* (4th ed.). Mountain View, CA: Mayfield.

Siedentop, D., P. Hastie, and H. van der Mars. 2004. *Complete guide to sport education.* Champaign, IL: Human Kinetics.

Singer, R.N., C. DeFrancesco, and L.E. Randall. 1989. Effectiveness of a global learning strategy practiced in different contexts on primary and transfer self-paced motor tasks. *Journal of Sport and Exercise Psychology* 11:290-303.

Slavin, R. E. 1996. Research on cooperative learning and achievement: What we know, what we need to know. *Contemporary Educational Psychology,* 21, 43-69.

Spackman, L. 1983. Invasion games: An instructional strategy. *British Journal of Physical Education* 14 (4): 98-99.

Stallings, J.A. 1989. *School achievement effects and staff development: What are critical factors?* Paper presented at the annual meeting of the American Education Research Association. San Francisco.

Stevens, P., and C. Collier. 2001. Shooting hoops: WallTar as an alternative. *Teaching Elementary Physical Education* 12 (1): 17-19.

Thorpe, R., D. Bunker, and L. Almond. 1986. A change in focus for the teaching of games. In *Sport pedagogy: The 1984 Olympic scientific congress proceedings,* vol. 6, ed. M. Piéron and G. Graham, 163-169. Champaign, IL: Human Kinetics.

Toh, K., and B. Woolnough. 1994. Science process skills: Are they generalisable? *Research in Science and Technological Education* 12:31-42.

Tucker, G.R. 1996. Some thoughts concerning innovative language education programmes. *Journal of Multilingual and Multicultural Development* 17:315-320.

Turner, A., and T. Martinek. 1992. A comparative analysis of two models for teaching games (technique approach and game-centered [tactical focus] approach). *International Journal of Physical Education* 29 (4): 15-31.

Veal, M.L. 1993. The role of assessment and evaluation in secondary physical education: A pedagogical view. In *Critical crossroads: Middle and secondary school physical education,* ed. J.R. Rink, 93-99. Reston, VA: National Association of Sport and Physical Education.

Wandersee, J., J. Mintzes, and J. Novak. 1994. *Handbook of research on science teaching.* New York: Macmillan.

Werner, P., and L. Almond. 1990. Models of games education. *Journal of Physical Education, Recreation, and Dance* 61 (4): 23-27.

Wrisberg, C.A., and Z. Liu. 1991. The effect of contextual variety on the practice, retention, and transfer of an applied motor skill. *Research Quarterly for Exercise and Sport* 62:406-412.

Zessoules, T., and H. Gardner. 1991. Authentic assessment: Beyond the buzzword and into the classroom. In *Expanding student assessment,* ed. V. Perrone, 47-71. Alexandria, VA: Association for Supervision and Curriculum Development.

About the Authors

Stephen Mitchell, PhD, is a professor of sport pedagogy at Kent State University. He received his undergraduate and master degrees from Loughborough University, England, where the tactical approach was first developed; and he earned a PhD in teaching and curriculum at Syracuse University. An avid soccer player and licensed coach, he has employed a tactical approach in teaching and coaching at the elementary, middle school, high school, and college levels since 1982. Dr. Mitchell is a member of the American Alliance for Health, Physical Education, Recreation and Dance (AAHPERD), the Ohio Association for Health, Physical Education, Recreation and Dance (OAHPERD), and the National Association for Physical Education in Higher Education (NAPEHE).

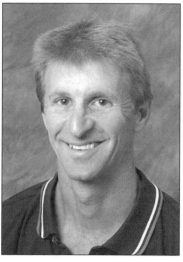

Stephen Mitchell

Judith Oslin, PhD, is a professor of sport pedagogy at Kent State University. She received her undergraduate and master degrees from Kent State and earned a PhD in sport pedagogy at Ohio State University. She has 30 years of experience as a physical educator and teacher educator. She has used the tactical approach with elementary, middle school, high school, and university students. Dr. Oslin has also presented numerous papers and workshops focusing on implementation of the tactical approach and the Game Performance Assessment Instrument at the international, national, regional, state, and local levels. She is a member of numerous professional organizations, including AAHPERD, NAPEHE, the American Educational Research Association (AERA), and the National Association for Girls and Women in Sport (NAGWS).

Judith Oslin

Linda Griffin, PhD, received her doctorate in physical education and teacher education from Ohio State University. As a physical educator and coach since 1976, Dr. Griffin has conducted extensive research, published nearly 30 articles and book chapters, and given numerous presentations on the tactical approach. She served on the planning committee for the first Teaching Games for Understanding Conference in New Hampshire in 2001. A former college volleyball player and coach, she is a professor and chair of teacher education and curriculum studies at the University of Massachusetts at Amherst and a member of AAHPERD and AERA.

Linda Griffin

*You'll find
other outstanding
physical education resources at*

www.HumanKinetics.com

In the U.S. call

1-800-747-4457

Australia	08 8277 1555
Canada	1-800-465-7301
Europe	+44 (0) 113 255 5665
New Zealand	0064 9 448 1207

HUMAN KINETICS
The Information Leader in Physical Activity
P.O. Box 5076 • Champaign, IL 61825-5076 USA